Abortion, Motherhood, and Mental Health

SOCIAL PROBLEMS AND SOCIAL ISSUES

An Aldine de Gruyter Series of Texts and Monographs

SERIES EDITOR

Joel Best, *University of Delaware*

David L. Altheide, **Creating Fear: News and the Construction of Crisis**

Joel Best (ed.), **Images of Issues: Typifying Contemporary Social Problems** (Second Edition)

Joel Best (ed.), **How Claims Spread: Cross-National Diffusion of Social Problems**

Cynthia J. Bogard, **Seasons Such As These: How Homelessness Took Shape in America**

James J. Chriss (ed.), **Counseling and the Therapeutic State**

Jeff Ferrell and Neil Websdale (eds.), **Making Trouble: Cultural Constructions of Crime**

Anne E. Figert, **Women and the Ownership of PMS: The Structuring of a Psychiatric Disorder**

James A. Holstein, **Court-Ordered Insanity: Interpretive Practice and Involuntary Commitment**

James A. Holstein and Gale Miller (eds.), **Challenges and Choices: Constructionist Perspectives on Social Problems**

Philip Jenkins, **Images of Terror: What We Can and Can't Know about Terrorism**

Philip Jenkins, **Using Murder: The Social Construction of Serial Homicide**

Valerie Jenness and Kendal Broad, **Hate Crimes: New Social Movements and the Politics of Violence**

Stuart A. Kirk and Herb Kutchins, **The Selling of DSM: Rhetoric of Science in Psychiatry**

Ellie Lee, **Abortion, Motherhood, and Mental Health: Medicalizing Reproduction in the United States and Great Britain**

John Lofland, **Social Movement Organizations: Guide to Research on Insurgent Realities**

Donileen R. Loseke, **Thinking About Social Problems: An Introduction to Constructionist Perspectives** (Second Edition)

Donileen R. Loseke and Joel Best (eds.), **Social Problems: Constructionist Readings**

Gale Miller, **Becoming Miracle Workers: Language and Meaning in Brief Therapy**

Elizabeth Murphy and Robert Dingwall, **Qualitative Methods and Health Policy Research**

James L. Nolan, Jr. (ed.), **Drug Courts: In Theory and In Practice**

Bernard Paillard, **Notes on the Plague Years: AIDS in Marseilles**

Dorothy Pawluch, **The New Pediatrics: A Profession in Transition**

Wilbur J. Scott and Sandra Carson Stanley (eds.), **Gays and Lesbians in the Military: Issues, Concerns, and Contrasts**

Jeffery Sobal and Donna Maurer (eds.), **Weighty Issues: Fatness and Thinness as Social Problems**

Jeffery Sobal and Donna Maurer (eds.), **Interpreting Weight: The Social Management of Fatness and Thinness**

Michael Welch, **Flag Burning: Moral Panic and the Criminalization of Protest**

Carolyn L. Wiener, **The Elusive Quest: Accountability in Hospitals**

Rhys Williams (eds.), **Cultural Wars in American Politics: Critical Reviews of a Popular Myth**

Mark Wolfson, **The Fight Against Big Tobacco: The Movement, the State and the Public's Health**

Abortion, Motherhood, and Mental Health

Medicalizing Reproduction in the United States and Great Britain

ELLIE LEE

Aldine de Gruyter
New York

About the Author

Ellie Lee is Research Fellow in the Department of Sociology and Social Policy, University of Southampton, Highfield, United Kingdom.

Copyright © 2003 Walter de Gruyter, Inc., New York

ALDINE DE GRUYTER
A division of Walter de Gruyter, Inc.
200 Saw Mill River Road
Hawthorne, New York 10532

∞ This publication is printed on acid free paper

Library of Congress Cataloging-in-Publication Data
Lee, Ellie.
    Abortion, motherhood, and mental health : medicalizing reproduction in the United States and Great Britain / Ellie Lee.
    p. cm.— (Social problems and social issues)
Includes bibliographical references and index.
    ISBN 0-202-30680-1 (cloth : alk. paper)—ISBN 0-202-30681-X (pbk. : alk. paper)
    1. Abortion—United States—Psychological aspects. 2. Abortion—Great Britain—Psychological aspects. 3. Motherhood—Psychological aspects. 4. Pregnant women—Mental health. 5. Post-traumatic stress disorder. 6. Postpartum psychiatric disorders. 7. Pro-life movement—United States. 8. Pro-life movement—Great Britain. I. Title. II. Series.
    HQ767.5.U5L42 2003
    363.46'0941—dc21
                                    2003010502

Manufactured in the United States of America

10 9 8 7 6 5 4 3 2 1

Contents

Acknowledgments   vii

Introduction   1

1   Reinventing the Abortion Problem   19

2   The "Syndrome Society"   43

3   The "De-moralization" of the Antiabortion Argument   81

4   Debating Postabortion Syndrome   115

5   Pregnancy and Mental Health in the United States and Britain   151

6   Motherhood as an Ordeal   189

7   Reexamining the Issues   221

Notes   251

References   255

Index   283

124661

Acknowledgments

There are four people who made it possible for me to write this book, and I would like to thank them particularly. They are Jennie Bristow, Adam Burgess, Frank Furedi, and Ben Metcalfe. Mary Boyle, Mike Fitzpatrick, James Heartfield, Brid Hehir, Sara Hinchliffe, Emily Jackson, David Nolan, David Paintin, and Derek Summerfield also took the time to read and comment on drafts of chapters and helped me enormously by doing so. I would also like to thank Joel Best, the series editor of Social Problems and Social Issues, for his help and encouragement throughout. And of course, thanks to Richard Koffler and Mai Shaikhanuar-Cota at Aldine de Gruyter.

Introduction

Abortion is inherently unsafe. Well over a hundred significant physical and psychological complications have been linked to abortion . . . The psychological effects of abortion can be particularly devastating, literally crippling a woman's ability to function in normal relationships with family or friends, and even at work.

—David Reardon, 1996

During pregnancy and in its aftermath, dozens of disorders may affect the reproductive process, or can be unleashed as complications . . . a catalogue of tragedies—depression, psychosis, abuse and other catastrophes—which make maternity seem like a risky venture.

—Ian Brockington, 1996

Whatever reproductive choices women make—whether they opt to end a pregnancy through abortion or continue to term and give birth—they are considered to be at risk of suffering serious mental health problems. According to David Reardon, an opponent of abortion in the United States, this is a big reason why people should consider abortion a problem. It "hurts women," he contends. Yet, on the other hand, as British psychiatrist Ian Brockington makes clear, becoming a mother is considered a big risk too. This book is about these representations of the results of reproductive choices. It examines how and why pregnancy and its outcomes have come to be discussed this way.

My interest in this aspect of the medicalization of reproduction—its representation as a mental health problem—arose in the first place in relation to abortion. Claims that associate abortion with mental ill health like those made by David Reardon, are, as Chapter 1 details, now primarily associated with those who oppose the provision of abortion to women. Such claims first came to my attention during the early 1990s, when I was involved in a research project on the campaigning activities of abortion opponents in Britain. Looking through leaflets and publications from Life and the Society for the Protection of Unborn Children (SPUC), the two main British organizations active in campaigning against abortion, I was struck by the prominence of medical (more precisely, psychological) terminology in their arguments. A leaflet from Life provided a long list of what it called "symptoms" of a "medical condition" termed Postabortion Trauma. The SPUC used the term Postabortion Syn-

1

drome and claimed that many thousands of British women—"victims of abortion"—were suffering from this illness and needed postabortion counseling as a result.

When I first came across these claims, it struck me as interesting that the antiabortion argument had apparently become far less "moralized" than in previous decades. Antiabortion literature from the 1970s and 1980s appeared much more focused on "moral problems," most centrally the question of "taking life." The alleged negative effect of abortion for women's health was, at this time, an incidental issue: just another reason that showed why abortion was a problem. But the real issue, for those opposed to abortion, was the destruction of "unborn life." Indeed, the names of organizations established to oppose the legalization of abortion—Life and the SPUC in Britain, or the National Right to Life to Committee in the United States—make this orientation clear. Discussion of the abortion debate—certainly that which I had come across in legal and philosophical texts—reflected this too. The philosopher L. W. Sumner, for example, thus explains: "Abortion is a moral problem. The existence of a moral problem presupposes some conflict of values or goals or interests. . . . What is at stake for the fetus is life itself. . . . What is at stake for the woman is autonomy—control of the use to be made of her body" (1981:5). In this approach, where abortion is a "moral problem," the conflict between those who defend abortion and those who oppose it is a conflict between women's autonomy on the one hand and the inviolate humanity of unborn life—"the life itself" of the fetus—on the other. The claim that abortion should be considered a problem because it is bad for women's health, and that what women need is counseling afterward, is clearly quite a jump from such moralized claims that defend "unborn life."

In particular, there is a very clear contrast between the construction of women who have abortions that is implied by moralized argument against abortion, and the construction that results when the claim against abortion focuses on its effects for women's mental health.

As the feminist political theorist Leslie Cannold notes, "fetal-centered" claims against abortion, which focus on the loss of "unborn life," concede that women "make rational and autonomous choices to have abortions" but criticize women for behaving immorally in doing so. In contrast, claims about the psychological effects of abortion focus on "pregnant women's lack of agency" (2002:172). Where the abortion problem is medicalized, women's psychological state following abortion allegedly proves they did not really choose to end their pregnancy. In the terms of this claim, women are "victims of abortion"—they are represented as fragile beings who are unable to make choices for themselves and who are not responsible for their actions. This is a construction that seems far removed from the previous typification of women as "acting callously, perhaps having multiple abortions, merely for their own convenience," as their representation in moralized argument against abortion has been described (Best 1995:9).

Why had abortion opponents adopted this kind of argument to convince others that abortion is a problem? What had led them to represent women as "victims" rather than rational, albeit selfish and immoral, actors? In part the pages that follow answer this question. Although I discuss only one particular aspect of the medicalization of the antiabortion argument in detail (it has taken place in other ways too, in claims about the physical health risks of abortion), I hope this book is a thorough examination of how and why abortion opponents came to make these new kinds of claims—in sum, their context. Through discussion of this issue, I aim in particular to show the value of a contextual constructionist approach to social problems, highlighted in other work on the abortion issue specifically (Linders 1998) and in relation to understanding social problems more generally (Best 1993).

The issue of the context for medicalized constructions of the abortion problem raises a further question, however. To what extent has the antiabortion movement managed to persuade those beyond its ranks, most importantly those involved in making law and policies on abortion, that women should be thought of as victims, traumatized by abortion? The second task of this book is to provide an account of this issue too. And to preempt what I have found, my case is that abortion opponents have experienced significant difficulties in finding support for their medicalized claims. They have met with considerable, effective resistance. The claim that women suffer from severe mental health problems after abortion and should be discouraged from having abortions because of this has not had the purchase that its proponents hoped for. At the time of writing, it has certainly not led to the legal and policy outcomes they expected.

It has also, notably, not led to a decrease in the popularity of abortion among women themselves. For some time, it has been estimated that one in three British women will have an abortion, and British women are in fact now more likely than ever before to terminate a pregnancy at some point in their lives (Office for National Statistics 2001). In the United States, it has been estimated that by the age of forty-five, 43 percent of women will have had an abortion (Henshaw 1998). Unlike in Britain, the abortion rate in the United States has fallen recently—it declined by 12 percent between 1992 and 1996, and by 5 percent between 1996 and 2000 (Finer and Henshaw 2002). This decline has been attributed to a number of factors, but it has been shown that the fall in the abortion rate has been most marked among young women (Finer and Henshaw 2002). The issue of why teenagers have become less likely to have abortion has itself become the subject of extensive debate, but it does appear to be the case that it is related to the fact that they have become less likely to experience unwanted pregnancy than in the past. Whether this is because teenagers are more likely to abstain from having sex, or because they have be-come more likely to use contraception when they do, is a controversial subject. But according to the Alan Guttmacher Institute (2002), as much as 43 per-cent of the decline in abortion in the United States between 1994 and 2000 can be attributed to the use of emergency contraception. Whatever the reason for the decline, however, it still remains the case that American women, like British women, are very likely to opt to end, rather than continue, pregnancies.

This outcome raises two further themes, and these form the other areas of discussion in this book. The first is the *limits* to medicalization. As I discuss in more detail here, engagement with medicalization processes from a socio-logical point of view has tended to draw attention to their strength in recent decades. For example, the way that claimsmakers often expand their rationale about why an issue should be considered a problem, to include claimsmaking about risks to human health, has been noted elsewhere (Burgess 2003). Claimsmaking about the problem of factory farming, for example, has moved from a focus on cruelty to animals to include claims about threats to human health (Kunkel 1995). But this is only one example among many—that we live in a society where claimsmaking is highly medicalized seems undeniably true. Claims, for example, that a food, lifestyle, or new technological develop-ment is a risk to health have become so ubiquitous they have ceased to stand out. Yet it has also been argued, as the summary later of sociological argument about medicalization shows, that there can be limits to medicalization, or at least differential extents to which claims that medicalize problems can gain ground in different contexts. It is important to investigate instances where limits to medicalized claimsmaking are apparent, and this book is intended to make a contribution to sociological inquiry in this regard.

At this preliminary stage, however, two points should be made clear about the limits to the medicalization of the abortion problem. First, claims that con-nect abortion with mental ill health have been limited in their influence, but this is not to suggest that they have not become a focus for discussion and have had no impact, and in later chapters I examine in detail instances in which this has been the case. Second, the limits to such claims about abortion do not, by any means, suggest limits to the process of the medicalization of pregnancy more broadly. They do not imply, I suggest, a process of *demedicalization*. This brings me to the final theme of this book—an account of a process that might be termed the *selective medicalization* of reproduction.

Discussion in the pages that follow, as this book's title suggests, is about motherhood as well as abortion. And, as later chapters in this book detail, when discussion of the medicalization of reproduction is extended to this is-sue too, it becomes very clear that this process has not abated overall. Whereas the putative category of mental illness Postabortion Syndrome has proved highly contentious, categories of mental illness that pertain to mothers, in con-trast, have not been. For example, as I detail in Chapter 6, the concept Postpartum Depression (Postnatal Depression in Britain) has become increasingly visible, as claimsmakers have drawn attention to the health risks that motherhood poses. In fact a plethora of mental illness categories, as Ian Brockington's comment at the beginning of this introduction suggests, have come to be associated with motherhood. Giving birth has been construed to be a cause of Posttraumatic Stress Disorder (PTSD)—a claim that is akin to that for Postabortion Syndrome, but which has had a very different response and effect. Most recently, a new category of mental illness called "tokophobia" has been named, which is considered by the proponents of this term to be "an unreasoning fear of childbirth" that makes its sufferers unable to face the prospect of pregnancy and motherhood at all. Indeed, when one starts to consider the general discussion about outcomes of pregnancy, it becomes clear that many aspects of motherhood—its planning through getting pregnant or avoiding getting pregnant, being pregnant, giving birth, the experience of being a mother and indeed the experience of parenting altogether—have come to be increasingly problematized through reference to their negative psychological effects.

While the idea of "abortion trauma" has been contested, therefore, where women's reproductive choices are considered more broadly, limits to medicalization are not so apparent. There is a discernible element in cultural, academic, and professional representations of childbirth and its aftermath that emphasize how this experience is at least a psychological ordeal for women, and very often a cause of serious mental illness. This suggests, I argue, that there is not so much a process of demedicalization of reproduction; rather we are witnessing a process of selective medicalization through which, at present at least, motherhood seems to be increasingly identified as a mental health problem, in way that contrasts with previous representations of this reproductive choice. An experience that was once most often represented as a source of joy and happiness has come to be considered one that may well leave women with a very high psychological price to pay.

This, I contend, raises an important and interesting issue; how might the different fortunes of claims about the psychological effects of abortion on the one hand, and motherhood on the other, be explained? In the final chapter I return to discuss this issue further. For now I want to set the scene in more detail for the chapters that follow, through a brief examination of sociology of medicalization processes, and thereby situate this study in relation to the existing body of work.

MEDICALIZATION

Investigation of "how it should be that certain areas of human life come—or cease—to be regarded as 'medical' in particular historical circumstances" is a well-established theme in studies of the construction of social problems (Wright and Treacher 1982:9). Medicalization has been described as the "process by which nonmedical problems become defined and treated as medical problems, usually in terms of illnesses or disorders" (Conrad 1992:209), and processes of medicalization and de-medicalization have attracted sociological interest since the 1960s.

A main observation of many early studies was that, overall, Western societies had moved from defining problems as sinful to defining them as criminal, and finally in terms of sickness. A therapeutic construction—an understanding of social problems in the idiom of medicine—had taken over from a religious or legalistic one (Fox 1977). Fox notes, for example, that the construction of problems in terms of illness, previously understood in other ways, was evident in the emergence of problems such as hallucination and delusion, which would once have been interpreted as signs of possession by the Devil. This is evident in the use of the term "Battered Child Syndrome" to describe a certain type of child abuse involving violence; in the way behaviors in children had come to be called alternatively hyperactivity, hyperkinesis, or minimal brain dysfunction, rather than badness or misbehavior; and in the emergence of so-called addictive disorders such as alcoholism, drug addiction, compulsive overeating, and compulsive gambling, which replaced the idea of sin (1977:11). In his famous work *The Illness Narratives,* Arthur Kleinman (1988) described how medicalization was the process exemplified by relabeling alcoholism as an illness and child abuse as a symptom of family pathology, and that society had come to define problems as medical that were previously defined and managed as moral, religious, or criminal.

It is important to note that this field of study can generally be characterized, certainly at the outset, as critical of medicalization, and that it has often been associated with radical thought. Irving Zola, a key scholar in this field of sociological examination, was one of the first to contend, in the 1970s, that the medicalization of life was a very distinctive feature of society, and he made the case that this development was problematic. His interest in medicalization was stimulated by "the realization of how much everyone has, or believes he has, something organically wrong with him" (1978:91). A society had emerged, argued Zola, in which there was a "belief in the omnipresence of disorder," exemplified and further enhanced by a plethora of warnings about "unhealthy" lifestyles: "From sex to food, from aspirins to clothes, from driving your car to riding the surf, it seems that under certain conditions, or in combination . . . virtually anything can lead to certain medical problems," he said, famously drawing the conclusion that he had become "convinced that living is injurious to health" (Zola 1978:92). In adopting a highly critical stance toward medicalization, Zola drew particular attention to the implications of eradicating other ways of thinking about human experience—for example, in moral or political terms:

[T]he debate over homosexuality, drugs or abortion becomes focused on the degree of sickness attached to the phenomenon in question or the extent of the health risk involved. And the more principled, more perplexing, or even moral issue, of *what* freedom should an individual have over his or her own body is shunted aside. (Zola 1978:95, emphasis in the original)

As the discussion below suggests, while the reasons for criticizing medicalization have varied and there have been debates within this field of sociological inquiry about what we should be critical of, it is generally the case that work within this field has tended to consider medicalization a problematic process.

Within the field of general interest in medicalization, certain themes and issues have emerged as particular foci for research and comment. Conrad (1992) identified two, in arguing that sociological literature considers the *process* of medicalization and *degrees* of medicalization. Studies, he explains, have detailed how medicalization takes place by considering who is involved in the process, in particular the extent to which medical professionals are involved, and how they are involved. More recently, attention has been paid to the degree to which medicalization has occurred, in particular whether or not medicalization is contested, and whether prior or alternative constructions are apparent and, if so, why. A third theme can also be identified: interest in medicalization through reference to the problem of mental ill health in particular. I will now briefly discuss each of these three themes.

Medicalization Processes

A key issue in studies of medicalization has been how this process occurs, and in particular whether and in what way medicine and the medical profession play a role in the process. Some accounts, especially those of the 1970s, presented the medical profession and medical organizations as central to the process. As Fox put it, medicalization has been viewed as "primarily the result of the self-interested maneuvers of the medical profession" (1977:13). Conrad (1992) notes that founding ideas in the "medicalization thesis" contended that this process entailed establishing the "jurisdictional mandate" of the medical profession over anything that can be labeled an illness, exemplified most clearly in the work of Illich (1976). Other studies, however, have considered whether medicalization is only, or primarily, about the extension of the power and control of the medical profession, and whether it is the case that the medical profession is always centrally involved. Indeed from the outset, the idea that medicalization is not only about "medical imperialism" or "medical colonization" featured in sociological work, and this has been a key area of debate within this field of sociological inquiry.

Thus, some accounts placed medicine at the heart of the process and attacked its effects for making people's lives worse. Some made the case, for example, that medicine has been directly opposed to the interests of oppressed social groups—for example, women and ethnic minorities (Ehrenreich and English 1978; Fanon 1978). Wright and Treacher note that feminism, in particular, led the way in advocating a negative attitude toward medicine and scientific knowledge: "[T]he women's movement has challenged not merely the domination of doctors, but also the supposed benevolent neutrality of the medical knowledge they employ" (Wright and Treacher 1982:1). Others, for example, Irving Zola, who are just as critical of the medical profession have argued rather differently, however, that the continuing growth of "the list of daily activities to which health can be related" involved more than activity on the part of the medical profession (1978:91). As Conrad has explained, medicalization has been understood by certain of its critics not so much as "medical imperialism" than as a "sociocultural process" that may or may not involve the medical profession, lead to medical social control or medical treatment, or be the result of intentional expansion by the medical profession (1992:211).

Studies that draw attention to variations in how medicalization occurs have become, rightly in this author's view, most numerous. Some have considered how historical examples of medicalization, which have sometimes been presented as early, important examples of the "colonization" of human experience by the medical profession, may not be so straightforward. The medicalization of homosexuality in the nineteenth century, for example, involved collaboration on the part of putative patients with doctors; homosexuals involved with such diagnoses were not "passive victims" of labeling. In the same way, women often collaborated in their diagnosis as hysterics (Hansen 1997). With reference to Rosen's work, Hansen (1997) also points out how developments in ways of understanding human behavior often constituted a movement from a conception of immorality and wrongdoing (as framed by religion or law) to a less and less punitive idea, through medicalization. Homosexuals, therefore, were "ill" rather than immoral, and the construction of the medical model of homosexuality involved collaboration on the part of those who were its focus. Others have shown how medicalization can comprise a process altogether different from that of "colonization" by medical professionals, in that other institutions and social actors are more centrally involved.

Of more recent medicalized problems, Conrad and Schneider argue that problems have entered the domain of the medical profession not as a result of doctors' activity, but by that of "various non-medical policy makers" or through the championing of pseudomedical arguments by "lay rather than medical claims-makers" (1980:75). Studies of anorexia nervosa, for example, indicate that that condition moved from relative obscurity (having been first identified in the 1870s) to become a highly visible social problem in the United States and Britain by the 1980s, and that the "epidemic" of anorexia nervosa that emerged at this time resulted less from the actions of medical professionals than from cultural changes and changes in the communication processes (Brumberg 1997). These changes include the emergence of a cult of "eat less, exercise more," the "circulation of news about eating disorders" through the media, and the fact that for governments in both the United States and Britain, the problem of the "self-image" of young women, exemplified by dieting to lose weight, became a focal point for campaigns to "raise awareness" about the perils facing the young in modern society. These processes, together with the activities of doctors, transformed anorexia nervosa from an "enigmatic and rare condition into a recognisable and accessible illness" (Brumberg 1997:141). In the United States, a psychiatric expert was at the center of this process, in that medicalization required the development of a theory that explained anorexia as a disease state, but broader cultural dynamics were also crucial to the construction of this social problem.

It has also been argued that claimsmakers who construct problems in medical-sounding terms may also in exist *in competition* with medical organizations and official medical opinion. "Medical ideology may arise independently from the medical profession," notes Conrad, and "for the medical profession to maintain dominance over this form of social control, it must publicly challenge those groups utilizing medical ideology" (1979:9). Studies of the construction of alcoholism as a social problem have, in particular, drawn attention to the way in which claimsmakers who are not part of the medical profession have played the key role in medicalization, and their claims have been disputed by medical professionals. Conrad notes that "Alcoholics Anonymous, a nonmedical quasi-religious self-help organization, adopted a variant of the medical model of alcoholism quite independently from the medical profession" (1979:6) and states that other self-help groups, such as weight-reducing groups, have adapted or developed their own "quasi-medical theories" independently from the medical professional (1979:8). Appleton has argued, on the basis of her study of alcoholism, that "Mainstream allopathic medicine generally has ignored attempts to medicalize alcoholism," and that medical practice rejects treating it as such (1995:65). Peele's (1995) study of the "diseasing" of alcoholism in the United States provides the most detailed account of this social problem and demonstrates that the prime movers in the construction of alcoholism as a biologically based or genetically inherited condition have not been those associated with the medical profession, and indeed some psychiatrists have outrightly rejected this explanation of the problem. On the other hand, the London-based general practitioner Michael Fitzpatrick (2001) suggests that some in the medical profession have played an important role in Britain in endorsing the addiction model of alcoholism and other forms of behavior.

Advocates of alternative medicine have also been shown to be important in current processes of medicalization. Sociologists Williams and Calnan note, with reference to research by Sharma, that the field of alternative medicine expanded rapidly over the 1980s and 1990s, and that those who use such therapies are "no longer confined to small groups of 'enthusiasts.'" Rather, their use is widespread and alternative medicine has become popularized (1996: 1617). The relationship of such therapies to scientific medicine is an interesting one with regard to the dynamics of medicalization. In the beginning at least, alternative therapies made an overt challenge to conventional, scientific medicine and were rejected by the medical profession (Jenkins 2002). According to some, therefore, their effect was to encourage demedicalization. However, others argue the effect of alternative medicine has been to extend medicalization in a new way. As Williams and Calnan note, the growing demand for and supply of such therapies have taken place *alongside* growing demand for conventional medicine, suggesting "a drastic increase in medicalization" (1996:1617). Additionally, the softening of hostility on the part of conventional medicine to such therapies, and their resultant relabeling as "complementary" rather than "alternative," also point to their advocacy and use constituting part of a process of medicalization. In this instance, therefore, medicalization is a process initiated outside and in response to "official" medicine, but which has increasingly become incorporated by it (Fitzpatrick 2002).

Following the case made by Appleton (1995), it can be concluded that the process of medicalization can take a variety of forms, and it may not always be the case that official medical endorsement is necessary for a condition to be successfully medicalized. A common feature of the medicalization process is the use of medical vocabulary, but the actors involved and their motivations can be very varied. Identification of the diffuseness of medicalization raises the question of why this process occurs. A number of explanations for this phenomenon have been put forward, but a common point is that medicalization often relates to social processes well beyond the confines of medicine and the medical profession.

One such account has been provided by Irving Zola, who argued that those not directly associated with medicine may use its language, since "the prestige of *any* proposal is immediately enhanced, if not justified, when it is expressed in the idiom of medical science" (1978:90–1, emphasis in the original). But such authority on the part of medical language may not be the result of medical "imperialism" specifically. It may rather reflect a broader social process, namely the emergence of an "increasingly complex technological and bureaucratic system—a system which has led us down the path of the reluctant reliance on the expert" (1978:81). The authority of medicine is only one part of a broader picture in which more and more aspects of life appear to demand recourse to expert knowledge. Medicine has acquired a particularly high degree of authority, but only as part of a society that has come to rely increasingly on expert knowledge of various kinds to attempt to solve problems of living. In this approach, medicalization expresses developments in the way in which society is organized. Thus, argued Zola, health has come to be identified as "a paramount value in society," representing a shift in cultural norms, and as a result medicalized constructions of problems could come to dominate, since health "is a phenomenon whose diagnosis and treatment have been restricted to a certain group" (1978:92). In other words, cultural developments had led "health" above all else to become considered as an unquestionable good, and in the context of a society increasingly reliant on experts, this had boosted the authority and dominance of the medical idiom. Medicine had come, "perhaps unwittingly," to be in a position of power, he argues. Christopher Lasch made a similar case, when he argued that the cultural climate in the late twentieth century was "therapeutic not religious." People, he suggested, had come to seek not salvation, but "the feeling, the momentary illusion, of personal well-being, health, and psychic security" (1980:17), which placed medicine in a new position of authority.

Others have also related medicalization to broader social processes, particularly over the last decade. As noted above, some have associated medicalization with the idea of the "victim" and the "victim culture." The representation of people as suffering from syndromes or depressive illnesses, as addicted or as codependent, forms part of a culture in which the idea that people are powerless and unable to find ways to exert control over their lives has become important. Medicalized claimsmaking thus intersects not only with the authority of medicine, but also with other social trends. Fitzpatrick (2002) has argued, in this vein, that the trend toward interpreting experience in emotional and psychological terms (a particular trend in medicalization introduced below, and detailed in Chapter 2) has emerged largely outside the world of medicine, but has gained increasing influence within it. For Fitzpatrick, it is a sense of heightened individual vulnerability that leads people to attribute responsibility for their behavior to someone or something over which they have no control. It is a culture in which people are assumed to be and consider themselves to be fragile and vulnerable that produces a demand for explanations that posit the reason for behavior and experience as external: as, for example, the result of a medical condition. Medicalization feeds off this culture, through providing answers and interventions that rely on treatment or therapy if the problem is to be overcome. For Fitzpatrick, more and more medical problems and psychological disorders appear to afflict people not because there are more illnesses that medicine has simply discovered. Rather, for "any observer who takes a historical or sociological perspective on the emergence of . . . novel illnesses, their origins in the existential distress of their sufferers is readily apparent." "The tragedy," he argues, is that those who come to suffer from such illness are primarily afflicted by a "lack of insight into this process, a deficit that is reinforced by the provision of a pseudo-medical disease label" (2002: 69). Culture, this approach suggests, at present encourages medicalization, with highly problematic effects.

THE LIMITS TO MEDICALIZATION

As well as processes of medicalization however, its *degree*—relating to the extent to which competing definitions of problems and trends toward demedicalization pertain—has also been highlighted as an important and underresearched question. As Conrad (1992) notes, in many cases medicalization is not complete, and "there is little doubt that some demedicalization has occurred along with medicalization" (Conrad and Schneider 1980:77).

A key example often cited in this regard, which could be considered to give further weight to the idea that processes beyond the actions of medical professionals are of importance, is the decision made by the American Psychiatric Association in 1973 that homosexuality should cease to be defined as an illness (Ingleby 1982; Conrad and Schneider 1980). That homosexuality was from this point no longer classified as an illness may have reflected more than simply the decision on the part of American psychiatry that it did not want to be considered the authority in explaining this behavior. An understanding of homosexuality as an illness was at odds with emergent ideas that construed it to be a lifestyle, equally valid to others—ideas that relate to broader developments in culture and changes in understandings of the family.

In relation to this example, and others, it has been argued that attention should therefore be paid not only to the power of processes that encourage medicalization, but also to competing trends. Phenomena, it has been argued, can be constructed in both medical and nonmedical terms because there is debate over definitions. Other kinds of definitions may coexist, and medicalized understandings may not be operationalized (for example, reflected in treatment that uses a medical model). Thus it may be advantageous to consider the question as a matter of degree. To what extent has a condition been framed in medical terms? Do competing definitions exist, and do prior nonmedicalized constructions continue to pertain? And it may be found that there are examples that contradict the general trend toward medicalization: "While evidence suggests that medicalization has significantly outpaced demedicalization, it is important to see it as a bidirectional process" (Conrad 1992:226).

The issue of the debate over problem definition has featured in accounts of, especially, the medicalization of women's experience. Studies have drawn attention to "the breadth of the medicalization of women's lives: battering, gender deviance, obesity, anorexia and bulimia, and a host of reproductive issues including childbirth, birth control, infertility, abortion, menopause and PMS" (Conrad 1992:222). Women's experiences have emerged as a notable site for medicalization, and many have drawn particular attention to the way in which pregnancy has become medicalized, expanding from childbirth to the "medical surveillance of obstetrics . . . to include prenatal lifestyles, infertility, and postnatal interaction with babies" (Conrad 1992:216).

An interesting and important aspect of this process is the role of feminist and women's movement claimsmakers in it. In some instances, such claimsmakers have acted as the main opponents of medicalization and have ensured that competing definitions of the problem exist (although, it has been argued, to a limited effect). The issue of the domination of the medical profession over pregnancy and childbirth, through its monopolization of ways of understanding and responding to these experiences, was formative in the origin of the critique of "medicalization" in the first place (Lupton 1994). The feminist critique of medicalization has argued that in their origins, obstetrics and gynecology in particular pathologized women's experience, and medicine in general tends to control women's bodies to women's detriment (Freund and McGuire 1991; Lupton 1994). While medicine that attends to the physical body has been strongly attacked by feminists, certain medicalized concepts that explain experience and behavior have also been criticized for pathologizing women. For example, the concept of "Premenstrual Syndrome" has been subject to debate, on the grounds that it represents women's biology as coterminous with irrationality (Figert 1996; Tavris 1992). Criticism of this concept links to a well-developed feminist argument that has demonstrated how in its origins, medicine viewed women's psychology as shaped by biological processes:

> If the uterus and ovaries could dominate women's entire body, it was only a short step to the ovarian takeover of woman's entire personality. The basic idea, in the nineteenth century, was that female psychology functioned merely as an extension of female reproductivity, and that woman's nature was determined solely by her reproductive functions. (Ehrenreich and English 1978:133)

A trend within feminist thought has, therefore, strongly opposed the way in which medicine has "reduced women" to their biology and emphasized the differences between men and women as a result (Lupton 1994). From the 1970s, part of the feminist project was to contest such representations of women. "Serious efforts have been made," noted Fox in 1977, "to heighten physicians' awareness of the fact that because they share certain prejudiced, often unconscious assumptions about women, they tend to over-attribute psychological conditions to their female patients." A related development, Fox rightly suggested, was the objection to the tendency to define pregnancy as an illness and the idea that childbirth had become too "technologized" (1977:18).

In sum, in regard to the medicalization of social problems, existing studies suggest that it is important to pay attention to who makes claims, and in particular to look at the relationship between different kinds of claimsmakers. And the degree of medicalization—whether competing problem definitions pertain, and why they might—has been considered an issue deserving of greater attention. The content of claims and what they represent can be situated, studies suggest, in relation to broader social and cultural trends. Where a process of medicalization (or demedicalization) takes place, it is likely that claims resonate with broader developments in society and culture.

Psychologizing Problems: The "Syndrome Society"

The study of medicalization processes that construct problems in regard to mental health forms the final part of the context for the present study. Sociological work about medicalization is extensive, involving examination of a very wide range of illness states, branches of medicine, different professionals, and different historical periods. Within this general field, a distinction can be made between processes that medicalize with regard to the physical body and those that relate to states of mind. This distinction cannot be drawn rigidly— claims about problems that draw attention to physical ill health and mental ill health often overlap [see, for example, the study of work stress by Wainright and Calnan (2002)]. A distinction can be made, however, insofar as claims about mental health often intersect with concepts emergent from psychiatry and psychology, and those about physical health with concepts from other branches of medicine. This book is primarily (although not exclusively) concerned with concepts that relate to understandings of problems associated with psychiatry and psychology, and the argument in the pages that follow can thus be situated in relation to studies that have examined claimsmaking about mental health that have also done so.

Chapter 2 provides a lengthy account of these studies, but at this point it should be noted that mental ill health is a long-standing theme in studies of medicalization. At the outset, critiques of medicalization as a form of social control pointed to the expanding domain of psychiatry. The ideas of those associated with "anti-psychiatry," most importantly Thomas Szasz (1977), have been considered important for the way they focused attention on the role of psychiatry in "making people mentally ill," through what Peter Sedgwick described as the "annexation of not-illness into illness" (Fox 1977:11). Second, a more recent body of work has emerged that considers mental illness and mental health more broadly, taking into account claimsmaking by those outside psychiatry as well as those involved with it. This work has shown that more and more forms of mental illness have come to be defined and recognized and has examined why and how this process has taken place; it considers what has been termed the "Syndrome Society" (Downs 1996). This body of work has a particular focus—the growing problem of mental ill health—but the two themes of the process and extent of medicalization again appear. The interaction between medical and other social actors (in this instance, psychologists, psychiatrists, psychiatric officialdom, and lay actors) has been described in detail, raising the issue of whether "psychiatric imperialism" is the best way to understand the current problem of mental ill health.

Studies of the development of the psychiatric diagnostic category Post-traumatic Stress Disorder (PTSD), for example, have described in detail how the intersection of lay interests with psychiatry led to the development of this category to account for the experience of veterans of the Vietnam War, and how nonmedical claimsmakers played the key role in "spreading" this category to apply it to other groups of people (Scott 1990; Dean 1997; Shepherd 2000). Ellen Herman contends, in her fascinating study of American psychology, that there has been a "curious courtship" of feminism and psychiatric and psychological constructions of women's problems, thus also pointing to the role of those outside the mainstream of psychiatry and psychology in medicalization processes (an insight of great relevance to the present study).

While feminists in the United States, Herman argues, have on the one hand opposed some psychiatric and psychological theories about women, on the grounds that they construed female independence as a pathological and socially damaging aspiration, it is also the case that psychology—albeit a different version of it—has come to be advocated and embraced by feminists. Psychology has "offered resources with which to support the ideas and actions of the women's movement" (1995:280), expressed through the feminist goal of improving women's mental health and through the representation of problems in terms of their detrimental effects for women's self-esteem and psychological well-being.

Others have shown, similarly, how feminist claimsmakers have sometimes acted to impel the medicalization of women's problems. Tierney notes, for example, that there was significant collaboration in the 1970s between feminist campaigners and official bodies that aimed to improve mental health, specifically the National Institute of Mental Health (NIMH). The NIMH began funding research into family violence, through which the issue of family and its problems came to be framed as a "mental health" issue. Feminist collaboration in this process was exemplified through the endorsement of the psychiatric concept of the Battered Woman's Syndrome, discussed in more detail later in this book. Violence against women was originally defined as a problem by women's movement activists in relation to broad social and structural issues. However, "Programs for battered women," argued Tierney in the early 1980s, "are already beginning to identify tensions in the marriage relationship, rather than patriarchal values or social inequality, as the source of wife beating; to give 'therapy' often to the woman alone" (1982:216). She noted that the official response was to define the problem for women in this way, par-

allel to the child abuse problem, which had also become medicalized and professionalized through the concept of the "Battered Child Syndrome" and its
link to the concept of the "toxic family."

Overall, such studies suggest that problems framed in medical, specifically
psychological, terms now appear as a ubiquitous part of the contemporary social landscape. Claims that an activity or phenomenon constitutes a mental
health risk or a health problem, and should therefore be taken seriously, are re-
lentlessly made. But some have gained more acceptance than others—not all
appear in psychiatrists' manuals, and not all are viewed as "real" mental illnesses. The question of the limits to this construction of problems is thus
raised. It is in this context that the present study is situated. Drawing on the
themes outlined above, it considers processes of medicalization with regard to
constructions of abortion and motherhood.

A COMPARATIVE STUDY

While my interest in the debate about the psychological effects of abortion
was provoked by claims made by British abortion opponents, it is in the
United States that such claims first emerged. This book therefore details medicalized claims against abortion, and the response to them, in both the United
States and Britain. It comprises in part a comparative analysis: an examination
of the similarities and differences in the context for the claim that abortion
causes Postabortion Syndrome, and the response to this claim in these two societies. Such an approach is necessary if the complete story of Postabortion Syndrome is to be told. Also, as Linders has argued in relation to her comparative
study of the construction of the abortion problem in the United States and
Sweden, a study of more than one case "has the potential to clarify some of the
relationships between claimsmaking and the context in which social problems
are constructed" (1998:491). By comparing the same problem in two contexts,
an assessment can be made of whether it is factors particular to one society that
determine the origins of and response to the claim, or whether common patterns are identifiable. I hope that in this study, through comparison of the
United States and Britain, useful insights have emerged about reasons for the
medicalization of this social problem and for the limits to this process.

In Chapter 1, I concentrate on outlining the features of the claim that abortion is a problem because it damages women's mental health. The first question posed by this framing of opposition to abortion is, what led to the
medicalization of antiabortion claims? Chapter 2 responds to this question
with a discussion of the "Syndrome Society," a context in which, I contend,
claims that problematize contemporary human experiences through reference
to the emotional and psychological problems that afflict people have become
increasingly visible and are rarely contested. I argue that the Postabortion Syn-

drome claim, in both the United States and Britain, can be understood in part as an attempt to "piggyback" other well-established medicalized claims.

If the claim that women who have had abortions can suffer mental health problems emerges out of this context, there is another dynamic, which I consider first in Chapter 3. The turn toward medicalized argument, I argue, also reflects the difficulties of arguing against abortion in other ways. I suggest the engagement of abortion opponents with the issue of the health risks of abortion—an engagement that has gained visibility and prominence from the mid-1980s—draws attention to the problems posed for them by relying on other moralities to make their case. I examine this issue first through a discussion of debates about abortion law in Britain and the United States and argue that attempts to gain support for restrictions on legal access to abortion through moralized claims, even in the context of very conservative political administrations, did not get very far.

Chapter 4 provides a detailed account of the intervention by abortion opponents that I suggest emerged as a result, in the debate about the psychological effects of abortion. Drawing on a range of sources—media reporting, documents produced by participants in this debate, records of parliamentary and congressional discussions—I draw attention to differences between the United States and Britain, but show that in both societies, medicalized arguments against abortion generated resistance, and ultimately such claims remained confined to their original owners. Indeed, as has been reflected in my discussion so far, the claim that abortion is traumatic and leads to a Postabortion Syndrome has remained very much identified with opponents of abortion. The remainder of this book examines why this has been the case.

Counterclaims, in opposition to antiabortion constructions of abortion as a health risk, have been associated primarily with psychiatric, psychological, and medical opinion. Such opinion has been forthright in contesting the attempt by opponents of abortion to frame their opposition in medical terms. What does this suggest? In Chapter 5, I argue that such opposition to the Postabortion Syndrome does not indicate a trend toward the demedicalization of abortion. Rather it indicates that abortion occupies a particular place in the more general medicalization of pregnancy. I make this case through examination of the construction of the problems of abortion, unwanted childbearing, and motherhood in medical opinion in the United States and Britain from the 1950s to the 1990s. My discussion indicates that abortion was not demedicalized over this time, but rather that its medicalization increasingly took place through its designation as a "low risk" problem for women, and through comparing its effects with those of its alternatives.

I suggest, therefore, that from the outset the strategy of the medicalization of the antiabortion argument faced arguably insurmountable problems, given that the alternatives to abortion had become increasingly problematized in medicalized terms. Chapter 6 develops this case one stage further, through an

examination of developments in constructions of motherhood, with a particular focus upon the role of lay claimsmakers.

I argue in this chapter that a new narrative of motherhood emerged over the
same period of time that abortion opponents attempted to find support for the
PAS claim. This is a narrative in which the association between motherhood
and mental ill health became increasingly prominent. From the 1980s to the
present, I suggest, ideas developed by psychiatry about the problem of motherhood have been adopted and given visibility by others. At the same time that
claims that ending a pregnancy through abortion can result in mental ill health
have been contested, a claimsmaking process regarding the problems of continuing a pregnancy, delivering a baby, and becoming a mother has taken
place.

Claimsmakers who argue that motherhood is a mental health problem are
very different from, and have sometimes been clearly opposed to, those who
have medicalized the abortion problem. But as Chapter 6 shows, the kinds of
claims that are made about motherhood, and the ways in which they frame
women's problems, in fact appear similar in many ways—in their structure
and language for example—to those made about the abortion problem by its
opponents. But the outcome of claimsmaking about the ordeal of motherhood
has been very different from that for Postabortion Syndrome; in both the
United States and Britain, there been a marked absence of competing claims.
Very few have opposed or contested the construction of motherhood as a risk
to women's mental health.

So why has one set of claims generated debate, but not the other? How can
this difference in the medicalization of reproductive choices be explained? In
the final chapter I respond to these questions. The most obvious explanation
would be that claims made about the problems of motherhood reflect scientific fact—they are based on research that shows motherhood has been proved
beyond question to be a cause of mental illness—whereas those made about
abortion are misrepresentations of what science shows. In my final remarks, I
assess whether this explanation makes sense, and put forward some thoughts
provoked for this author by the story of the medicalization of abortion and
motherhood in the United States and Britain.

1

Reinventing the Abortion Problem

According to counselors working for Life, Britain's most prominent anti-abortion organization, terminating a pregnancy can cause serious mental health problems. Geraldine, a Life counselor in London, claims of women she sees who have had an abortion:

> . . . some will present themselves with symptoms that are serious, with the definitions of Post Traumatic Stress. The types of exaggerated, extreme responses to big events in your life. . . . So what we are looking at is extreme symptoms. Sleeplessness, eating problems, bad dreams, weepiness. Issues where you realise you are not functioning normally.

Diana, also a counselor for Life, contends: "Post Abortion Syndrome is what happens to a woman when she's had an abortion, she hasn't recognized she is traumatized by it, she's pushed it under and hasn't been allowed to grieve, and she gets post-abortion stress. Some can have really serious psychological disturbances."[1] Geraldine and Diana represent, in a particular way, women's feelings and behavior following abortion. These feelings are evidence, they argue, that the woman concerned is suffering from a medical problem termed Postabortion Syndrome (PAS), or from "a kind of Post Traumatic Stress." Certain forms of behavior or feelings are "symptoms"—they are evidence that the woman is suffering from ill health. And such symptoms emerge as a response to a definable pattern of events, where a woman's feelings about abortion are "pushed under" or repressed. Her experiences are not unique or unusual but have a predictability that justifies conceptualizing them as a medical problem, with roots in a specific pathogen, abortion.

As the Introduction suggested, this claim is interesting because it appears to depart significantly from the familiar terms of the antiabortion argument—terms that can be described as "moralized." Moralized argument relies upon the representation of the fetus as a person, and abortion is construed as a problem because it is morally wrong to kill a fetus ("to take a life"). Claims for fetal personhood have been made through reference to religious (God deems human life to begin at the moment of conception) and "scientific" or "medical" tenets. Studies of the antiabortion argument and of images used by the antiabortion movement have shown how extensive use has been made of medical technologies to substantiate claims for fetal personhood. Ultrasound images of developing fetuses have been used in particular to show that the fetus looks like a born baby, and these images have been used to substantiate the claim that the fetus counts as a person (Franklin 1991; Newman 1996). They also emphasize medical facts—for example, that the fetal heart starts beating at six weeks' gestation or that a fetus can respond to stimuli such as sound—and on this basis contend that it has been proved that the fetus is a person.

These different arguments all focus on the fetus's "personhood," however, and draw attention to the loss of human life abortion allegedly entails. Abortion is, in this frame, construed a "moral" problem in a profound sense since it "takes a life." Abortion is considered an act that can only possibly be justified in very unusual and particular circumstances and is in general to be considered "wrong." Moralized claims about the problem of abortion are, of course, still evident in the abortion debate, especially in the United States. But in addition to this, the claim that abortion is a problem because it is bad for women's health has become a feature of the antiabortion argument. Indeed, in Britain this type of argument has become more dominant than that which problematizes abortion on moralized grounds.

The claim that abortion is a problem because it damages women's health departs significantly from claims that emphasize the sanctity of life. Appeal to this moral precept is replaced by claims that lack such overt moralistic tones. The aim of this chapter is to examine in more detail the facets of this "de-moralized" claim about why we should consider abortion a problem. I make no attempt here to explain why this claim has emerged—I leave this task to later chapters. For now, my aim is simply to detail its features. What is Postabortion Syndrome? Exactly how does the claim that abortion is a problem because it damages women's health differ from the construction of abortion as a moral problem?

POSTABORTION SYNDROME

The most obvious aspect of the Postabortion Syndrome claim is that abortion is a problem because it can make women ill. This representation of behavior or feelings that might follow abortion is prominent in books and leaflets distributed by British organizations opposed to abortion. According to Life, "the sequelae of abortion, especially post-abortion trauma, are major medical conditions affecting the health and welfare of women" (1992:8). A Life leaflet titled *Had an abortion? Feeling bad?* discusses feelings and forms of behavior as "symptoms" of a condition women "suffer from," which the leaflet describes as follows:

When you're hurting inside and can't understand why you feel:

Grief; guilt/shame; anger—against your partner, against your parents, against your doctor, against those who suggested abortion; self-pity; depression; you're moody, withdrawn, constantly crying; you're playing around with drugs; you're overeating; you've gone off your food; you're having nightmares; you can't sleep; you've gone off sex, or to overcome your pain you're using sex; you don't like yourself very much; you feel ashamed. These feelings are all symptoms of what is known as POST-ABORTION TRAUMA. A lot of women suffer from it.

Care for Life, a project initiated in Britain by Christian Action Research and Education (CARE) (an organization that was named the Festival of Light until 1983), organizes the CARE Centres Network in Britain. This network offers counseling to women who are considering, or who have had, an abortion and claims that abortion can cause health problems. These include physical health problems, contends CARE, but "more significantly, there are emotional effects," including numbness, sadness, guilt and shame, a sense of loss, emptiness, grief, anger and depression (CARE n.d.). Difficulties that women experience as part of such mental health problems, CARE alleges, are tensions in relationships, bad dreams and nightmares, flashbacks, loss of self-esteem, and a preoccupation with babies.

In Britain, the term "Postabortion Syndrome" first appeared in public debate about abortion in parliamentary discussions in the late 1980s. During a debate about the Alton Bill in the British Parliament in 1987, a bill that was intended to restrict the legal time limit for abortion to 18 weeks, Liberal Democrat Member of Parliament David Alton, the bill's sponsor, described Postabortion Syndrome as "the psychiatric morbidity experienced by a woman after an abortion" (Steinberg 1991:181). Three years later, during a debate about the Human Fertilisation and Embryology Bill (a bill that was concerned mainly with regulation of experiments on embryos and fertility treatment), Dame Elaine Kellett-Bowman claimed that research carried out in the United States showed that 82 percent of women who have had their pregnancy terminated suffer from Postabortion Syndrome. One section of this bill concerned the time limit for abortions, and it was proposed that the time limit should be lowered. Kellett-Bowman argued in favor of this proposal. Her argument was that it is wrong to make it easy for women to get abortions, and particularly to allow them to terminate pregnancies at later stages in gestation, because of this risk to their mental health. To the contrary, she argued, it should be compulsory for women to be counseled before abortion, preferably by a doctor, to make them aware of the psychological problems that were likely to result if they went ahead. Newspaper articles at this time also began to refer to the PAS claim, when they included comment from representatives of antiabortion groups (Legh-Jonson 1989; *Scottish Catholic Observer* 1992; *Education Guardian* 1992; Macdonald 1992).

This claim has subsequently made regular appearances when abortion has been the focus for public debate in Britain, and its proponents have emphasized that abortion makes women ill. For example, following the announcement in 1997 that the abortion provider Marie Stopes Clinics was to begin providing an abortion service so simple that a woman could end her pregnancy during her lunch break, opponents of abortion made the PAS claim their central objection to this new service. According to Tim Black, Marie Stopes Clinics' chief executive, the new service was a boon for women, since it would make "early abortion a minor procedure that could quite easily be completed during a working woman's lunchtime break" (Brown 1997:2). This would be possible because of the use of a new abortion technique, whereby an abortion is performed in the first twelve weeks of pregnancy, with a local anesthetic. A woman can attend a clinic, undergo the abortion, and leave the clinic within two hours. However, opponents of abortion were outraged by the argument that it should be made as easy as possible for a woman to end a pregnancy. Jack Scarisbrick, Life's chairman, drew attention to the idea that abortion makes women mentally ill. He called the service "bad news for women," claiming that "Post abortion trauma is becoming a major women's disease when they try to come to terms with the guilt, grief and anger at the loss of life" (Brown 1997:2).

In the United States as well, antiabortion organizations claim that abortion is a health risk for women because it can lead to Postabortion Syndrome. Indeed, this claim against abortion has its origins in the American abortion debate. As Chapter 3 details, the term "Postabortion Syndrome" first emerged in the abortion debate in North America in the early 1980s. Antiabortion literature in the United States routinely details the alleged health risks of abortion and sets out lists of feelings and forms of behavior that are claimed collectively to comprise the symptoms of the psychiatric disorder Postabortion Trauma/Syndrome. The National Right to Life Committee (NRLC) contends,

> Clinical research provides a growing body of scientific evidence that having an abortion can cause psychological harm to some women. . . . Researchers on the after-effects of abortion have identified a pattern of psychological problems known as Post-Abortion Syndrome (PAS). Women suffering from PAS may experience drug and alcohol abuse, personal relationship disorders, sexual dysfunction, repeated abortions, communications difficulties, damaged self-esteem, and even attempted suicide. (National Right to Life Committee n.d.)

The claim that abortion is a mental health problem has informed the activities of abortion opponents. They set up organizations in the United States in the 1980s that prioritize publicizing the negative psychological effects of abortion, for example, American Victims of Abortion (which has a sister organization based in Britain, named British Victims of Abortion) and Women Exploited By Abortion (WEBA). Feminists for Life was established in 1973 to draw attention to the contradiction that it alleges exists between women's interests and the legalization of abortion, and this group has incorporated into its arguments the claim that abortion brings with it significant emotional risks for women. To meet the health needs of U.S. citizens, Feminists for Life argues, the U.S. Department of Health and Human Services should conduct a "comprehensive study" of the emotional effects of abortion, to make clear the significant risk abortion poses for women's mental health (Ciampa 2001:12). Women Deserve Better is the most recently formed initiative aimed at publicizing the supposed impact of abortion upon women's mental health. This campaign, organized by Feminists for Life and backed by the Family Research Council and Concerned Women for America, was launched in 2002 and promotes the slogan "Abortion Hurts Women."

The Elliot Institute, founded in 1988 under the directorship of David Reardon, has emerged as a key proponent in the United States of the link between abortion and mental ill health. The Institute, according to its website, was founded "to perform original research and education on the impact of abortion on women, men, siblings and society." It publishes "research and educational materials and works as an advocate for women and men seeking post-abortion healing." The claim that abortion causes significant psychological problems for women is central to such advocacy work. The Elliot Institute contends that, although present research has not established accurately how many women suffer from any specific symptom of postabortion trauma, "it is clear that post-abortion psychological disorders do occur." Making this alleged health risk of abortion into an issue is, David Reardon argues, central to a prolife strategy that can make "post abortion healing" widely available in American society. The argument that abortion harms women's health, he says, will ultimately discredit legal abortion altogether (Reardon 1996a).

An array of therapeutic services initiated by or linked with organizations that oppose legal abortion has emerged, which offer counseling to women who have had abortions. One such initiative in the United States is Rachel's Vineyard, a "therapeutic support group for post abortive women," which started out as the Center for Post Abortion Healing in 1986, and which now operates as part of the activities of the American Life League. Rachel's Vineyard lists the following as "symptoms of Post Abortion Syndrome/Trauma":

> Bouts of crying, guilt, intense grief/sadness, emotional numbness, eating disorders, drug and alcohol abuse, suicidal urges, anxiety and panic attacks, depression, inability to forgive yourself, anger/rage, sexual problems or promiscuity, lowered self esteem, nightmares and sleep disturbances, difficulty with relationships, flashbacks. (Rachel's Vineyard n.d.)

Rachel's Vineyard takes its name from the woman described in the Bible weeping for her lost children, as does Project Rachel, a "ministry of healing directed toward those who suffer from Post-Abortion Syndrome" (Kupferman 1994: 11). While affiliated with the Catholic Church, and thus religious in orientation, the advocates of such "healing" blend religious rhetoric with the language of psychiatry and medicine. Reverend Larry Kupferman, a priest who works as a postabortion counselor for Project Rachel, devised a "Rachel rosary" to be recited by "victims of abortion." The rosary includes a Hail Mary ("For the woman whose pain and guilt over a previous abortion manifests as clinical depression years later") and a prayer to God ("For an increase in education in the areas of sexuality and relationships") (Kupferman 1994:22–35).

Therapist Teri Reisser, who wrote a book promoted by organizations advocating a more widespread diagnosis of PAS, medicalizes the problem of abortion as a "silent epidemic." According to Reisser, during the 1980s hundreds of "Crisis Pregnancy Centers" (CPCs) were founded in the United States to "provide meaningful alternatives to abortion," and their activities came to include counseling women after abortion for "post-abortion pain." The problems that women can experience following abortion, states Reisser, have been designated a form of psychological disorder termed Postabortion Syndrome. Reisser (1999) cites papers published by Anne Speckhard, Vincent Rue, and David Reardon to substantiate this claim. Nancy Michels, whose book *Helping Women Recover from Abortion* was written as a result of her experience counseling women in a project organized by Lutherans for Life, describes feelings of guilt, anger, and fear among women following abortion as "a few of the common reactions now identified in Post Abortion Syndrome (PAS), the condition that occurs when women repress the grief that results from the loss of their aborted child" (1988:30).

Such campaigns and projects each promote their activities on the basis that they have something unique to add to the prolife cause and can in their own unique way assist women who have had abortions. A point of agreement, however, is that abortion is a problem because it places women's mental health at risk.

Postabortion Syndrome as a Form of Posttraumatic Stress Disorder

To posit the existence of Postabortion Syndrome is not, however, simply to make a claim that abortion leads to mental illness. Claimants are more specific. The condition is a form of Posttraumatic Stress Disorder, they argue. The National Office of Post-Abortion Reconciliation and Healing, Inc., founded in 1990 in the United States to "network researchers and psychotherapeutic professionals working in the field within the U.S and abroad," claims, for example, that "there is a wide variety of symptoms of abortion's aftermath," ranging from "mild grief" to "Post-Traumatic Stress Disorder" (n.d.). According to Feminists for Life, "Many women [following abortion] experience symptoms similar to other forms of post-traumatic stress disorder" (Ciampa 2001: 14). Margaret Cuthill, the founder of British Victims of Abortion, claims that "Post Abortion Syndrome has been classified as a type of Post Traumatic Stress Disorder" and that women who have undergone abortion fall into two groups, those who suffer from PTSD "on an acute or chronic basis" and those who have no symptoms at present, "but are at risk at some future stress point" that may act as a trigger for the development of the illness (Cuthill 1996:xvii).

It is commonplace for the experiences of women who have had an abortion to be compared to the experiences of groups of people who have come to be recognized as vulnerable to PTSD. Comparisons to Vietnam veterans, the first group of people diagnosed as suffering from this illness, are often made. John Wilke, then president of the National Right to Life Committee, drew attention to the apparent similarity between women who have had abortions and Vietnam veterans in the late 1980s, the point when PAS first began to gain visibility in the United States. He explained that the "antiabortion forces' next big move" would be to increase their political power by recruiting women who feel guilty about having had abortions. Scientists, Wilke argued, have "uncovered dramatic new findings indicating that the millions of women who have undergone abortions are in danger of suffering from the same sort of 'shell shock' problems that afflict many Vietnam War veterans" (Coates 1986:3). American proponent of PAS Vincent Rue visited Britain in 1989, to speak to a meeting of politicians opposed to abortion. Rue warned that women who have had abortions "may experience the same kind of guilt and misery as Vietnam Veterans who cannot chase off the nightmare of life under fire" (Illman 1989). According to Michael Jarmulowicz, a British advocate of PAS, "Post Abortion Syndrome is a variant of 'Post Traumatic Stress Disorder,' first described in Vietnam war veterans." He argues, "The wives of the men suffering described how they had changed—they might be violent or abuse alcohol. . . . So it is with abortion. The feelings about the abortion are suppressed, but the subconscious must have some mechanism of release and other apparently unrelated symptoms emerge" (1992:9).

The claim that PAS is a form of PTSD was, according to many accounts of the origin of the term "Postabortion Syndrome," pioneered in particular by Anne Speckhard and Vincent Rue (Michels 1988; Doherty 1995). During the 1980s Rue gave a number of papers and published a number of articles about PAS, the first of which was given in testimony before the U.S. Senate in 1981 (see also Rue 1984, 1986). Anne Speckhard's unpublished doctoral thesis is titled "The Psychological Aspects of Stress after Abortion," and its findings are referred to in writings by antiabortion claimsmakers as evidence for the existence of the syndrome.

Rue developed "diagnostic criteria" for PostAbortion Syndrome,[2] modeled on those for PTSD that appear in the American Psychiatric Association's *Diagnostic and Statistical Manual of Mental Disorders* (DSM). The diagnostic criteria for PTSD were developed to account for the experiences of soldiers returning to the United States from the war in Vietnam. Rue explicitly compares the symptoms of PAS to those considered characteristic of Vietnam veterans diagnosed with PTSD. He has argued that "the symptoms are the same: flashbacks, denial, lost memory of the event, avoidance of the subject" (Rourke 1995:E-1). Rue's diagnostic criteria for PAS appear in other U.S. accounts that promote the need to consider abortion a cause of mental ill health (Reisser 1999).

For Rue and Speckhard, comparing women who have had abortions to soldiers emphasizes that the psychological effects of terminating pregnancy should not be underestimated; rather, it is "possible that the decision to elect abortion can generate significant resulting psychosocial distress" (Speckhard and Rue 1992:96). According to Rue:

> . . . while abortion may indeed function as a "stress reliever" by eliminating an unwanted pregnancy, other evidence suggests that it may also simultaneously or subsequently be experienced by some individuals as a psychosocial stressor, capable of causing posttraumatic stress disorder (PTSD). . . . We suggest that this constellation of dysfunctional behaviors and emotional reactions should be termed "Postabortion syndrome (PAS)." (Rue 1995:20)

One potential difficulty that proponents of this argument face is that, as Chapter 2 details, when the diagnostic criteria for PTSD in the DSM were first formulated, they specified that a "stressor" that could lead to the disorder would be "outside the range of usual human experience" (for example, fighting in a war). This criterion for a PTSD stressor has been described as the "gatekeeper" for the diagnosis of PTSD (Joseph et al. 1997). It is on these grounds that experiences like "marital conflict" or "simple bereavement" were, in the 1980s, excluded as events sufficiently traumatic to lead to PTSD. Regardless of how upsetting the individual concerned finds a divorce or the death of a loved one, or how she responds psychologically to that experience, it was argued that she could not be diagnosed as suffering from PTSD.

On this basis, one U.S. critic of PAS, Henry David, contends that the PAS diagnosis makes no sense (1997). He argues that, given the numbers of women who have had abortions (it is estimated that around one-third of American and British women will have an abortion at some point in their life), it is difficult to see how abortion can be defined as an event that is "outside the range of usual human experience." For David, abortion is part of everyday experience for so many women that it simply cannot be defined as potentially traumatic. By contrast, Speckhard and Rue maintain that abortion can legitimately be defined as a "trauma" on the grounds that many women perceive it that way. They argue: "Stress begins with one's perception of it" (1992:106). Hence there can be no generally applicable definition of what events can be traumatic, and a more subjective definition of stress should be accepted. Although some women may not perceive abortion as a stressor, others will. Where abortion is perceived as stressful by the woman, according to these claimsmakers, symptoms characteristic of PTSD are likely to emerge, and in this circumstance women can legitimately be "diagnosed" as suffering from PAS.

Rue also links abortion as a "stressor" to the PTSD diagnostic criteria by defining abortion in a particular way. The DSM states that the kind of "stressor" that can lead to PTSD includes threats to the lives of one's children. PAS, argues Rue, can be considered a form of PTSD since it involves "exposure to or participation in an abortion experience i.e. the intentional destruction of one's unborn child, which is perceived as sufficiently traumatic and beyond the range of usual human experience" (1995:21). Throughout his writings the claim that abortion, for some women, is perceived as the "death of a child" is key to the argument that abortion can lead to a form of PTSD. Rue has described abortion as a "death experience," stating

> If elective abortion is nothing more than the removal of nondescript cells or tissue, then it would be highly unlikely that such a procedure could cause any significant psychological harm, much less resemble the symptom picture of post-traumatic stress disorder (PTSD). On the other hand, if elective abortion is an intentionally caused human death experience, then it is likely that some women, men and significant others could manifest profound symptoms of intrusion/re-experience, avoidance/denial, associated symptoms, depression, grief and loss. It is also true that stress and trauma begin with one's perception of it. (Rue 1995:19)

Rue presents two possible perceptions of abortion, the "removal of nondescript cells" and a "human death experience." If abortion is perceived as the removal of "nondescript cells" there would be no reason to believe that the psychological response to abortion would be negative, certainly not to the extent that the woman could suffer from PTSD. If abortion is perceived, in contrast, as a "human death experience," then severe psychological problems could be predicted postabortion on the grounds that the woman, and those who associated with her when she had an abortion, participated in the killing of a human being. Rue thus construes abortion as "outside the range of usual human experience" and links PAS to PTSD.

It is in this aspect of the PAS claim that the familiar concern of abortion opponents, the loss of fetal life, appears. It is noteworthy, however, that this concern is implicit, not explicit, in the PAS claim and that it is less overtly moralistic than claims that emphasize that abortion "takes a life." Rue acknowledges that abortion can be understood in different, competing ways and states that what counts is the subjective view of the woman who has had an abortion. Only where abortion is perceived as a "death experience" is PAS likely to develop. The personhood of the fetus is thus construed as a matter of opinion rather than fact.

A further noteworthy feature of the PAS claim, in regard to the diagnostic criteria for PTSD, is the representation of the symptoms of PAS. According to the diagnostic criteria developed by Rue, the abortion experience is defined as a stressor, sufficiently traumatic to cause the "symptoms" of "re-experience, avoidance and impacted grieving." To be diagnosed as having PAS, the woman has to reexperience the abortion trauma in one of four listed ways (for example, having recurrent, distressing dreams of the "unborn child"); she has to show three manifestations of a possible seven listed examples of avoidance (such as avoiding thoughts about abortion or feeling detached from others); and she has to have two of a possible eleven "associated features" (such as difficulty in falling asleep or eating disorders) (Rue 1995:27–28). The PAS claim is therefore formally modeled on the existing, accepted psychiatric criteria for PTSD.

However, the writings of PAS claimsmakers reveal a shift from a definition of the symptoms of PAS where the proposed comparison with PTSD is made clear to a much broader collection of symptoms. As American feminist theorist Valerie Hartouni notes in her discussion of the PAS claim, the syndrome has a "vast range of indications," including "guilt, remorse, despair, unfulfillment, withdrawal, helplessness, decreased work capacity, diminished powers of reason, anger and rage, seizures, loss of interest in sex, intense interest in babies, thwarted maternal instincts, residual 'motherliness,' self-destructive behavior, suicidal impulses, hostility and child abuse" (1997:43). Thus, where Rue presents the diagnostic criteria for PAS, he also lists a wide range of feelings and forms of behavior that he argues might be evident in women who have had an abortion. These include feelings of helplessness, hopelessness, sadness, sorrow, lowered self-esteem, distrust, regret, relationship disruption, communication impairment, and/or restriction and self-condemnation (Rue 1995:20).

Following Rue, other PAS claimants have taken a similar approach. The Elliot Institute includes as symptoms of PAS sexual dysfunction (comprising loss of pleasure from intercourse, an aversion to males in general, or promiscuity); increased cigarette smoking; child neglect or abuse (including "replacement pregnancies," that is, becoming pregnant after an abortion); reduced maternal bonding with children born after the abortion; divorce; and repeat abortions (having another abortion in the future). Peter Randall, in his introduction to a book about the effects of abortion distributed by the SPUC, contends that women who become "shopaholics," consume "excess alcohol," or "engage in frenetic activity within their homes and with voluntary causes" have the syndrome, as do those who experience "sleeplessness, appetite disorders, parenting problems over the management of other children, depression, psychosomatic illness which may include anorexia and bulimia and. . . . a profound fear of becoming a parent." Among the common symptoms of Postabortion Syndrome, argues Randall, are "guilt, depression, grief, anxiety, sadness, shame, helplessness and hopelessness. These may result in lowered self-esteem, distrust, hostility towards self and others, insomnia, or recurring dreams and nightmares" (1996:ix–xiv). The benefit for PAS claimants of associating this broad range of symptoms with a diagnosis of PAS is obvious, in that it lets claimants argue that large numbers of women may suffer from the syndrome. As the diagnostic criteria for PAS become broader, it is easier to claim that many women may suffer from it. British Victims of Abortion states, in this way, that "PAS displays the hallmark of repressed mourning: guilt, pain and impacted grief. . . . the number of women at risk here in Great Britain is staggering. Since 1967, approximately 4.5 million abortions have taken place. . . . [which] would indicate that some 45,000 women have been experiencing trauma which could affect their lives" (Cuthill 1996:xvi–xvii).

Speckhard and Rue formalize the elastic definition characteristic of PAS symptoms when they suggest that "as a psychosocial stressor, abortion may lead some women to experience reactions ranging from mild distress to severe trauma, creating a continuum that we conceptualize as progressing in severity from postabortion distress (PAD) to PAS to postabortion psychosis" (1992:104–5). Positing women's reactions to having an abortion as a continuum is significant, in that it creates a link between mild and severe responses: all become less serious versions of the same medical condition. Feelings that a woman might experience after abortion, such as sadness or regret, come to be seen as a version of a psychiatric disorder. As later chapters detail, however, such an approach is not unique to those who claim there is a psychological illness they call Postabortion Syndrome. Such "concept slippage"—use of very inclusive definitions of illness symptoms—is in fact characteristic of the wider discussion of trauma and its effects for mental health. What is at issue, as this book discusses later, is the extent to which such an approach comes to be contested by others.

A Common Illness

The argument that large numbers of women suffer from PAS is developed through reference to a key symptom of the syndrome, "denial." Denial is considered to stretch through the duration of the pregnancy and comprises all of the reactions that a woman who has an abortion might have in relation to her pregnancy. Rue refers approvingly to the therapist Selby, who argues that the stages of denial are

> 1) preabortion denial (a) of the pregnancy itself; (b) of the responsibility for the pregnancy; (c) of the baby or the humanity of the product of conception; or (d) of how she became pregnant; 2) during the abortion event denial (a) of the physical experience itself; (b) of her emotional reactions to the procedure; and 3) post-

abortion denial (a) of certain aspects of the abortion; (b) of all memory of the abortion and (c) of any relationship between abortion and self-defeating behaviors. (Rue 1995:23)

Thus, when a woman before an abortion expresses surprise that she became pregnant since she was using contraception, but puts the pregnancy down to contraceptive failure, she can be considered "in denial" of "responsibility" for the pregnancy. Equally, her claim that she does not consider a fetus to be a person is denial of the humanity of the "baby."

However, the main focus for PAS advocates is the time following an abortion. Rue suggests that, following abortion, to cope with its trauma, women employ "a mechanism known as 'psychic numbing.'" This means that women deny the trauma of the abortion and repress the memories of it, "thus enabling the person to present a reasonably calm exterior." But, according to Rue, there is every possibility that "a degree of anxiety and depression may re-emerge later" (1995:10). Following Rue, Peter Randall argues:

> Early psychological studies on the aftermath of abortion reported some damage, but found it in only a small minority of women. This does not contradict our experience of PAS, because symptoms of repressed grief are most likely to surface from six months to two years after the trauma occurs. . . . Most of those we see and counsel have had their abortions between 8 and 35 years ago. (1996:xvii)

The significance of this claim about women's psychological response to abortion is that the absence of evidence for PAS in the present does not invalidate it. According to the Elliot Institute, "many women who have had an abortion use repression as a coping mechanism." There may be a long period of denial before a woman seeks psychiatric care, and "indeed for many women, the onset or accurate identification of PTSD symptoms may be delayed for several years" (1997). Hence, while there may not be large numbers of women with PAS at the present time, there will be many PAS sufferers in the future. Moreover, any of the many symptoms ascribed to PAS, at whichever point they exist following an abortion, can be used as evidence of PAS. Since the woman has denied and repressed her feelings, these symptoms can emerge much later in her life and appear to her and to other people to be unrelated to the abortion experience. Thus any future depression, or other more or less severe negative feelings experienced by a woman who has had an abortion, can be attributed to having ended a pregnancy earlier in her life.

Presenting denial as a significant response to abortion permits the claim that large numbers of women have in fact experienced abortion as trauma, whether they know it or not. As Hopkins, Reicher, and Saleem have noted, through their analysis of the PAS claim, this claim "allows a woman's declaration that her psychological health is unaffected by abortion to be dismissed" (1996:547). To illustrate this effect of the PAS claim, they point out that a Life briefing paper on the psychological effects of abortion contends that because of denial, "it is no surprise that studies soon after an abortion find the women feel relieved and so claim that they suffer no adverse affects." This means that the broad range of symptoms deemed characteristic of the syndrome can be presented as effects of the illness, even if the woman concerned does not herself connect them to having had an abortion (Hopkins et al. 1996:547-8). Wanda Franz, as president of the U.S. NRLC, has used Rue's argument about denial to contend that even women "damaged" by their abortion experience can claim, in good faith, to have no negative psychological reactions. Psychological problems are suppressed, and therefore after abortion women have no conscious awareness of them (Franz n.d.). The emergence of PAS as a health problem can then be projected into the future. According to Rue: "It took the Vietnam veterans over 10 years to convince the American Psychiatric Association that there is such a thing as post-traumatic stress syndrome. . . . We believe PAS is experiencing a similar journey" (Brotman 1990:4). Rue claims that PAS will come be recognized by the American Psychiatric Association as a form of PTSD when the symptoms of "repressed trauma" emerge in women who had abortions in the past.

PAS AND THE POLITICS OF ABORTION

Postabortion Syndrome, it is therefore claimed, is a particular form of mental illness. The abortion problem is medicalized, but those who frame it in this way do not simply borrow the language of psychiatry and therapy. This process also entails a reworking of antiabortion movement claims about women, about those who provide them with abortions, and about the motives behind the actions of those involved in the abortion debate. In sum, this process entails a reconstruction of the politics of abortion.

As Loseke has argued, claimsmaking involves constructing certain types of people, often "victims" and "villains" (1999). Such constructions carry with them encouragements to apportion blame for social problems. "Victims" do not bear responsibility for the condition they find themselves in, even if the condition is deemed problematic, whereas "villains" do. In claims about the problem of abortion, moralized antiabortion rhetoric has tended to construct women as actors who commit wrong, thus contending that women who have had abortions have made a moral mistake. Often projected through the notion that such women have behaved "selfishly" or "irresponsibly," women are thus construed more as villains than victims. The PAS claim, which relies upon a construction of women who have abortions, is different, however. Like other groups deemed to suffer from PTSD, or to be at risk of it, women who have abortions or who are considering doing so are framed explicitly as "victims" by PAS advocates. Women, in this form of the antiabortion argument, are no longer immoral, to be considered wrongdoers because they have acted selfishly and taken life, but are victims to be pitied and helped. As I go on to discuss, this construction of women brings with it both a new focus for the antiabortion argument about responsibility for the abortion problem and a reconstruction of the aims of those who are involved in opposing abortion.

Women as Victims

In claimsmaking about PAS, a comparison is often made between women who have had an abortion and other women who have come to be considered victims of PTSD. Rue argues that "Other variants of PTSD, not dissimilar to PAS, are 'Rape Trauma Syndrome,' 'Battered Wives' Syndrome,' and 'Post-Hysterectomy Syndrome,' all of which are also not included in the DSM-III-R [as is the case for PAS], but which are widely accepted" (1995:21). Linking claims about PAS to the representation of women who have been raped is particularly prevalent. "Some women feel coerced and physically violated by their abortion experience. Their feelings and symptoms are similar to women who have been physically or sexually assaulted. Issues to be addressed in counselling include anger, self-blame and punitive behaviours, low self-esteem, re-victimisation and regaining a sense of control in their lives," argue Rue and Banhole (1998:25).

Reardon says in his book *Victims and Victors,* of women who become pregnant from rape or incest, "Many women report that their abortions felt like a degrading form of 'medical rape.' . . . Abortion involves a painful intrusion into a woman's sexual organs by a masked stranger. . . . For many women this experiential association between abortion and sexual assault is very strong" (Matthewes-Green 2000). Olivia Gans, of American Victims of Abortion, argues that her abortion led to postabortion trauma: "I honestly feel like I was mechanically raped that day," she has claimed (Schmich 1989:1). Abortion, argues Gans, is "an act of violence against women, an act of violence against our children" (Crawley 1989:14). Reardon also links abortion to violence against women by comparing doctors who perform abortions to rapists, on the grounds of the similarity in the psychological effects of the two experiences. He argues, "Both rapists and abortionists injure women in a way which creates so much shame that their victims actually help to conceal the crime . . . the victims of rape and abortion are both inclined to blame themselves for the 'stupidity' of having put themselves in the hands of their abuser" (Reardon 1996b).

The PAS claim continually invokes the notion that women are victimized by abortion. As journalist Cathy Young has argued, this representation of the woman who has an abortion constitutes a "transformation" in the terms of antiabortion claims. "No longer is she a selfish monster . . . instead . . . she is a passive victim. . . . The new rhetoric of the anti-abortion movement employs feminist language, terming abortion 'surgical rape,' and borrows from the more extreme brands of feminist rhetoric that label 'rape' every real or imagined injustice toward women" (1989:D-05).

Constructing Villains

The construction of women as victims of abortion carries with it claims about who might be considered villains. The corollary of the argument that women are victims when they abort a pregnancy is that those who enabled or encouraged them to do so are the villains. Who, in particular, is constructed this way?

A key theme in arguments made by proponents of PAS—in common with other claims for victims (Best 1999)—is that the trauma of abortion is unrecognized. In this instance, the villain of the piece is sometimes presented in very general terms, as "a society" that does not care sufficiently for its victims and thus refuses to recognize the trauma of abortion. Thus, according to Margaret Cuthill, spokeswoman for British Victims of Abortion, "Society today denies women who have had abortions permission to grieve." She aims to expose "the truth about abortion so that those suffering from trauma will know there is help available to them" (Marsh 1997:6).

Rue also contends that the lack of recognition of the trauma of abortion is key to the psychological problems experienced by women who have had an abortion. He links his argument to a more general claim that society refuses openly to acknowledge grief after traumatic events, described as the problem of "disenfranchised grief," and argues, in this vein, "When a pregnancy loss such as induced abortion is traumatic, and it cannot be openly acknowledged, publicly mourned or socially supported, the parent lives in isolation. For such an individual, grief is 'disenfranchised'" (1995:17). Rue draws directly upon the argument that women, in particular, are victims of socially unrecognized traumatic experiences. He refers frequently to the work of Judith Lewis Herman, whose views have been highly influential with regard to women's experiences of rape and sexual violence. Herman argues that women and children "may find that the most traumatic events of their life take place outside the realm of socially validated reality" and hence that their experience becomes "unspeakable" and their victimhood is made "invisible." Rue claims that, when it comes to abortion, a woman's experience is the same: "many women are traumatized not only by their abortion experiences but also by an unsympathetic society. These women are prevented by shame or denial from voicing their experiences . . . society implicitly or explicitly encourages them to remain 'invisible'" (1997:8).

A more specific target for the role of villain is people involved in the mental health professions. They are condemned by PAS claimants for their alleged failure to recognize the problems faced by women who have abortions. Rue argues: "In the mental health community, resistance has all too often been considerable in acknowledging the profound effects of human trauma. . . . This is particularly the case regarding induced abortion" (1995:15). Those who work in mental health services are considered either reluctant to acknowledge the trauma of abortion, "for fear of lending support to a political position in opposition to their own," or insufficiently alert to the problem; they "never bother to question the patient about past pregnancy losses and any possible resulting behavioural, cognitive and/or emotional changes" (1995:15).

PAS advocates also blame researchers who have investigated the psychological effects of abortion for failing to recognize the problems women allegedly face. The purported lack of research about the psychological effects of abortion is used to emphasize the potentially widespread nature of the problem. For former president of Feminists for Life Rachel McNair, PAS is not accepted as an important mental health problem because researchers refuse to take women's problems seriously. "As with breast cancer," she argues, "the definitive unassailable study [of the psychological effects of abortion] remains to be done. . . . Too much of the material is anecdotal, or shallow questionnaires done of biased samples. . . . Once again, women do not get unassailable answers on this point . . . because a widespread problem that affects only women is not regarded as sufficiently important to expend resources upon" (1997:81).

It is claimed that, since the extent of PAS is underresearched, there may be many more women suffering from it than anyone currently recognizes: "The incidence of PAS can only be estimated. . . . It is estimated that 7–17% of women who elect abortion may meet the diagnostic criteria for PAS and 25–45% experience multiple post-traumatic stress-related symptoms" (Rue and Banhole 1998:29). A point also emphasized throughout the literature produced on PAS by the antiabortion movement is that existing research about the psychological effects of abortion is unreliable. Most research carried out following the legalization of abortion in the United States and other countries, as Chapter 5 details, has found that abortion does not lead to severe psychological difficulties. However, according to PAS claimsmakers, research findings to date do not invalidate their argument. Rue argues that even those who believe that abortion does not cause significant psychological harm have accepted that there are methodological shortcomings to existing research, that conclusions about the long-term effect of abortion cannot be drawn from them, and that women who might find abortion stressful are underrepresented in survey samples. Therefore, he argues, "these limitations would certainly seem to question the validity of making such sweeping claims about the psychological safety of induced abortion" (1995:15).

Of these alleged limitations, claims about PAS focus in particular on the lack of evidence about the long-term psychological effects of abortion. Since, argues Rue, "Women with PAS may employ repression in an attempt to 'forget' parts or the whole of the postabortion trauma, creating 'psychogenic amnesia'" (Rue 1995:24), data about the psychological effects of abortion gathered shortly after the procedure do not invalidate the PAS claim. According to PAS claimants associated with the Pine Rest Christian Hospital, Michigan, "most studies covered a year or less following the abortion," and their results cannot be taken as reliable evidence for the benign effects of abortion, since it would be "some time later that psychological sequelae would likely manifest" (Anderson et al. 1995:103–4). It is argued that, given this research gap in the case made by supporters of legal abortion, "pronouncements concerning the psychological safety of induced abortion are at this time premature at best, and at worst, misleading and harmful to women's health" (Rue 1995:26).

Other villains, according to PAS advocates, are those involved in the provision of abortion services. Doctors and abortion providers are often constructed as villains because, it is claimed, they pay little heed to the damaging consequences for women of the abortions they provide. U.S. proponents of the PAS claim are particularly forceful in their condemnation of abortion providers. Often their claims invoke the notion that abortion provision is an "industry" that aims only to make money, not care for women. Abortion providers are castigated for "hurting women" for financial reward.

As Woliver (1996) notes, in her study of amicus briefs filed for the 1989 Supreme Court case *Webster v. Reproductive Health Services,* attacks were directed by prolife groups at clinics where abortions were performed, as such clinics were described as part of the "abortion industry" (see Chapter 3 for a discussion of this case). Doctors, it was argued, have a direct financial interest in promoting abortion and disregard women's health; they are, it was claimed, little more than "abortion profiteers." Doctors were also described as "technicians," thereby implying that they are unable to act in a way that can take into account the emotional needs of their patients.

PAS claimants often present themselves as doing battle with "the abortion industry" to defend the victims of abortion and ensure their rights are protected. David Reardon contends that at present "abortionists are both violating their duty and denying women rights" (1996a:43). For Reardon, it is not the moral arguments against abortion that will create opposition to the provision of the procedure, but women's rights, in particular "the right to know about abortion's risks," "the right to be screened for predisposing risk factors," "the right to be offered safer alternatives," and "the right to sue abortionists," which will hurt the only thing Reardon alleges they care about, "their bank accounts."

The argument that doctors and clinics are the villains of the piece is less visible in Britain, perhaps because abortion is usually funded by the state and is often provided in National Health Service (NHS) hospitals. There is, therefore, no "profit motive" involved. In the United States, by contrast, abortion is removed from the system of state-allocated funding and is therefore frequently privately funded. This makes the presentation of abortion as an "industry" more likely to emerge. This difference between the systems of provision of abortion in the United States and Britain is itself a product of the difference in the construction of the abortion issue, which I detail in Chapter 3.

However, despite these differences, British abortion opponents have represented specialized clinics that provide abortions as "villains." Their response to Marie Stopes Clinics' provision of "lunch-hour" abortion was to claim: "This is the ultimate in a fast economy, fast food and now fast abortion." The clinics were "part of a huge money-making industry," a spokeswoman for Life contended (Borrill 1997). British Victims of Abortion (BVA) justify their castigation of doctors by contending that "the medical profession have largely ignored this syndrome [PAS], denied its reality, or minimised its impact on the lives of countless women and men" (British Victims of Abortion n.d.).

Other "villains" often targeted by PAS advocates are women's partners, husbands, friends, and families, who, it is alleged, care less for their wife, partner, or daughter than for themselves. Bernadette Thompson, speaking for BVA, argues: "Of the many women I've counselled [for PAS], I would say that well over 90 per cent of them aborted their babies to please someone else: their husband, boyfriend, parents or peer group" (Bowman 1996:9). Feminists for Life contend that, like them, "early feminists" opposed abortion because they knew that women "resorted to abortion because they were abandoned or pressured by boyfriends, husbands and parents." They argue that women have abortions because they are "pressured by partners who say they will pay $300 for an abortion but won't pay a dime in child support" (2000). One leaflet distributed by BVA that discusses PAS states: "[W]e know that the majority of women who have had abortions would have preferred another solution to the problem. They are clearly victims of someone else's decision making" (Franz n.d.).

When the abortion problem is constructed in terms of its psychological effects, rather than its morality, women who have had abortions are no longer presented as the villains. Instead, they are represented as victims who have not chosen abortion. Their experience of PAS indicates they are victims of others' actions.

"ProLife, Prowoman": The Feminization
of the Antiabortion Cause

Opposition to abortion, where the problem is construed in terms of damage to a woman's health, clearly focuses attention upon the woman. In their interesting and informative study of the antiabortion argument, Hopkins, Reicher, and Saleem argue that, through the PAS claim, opponents of abortion are in fact responding to the criticism that they ignore the experience and needs of women. They argue that this criticism represents the "rhetorical Achilles' heel" of the antiabortion argument:

> . . . the anti-abortionists' focus upon the foetus means that they remain vulnerable to the charge of ignoring the woman and her experience. Indeed whilst the image of the foetus as a free-floating independent individual able to claim "rights" is actually dependent upon what Rothman (1986) describes as the reduction of the woman to invisible "empty space," this treatment of women con-

stitutes something of a rhetorical Achilles heel. Put simply, it gives pro-abortion activists the opportunity to castigate anti-abortionists for ignoring the woman. (1996:542)

Through their construction of women as victims, those who argue that there is a Postabortion Syndrome reconstruct abortion opponents as the interest group that is truly concerned with women's health and well-being.

An amicus brief for *Webster v. Reproductive Health Services* from Feminists for Life illustrates this point. The brief included testimonies from a book titled *Rachel Weeping,* which recounted women's bad experiences with legal abortion. Another from the prolife "crisis pregnancy" organization Birthright similarly made "feminized" claims against abortion through its argument that abortion is not a choice women make, "but an act of despair on the part of women." Abortion, argued Birthright, "has become an excuse for not offering real aid to pregnant women. . . . Abortion is indeed a woman's issue, but it is an issue not of women's rights, but of women's oppression" (Woliver 1996:17).

Some even argue that the original feminist argument from the nineteenth century opposed abortion and that it is those who advocate the need for legal abortion who have co-opted the feminist stance. In this vein, advocates of the Women Deserve Better campaign claim they are "fed up with pro-abortion groups co-opting pro-woman language" and that "pro-life organizations plan to take back the abortion issue by focusing on what abortion advocates have forgotten: the needs of women who are pregnant, parenting or who have had an abortion." In the period just before the thirty-fifth anniversary of the *Roe v. Wade* Supreme Court ruling, which legalized abortion in the United States, Women Deserve Better claimed that it planned to focus attention on the need to "meet the physical, emotional, and practical needs of women— needs that are categorically neglected by the abortion industry" (Ertelt 2002b). A commentary from a "prolife feminist" contests what it claims is the "phoney" argument that prochoice feminists make in connecting abortion with women's liberation: "Abortion doesn't 'liberate' women—it 'liberates' the people around them. For instance, employers do not have to make concessions to pregnant women and mothers. Schools do not have to accommodate to the needs of parents, and irresponsible men do not have to commit themselves to their partners or their children" (Garago n.d.).

The British antiabortion organization Life also contests the association between women's interests and a prochoice position on abortion. Its leaflet titled "A Woman's Right to Choose? Women and the Problem Pregnancy" asks, "When pregnancy is unwanted what real choice is there?" The answer is that women really have no choice:

> The choice is between abortion, with its physical and emotional after-effects, or continuing the pregnancy. . . . For selfish partners, parents, friends, the choice is simple. They do the choosing, not her. Sometimes the pressure is gentle. Of-

ten it isn't. There is little freedom of choice when those who should give love and support walk away leaving her to cope alone. Readily available abortion has made women more vulnerable. (n.d. a)

Such reconstruction of the antiabortion case leads to the claim it is not only the impact of legalized abortion upon the fetus that should be considered— its benefits for women should also be questioned. For example, the claim that the trauma of abortion is unrecognized responds to the argument that access to legal abortion is beneficial for women. In the prochoice argument, the greater social acceptance of abortion, brought about through its legalization, has been construed to be in women's interests. The PAS claim inverts this argument. Rue and Speckhard claim that social acceptance of abortion "may discourage women from revealing their postabortion feelings and may result in labeling women with emotional difficulties after their abortion as deviant and in need of psychotherapy" (Speckhard and Rue 1992:96). According to this approach, the legalization of abortion means that either the trauma of abortion is suppressed, or that those women who do admit to their psychological difficulties are labeled abnormal, and it is those who recognize the suffering abortion brings for women, and who therefore oppose its legality, who are truly "prowoman."

Central to the PAS claim is a critique of the legal concepts and arguments that have tended to legitimize abortion. According to the Elliot Institute, U.S. national policy on abortion is built on the idea that abortion is a safe procedure—as the Supreme Court found it to be in its deliberations in *Roe v. Wade*. However, "if it is found that abortion may actually be dangerous to health of women," as the Institute believes it to be, "there is just cause for governments to regulate or prohibit abortion in order to protect their citizens" (1997). Similarly, Life presents legal abortion as a danger to women's health:

> The Abortion Act was also a grievous setback for true feminism, because every time a pregnancy is deliberately destroyed a woman is abused. From our nationwide care service for women facing an unintended pregnancy or suffering from the effects of abortion, we know that the true human cost of twenty five years of abortionism has been thousands of women deeply wounded in mind and often in body, as well as nearly 4 million innocent human lives extinguished. (1992:1)

The PAS claim against the current abortion law thus represents opponents of legal abortion as speaking on behalf of women and their rights. Most significantly, PAS claimants set out to undermine a key idea that underpins support for legal abortion—that women should be able to choose for themselves whether or not to have a child. For example, in Olivia Gans' comparison of her abortion to rape, the analogy suggests that she had no choice. Women suffering from PAS are not, in this framework, people who have freely chosen abortion, and have therefore been well served by legal abortion. Rather they are "victims" of others' choices, who had an abortion against their own desires, because others persuaded them into it.

The question of what is meant by women's rights is, therefore, reversed in comparison with its usual definition with regard to abortion. Where those who argue that legal abortion is an aspect of women's rights place emphasis on women's freedom *from* state interference in their lives, PAS claimants argue just the opposite; that women's rights require that the state intervene *to protect women* from ending pregnancies through abortion. The rights of women are redefined as the right to be protected by the state from the psychological harm done by abortion, from the actions of doctors who perform abortion, and from women's relatives and friends, who allegedly pressure them to end pregnancies.

Feminized antiabortion claims also relate to arguments and strategies for the introduction of new kinds of laws governing abortion. Since the early 1990s, as Chapter 4 explains, legislative initiatives termed "Women's Right to Know" laws have been advocated by abortion opponents, especially in the United States. Such laws mandate the provision of certain kinds of information to women by abortion providers, and proposals often include that they be told of the supposed psychological risks entailed by abortion. Such laws, claim Feminists for Life, empower women: "As with any other medical procedure, women have a right to full disclosure of the nature of the abortion procedure, risks and potential complications," they contend (2000). Americans United for Life advocates such laws, since they "seek to protect women from the risks of abortion. . . . In order for women to make an informed choice, they must be given information that provides them with accurate and adequate information" (1999). State requirements that doctors inform women of the supposed risks of abortion are thereby construed as a woman's right.

The feminized reorientation of the antiabortion argument, however, not only focuses on the issue of the law. The PAS claim also brings with it arguments about the kind of health care pregnant women need, a concern that has been associated with those who advocate the wider availability of abortion. As Chapter 4 discusses in more detail, many different "postabortion healing" and "crisis pregnancy counseling" projects in the United States have been initiated by abortion opponents, the justification for which is the psychological damage supposedly caused by abortion.

In Britain, Life, the SPUC, and CARE advertise and provide counseling for women seeking abortion and counseling for women after abortion. BVA exists specifically to provide such counseling and to educate others through media work and "speaking engagements" about the problem of Postabortion Syndrome (Bowman 1996:xviii). Life has 130 counseling centers, which exist, argues Life, because "Women are often badly damaged by abortion. They say how they regret they were not fully informed and counselled beforehand." Such women, explains a Life leaflet, have commented: "I had an abortion 12 years ago which caused me tremendous psychological problems, resulting in 18 months of psychiatric help," and "On several occasions I hit the bottle. . . . I couldn't stand seeing pregnant women or young children" (n.d. b).

PAS claimants also criticize attempts to make it easier for women to get abortions, not on the basis that unborn children are killed, but on the basis that more women will suffer. In Britain, for example, it was reported that antiabortion groups were "dismayed" by "calls for abortion on request" made by groups supportive of legal abortion. An argument was put forward at a conference that "abortion should be made available on request during the first three months of pregnancy," in contrast to current British law, which states abortion can be provided legally where two doctors agree "in good faith" that the woman concerned meets one of the grounds for abortion specified in law (see Chapter 3 for further discussion of these regulations). In response to this proposal, a spokesperson for Life commented: "We believe the rising number of abortions has already led to problems and we are counselling more and more women who are suffering trauma after having a termination" (*Yorkshire Post* 1999; Hall 1999).

A similar debate emerged in 2001, in response to a document from the British government's Department of Health, which stated that women who are legally entitled to abortion should be able to have the procedure within three weeks of requesting it. The British Pregnancy Advisory Service (BPAS), Britain's largest specialist abortion provider, argued that more use should be made in Britain of the "abortion pill" (RU 486). This approach, claimed BPAS spokesperson Ann Furedi, would better meet women's needs: "Women want abortions that are convenient to slot into their lives. They want to be able to come into the clinic and to be able to be treated and to be able to leave within a couple of hours." Life's chairman, Jack Scarisbrick, opposed this view by emphasizing that psychological problems would result from such an approach and pointing to the need for women to have "time to think and reflect on what they were doing." "What women want is the chance to calm down. They need to have more space. We want the abortion industry to wither away because that is what is best for women" (BBC News Online 2001).

As this chapter has demonstrated, the key feature of the PAS claim is that it constructs abortion as a problem on grounds that are "de-moralized." The moral claim that abortion is a problem because it "takes a life" is, in this construction of the abortion problem, moderated—or even abandoned altogether. The claim focuses, implicitly at least, less on the problem of killing a fetus and more on the health of women. In turn, women who have abortions are constructed less as villains than as victims; and the antiabortion movement, it is claimed, has feminist motivations when it opposes the provision of abortion. The PAS claim is not neutral in regard to social and political issues. Rather, the medicalization of the abortion problem involves claimsmaking about the people who are involved with abortion and about how the procedure should be thought about and regulated. What has led to this reconstruction of argument against abortion? What is the context for such medicalized claims and activities that relate to them? These are the questions at the heart of the following two chapters.

2

The "Syndrome Society"

Why have abortion opponents come to argue abortion is a problem because of its effect upon women's health? What advantages do claims framed in medicalized terms seem to offer? In Chapter 3 I argue that the emergence of claims of this kind can be understood as a response to the limitations of explicitly moralized claims against abortion. But why might abortion opponents *medicalize* their claims? There are, after all, other ways in which claims could be made against abortion that do not rely centrally on emphasizing the "sanctity of unborn life." My aim in this chapter is, therefore, to explain why the specific claim that abortion causes mental illness emerged. I argue that this way of framing the case against abortion was influenced by the context of more general trends in which human experience has been extensively medicalized; a development that has been termed the "Syndrome Society" (Downs 1996). Through exploring this development, I show why claiming there is a Postabortion Syndrome became an option.

THE CONTEMPORARY MEDICALIZATION
OF HUMAN EXPERIENCE

As I discussed in the Introduction, the issue of the medicalization of human experience is a relatively long-standing focus for sociological research. But a development that has caught the attention of some is the growing propensity for human experience to be described and explained with reference to mental illness and disease. As Horwitz argues, whereas thirty years ago many people experienced social and person difficulties in their lives, these were not considered "medical problems" and were certainly not taken to mean that people were afflicted by specific, discrete kinds of mental disorder. What is highly significant about the period of time in between, he contends, is that such "general disturbances of living" metamorphosed into "specific psychiatric diseases that afflict the clients of mental health professionals today" (2002:ix). Like Horowitz, others also argue that this development is of great sociological interest. According to sociologist Frank Furedi, it is the emergence of a "variety of new disorders and conditions" in contemporary British and American societies that constitutes "the most dramatic effect of the medicalization of experience" (1997:92).

Some consider the most developed example of this trend to be the use of the term "addiction" to explain patterns of behavior deemed problematic or troublesome. In the terms laid out by the addiction model of human behavior, people do things they know they should not, and behave in ways they later come to regret, as a result of the presence of a medical, specifically psychological, disorder (Peele 1995; Fitzpatrick 2001). The explanation of behavior in these terms now stretches beyond the long-established examples of alcoholism and cigarette smoking to include gambling, shopping, and sexual behavior. Indeed, according to Sutherland, although alcoholism and substance abuse remain at the core of the concept of addiction, "sex addiction" has become the fastest growth area for groups advocating psychological treatment in the United States through the twelve-step program (the program first established as a treatment for alcohol addiction) (2002).

It has also been argued that the widespread use of the term "syndrome," characteristic of the medical idiom, to account for people's feelings and behavior, shows how contemporary society has come to understand and problematize human experience in medicalized terms. Downs coined the term "syndrome society" to describe this phenomenon, and he argued that "seemingly every trend that involves conflict or potential emotional stress is designated a 'syndrome'" (1996:24).

Downs explained that by the mid-1990s, a rapidly expanding number of syndromes had come to be socially recognized and had emerged as a subject of discussion in scholarly and popular media. His review of articles in law journals found that, whereas in 1950, 1960, and 1970 not a single article used the word "syndrome," by 1985 the word appeared in 86 articles, in 1988 in 114 articles and by 1990 in 146 articles. In newspapers and periodicals, in one month in 1993 alone, more than 1,000 articles used the term (1996:25). Downs's focus is on the incorporation of syndrome diagnoses into legal discussion and their use as part of legal defenses to explain allegedly criminal behavior. But the recognition of new syndromes has been apparent in many arenas. Some, such as Battered Woman's Syndrome and Premenstrual Syndrome, have been highly visible for some years, but the list of syndromes is extensive and growing. Raitt and Zeedyk (2000) cite Battered Child Syndrome, Parental Alienation Syndrome, Child Sexual Abuse Accommodation Syndrome, Failure Syndrome, Gambler's Syndrome, Racial Hatred Syndrome, Internet Addiction Syndrome and Hope Deficiency Syndrome as examples that sit alongside Battered Woman's Syndrome and Premenstrual Syndrome.

The proliferation of categories of mental illness included in the diagnostic manuals used by mental health professionals is perhaps the most important indicator of the strength of this tendency toward the medicalization of human experience (Horwitz 2002). The relevant American manual is the *Diagnostic and Statistical Manual of Mental Disorders* (the DSM) produced by the American Psychiatric Association, and the European version, published by the World Health Organization, is the *International Classification of Disorders* (ICD). Although not all of the conditions listed above have made their way into the official manuals, there has been a noteworthy expansion of the number of categories of mental illness that more recent editions of these manuals include. As Kutchins and Kirk, the North American authorities on psychiatric diagnostic categories, explain, whereas descriptions of madness and its subtypes have been around since the ancient Greeks, by 1994 "the count [in the DSM] had grown to over 300 categories, and the number appears to be rising." This number of official categories, they argued, should be compared with the handful of unofficial, broad categories that "appeared to be sufficient until the last half of the 20th century" (1997:38).

Running alongside the expansion of mental illness categories has been a growth in the number of people considered to be mentally ill. Oliver James, a high-profile British psychologist, argued that by the mid-1990s around one-third of British adults could be diagnosed as having some kind of "psychiatric morbidity" (1997:301). James contended that, if those manifesting tendencies toward "violence and aggression" were added to this number, it brought the number of those who require some form of treatment to "perhaps 20 million people" (1997:308–9). Of course, there have been disagreements about numbers—not all psychologists and psychiatrists have agreed with James' assessment of 20 million people. But the notion that mental illness is common, that the number of people who are ill has been underestimated in the past, and that more needs to be done about mental illness has come to be widely held and officially endorsed.

The British Department of Health, for example, launched a new campaign called "Mind out for Mental Health" in 2000, in recognition of the fact that "Mental health problems are extremely common. In fact, each year, one in four people experiences one" (Department of Health 2001a). The British Royal College of Psychiatrists now contends that mental illness is a problem that affects a large section of the population and that it is a problem that has been badly neglected in the past. Its campaign called "Changing Minds" includes a film shown at cinemas in Britain titled *1 in 4*. One in four people, the film explains, suffers from mental illness. "1 in 4 could be your brother, your sister. Could be your wife, your girlfriend. . . . 1 in 4 could be your daughter. . . . 1 in 4 could be me. . . . it could be you," states the commentary. Children have come to be considered particularly prone to mental illness and afflicted by "common conditions," including "emotional disorders" (for example, anxiety, depression, phobias, and stress), "conduct disorders" (for example, stealing, truancy, aggression, and delinquency), "attention deficit disorders," and "eating disorders" (Department of Health 1999b). The British government, in 2000, set aside more than £300 million to be invested in mental health "to help the NHS make up for its past neglect," and a National Institute of Mental Health was launched "to co-ordinate research and development as well as carrying out the biggest ever studies into mental health."

If England now has a National Institute of Mental Health, established because the problem of mental illness has been placed at the center of government health policy, its elevation as a social problem is a longer-standing trend in the United States. The American National Institute of Mental Health (NIMH) was established in the 1940s, and it has made "raising awareness" of the problem of mental illness central to its work. In the late 1980s, the NIMH launched the Depression Awareness, Recognition, and Treatment (DART) program to encourage people to come forward for treatment, with considerable success. Between 1979 and 1997, rates of outpatient treatment for depression tripled from 1.76 to 6.33 million people (Kupersanin 2002). The Institute currently claims that more than 20 million Americans—one in ten of the population—have a "mood disorder," most likely depression. Where all kinds of mental illness are taken into account, its prevalence in the United States is considered very widespread. In the mid-1990s, the NIMH argued that its research, carried out by "lay interviewers," had found that 25 percent of American adults have a psychiatric disorder in any one-year period (Downs 1996:26). In 1997, the NIMH was reported to estimate that one third of Americans will suffer from mental illness in any one year, and more than half will suffer from mental illness at some point in their lifetime (Sharkey 1997).

Why has it become so accepted that there are now more forms of mental illness, and more people suffering from it, than ever before? How can the emergence of the "Syndrome Society" be explained? Studies of particular disorders—how they came to be named and the response to them by others, health professionals and official medical bodies in particular—have accumulated over the past two decades and provide some answers to these questions (Scott 1990; Young 1995; Figert 1996; Kutchins and Kirk 1997; Tavris 1992). Such studies have revealed that although each new diagnostic category has a context of its own, these new categories have at least three features in common. The remainder of this chapter discusses these features with particular reference, given its relevance for the Postabortion Syndrome claim, to Posttraumatic Stress Disorder (PTSD).

REDRAWING THE BOUNDARY BETWEEN THE NORMAL AND THE ABNORMAL

Examination of current mental illness categories, from a sociological point of view, has drawn attention to the way in which they are characterized by lists of symptoms that tend to be expansive and diffuse. The first feature of syndromes and disorders, therefore, is that they tend to provide a broad definition of abnormal behavior. One characteristic is, in fact, the *absence* of symptoms. As Best has noted, "a failure to display any symptoms need not be significant" (1999:110). Some have argued that people can be considered to be suffering from certain conditions even when they do not appear to be mentally ill. This approach is particularly characteristic of syndromes and disorders such as Recovered Memory Syndrome, which connect the present psychological state of an individual to their past experience of an adverse life event.

Where manifest symptoms constitute the evidence for the presence of a disorder, the diffuse quality of the symptoms is also notable. Kutchins and Kirk have drawn attention to the way in which the DSM has come to list a very wide range of forms of behavior throughout as symptoms of mental illnesses of one kind or another. The same point could also be made about many books and articles detailing symptoms of particular disorders. Such symptoms include frustration, anger, difficulty concentrating, restlessness, increased appetite, weight gain, often losing one's temper, being easily fatigued, muscle tension, avoidance of almost all genital contact with a sexual partner, recurrent inability to maintain adequate erection, recurrent delay in orgasm (for a woman) following normal sexual excitement, having extremely frightening dreams, being inappropriately sexually seductive, theatricality, showing arrogance, lacking empathy, being preoccupied with being criticized, and difficulty making everyday decisions (1997:20). Lists of symptoms like this indicate that many everyday experiences and feelings have come to be taken as evidence of illness. The same symptoms frequently recur as part of the diagnostic criteria for different conditions, making it difficult to discern how a person could be diagnosed as suffering from one illness rather than another. Symptoms are often contradictory (for example, both overeating and loss of appetite appear as criteria, as do loss of interest in sex and promiscuity), and of course they apparently exist in people who do not consider themselves ill, as well as those who do.

This feature has been highlighted by Tavris, in her argument about Premenstrual Syndrome (included in the DSM as Late-Luteal Dysphoric Disorder). She pointed out that "the list of symptoms thought to characterize 'PMS' doesn't leave much out." The "complete checklist" compiled from her review of literature on the subject includes:

> . . . weight gain, eye diseases, asthma, nausea, blurred vision, skin disorders and lesions, joint pain, headaches, backaches, general pains, epilepsy, cold sweats and hot flushes, sleeplessness, forgetfulness, confusion, impaired judgements, being prone to accidents, difficulty concentrating, lowered work performance, lethargy, decreased efficiency, drinking and eating too much, mood swings, crying and depression, anxiety, restlessness, tension, irritability and loss

of sex drive, allergies, alcoholism, anaemia, low self-esteem, problems with identity, and craving for chocolate. (1992:135)

Some physicians, argues Tavris, identified as many as 150 different symptoms of PMS, a characteristic of this syndrome that gives it much in common with other disorders. Attention Deficit Hyperactivity Disorder (ADHD), for example, a disorder first designated to explain problematic behavior in children, also has a very wide and diffuse range of symptoms. Its three cardinal symptoms are inattention, hyperactivity, and impulsivity. According to the DSM, inattention can be indicated by children becoming easily distracted, failing to pay attention and making careless mistakes, rarely following instructions carefully, and losing or forgetting things like pencils and books. Signs that may show the presence of hyperactivity and impulsivity are feeling restless and fidgeting; running, climbing, and leaving a seat when quiet behavior is expected; blurting out answers before hearing the whole question; and having difficulty waiting in line (National Institute of Mental Health 1996). Given this definition of its characteristics, it is understandable that ADHD has been described as "a vaguely defined disorder implicated in a broad set of behaviors often typical of children and young people, with no defined medical basis" (Downs 1996:26).

Official medical bodies appear to have an ambivalent relationship to the obvious diffuseness of its symptoms. On the one hand, the NIMH notes, "everyone shows some signs of these behaviors at times," and it states that the DSM therefore has "very specific guidelines" for determining when a child has a condition. On the other hand, the NIMH is keen to emphasize that ADHD is a serious medical problem for a very large number of American children. The NIMH emphasizes this point by describing ADHD as "one of the most common mental disorders among children," stating that it affects 3 to 5 percent of children—that is, "perhaps as many as two million American children" (National Institute for Mental 1996:1). Even if psychiatry has attempted to restrain the process by which its definition of abnormal behavior spills over to encompass the behavior of more and more people, this appears to have been a futile exercise. The propensity to understand children's behavior as symptomatic of psychological disturbance is demonstrated in the popularization of the category ADHD, evidenced by the growing number of websites and publications about this problem in children and its appearance in the popular media. Most significantly, ADHD has now expanded to explain adults' behavior. As Downs noted in 1996, "the disorder appears to be highly socially constructed, and practitioners are currently bent on expanding its application to adults," a process of expansion that has now taken place (Conrad and Potter 2000).

The redrawing of boundaries has also taken place for more long-standing categories of mental illness. According to Dworkin, a link has been established between clinical depression and "everyday unhappiness." It is not only ordinary people in everyday life who now use the term "depression" loosely, so as to include familiar feelings of sadness and "the blues." Science, argues Dworkin, has established and endorsed such a link through the DSM. Whereas prior to the development of the manual, there was no conceptual relationship between clinical depression and sadness, this was changed through the DSM, "creating large categories of mental illness and then ever-increasing subcategories, replete with subtypes and specifiers" (Dworkin 2001:88). "Major depression" was broken down into many subtypes, which include "minor depression" with symptoms like pessimism, hopelessness, and despair. Everyday unhappiness "suddenly gained a fixed position in medical science, if only as a subcategory of a major mental illness" (Dworkin 2001:88). Dworkin also notes that the blurring of categories is encouraged because each is so porous, thus allowing everyday unhappiness to pass into the category of a more significant disease. "Minor depression," a subcategory of "major depression," requires only that a person feel sad and lose pleasure in everyday activities—which, of course, is also what characterizes everyday unhappiness. The same experience can be understood in two ways: as a less serious version of clinical depression, requiring that the person be treated with medication or therapy, or as part of day-to-day life.

This approach to the identification of symptoms of mental illness has become noticeable in arguments made by official bodies. According to the U.K. Department of Health (DoH), for example, it is now necessary to predicate diagnosis of mental illness on an understanding of the relationship between "mental health and behavioural problems, violence, child abuse, drug and alcohol abuse, health in the workplace and risk-taking behaviour such as smoking and unsafe sex" (2001b:16). These forms of behavior, for the DoH, have all become symptomatic of mental illness; people may take drugs, smoke cigarettes, have sex without using a condom, or abuse children because they are not of sound mind. According to Kutchins and Kirk, the incorporation of these kinds of experiences as symptoms of mental illness is well established in the United States and distinguishes the current understanding of people's problems from that of the past.

This trend suggests there is a "growing tendency in our society to medicalize problems that are not medical" and "to find psychopathology where there is only pathos" (Kutchins and Kirk 1997:x). The diagnostic category PTSD can be considered an exemplar of this process. PTSD has its origins in the United States—it was first officially specified in the DSM in 1980, when the third edition of the manual was published. By this point, therefore, American psychiatry had accepted that there was a specific form of mental illness that followed from, and was directly a result of, a traumatic event.

POSTTRAUMATIC STRESS DISORDER

According to DSM III, PTSD has a particular group of symptoms—certain forms of behavior or emotional states are deemed to be evidence of the existence of the specific mental illness. In DSM III, the symptoms of PTSD are grouped into three sections: (1) reexperiencing the traumatic event; (2) persistent avoidance of stimuli associated with the trauma; and (3) persistent symptoms of increased arousal. In each of these sections, there is a list of examples of symptoms—the third section, for example, includes "difficulty falling or staying asleep" and "difficulty concentrating" as examples of "increased arousal." These symptoms are, according to these criteria, the result of the individual experiencing a "stressor event":

> The essential feature of this disorder is the development of characteristic symptoms following a psychologically distressing event that is *outside the range of usual human experience* (i.e., outside the range of such common experiences as simple bereavement, chronic illness, business losses, and marital conflict). The stressor producing this syndrome would be markedly distressing to almost anyone. . . . The trauma may be experienced alone (e.g., rape or assault) or in the company of groups of people (military combat). Stressors producing this disorder include natural disasters (e.g., floods, earthquakes), accidental man-made disasters (e.g., car accidents with serious physical injury, airplane crashes, large fires), or deliberately caused disasters (e.g., bombing, torture, death camps). (American Psychiatric Association 1980:247–8) (my emphasis)

The linking of a specific event or experience from the past ("the stressor") to behavior in the present ("the symptoms") is, thus, the defining feature of the diagnostic criteria for PTSD.

It is important to emphasize that, in 1980, an event capable of leading to the development of PTSD was defined as one that is "outside the range of usual human experience." Indeed, as the previous chapter noted, the particular event that gave rise to the naming of this form of mental illness was involvement in the Vietnam War (American veterans were the first group to be diagnosed with the disorder), and this experience was clearly not part of day-to-day life. Similarly, DSM-III-R (1987) stated:

> The person has experienced an event that is *outside the range of usual human experience* and that would be markedly distressing to almost anyone, e.g. serious threat to one's life or physical integrity; serious threat or harm to one's children, spouse, or other close relatives and friends; sudden destruction of one's home or community; or seeing another person who has been, or is being, seriously injured or killed as the result of an accident or physical violence. (Joseph et al. 1997:10) (my emphasis)

But if PTSD was first conceptualized by psychiatry in response to the experience of Vietnam veterans, was considered to be a rare disorder that might result from unusual situations, and was characterized by clearly definable symptoms, it has subsequently become a very different entity. As Kutchins and Kirk note, it came to be the case that a more diffuse approach to defining the disorder gained ground, one that "broadens the concept of trauma and increases the number of potential candidates for a diagnosis of PTSD" (1997:118).

Redefining PTSD

This redefinition of the disorder is most obviously apparent in the way in which its causes and symptoms have come to be defined. A new edition of the DSM, DSM IV, appeared in 1994. In this edition, Criterion A for PTSD had been amended to the following:

> The person has been exposed to a traumatic event in which both the following were present:
>
> (1) The person experienced, witnessed, or was confronted with an event or events that involved actual or threatened death or serious injury, or a threat to the physical integrity of self or others.
>
> (2) The person's response involved fear, helplessness, or horror. *Note:* In children this may be expressed instead by disorganized or agitated behavior. (Joseph et al. 1997:13)

Criterion A serves as the "gatekeeper" for the diagnosis of PTSD. As two commentators on the original definition of the disorder put it:

> If a person does not meet the required definition of a stressful event, it matters little whether all the other criteria are met because the person cannot be diagnosed with PTSD. If criterion A is loosely defined and over inclusive, then the prevalence of PTSD is likely to increase, whereas a restrictive definition will reduce its prevalence. (Davidson and Foa 1991: 346)

As this comment indicates, the creation of a looser definition of Criterion A by 1994 inevitably suggested that more people could be defined as suffering from PTSD. To make the importance of this change clear, the definition of the "stressor event" as "outside the range of usual human experience" had disappeared by 1994. The revision of Criterion A in DSM IV in this way indicates that by this point a looser definition had come to be considered preferable. How did this come to be the case? What claims were made for rethinking what constitutes a traumatic event?

There is a very substantial literature about this issue, and it is not possible to discuss it in detail here. But some claims about the problem of defining what constitutes trauma highlight the relevant concerns particularly clearly. Psychologists Scott and Stradling, for example, argue in way that showed how the validity of a single, objective definition of trauma came to be questioned. They argued in the early 1990s that "according to DSM III-R a diagnosis of PTSD cannot be made if such an event [a major trauma] has not occurred. But this raises . . . important questions. . . . what makes an event traumatic as opposed to simply being stressful?" (1992:18). The question, what makes an event traumatic or stressful? invites us to consider whether it is the case that some events simply are traumatic, and will always generate severe psychological symptoms, whereas others, while unpleasant and difficult, will not. In answer, Scott and Stradling contended, "Different people react to objectively similar situations differently. For example one person may react to a divorce with disappointment and sadness whilst another becomes suicidal" (1992:19). If this is true, then the case made in DSM III-R that "usual marital conflict" does not constitute a traumatic event is called into question. Given that divorce is very common, it cannot be defined as "outside the range of usual human experience"; but according to Scott and Stradling it can generate PTSD-like symptoms.

The case argued by therapist Frank Parkinson typifies this approach. He also criticized the DSM III-R definition of a traumatic event, arguing:

> Post-Traumatic Stress Disorder is defined in the American Psychiatric Association publication *Diagnostic and Statistical Manual of Mental Disorders* (revised 1987), as "The development of certain characteristic symptoms following a psychologically distressing event which is outside the range of normal human experience." . . . the problem is with what is and what is not "normal" (1995:95).

Parkinson gave his own answer to the question, what is and what is not normal? when he argued: "Post-trauma stress can result from any experience which, for me is not normal; because it is not normal it can cause traumatic reactions" (Parkinson 1995:36). As a result, almost any life experience can be said to produce PTSD, including, for Parkinson, bereavement, divorce, moving house, and marriage breakdown. Any such "abnormal" event can lead to "posttrauma stress" because any event that involves change or loss can be traumatic: "There are many situations in life where the stress generated becomes 'dis-stress' and we may find it very difficult to cope," he argued (Parkinson 1995:31).

In this approach, events are deemed traumatic on the grounds that they involve "change and loss." Many difficult life events or experiences can therefore be, in Parkinson's terms, construed as traumatic, since most things that happen to people inevitably involve change of some description, and it is in the nature of change that there will be loss. Parkinson makes this argument about the traumatic effects of "ordinary" life events clear in his description of the transition from conception to death:

> . . . losses are due to the changes we go through as we grow and develop from conception and birth to death: in childhood separation anxiety, going to school, puberty, making and breaking relationships, leaving school and home, starting work, unemployment and redundancy, falling in love, marriage, pregnancy, miscarriage and abortion, having new children in a relationship, separation and divorce, moving home, a hysterectomy, the menopause, retirement and adjusting to old age, the death of a spouse and the inevitability of one's own death. All of these, including natural and man-made disasters, entail loss, and therefore involve reactions of grief and post-trauma stress. (1995:45)

Discussion about PTSD in the relevant literature indicates that some psychiatrists have been wary about adopting an approach that involves such a broad definition of the "stressor event" capable of producing PTSD. Given the status of psychiatry as a medical discipline that bases its approach in scientific method, it is vital that diagnostic criteria appear objective and scientifically verifiable, rather than subjective and open to interpretation. There is, however, a commonsensical character to the approach taken by those like Parkinson, which was arguably codified in DSM IV. There are obvious difficulties with maintaining a very strict definition of what constitutes an experience "outside the range of usual human experience." It is arguable that once it came to be considered the case that a particular traumatic event could be the cause of certain symptoms, there would be a debate about what such an event was constituted in.

This trend toward redefining what constitutes a traumatic event, in a broader and more inclusive way, has also been evident in claims that such experiences are often ignored or are not recognized for what they are (Furedi 1997). This tendency has been evident in some mental health professionals' warnings that populations that have not yet been diagnosed with PTSD are "at risk" or the claim that the condition is "underreported" and "underdiagnosed." The case for diagnosing PTSD following childbirth, an issue discussed further in Chapter 6, illustrates this point.

Such claims were first made in the early 1990s and have been visible ever since. Thus, according to Dr. Fiona Blake, of the John Radcliffe Hospital in Oxford, England, PTSD is an "under-recognised complication of difficult childbirth" and can be caused by "insensitive obstetric care." Blake claimed that women may suffer lasting distress, as well as symptoms such as flashbacks, and the delivery need not have been abnormal from the clinician's perspective for the syndrome to occur (Gold-Beck-Wood 1996). Other medical professionals who deal with women giving birth agreed. Dr. Janet Menage, a GP and counselor, contended that one in five women find obstetric and gynecological procedures "very distressing" or "terrifying" and that 1.5 percent of those undergoing such procedures suffer from PTSD (Gold-Beck-Wood 1996). According to one study, the incidence of PTSD in women who have babies is more severe still. One in four suffers from the disorder one and a half months after giving birth, claimed psychologists at the University of Sheffield. They found that 3 percent of new mothers surveyed showed "signs" of PTSD six weeks after birth, and that at least 24 percent had at least one of the three groups of symptoms for the disorder. This problem "has gone unacknowledged and often masqueraded under other forms, such as anxiety," argued Dr. Slade, who carried out the research (Irwin 1999:9).

Alongside claims that expand the range of experiences that are said to constitute causes of PTSD have been claims about the disorder's symptoms. To be more precise, the symptoms of PTSD as listed in DSM are open to interpretation and have arguably been interpreted in an increasingly inclusive manner since 1980. Kutchins and Kirk have drawn attention both to the wide variety of symptoms that have been claimed to characterize the effects of the syndrome (there are 175 combinations of symptoms by which PTSD can be diagnosed) and to their imprecision: "Many of the defining features of PTSD are shared with dozens of other diagnoses. Furthermore it is difficult to distinguish between maladaptive and health responses to stress or pressure" (1997:125).

The trend of defining the disorder's symptoms inclusively is very apparent in the way in which enthusiastic proponents of PTSD have made their case. An advertisement for a book on PTSD explains, for example, "Half the population suffer from PTSD. Most only recognise it . . . when they read this list." This statement is followed by a catalogue of symptoms that include being off work with stress, nervousness, anxiety, fatigue, fragility, sleep problems, flashbacks and replays, trauma, tearfulness, anger, irritability, headaches and frequent illness, skin problems, poor concentration and memory, sweating, palpitations, obsessiveness, hypervigilance, exaggerated startle response, isolation, embarrassment and guilt, low self-esteem, loss of self-worth, and "etc." (Kinchin 1998). Most medical texts do not overtly adopt such a generalized approach and tend to use scientific terminology when discussing the symptoms of PTSD—for example, "reexperience" or "avoidance behavior." However, as the psychiatrist L. H. Field, a critic of the concept PTSD, has explained, the use of such terminology may only create a scientific veneer for the kind of approach that is taken by the leaflet described above. It may be that the symptoms that have now come to be considered characteristic of PTSD are, in many cases, "nothing more than a collection of the psychological reactions that may occur after exposure to an emotionally traumatic event" (1999:36).

In explaining this point, Field argues that all three of the key criteria can be challenged, because the psychological responses they might describe are so diffuse. The category of "persistent reexperiencing of the traumatic event" could just be a description of what human beings do following "emotionally significant events." Be they pleasurable or traumatic, they leave lasting memories, which may be "triggered" from time to time by an external event. Similarly, "persistent avoidance of stimuli associated with the trauma," argues Field, may be normal, not a sign of pathology: "When a person has been exposed to an emotionally traumatic event, exposure to similar circumstances will induce anxiety." Finally, "increased arousal" can be considered symptomatic of either previously recognized psychiatric conditions (for example, "phobic anxiety"), or, again, it could be considered quite normal. "Being jumpy" is not, in itself, an indication of mental illness, contends Field. Indeed, the existence of "increased arousal" as symptomatic of PTSD could be diagnosed where the person concerned had "difficulty concentrating" and "irritability and outbursts of anger." Such states are predictable, for example, after a loved one has died, or after a bad accident (1999:36–37).

The conclusion drawn by Field is that, in many cases, symptoms that have come to be taken as evidence of mental illness in diagnoses of PTSD may not be so, and that, if the symptoms are sufficiently serious for a diagnosis of psychiatric disorder to be made, long-standing categorizations of mental illness are sufficient and there is no need for "special terminology." Whether an individual is diagnosed as having PTSD depends on the approach taken by clinicians; and of course, not all will adopt an approach in which they eagerly diagnose people as having the disorder. But I will now argue there is a clear trajectory toward taking this problem seriously and encouraging its diagnosis. I contend that the problem of "traumatization" and its manifestation in symptoms of "stress" has come to be considered very significant and widespread.

A New Epidemic?

If PTSD was first officially recognized in 1980, the term appeared with increasing frequency in the medical literature over the 1990s (Ashmore 1996) and has "fast become a recognized mental health problem" (Thompson 1997:349). One search of on-line data services found over 50,000 indexed references to PTSD (O'Brien 1998). British psychiatrist Derek Summerfield notes that the National Center for Post-Traumatic Stress Disorder in the United States, which tracks journal articles, books, and technical reports, had by September 1999 indexed more than 16,000 separate publications on the subject (2001).

As part of this development, the concept has moved in its practical application far beyond psychiatry (some psychiatrists were important in advocating the early use of the PTSD concept, and early diagnosis of PTSD was mainly restricted to this group of people) to a much broader group of professionals. Many different mental health professionals now diagnose this disorder and offer expert opinion about it in specialist and popular literature, in relation to a

widened range of experiences. This group includes psychologists, clinical social workers, psychoanalysts, therapists, and counselors. The difficulties in
making rigid distinctions between these different kinds of mental health professionals (in particular, between therapists, psychotherapists, and counselors)
have been discussed elsewhere (Dineen 1999; Howard 1996). It is clear, however, that their number has increased dramatically in recent years. According
to Horwitz, in the United States between 1970 and 1995, the number of mental health professionals quadrupled (2002:4). There is one mental health professional for every 250 people in the United States, according to Dineen
(1999:134). This trend is evident in Britain, too. As Smail notes, "[T]he days
are long gone when the British could laugh at America for its self-indulgent
preoccupation with therapy and counselling" (Dineen 1999:xiv). It has been
estimated that, by 1999, there were half a million people employed full-time
or part-time as counselors in Britain, and counseling has been considered one
of Britain's few "growth industries" (Furedi 1997).

Not only do mental health professionals include diagnosis and treatment of
new forms of syndromes and disorders as part of their work—many specialize
in these areas. The effects of trauma, stress, and addiction have become specialist fields in their own right (Dineen 1999:8). Perhaps as a result, discussion of the problem of PTSD has become more and more widespread, and the
number of people deemed to have the disorder has become very large indeed.
Rates of PTSD have been defined, and its prevalence is used to make claims
that this disorder merits recognition as a very significant mental health problem in the general population.

Mezey and Robbins (2001) thus suggest that studies in the United States
have found PTSD rates of between 1 and 7.8 percent of the population, and
they argue that rates are similar in other developed countries. According to
a report from the Food and Drug Administration, more than 10 million
Americans each year (about 4 percent of the population) "experience the life-
disrupting symptoms of PTSD" (Nordenberg 2000), although the National
Institute of Mental Health puts the figure at 5.2 million (3.6 percent of the
population) (2001a). Foa and Rothbaum contend that the "lifetime prevalence
of PTSD in the general population is estimated at 9%, with over a third of
these cases having chronic PTSD"; but when "subthreshold cases" are added,
the prevalence increases to 15 percent, with a prevalence of 24 percent among
"trauma victims" (1998:xi). They argue that "because PTSD is such a prevalent and debilitating disorder, one of the top priorities for mental health professionals around the world is to develop effective and efficient treatments for
it" (1998:8). Many more people than these figures suggest, however, are said
to be "at risk" of suffering from PTSD. As has been noted by many who have
studied the subject, the claim that anyone present at, or in some way related
to, a disaster or accident may later suffer from PTSD has become commonplace
(Dineen 1999; Bailey 2001; O'Brien 1998). As a result, some very large fig-

ures are sometimes reported. One British article in a journal for nurses claims that "Research in America suggests that 75 per cent of the US general population has been exposed to a traumatic event which is significant enough to cause PTSD" and states that one study found 89.6 percent have been exposed to such an event and thus were at risk of developing the disorder (Rogers and Liness 2000:48).

The result of all of this, Kutchins and Kirk suggest, is that PTSD has become the dominant label "for identifying the impact of adverse events on ordinary people." These writers also note that this process has resulted in an approach to PTSD that would have been unrecognizable in the 1970s: "It would be hard for the Vietnam veterans and psychiatrist allies who fought for recognition of the syndrome to recognize the diagnosis as it is presently formulated" (1997:123).

EXPLAINING PROBLEMS IN MEDICALIZED TERMS

A second point that some sociological studies of mental illness categories have made is that they relate to the way in which human experience is conceptualized; they constitute a way of thinking about human beings and their experience (Furedi 1997; Hacking 1995). Some have argued that the tendency to view human experience through the prism of mental illness can be problematic, because it can emphasize "medical problems" at the expense of social ones. Thus the experience of the person who, for example, drinks alcohol frequently, feels angry a lot, or finds it difficult to establish relationships with others (all symptoms of certain disorders) is to be explained by the condition they are diagnosed as suffering from: it is the "illness" that accounts for the "symptoms." Hence the most appropriate explanation for the difficulties and problems experienced by an individual is a medicalized one, the explanation provided by therapists and medical experts who "have the appropriate knowledge and skills for diagnosing and treating psychological problems" (Best 1999:106).

Such accounts tend to dispute the "discovery" model of mental disorders, which the American Psychiatric Association (APA) uses to explain its revision of its classification system for mental disorders, the DSM. The DSM has been revised three times since 1979, and each time the APA has claimed that the expanded list of disorders is based on scientific research through which new ones have been "discovered" (Kutchins and Kirk 1997; Horwitz 2002). According to this approach, at a particular point, as a result of scientific enquiry and investigation, these illnesses came to be properly understood. Their causes and symptoms have been mapped out and specified in a way that makes it possible for the diagnostic categories that result to be used by mental health professionals to diagnose and treat those who suffer from these conditions. They have been labeled and specified in the same way that cholera, diphtheria, and polio were labeled and specified at earlier points in the history of medicine. This account suggests that the increase in the number of mental illnesses in recent years (and in those diagnosed as suffering from them) is the result of scientific discovery and the progress of medical science (Raitt and Zeedyk 2000).

Some contest this argument about how new mental illnesses have come into existence. It is not disputed that there are individuals and groups of people who experience profoundly negative emotions, behave in ways that appear problematic for them and others around them, or feel ill. Rather, what is contested is the way in which such experiences come to be defined as particular conditions. It is argued that the "rational account"—that the growing list of psychiatric conditions is a result of empirical evidence, and objective, scientific enquiry—disguises and obscures a different process altogether, that which has been termed the "construction" or "invention" of new mental illnesses.

This argument has been made in various ways, but at its center is the proposition that, broadly speaking, "nonscientific" factors are determinant in the way in which psychiatric conditions are newly defined. It has thus been argued that "New diagnoses rarely emerge simply as a result of new scientific discoveries" but that, by contrast, such diagnoses "are the product of socio-historical circumstances and the claims-making of particular interest groups" (Conrad and Potter 2000:560). Cottle summarized this argument as follows:

> Definitions of illness and health do not belong solely to the white-coated realm of pure science. They are social, cultural, and economic phenomena as well. They are not invented exactly, but coaxed and shaped into public acceptability by a cadre of medical researchers, and advocacy groups. . . . This is often a long and arduous process. . . . it can take years for the populace to be taught that what was long thought to be a behavioural quirk is in fact a mental illness. (1999:25)

Cottle made this argument in relation to the conditions Social Phobia and Attention Deficit Hyperactivity Disorder, and her investigation of the development of the diagnostic criteria for these conditions, and their application to explaining certain forms of behavior, led her to emphasize aspects of these developments that are outside the realm of "pure science." These developments, she argues, suggest that attention needs to be paid to the forces "that help draw the boundary between what we are told to think of as normal and what we are told to consider pathological" (Cottle 1999:25).

Different social actors have been discussed as playing a role in the development of this explanation of human experience. It has been argued that political forces often contribute to decisions about what is normal and what is pathological. Medical sociologist Bryan Turner argues that the evidence for this account of mental illness categories is provided by the "rapid movement" of such categories into and out of diagnostic manuals. He points, in common with others (Kutchins and Kirk 1997; Figert 1996), to the removal from the DSM of homosexuality as a category of mental illness in 1973 and the inclusion, despite protests from women's movement organizations, in DSM III-R of "three new illness classifications—masochistic personality disorder, paraphilic rapism disorder (having fantasies of rape or sexual molestation) and late luteal dysphoric syndrome or premenstrual syndrome" (1995:79). For Turner, it is the relative strengths of competing groups of people who hold differing perceptions of the behavior of, for example, homosexuals or women, that ultimately decide whether a certain form of behavior should be deemed a form of mental illness. Kutchins and Kirk (1997) forcefully argue that many psychiatric categories are highly influenced by perceptions of what constitutes "normal" or "abnormal" behavior and mental states. They contend that the boundary where normality (feeling sad or anxious) turns into mental illness (clinical depression or ADHD) is very open to dispute and disagreement, and it is the outcome of such disagreements, rather than objective calculation, that decides whether a new psychiatric condition comes into being. Understanding the "Syndrome Society," therefore, does not involve grasping how disinterested science has discovered disorders, but rather involves uncovering a process where interest groups, the psychiatric profession, and other institutions "struggle over whether to create categories of mental disorder" (Kutchins and Kirk 1997:16).

Other accounts have emphasized the role of pharmaceutical companies in the creation of the "Syndrome Society" (Cottle 1999; Koerner 2002; Dworkin 2001). New drugs need markets (in other words, new diseases), and the impulse to develop more and different variations of drugs has therefore required the development of new and different mental illnesses, each of which needs a cure. British physician James Le Fanu has argued that, having failed to create cures for "serious" diseases such as cancer and dementia, the pharmaceutical industry switched its attention to what he calls "lifestyle" problems such as unhappiness, obesity, and forgetfulness. In doing so, the pharmaceutical industry encouraged the designation of such problems as medical conditions (Horrie 2001).

Moynihan, Heath, and Henry claim that "There's a lot of money to be made by telling healthy people they're sick" and accuse pharmaceutical companies of being "actively involved in sponsoring the definition of diseases and promoting them to both prescribers and consumers" (2002:886). Kutchins and Kirk have emphasized that drug companies have pursued their financial interests by medicalizing more and more aspects of human experience: "For the drug companies, the unlabelled masses are a vast untapped market, the virgin Alaska oilfields of mental disorder" (*The Times* 1997:15).

David Healy has provided the most detailed accounts of this process, with regard to the issue of depression. In his discussion of the "anti-depressant era," he shows how, because of factors including developments in the regulation of

drugs and the ascendancy of biological models for understanding mental
states, an "arsenal of magic bullets" was developed in the United States. A variety of different drugs have been developed, each of which, drug companies
claim, is a cure for a different type of depression. Thus, more and more new
disease states have come into existence (1997, 2002).

Drug companies, by these accounts, have encouraged the designation of
more and more experiences and forms of behavior as evidence of specific disease states, with biological causes. Some critics of this development contend
that it downplays the social causes of the problems that people face. Hence,
drugs come to be construed as the cure for a mental distress that in fact has
other origins. Furthermore, such treatments encourage the construction of the
problem of "mental ill health." Treatments for mental illness play a crucial role
in encouraging the blurring of the distinction between everyday unhappiness
and medical problems. New drugs offer treatments for newly defined disorders, and in doing so they encourage the emergence of "mental ill health" as a
major preoccupation and highly visible social problem. Concern grows about
an "epidemic of mental illness," whereas in fact what has taken place is the re-
designation of experiences and behavior that existed previously, but which
were not constructed as major "problems."

There seems little doubt that the development of new drugs has played a
role in the medicalization of human experience. As Dworkin (2001) notes,
drugs for mental illness are increasingly prescribed; in the United States over
the 1990s, the use of psychotropic medication in depressed patients increased
by more than 40 percent, from 32 million office visits resulting in drug pre-
scription to over 45 million. In Britain, the annual number of antidepressant
prescriptions more than doubled, from 9 million to 22 million, over the 1990s
(Double 2002). This number of prescriptions suggests a relationship between
the availability of medication and a society in which people's mental states
have become a powerful preoccupation, for both patients and their physicians.

But the same preoccupation, it has been argued, is also indicated by the
popularity of treatments that do not rely on drugs. It is not only drugs manufactured by pharmaceutical companies that are now used at an unprecedented
rate. Complementary and alternative medicine (CAM) has also become very
widespread in its use. Around 5 million people use some kind of CAM annually in the United Kingdom, and there are at least 50,000 registered CAM
practitioners (Hehir 2001). CAM's influence is also apparent it the ubiquity
of complementary and alternative medicines on supermarket shelves and in the
advocacy of such medicines in mainstream debate and the popular media
(Jenkins 2002). Although not all CAM purports to treat mental illness, much
of it does; its underlying emphasis on a "holistic" approach, in which mind
and body must be considered and treated as dependent upon each other, suggests that treating people's state of mind has assumed an increased significance
in perceptions about how physical illnesses might be cured.

For many, there would seem to be a great deal of difference between med-icalization through the marketing and use of drugs, and the advocacy and use of CAM. Indeed, these approaches are often considered to be the opposite of each other, and some proponents of CAM are very hostile critics of "conven-tional" drug treatments. Without doubt, the ways in which those who advo-cate the use of drugs and those who advocate CAM explain the causes of people's mental states are very different. But when the issue of interest is the expansion of the problem of mental ill health, these differences are of less sig-nificance. The growth in and use of various kinds of complementary and al-ternative medicines also indicate that people's state of mind has emerged as a major concern. In this vein, some accounts of the problem of mental illness also focus on the role of the "psychology industry." This includes therapists, psychologists, and counselors, whose numbers have increased significantly in the past three decades and who, it has been argued, make a living from en-couraging the "psychologizing" of human behavior (Dineen 1999). The growth of this industry has been viewed as part of the growth of alternative medicine (Fitzpatrick 2001).

Evidence suggests that the influence of the "psychology industry" is sig-nificant. The notion that a convincing explanation for certain kinds of behav-ior and human experiences derives from a psychological model, and that it is to be supplied by experts through such models, is now rarely questioned, and the need for counseling or therapy to cure mental illness is widely promoted (Summerfield 1999; Fitzpatrick 2002; Furedi 2002b). The explanation of a person's problems in the present as resulting from psychological disturbance in the past is commonplace. Traumatic events or troubled relationships, espe-cially those that take place in childhood, are often put forward in particular as the reason for current feelings and forms of behavior. The powerful imperative to emphasize the problem of "poor parenting" (including smacking or shout-ing at children) certainly seems to suggest that childhood experience has as-sumed a significant place current conceptualizations of the origins of people's problems (Furedi 2001; Hardyment 1995). According to psychologist Oliver James (2002), for example, it is the emotional attachments with parents in the first few years of life that shape people's future relationships and their very sense of self. People are seen as potential victims of their childhood experience, and if parenting is done badly, they will suffer from mental health problems as a result.

This explanation of people's problems is promoted, championed, and pop-ularized, unsurprisingly perhaps, by some mental health professionals (Dineen 1999). It has been argued that it has also become incorporated into the think-ing of policymakers concerned with social problems in Britain and the United States who have also therefore contributed to encouraging the dynamic toward medicalization. As Pupavac notes, such perspectives "have become central to Western domestic social policy, to how Western governments relate to their own citizens and also how individuals in the West understand themselves" (2001:359). Certainly the issue of "parenting" has assumed a greatly significant place in policy agendas, with those planning to have children or who already have them routinely encouraged to attend "parenting classes" in Britain and the United States. These programs are justified in part on the basis that they can help prevent mental ill health in future generations.

A number of different factors have therefore been considered important in generating a culture in which people's problems are understood with regard to mental illness. The problem of mental illness has gained increasing visibility as the explanations for problems discussed above have gained more currency. Over time, people's experiences, in consequence, have come to be understood less as the result of concrete, definable economic problems, social policies, or social trends in the present, than as a product of the existence of specific, objective types of mental illness. As I now discuss, the rise of PTSD directly relates to this process.

INVENTING PTSD

Many, indeed most, accounts of PTSD insist that the disorder was "discovered" and that people have always developed PTSD following traumatic events. In his review of the psychiatric literature, O'Brien (1998) notes that many therefore read PTSD back into history. His own favorite example is the diagnosis of PTSD in Merlin, the wizard, in the tales of King Arthur. Apparently, descriptions of Merlin's state following involvement in battle indicate that he suffered from the condition. Samuel Pepys' seventeenth-century accounts of his feelings and experiences following the fire of London are a commonly cited example of PTSD-like symptoms. Papers about railway accidents in the nineteenth century abound with examples of symptoms said to be characteristic of PTSD, as do those about the American Civil War. In this approach, all that happened since the early 1980s is that psychiatrists have come to define and understand such experiences as PTSD. Some studies of the development of the category, however, have disputed the "discovery" model of its origins. The disorder, it has been argued, was not so much "discovered" as "invented," and those who have drawn this conclusion have shown how PTSD, too, psychologizes experience at the expense of social explanations.

It is the process through which the category PTSD developed in the first place, as an illness suffered by American soldiers who had been involved in the Vietnam War, that has been most extensively detailed (Scott 1990; Young 1995; Dean 1997; Shepherd 2000). The point of such studies is not, as Scott has argued, to adopt an "ironic stance" by suggesting that PTSD is "merely" a social construction or invention. They do show, however, how what comes to be considered as "objective knowledge," in particular that which achieves the status of medical or scientific fact, is "produced, secured, and subsequently creates other objective realities" (Scott 1990:308). That is to say, these studies point to the importance of understanding how and why the category PTSD emerged, and how and why it has subsequently developed. In doing so, such sociological investigation has drawn attention to some very significant issues. A key observation has been about the importance of the role of lay actors in the "invention" and development of the category PTSD and the importance of their role in promoting a medicalized understanding of human experience.

In regard to PTSD, Dr. Arthur S. Blank has argued, "There is no trauma field without advocacy" (Shepherd 2000:356). In common with others who have studied the development of PTSD as a specific category of mental illness, Blank contends that the idea of a connection between past adverse life events and the appearance of "symptoms" in the present is not a self-evident fact. Rather, for this connection to become accepted as the explanation for behavior and experience, the intervention of social actors who speak on behalf of putative "victims of trauma" is required. Furedi (1997) has argued similarly that the self-identification as victims by those who have had adverse experiences, and who consider themselves to suffer illness as a result, requires, at least in part, that they are defined this way by those who claim to advocate their interests. This is illustrated by the following account of the social history of PTSD.

War and Male Violence

As noted previously, in the 1980 edition of the DSM, PTSD appears as a clearly defined condition, with specified causes and symptoms. But this definition of it, as a scientific entity, it has been argued, disguises another story altogether. Its appearance as a recognizable illness, some contend, was in the first place a consequence of a particular set of arguments made on behalf of Vietnam War veterans, rather than a consequence of objective medical research.

O'Brien has described the process that led to the development of the concept of PTSD in broad terms, as the emergence of an association between fighting in Vietnam and veterans' "social problems, poor integration in society, criminal behaviour and mental health problems" (1998:12). Crucial in bringing into being this association were the political and campaigning activities of those who took up the veterans' cause, in particular antiwar activists, and psychiatrists and social workers opposed to the war (Scott 1990; Young 1995). They argued that as a result of the war, veterans were experiencing a specific type of mental disorder, originally named post-Vietnam Syndrome. Scott argues that it was the activities of these advocates for the veterans that laid the foundation for the argument for PTSD, and he presents a detailed study of their claimsmaking activities to demonstrate this point. This study shows how "the struggle for *recognition* of PTSD by its champions was profoundly political, and displays the full range of negotiation, coalition formation, strategizing, solidarity affirmation, and struggle—both inside various professions and 'in the streets'—that define the term" (1990:295, emphasis in the original). In this analysis, it is the extensive, effective campaigning of the champions of the veterans that finally led to the official recognition of PTSD in the DSM.

In his fascinating study comparing soldiers in the American Civil War with those in Vietnam, and the responses to the experience of both groups, Eric T. Dean, Jr. similarly points to the arguments and activities of those opposed to the war in Vietnam. He argues: "The entire concept of PTSD and its close association with the Vietnam Veterans were very much products of the antiwar fervour in the early 1970s, and the determined agitation of a number of antiwar psychiatrists and psychologists" (Dean 1997:200). For Dean, mental health professionals opposed to the war in Vietnam functioned as "unbridled advocates," rather than as neutral scientists. The psychiatrist Simon Wessely, too, sees the emergence of PTSD primarily as a result of such advocacy. The disorder emerged not as the result of "any careful hypothesis, epidemiological investigation or even serendipitous inquiry," but "in response to America's own traumas associated with the Vietnam War." PTSD was created "consciously and deliberately" by a section of the mental health community, and research tended to follow (1995:662). Such a conclusion is also suggested by Shepherd's study of PTSD. He argues that in the 1970s, psychiatrists, in their response to the putative category, divided into "doves" and "hawks." The hawks maintained that psychiatry did not recognize disorders that had their origin in a catastrophic event, such as war. They saw the acceptance of the idea that war leads to mental illness as the elevation of the "pathological into the mainstream" and emphasized the destructive consequences of this for the armed forces. The doves, by contrast, believed that mental illness resulting from catastrophes was an unrecognized problem of major proportions, which could have disastrous social effects. As the psychologist Figley put it, "'dovish' psychiatrists and other practitioners believed that emotional disorders among returning veterans could reach epidemic proportions . . . post-Vietnam syndrome [as it was first labelled] become a frightening buzzword among clinicians and journalists, but in fact was a thinly veiled position of opposition to the war" (Shepherd 2000:359).

In short, opposition to the war was articulated through the claim that it resulted in psychiatric illness for soldiers. The claim that there was a psychiatric illness eventually labeled PTSD functioned as a metaphor for arguments against war. Indeed, it has been argued that it is this cultural context that makes PTSD a specific disease category distinguishable from, for example, "shell shock," the psychiatric disorder associated with involvement in combat in the First World War. Both disorders were influenced by cultural forces, contend Jones and Wessely; and whereas "shell shock" reflects ideas of the early twentieth century, especially the "terrifying qualities of trench warfare," PTSD "expresses many of the conflicts of the [Vietnam] war" (2000:353). In particular, it expresses conflicts about who is to blame for the veterans' problems, and what should be the role of the U.S. state in relation to soldiers who fought in that war.

In this regard, the particular case made by such opponents of war about the mental state of the Vietnam Veterans has been considered highly significant. As Shepherd has argued, through developing the idea that a general, loosely defined "syndrome" could be a delayed result of exposure to a traumatic event and lead to significant mental health problems, "the balance was shifted between trauma and victim, putting much greater emphasis on victimhood than endurance" (2000:360–1). The most important component of the argument made by advocates of PTSD was that the veterans' feelings and experiences—alcoholism, problems in their marriages, nightmares about the war—were not evidence of the inability of vulnerable individuals to cope, or an acceptable outcome of war. Rather, they were proof that war inflicted terrible damage on those involved (including those who were perpetrators of atrocities, rather than victims of them), resulting in mental illness. Through the argument that traumatic memories of war were being relived in the present, a key shift in the representation of the soldier who fights in war thus took place. Scott summarizes this development as follows:

> This orientation shifted the focus of the disorder's cause from the particular details of the individual soldier's background and psyche to the nature of war itself. Its advocates claimed: soldiers disturbed by their combat experiences are not, in an important sense, abnormal; on the contrary, it is normal to be traumatized by the abnormal events of war. (1990:308)

Such an approach therefore construes ex-soldiers who are experiencing psychological problems as victims of war, rather than as psychologically weak individuals. The experience of war is presented as the problem since those who have taken part are likely to be traumatized by this experience. Summerfield has argued that the significance of the new diagnosis was to shift attention away from the psyche of the individual soldier to the "fundamentally traumatogenic nature of war." This, argues Summerfield, was a highly significant development, since it meant that Vietnam veterans were no longer to be seen as perpetrators or offenders but as people traumatized by roles thrust on them by the U.S. military: "Post-traumatic stress disorder legitimised their "victimhood," gave them moral exculpation, and guaranteed them a disability pension" (2001:1995). PTSD, therefore, also generated a particular kind of argument against war; namely that war is a problem because it is traumatic for those involved in it, and therefore makes them ill. Attention is drawn less to the problem of the social and political dynamics that lead to warfare than to its effects for the mental state of participants involved in conflict.

For the veterans, the emergence of a psychiatric diagnostic category to explain their problems can be considered understandably advantageous. It enabled them to gain access to resources and allowed them to be considered as a section of society that should not be despised and hated for their role in Vietnam, but pitied for their suffering. The implications of the emergence of PTSD, however, stretch far beyond the experience of these soldiers. If the experience that gave rise to this category of mental illness in the first place was the Vietnam War, it very quickly came to be applied to other groups. In this process, the role of advocates has again been identified as crucial; and again, a shift of emphasis from the social to the psychological is apparent.

Anthropologist Allan Young's authoritative study of PTSD indicates the precedent-setting effect of diagnosing the Vietnam veterans as victims of this disorder. Young notes: "Vietnam veterans . . . [were] followed by victims of other suppressed traumas such as childhood incest and domestic rape" (1995:142). The spread of PTSD, as this argument suggests, is linked to the emergence of claims brought on behalf of further groups of people, which rest on the argument that they, too, have symptoms of mental illness brought on by past trauma. The concept of PTSD created a model of how people respond to adverse life events, which allowed bridges to be built between "the 'trauma of war' and other kinds of trauma such as rape, child abuse, and civilian disasters" (Shepherd 2000:385).

The PTSD diagnosis thus did not remain confined to Vietnam veterans. It has been argued that the first major impetus behind the application of PTSD to other groups came from the women's movement. "Male violence," as it came to be termed, emerged as the next exemplar of a traumatic experience that could generate mental illness. Judith Lewis Herman, a key proponent of this understanding of women's lives, draws a direct comparison between women's experience and that of male soldiers and contextualizes the way in which women emerged as traumatized victims of male violence in relation to the influence of feminism. Not until the women's liberation movement of the 1970s, she argues, "was it recognized that the most common post-traumatic disorders are those not of men in war but of women in civilian life" (1992:28). For Herman, just as "hysteria" came to public attention in the late nineteenth century in the context of the contemporary republican anticlerical movement in France, and the antiwar movement gave rise to the recognition of combat neurosis, so the political context for public awareness of male violence "is the feminist movement in Western Europe and North America" (Herman 1992:28).

Herman draws attention to the way in which some feminists, at a time when arguments about the traumatic effects of war were gaining visibility, used the already existing concept of PTSD to construct women as victims traumatized in the everyday life of their sex. Downs notes also how "victimization syndromes" specific to women emerged as a result, namely Battered Woman's Syndrome and Rape Trauma Syndrome, which were "considered part of a broader psychiatric disorder, post-traumatic stress disorder (PTSD). . . . [and which] capture the psychological effects of long-lasting oppression in the context of the family or of violent acts against the self" (1996:19). Westervelt (1998), who, like Downs, has examined the relationship of such concepts to the development of the law, also draws attention to the activities and arguments of feminist campaigners, specifically those who wanted to develop legal defense strategies for battered women who had injured or killed their partners and who might be criminalized as a result. Feminist lawyers and social scientists, she explains, developed a strategy—expressed through the concept of Battered Woman's Syndrome—in which women were represented as victimized through their experience at the hands of their partners and thus as not responsible for their violent actions.

Such activity took place in a "social landscape where arguments and ideologies of the women's movement became a focus for public attention" (Westervelt 1998:11). The attention paid to how the law treats *women* and the development of gender-specific legal concepts and understandings can be understood, for Westervelt, in this context. If, broadly speaking, the context for extending the PTSD diagnosis to women can be understood as the movement for women's liberation and the attention paid to the claims of this movement, however, it is perhaps more accurate to emphasize that one strand of thinking in the women's movement promoted the need to understand women's experience through the lens of victimization. It has very frequently been pointed out that, following its emergence, the women's movement developed in different and often contradictory directions. Where it may have been possible in the late 1960s and early 1970s to speak of "the" women's movement, this movement very rapidly developed a number of strands of thinking and different campaigns that have emphasized different problems.

It is important to note that the problem of violence is not immune to this process of differentiation; it is a problem that feminism has understood in different ways. Differences of opinion about how to understand and represent the issue of "male violence" and its effects for women can be considered part of a debate about how to understand women's problems more generally. Themes important for the women's movement in the 1970s and 1980s were gender equality, sex bias, and victimization, argues Westervelt; and she highlights how these themes all played a role in the process through which PTSD was extended to women, in the form of BWS. But there is also an important distinctiveness to arguments about women's problems that are framed in this way. In particular, there is a specific conceptualization of what is meant by equality, which carries with it a concomitant elevation of the problem of victimization. In this approach, it is claimed that feminism's aim should be less to emphasize how women and men can be equal if certain barriers to equality are removed, than to construe equality as contingent on special treatment for women. In other words, for women to be equal requires *recognition* of their *dif-*

ference from men. Equality can come about not through extending to women ideas and practices that have been considered only relevant to men, but rather by taking into account the special and "un-male" experience and characteristics of women.

Those adopting this approach found that gender-specific conceptualizations of violence, and their expression in certain categories of mental illness, made sense. For women to be equal required not that they be treated like men, but that their unique experience of degradation at the hands of men be taken seriously. The problem *women* suffer from is *male* violence, and treating women as equal to men means taking their difference and particular experience seriously. In relation to victimization defences, for example, this meant arguing that the law had been "male centered" and reliant upon "gender-based assumptions," as it had defined the concept of self-defense with regard to men's experiences. This way of thinking about experience failed to take into account what happened to women responding to violence carried out by men— women's primary encounters with violence—and thus the law needed to be changed to take this experience into account (Westervelt 1998). The demand, in this frame, was not so much for men and women to be treated equally in law, but for the law to enact special measures to protect women from men, or to avoid criminalizing women's actions when they attack violent men, and BWS provided a means for doing so. More broadly, where the problem of "male violence" was emphasized, change that can lead to equality meant enacting programs and policies that are organized around fundamental differences in the behavior and even the nature of men and women.

Not all feminists advocated concepts that draw on PTSD, like BWS and Rape Trauma Syndrome. "[D]omestic violence is political, an oppression of women, an expression of sexism," one critic of the concept BWS has argued, to draw attention to such differences (Downs 1996:12). Such an approach to violence against women relates this problem to the organization of the society in which women are oppressed. It is the structures of society, in particular women's lack of economic independence and political power, that cause violence against women, and the remedy lies in the transformation of these structures. In this approach, the concept of BWS is considered problematic because it fails to draw sufficient attention to these issues. Through the concept of BWS, it is men's behavior and men's allegedly aggressive nature that are predominantly problematized, and the solution is therapeutic interventions for women and punishment for men. For feminist critics of BWS this is, at best, inadequate; and at worst it can infantilize women by emphasizing their weakness and vulnerability.

But if the female victim emerged in the 1970s as a contested strand in feminism, this construct has subsequently come to exert a great deal of influence. The notions that male violence is a widespread and often still underrecognized problem for women and that rape is a ubiquitous female experience have been widely adopted as typifications of women's problems. A huge literature has emerged that focuses on this problem, now named "intimate partner violence," "spousal abuse," or "family violence," in addition to "sexual violence" and "domestic violence." The problem of female victimization has helped shape law and policy in many arenas in the United States and Britain (Patai 1998; Coward 1999; Young 1999). The need to respond to the problem has been endorsed by important institutions, most obviously the law and the criminal justice system (Westervelt 1998). As Kutchins and Kirk (1997) point out, on this issue traditionally hostile social groups—feminist campaigners and antifeminist politicians—both supported the claim through the 1980s that women are victims of male violence. Now, however, advocating policing strategies and legal reforms to take this agenda farther has a place in political programs generally.

The growth of health policies and programs to deal with PTSD and related gender-specific syndromes also reflects this development. Those involved in the provision of medical care to women have increasingly come to consider PTSD a clinical matter and include identifying and responding to its occurrence and risk of its occurrence as part of health-care provision. The definition of women's problems as "mental health issues" that result from rape and domestic violence has also become commonplace, and responding to this problem has assumed a central place in the agenda and practice of mental health care. For Foa and Rothbaum, PTSD resulting from male violence thus constitutes a "monumental problem." They draw attention to studies finding that 12.4 percent of women develop PTSD following rape and claim that since 12 million American women have experienced "completed rape," "right now about 1.5 million adult rape victims . . . suffer from this devastating disorder." "The problem of PTSD following assault is monumental and growing as women are attacked every hour" they contend, concluding, "It is incumbent on health care professionals to provide effective and efficient treatment for these women to alleviate their suffering" (1998:xii).

In the United States and Britain, women are generally identified in policy agendas as being at greater risk of mental ill health than men, with the problem of the effect of "violence and abuse" highlighted as a key concern. The British Department of Health recently launched a new strategy, "Women's Mental Health: Into the Mainstream," which was needed, claimed the Department, because of "clear gender differences" in occurrence of and kinds of mental illnesses women and men suffer from. The Department highlighted in particular that "violence and abuse" is one of the "most devastating life events" that can affect women's mental health and claimed that "between 18 and 30% of women experience domestic violence during their lifetime and between 14 and 40% of women have experienced sexual violence" (2002:8).

New Victims

Whatever assessment is made of the way in which soldiers and women have been constructed as traumatized victims who are likely to suffer from PTSD, it is notable that PTSD moved on to other groups. This is perhaps one of the most interesting aspects of the story of PTSD since the early 1980s. A category that first emerged to explain a very particular experience—of soldiers fighting a war—gained far wider applicability.

As Kutchins and Kirk explain, "Most people who have received the diagnosis of PTSD . . . have a very different history from the Vietnam veterans" (1997:116). According to Dean, in the United States, PTSD in fact quickly became the "disorder *du jour.*" He contends that in the 1980s, "the possibility was raised that practically the entire population of the United States was suffering from some sort of PTSD or associated guilt syndrome related to the Vietnam War" (1997:15), a process that has not abated. In 2000 it was reported that around 1000 women who served in the U.S. army in Vietnam, in noncombat but nonnursing roles (for example, as flight controllers), were the "hidden victims" of that war, whose traumatic experience the "world forgot" (Krum 2000). It has also been noted how the concept of PTSD has been applied very generally to populations who live in war zones, not just combatants: "Programmes costing millions of dollars to address 'posttraumatic stress' in war zones have been increasingly prominent in humanitarian aid operations, backed by UNICEF, WHO, European Community Humanitarian Office and many nongovernmental organisations," notes Summerfield (1999:1449).

Thus a diagnosis that was originally developed to explain the experiences of those who had *committed* acts of violence against others has come to be most commonly applied in relation to those who have had such acts committed against them, or who have witnessed such acts. Westervelt observes, in a different sense, that the way in which the concept of PTSD developed is intriguing. She makes the important point that the effect of syndrome claims for women has been paradoxical. The concept of victimization, which for its feminist advocates was mobilized to highlight precisely the *unique* experience of women subject to male violence, has become more and more *universalized.* "[N]o doubt feminist reformers who fought for this institutionalization [the recognition of victimization by the law] also contributed to the victimization culture by encouraging the further use of victimization as a culturally valid excuse," she argues, creating a "culture of victimization" (1998:12).

Young also suggests that PTSD became increasingly culturally validated over the 1980s and 1990s; it acquired, in his terms, "factity." The existence of the diagnostic category shaped, from the 1980s on, "the self-knowledge of patients, clinicians and researchers" (1995:5). Once established as a recognized condition through the experience of war veterans and women, PTSD diffused to influence claims made about the experiences of many people and how society should treat them. According to Tana Dineen, PTSD "quickly became a buzzword, going far beyond the original patient population. . . . it led to a battlefield being seen as 'a microcosm of trauma,' resulting in virtually any scene from everyday life having the potential to be seen as a battlefield" (1999:71).

Over the 1980s and 1990s in the United States, Kutchins and Kirk contend, PTSD became a "catchall category" for mental health professionals. It was used to diagnose people who in the past would not have been considered mentally ill, as it gained application in relation to an "increasingly wide pool of problems that originate in traumatic life events and are not attributable to pre-existing intrapsychic malfunctions" (1997:116).

It has been argued that a similar development took place in British society, although later than in the United States. PTSD first became highly visible in public discussion in Britain in 1985, when the syndrome was diagnosed in firefighters who tackled a fire at Bradford football stadium that killed thirty-six fans. The 1987 fire at King's Cross train station, and a major disaster at Hillsborough football stadium that killed ninety-five fans, were followed by a plethora of diagnoses of PTSD among both survivors and service personnel (Toolis 1999). Although more recent cases still have tended to center on service personnel, they have not always involved tragedies or disasters. Ambulancemen, policemen and women, paramedics, firefighters, and members of the armed forces have regularly claimed that they have PTSD following the performance of their regular duties (Summerfield 2001). Summerfield argues that those involved with mental health care have come to associate PTSD with "a growing list of relatively commonplace events: accidents, muggings, a difficult labour (with a healthy baby), verbal sexual harassment, or the shock of receiving (inaccurate) bad news from a doctor" (Summerfield 2001:96).

The disorder has, therefore, now moved far beyond the scene of wars, male violence, and even accidents and disasters. It remains the case, of course, that those who experience such events are certainly often represented as victims of PTSD. A landmark class action was brought against the U.K. Ministry of Defence (MOD) in 2002 by former soldiers of the British army, who alleged that the MOD had neglected its "duty of care" to them, because they had been traumatized by their involvement in wars in Northern Ireland, the Persian Gulf, the Falkland Islands, and Bosnia, and were not warned of this possibility in advance (Dyer 2002). A 1997 survey claimed that its results showed that 750,000 British women are still suffering from the stress and trauma of the Second World War (Furedi 2002b). But in addition to these claims, PTSD has come to be implicated in explanations for the problems of everyday life and diagnosed in relation to them.

Some accounts draw attention to bizarre examples of this. Field cites examples of people involved in claims for compensation who have been diagnosed as suffering from PTSD, including people involved in minor car accidents, sometimes while asleep in a lay-by; a person knocked down by a bicycle; a shopper who was struck on the head by merchandise falling from a shelf; and subjects who had suffered serious head injuries, but who on regaining consciousness were unaware they had been involved in accidents (1999). One British case in 2000 involved a supermarket employee, who successfully claimed that he had been victim of discrimination because of mental disability. He was made redundant after four months' sick leave and claimed unfair dismissal because he was suffering from PTSD that had developed after many shoppers had contracted dysentery from the salad bar he managed. At the court hearing for his case, which went in his favor, a representative of the Trauma Aftercare Trust testified they were certain that the man had suffered from PTSD, and that he should qualify as "a disabled person" (*The Guardian* 2000).

Perhaps more significantly, sites in which millions of people interact every day have come to be represented as places where people are "at risk" of PTSD. Summerfield (2001) notes how the British workplace is increasingly presented as a site of traumatic events, and PTSD is more and more frequently diagnosed following disputes between colleagues. The experience of school in Britain (and the United States) is now routinely discussed as an arena in which "traumatization" may occur. The fact that schools frequently "buy in" counselors following events involving pupils such as injuries and fatalities, or employ counselors as part of the staff, indicates that they consider "traumatization" more or less inevitable and assume that families and teachers will prove unable to help children to cope with such events. Other children are also increasingly viewed as a risk factor for their fellow pupils. Recently published British research links bullying in school by pupils to a variety of mental health problems developed later in life: depression, alcoholism, suicide and PTSD in adults are all considered to be caused by previous experiences at school. The problem this poses for the future is considered to be of epidemic proportions, since more than half of British children are considered subject to bullying (McVeigh 2001).

Through this process, PTSD has emerged as a disorder that is not confined to the hospital or the treatment room. Recognition of PTSD does not comprise simply the interaction between mental health professionals and their patients. Although this dimension is central to the concept of PTSD, the disorder is also intimately connected with nonmedical activities and developments. As Farrell notes, the "clinical concept" of trauma has come to interact with "a host of ideological concerns outside the doctor's office, from the defeat in Vietnam to massive layoffs. The term has become metaphorical even as its clinical significance persists, contributing to increasingly psychologized and medicalized explanations for behavior" (1998:x). PTSD exists both as a medical condition and as a form of argument about how individuals and groups of people should be perceived and treated by others, and how we should perceive ourselves.

SYNDROME EXPLANATIONS ARE CULTURALLY SANCTIONED

The tendency to explain problems in medicalized terms and the linked effect of the construction of mental illness as a very common problem point to a third feature of the "Syndrome Society": that these accounts of human experience are culturally sanctioned. Particular putative disorders and mental illness have met some resistance from certain quarters. As noted previously, attempts to explain in terms of PMS why women may have certain experiences before they menstruate, or attempts to characterize forms of behavior that are most frequently exhibited by women as mental illness (Masochistic Personality Disorder), have been disputed and criticized by some feminists as damaging to women and their interests. In the context of certain institutional settings, illness explanations have also been disputed. For example, in the legal arena, it has not always been the case that syndrome defenses succeed in convincing a jury or judge that the person who committed the alleged crime should be considered excused because his or her behavior was the product of the relevant syndrome (Downs 1996; Westervelt 1998; Raitt and Zeedyk 2000). The fact that there is some such contest does not detract, however, from the dominant trend of acceptance of medicalized explanations of human behavior.

The perception at the center of this trend is that it is *advantageous* for behavior to be understood in this way. The idea that people benefit from explanations that construct their problems as resulting from the presence of a psychological condition, and are therefore likely to do better if they are subject to therapeutic intervention of some kind, is frequently accepted and championed. The notion that *recognition* of suffering and illness is essential, and too often absent, is promoted widely. Hence many groups of people have been construed as "suffering in silence" or as being the "hidden victims" of one form of medical problem or another (Best 1999). In the United States and Britain it has become entirely predictable that following any kind of disaster, accident or conflict, the need for counseling will be advocated and provided to those affected.

A great deal of importance is now attached to the recognition of psychological suffering, and in turn the moral high ground has come to rest with those who advocate such recognition. The cultural dominance of the importance of recognizing suffering is most obviously shown by the language and practice of institutions. Now key to the self-advocacy of law enforcement agencies is the claim that they take the experience of victimization seriously. Accounts abound of how, following muggings, people are encouraged to contact "victim support" to obtain counseling for trauma, and those whose houses have been robbed, posing no threat to personal safety, are encouraged to do likewise (Wessely 1999). Assisting victims of violent assault, especially in relation to sexual violence, has become a specialist aspect of policing. The rise of the "victim of crime" is illustrated by the increasingly widespread use in Britain of the term "Victims' Justice System" rather than "Criminal Justice System," to describe the institution responsible for prosecuting those accused of committing crimes. Institutions concerned with education have become increasingly aware of the need to recognize ADHD, and the notion that schoolchildren are likely prone to traumatization from bullying is central to local and national policies.

In many universities, too, the need to anticipate the problems students might face as a result of stress produced by leaving home and by studying has been formalized in policies and new practices (Furedi 1997). And promotion of the need to recognize the problems faced by victims of disorders and anticipate the emergence of new groups likely to suffer is widespread in media reporting of human experience. The cultural dominance of this perception of what is best for people is perhaps the most important feature of the "Syndrome Society" and is very evident in the case of PTSD.

POSTTRAUMATIC CULTURE

It has been argued that the cultural resonance for PTSD, as a particular form of mental illness, is shown by the way terms such as "stress," "trauma," and "emotional scarring" have become commonplace, used both metaphorically and to indicate that professional help is needed by those suffering from distress (Summerfield 1999). The phenomenon is, according to Summerfield, one aspect of a culture in which a particular version of "personhood" has become culturally dominant.

Prior to the development of the "Syndrome Society," personhood in British society invoked notions of stoicism and understatement. The culturally dominant expectation of personhood construed the "normal" to include such psychological states as resilience and composure. Today the conception of the "normal" has shifted: "When a psychiatrist or psychologist attests that an unpleasant but scarcely extraordinary experience has caused objective damage to a psyche with effects that may be long lasting, a rather different version of personhood is being posited" (Summerfield 2001:96). Even if the reality of the stoicism and understatement of the British people was overstated in the past, nowadays such characteristics are rarely claimed to be desirable. The culturally dominant version of personhood considers it usual for people to respond to adverse life events by becoming overwhelmed and engulfed by them, and desirable that they should admit to being so. The expectation is not that people will be able to cope, but that they will find it difficult, perhaps impossible, to do so. Psychologist Peter Cotton claims similarly that the rise of PTSD represents the emergence of a "precarious self" in which the individual, in a context where traditional cultural, religious, and familial frames of reference have receded, appears to be left isolated. In consequence, the idea of psychological fragility and vulnerability of the self has become the dominant cultural point of reference (1996).

This version of personhood, and the resultant argument that it is advantageous to recognize people's difficulties in coping, is apparent in the claims made by those who advocate the use of the concept of PTSD. In response to an article published in the *British Medical Journal* criticizing the concept, for example, a psychiatrist writing in support of PTSD argued, "[T]he birth of post-traumatic stress disorder exemplifies how good it is that despite orthodoxy and haughtiness the medical profession is sometimes forced to listen to people's pain. . . . Doctors should encourage their patients to disclose distress and seek help" (Shalev 2001). Another respondent contended that psychiatrists who diagnose PTSD are doing the right thing, compared with "unsympathetic psychiatrists [who] deny suffering and disability" (Ellis 2001). One correspondent claimed that PTSD "may well be the medicalisation of everyday life, but . . . it is a necessary evil" (Litvea 2001) and yet another, that "Negating it [recognition of PTSD] can be a disenfranchisement of the patient" (Devilly 2001).

Mental health professionals who embrace this conceptualization of patients' problems can, it is argued, do a great deal of good, certainly compared with those who dismiss patients' problems as nonmedical in origin. As a result, a moral contrast emerges between those who advocate medicalizing the effects of adverse life experiences (sympathetic to the patient) and those who do not (cold, haughty, and dismissive of the patient). For the former group, it is positive when people discuss their feelings and problems with mental health professionals and look to them for help, rather than attempting to deal with their problems on their own. Attempting to "cope alone" with the effects of adverse life events (or even with the assistance of family and friends) is often considered, at best, inadequate and, at worst, highly damaging. In this approach, the fact that PTSD is more visible and recognized than ever before is considered a positive development. As Toolis notes, to some of those who support the concept of PTSD, the fact that people are increasingly diagnosed as suffering from it constitutes as positive development, since it indicates "belated recognition of the effects of psychological harm and trauma across a whole range of human activity" (1999:27).

Claims for the merit of recognizing psychological harm and trauma are evident in many other arenas and institutions. The legal profession has been very active in promoting the need for recognition of the experience of trauma; according to some, it has been more active than any other body of people (Field 1999). In Britain, the significance of PTSD for the law has been considered particularly important, since in order for compensation for damages to be claimed, the claimant must be considered to suffer from a recognized psychiatric injury. Hence PTSD has emerged as a vital concept in compensation claiming (Napier and Wheat 1995). Legal professionals work with psychiatrists or other mental health professionals in making claims for compensation on behalf of those who have experienced adverse life events and are deemed to suffer from PTSD as a result, where it can be proved that those events were the fault of another party. According to Field, such legal claims are commonplace: "It is virtually impossible nowadays," he argues, "to study a medicolegal report by a psychiatrist or psychologist instructed on behalf of a plaintiff in personal injury litigation which does not conclude that he or she is suffering from post-traumatic stress disorder" (1999:35).

Legal experts have also noted how the increasing recognition by judges that psychiatric injury is a form of genuine and nontrivial damage is one of the most significant developments of the past decade (Atiyah 1997). Farrell has investigated the phenomenon he calls the "post traumatic culture," and he draws attention to the importance of the law. Writing about the United States, he argues that concerns about compensation have always accompanied ideas about trauma. This is true of legal defenses used for veterans in trouble with the law and of the relationship between PTSD and compensation. The women's movement has also prominently used the concept of trauma to give weight to legal arguments, but "the phenomenon has expanded into many areas of tort and criminal law" (Farrell 1998:24).

Advocates of claims for compensation for the injury of PTSD contend that legal recognition of psychiatric damage is a positive step forward; for them the effect of enabling people to be viewed by the law as subject to traumatization is empowering. The redefinition of PTSD in the DSM to include a wide range of experiences as traumatic has been welcomed as rightful recognition of "the diversity of the ways in which human beings can experience and be affected by stress" (Napier and Wheat 1995:41), and it had been argued that it is right for the law to prioritize putative victims' perceptions of what took place. Even if the accident is "relatively minor"—for example, a road accident or "near miss"—it is deemed right that a claim can be brought if the accident is viewed as threatening by the person concerned (Napier and Wheat 1995:43). Hence, widening the range of events that can be considered traumatic is deemed an important and useful development.

The effect of such developments in the realm of the law has important cultural effects. Law, argues Westervelt (1998), reflects cultural premises—innovations in law thus emerge in a way that tends to resonate with broader cultural imperatives—but law contributes to cultural change as well, by encouraging certain trajectories. So, as the law reflects a culture that wants to recognize the experience of those who have come to be considered victims, its reformation to allow this experience to be recognized facilities further moves in this direction. Where the law bends to accommodate the experience of certain victims, so others are encouraged to tread the same path, and thus the law contributes to the process through which the victim attains cultural legitimacy.

Farrell's examination of "post traumatic culture" draws attention to another arena that supports the representation of experience in terms of trauma, namely media representations of experience. Farrell (1998) considers mainly fictional accounts in films and novels, and while his case is that such representations draw attention to broader social developments—dislocations and loss of coherence that lead people to feel out of control and unable to maintain their sense of self, thus generating the experience of trauma—his work documents powerfully how commonplace the portrayal of trauma has become. O'Brien also notes how media representations have played an important role in popularizing this representation of experience—"newspapers and magazine articles, popular books and films, television documentaries, all played a part in bringing the plight of Vietnam veterans to the attention of America" (1998:3)—and have done so subsequently. On this basis, PTSD has become a "sort of psychiatrists' 'dish of the day,'" comprehensible and accessible for mass media, which adds "human interest" to disasters and which commands enormous popular as well as professional interest (O'Brien 1998:3). As this writer notes, every time there is a tragedy, broadcast and print media discuss the trauma that survivors have experienced and inform the audience that trained counselors are being deployed to help survivors come to terms with the trauma of the event.

A recent example of this phenomenon is the way in which people's responses following the attacks of September 11, 2001, were discussed in relation to their developing PTSD. It was automatically assumed that many were likely to be traumatized [indeed, one commentary claimed that even journalists who reported the event would suffer PTSD and be in need of counseling (Braynes 2001)]. Following September 11, the widely reported research findings that appeared less than a year later found that 11.2 percent of New Yorkers had PTSD. Headlines appeared stating: "'Millions' suffered 11 September trauma." One very interesting finding that did not make the news, however, was that outside New York "overall distress levels . . . were within normal ranges" (Schlenger et al. 2002:581). The finding that most Americans did not develop this mental illness following September 11 was, apparently, not considered significant by the press.

Where there is such cultural support for PTSD, it is perhaps not surprising that people do often understand their experience of adverse life events in terms of the disorder. Indeed, according to some, the experience of PTSD is a *result* of the disorder being culturally sanctioned. This point has been made in relation to the reinterpretation of past experience, through the emergence of new memories and feelings. Writing of the experience of a veteran of the Second World War who had been diagnosed, 40 years later, as suffering from PTSD following the experience of disturbing memories of the war, Summerfield and Hume argue: "a person processes trauma as a function of the social meaning attached to it." In a context where, since 1945, Western culture has seen a "dramatic rise in the power of psychological explanations for the world," popularized through the medicine, law, and the media, it is to be expected that "traumatic memories" emerge (1994:873). The rise of "trauma" as a medical and cultural category has meant that people, for example, ex-servicemen, have reevaluated their past experiences in light of the social meaning that has more recently come to be attached to them.

It has also been argued that it is cultural endorsement of the idea of trauma that accounts for the experience of those newly traumatized. Anthropologist Allan Young describes this phenomenon as a self-perpetuating "cultural loop." "If it becomes socially axiomatic that all traumatic events will produce PTSD, then some individuals involved in these events will believe that their understandable short term distress is a psychiatric illness" (Toolis 1999:29). For Farrell, in the "post-traumatic culture," while the concept may often be "overstated or implausible," it is nonetheless the case that "people feel, or are prepared to feel . . . as if they had been traumatized" (1998:x).

Attention has also been focused on how, in specific contexts, endorsement of PTSD *accounts* for the experience of traumatization. For example, it is involvement in litigation that, according to some, accounts for the persistence of the "symptoms" of PTSD. Field has argued that litigation is formative in relation to the phenomenon of symptoms identified as "reexperience." He contends that litigation will lead to this "symptom," since those claiming compensation for PTSD will be required to constantly relive what happened, as they are examined for the preparation of medico-legal reports and discuss their experience with their lawyers. "In other words, ongoing litigation acts as an artificial reinforcing factor for unpleasant memories and their accompanying effect" (1999:36). Wessely, similarly, contends that: "The charge is no longer that people routinely fake symptoms to gain compensation, but that the process of litigation reinforces disability to the extent that it becomes perpetuated. . . . Once embarking on litigation, there are no rewards for getting better—rather the reverse" (1995:664). Posttraumatic Stress Disorder, these accounts suggest, has become a concept through which people understand and experience their problems; it has become a culturally endorsed option.

The three features of the "Syndrome Society" discussed above suggest, therefore, that a powerful dynamic in both the United States and Britain lends legitimacy to the problematization of human experience in terms of mental illness. The concept of PTSD has been examined in this chapter as an example of this trend. The contribution of different groups of social actors to its construction has been discussed, to show how PTSD results from the intersection of lay interests, medical professionals, and other institutions. From this standpoint, PTSD constitutes not so much a scientific or medical category as cultural concept of personhood, framed in psychiatric terms. The diagnostic criteria for the disorder constitute a representation, in the language of medicine, of the perception of the ability (or inability) of people to cope with adverse life advents.

Chapter 4 explores the extent to which the experience of abortion has come to be included in the "Syndrome Society." As Chapter 1 illustrated, the PAS claim draws explicitly on the concept of PTSD. Its proponents have attempted to co-opt the framing of human experience in the "Syndrome Society" and construct abortion as an experience capable of producing PTSD. In common with other aspects of the medicalization of human experience, the language of the PAS claim emphasizes and elevates women's vulnerability and difficulties in coping with abortion, in order to problematize the procedure. How far has this construction of the problem of abortion been endorsed by others? To what extent has the notion that abortion can be a pathogen, which leads to mental illness, become accepted? Before considering these questions in detail, however, it is necessary first to provide an account of why abortion opponents in the United States and Britain considered it necessary to modify the moralized framing of their case, by adopting medical-sounding language.

3

The "De-moralization" of the Antiabortion Argument

In the context of the "Syndrome Society," it is easy to see why abortion opponents might claim that abortion is a problem because it damages women psychologically. As this chapter explains, the medicalization of the antiabortion argument was made more appealing still by the difficulties presented by explicitly moralized antiabortion claims. I make the case that framing abortion as a medical problem was, and remains, a response to a context that was, and is still, either inhospitable to or ambivalent about the claim that abortion is morally wrong. Much of the debate about abortion in the United States and Britain has focused on what the law should allow, and claimsmakers involved in the abortion debate have dedicated their time and resources to attempting to influence the outcome of debates about the law. The subject of this chapter is, therefore, the legal debate about abortion, and what this tells us about why abortion opponents might reframe their claims in medicalized terms.

ABORTION LAW IN BRITAIN

The main statute that regulates abortion in Britain was passed by Parliament in 1967. The 1967 Abortion Act has been amended only once, in 1990, through section 37 of the Human Fertilisation and Embryology Act. The main part of the resulting statute reads:

> A person shall not be guilty of an offence under the law relating to abortion when a pregnancy is terminated by a registered medical practitioner if two registered medical practitioners are of the opinion formed in good faith—
>
> (a) that the pregnancy has not exceeded its twenty-fourth week and that the continuance of the pregnancy would involve risk, greater than if the pregnancy were terminated, of injury to the physical or mental health of the pregnant woman or any existing children of her family; or

(b) that the termination is necessary to prevent grave permanent injury to the physical or mental health of the pregnant woman; or
(c) that the continuance of the pregnancy would involve risk to the life of the pregnant woman, greater than if the pregnancy were terminated; or
(d) that there is substantial risk that if the child were born it would suffer from such physical or mental abnormalities as to be seriously handicapped.

This statute permits abortion on terms that have had an important effect in shaping the British abortion debate. Under the 1967 Abortion Act, abortion remained formally a criminal offense, since the existing legislation was not repealed. The procedure remained regulated by Sections 58 and 59 of the 1861 Offences Against the Person Act, which made the attempt to "procure a miscarriage," by a woman or any other person, a criminal offense that could be punished by imprisonment. However, from 1968 on (when the 1967 Abortion Act came into force), the 1861 Act had to be read in conjunction with the 1967 Act. A defense was provided in the latter statute against the offenses defined in the prior legislation because, in the 1967 Act, doctors were empowered to carry out legal abortion on the grounds specified in its clauses (Bridgeman 1998; Simms 1985). Under British law, women therefore have no right to abortion; the right to decide whether or not a woman can legally end a pregnancy rests with two doctors, who can agree to the request for abortion on specified grounds.

According to the British philosopher Janet Radcliffe-Richards (1982), the key feature of this law is that it does not have any overt moral basis. British law is not based on stated principles regarding the morality of abortion, and rights are ascribed neither to the pregnant woman nor to the fetus. Rather, throughout pregnancy, the abortion decision is made according to medical judgment. The "de-moralization" of abortion is, therefore, at the heart of the terms of this statute. On the one hand, abortion remains constructed as a "wrong." The 1861 Act that criminalized abortion as an "offence against the person" was not repealed in 1967. However, abortion came to be considered, through the 1967 Act, a wrong that can be justified on a number of grounds. Abortion should be permitted, according this Act, where certain conditions pertain.

The type of condition under which abortion is deemed legally permissible adds a further, crucial dimension to the "de-moralization" of abortion in British law. There is no mention of the concepts of liberty, freedom, autonomy, or any other moral precept as a ground for abortion in British law. The reasons why an abortion can be considered legally justifiable are medical ones. It has to be the case that two doctors consider it medically necessary that an abortion is performed because a woman's health, or that of members of her existing family, is "at risk" if she continues the pregnancy. The construction of the terms under which women can legally terminate abortion in Britain, as a matter best decided by medical discretion, has been termed the "medicalisation of abortion" (Sheldon 1997:3).

Reform of the law to allow abortion on these medical grounds went through a long evolution. It was preceded by attempts to reform the law from the 1930s on; consequently the issue had already been raised many times before 1967 (Simms and Hindel 1971) and has, according to scholars who have considered the terms of the abortion law, deep cultural roots. Davies (1992) argues that legal reform on the terms outlined above accorded with a set of assumptions that he terms "causalism." Those adopting a causalist approach, contends Davies, are unlike moralists in that they do not consider the law to be an instrument that is intended to identify and penalize the guilty and identify and protect the innocent. The frame of reference is not right and wrong, and guilt and innocence. Rather, causalist thinking is concerned with "questions of cause and consequence," and the aim is to minimize harm overall and reduce suffering. In essence, the causalist goal is welfare, whereas that of moralist thinking is justice. So in considering how to frame laws, the causalist aims above all to reduce suffering, which is considered to be "the greatest of all human evils." Such an approach to the law, argues Davies, does not imply hedonism, and its proponents are not visionaries: "They are only concerned with present disutility, with the avoidance of today's tangible but visible suffering, distress, harm and conflict" (1992:105). Boyle (1997) has also drawn attention to the way that the abortion law primarily attempted to reduce suffering and argues that this approach to the regulation of abortion was in line with the broader development of "therapeutic law" during the post–Second World War period in Britain.

Davies presents causalists as an ideal type, but the arguments made by those supporting abortion law reform in 1967, which had majority support in Parliament, do conform to this characterization. Those who advocated reform did not argue for abortion in any sense as a facet of moral concepts of freedom or liberty. They rather presented it as a lesser evil. Legalizing abortion was presented as a way of alleviating suffering for women who risked being maimed through illegal abortion procedures. It was also presented, as I illustrate further in Chapter 5, as a solution to the social ills that were considered to be created by overly large families and unwanted childbearing, particularly among the poor. Thus supporters of law reform argued that abortion was a lesser evil than illegal abortion or "over-large" families and could therefore be justified as acceptable in preventing the mental or physical suffering that might result from these problems. The causalist law that resulted from this thinking avoided any reference to moral precepts, whether supportive of or opposed to abortion, and in the event it was the causalist law that most in Parliament wanted to support.

Organizations whose stated aim is to oppose the legalization of abortion were established in response to the 1967 reform of the law (Francome 1984), and their founding aims are clearly moralistic. Life's chairman wrote in 1971, shortly after the organization was established, "The unborn child has as much right to life as his mother has. . . . It must be wrong deliberately and directly to kill either, even for the sake of the other" (Francome 1984:161). The aims of Britain's other main antiabortion organization, the SPUC, include "To affirm, defend and promote the existence and value of human life from the moment of conception" (Society for the Protection of Unborn Children n.d.). The implication is that the organization's aim is to repeal the 1967 Act and return abortion to its prior legal position, and that it hoped to persuade politicians in Britain to adopt a moralistic mode of thinking and consider abortion law as a mechanism for drawing lines about right and wrong. How have abortion opponents fared in the face of this difficult task? What is noteworthy for the purposes of my argument is the fact that the statute has proved to be remarkably durable. Since 1967 MPs, including those who consider the statute problematic because it fails to recognize in law the interests of the "unborn" or the interests of pregnant women, have decided to accept the de-moralized regulatory framework represented by medicalized abortion law.

Parliamentary Debates, 1967–1989

Parliamentary debate about abortion was most prevalent over the 1970s and 1980s, and its impetus was sentiment opposed to increased access to abortion. There were fifteen parliamentary bills between 1967 and 1989 that were intended to restrict the terms on which abortion could take place (Moore 1992). The main bills were introduced in 1974 (the White Bill), 1979 (the Corrie Bill), and 1987 (the Alton Bill). Others were introduced in 1977, 1978, 1985, 1986 and 1987 (there were three antiabortion bills in 1987 other than the Alton Bill). It is notable that none of these bills were intended to outlaw abortion or introduce a "right to life" into the law; such a project, it seems, has never seemed realistic to parliamentary abortion opponents.

These bills can be considered "antiabortion," however, since they sought to alter the terms of the 1967 Abortion Act in a restrictive direction. They sought to do this by amending the clause in the act that deals with conscientious objection on the part of doctors, to make it easier for doctors to opt out of providing abortion; by specifying that one of the certifying doctors has to be a consultant or doctor of equivalent status; by limiting the terms under which abortion was provided by the independent sector (by abortion providers who are not part of the National Health Service); by tightening the wording of the act, to allow abortion only in cases of "serious" risk of "grave" injury to the woman or her family; or, most commonly, by lowering the gestational "time limit" for abortion (Millns and Sheldon 1998:11). Such bills fell short of the central goal of antiabortion organizations (a ban on abortion), but support was offered to MPs who put them forward, in the form of publicity, and lobbying and campaigning activities. Through achieving more limited aims, antiabortion organizations hoped that they would eventually move forward to their final goal of recriminalizing abortion.

This assessment of the situation in the event proved misplaced; none of these bills succeeded in bringing about legal change. Although they did succeed in generating an unusually full debating chamber, and much heated discussion, none had a legislative effect, and the result has not been the emergence of a political climate amenable to more thoroughgoing restrictions on abortion. Indeed, it is arguable that the opposite has been the case. Not only did no antiabortion measures succeed in Parliament, but, as I discuss later, the end result of this period of debate was the further consolidation of support for the regulation of abortion through the existing legislation.

That the abortion debate turned out this way is interesting given that much of it took place at a time when the issue of the "moral crisis" allegedly facing Western societies was a major public and political preoccupation. The 1980s as a whole have been considered a decade in which "'moral panics' over issues such as AIDS, abortion, child abuse, hooliganism and delinquency" emerged in many advanced industrialized countries, reflecting a "widespread sense of a loss of consensus concerning basic values and beliefs" (Furedi 1992:88). In the 1980s, the notion that Britain was facing a collapse of values and that a process of moral regeneration was in order had visibility and apparent social resonance. As political scientist Martin Durham describes it, in his informative study of this period, "in article after article" at this time "rising divorce rates, one-parent families, abortion, homosexuality, pornography—all have been cited as indices of a nation facing moral collapse" (1991:5).

Within this complex of issues, abortion figured prominently. It was commonly discussed as an exemplar of the problem of moral decline in British society. According to the right-wing philosopher Ronald Butt, for example, "The old restraints that once governed conduct have been dismantled and new conventions created. . . . It has been morally respectable, if regrettable, for life to be conceived only to be destroyed within 28 weeks" (1987). Some considered that this view of moral decline was politically influential. As Somerville (2000) notes, profamily crusades did "catch the ear" of a faction of the Conservative Party, and from the 1979 general election the idea was promoted that this was the "Party of the Family." Moralistic organizations, and those formed specifically to oppose abortion, appeared to gain new confidence in this environment, and to some it appeared there was evidence that a political "Moral Right" was emergent in Britain that was akin to the politically influential "Moral Majority" in the United States. At the very least, moralization of the political agenda was considered a significant component of Thatcherism (Weeks 1989). The abortion issue was considered to have a place in this political agenda, and, it was argued, the trajectory would be for policy in general, and abortion policy in particular, to move in an increasingly restrictive and conservative direction (David 1986).

There did appear, at certain points, to be significant support in Parliament for antiabortion bills. For example, on the day of publication of the Alton Bill in 1987, daily papers carried a full-page advertisement sponsored by fifty-two MPs depicting a photograph of a fetus with the caption, "We've abolished the death sentence for murderers and terrorists, shouldn't we abolish it for him?," and newspapers devoted many pages to informing readers of the things that twenty-eight-week-old fetuses that could still be legally aborted could do (for example, dance to pop music) (Phillips 1988). Yet the predictions that a new "Moral Right" would prove decisive in politics proved wrong, at least if the measure is taken as actual legislative and policy initiatives. As Berer has noted, looking back on the 1970s and 1980s, "every one of the now fifteen bills to restrict abortion . . . have always seemed to have a majority of Parliamentary support, yet every bill has fallen" (1988:28).

In no instance was it the case that such bills were clearly defeated by an opposing "prochoice" point of view. Rather, they tended to fail because of the procedural tactics used by opposing MPs (walking out of committees to ensure they were inquorate, or filibustering to stop a vote from taking place). Those that got farthest were the White Bill, the Corrie Bill, and the Alton Bill. The first lapsed at the end of the parliamentary session in which it was introduced. The second, which reached the stage of its second reading in 1979, at the point when the Conservative Party had a very large parliamentary majority, was "talked out" through the tabling of a large number of amendments. The Alton Bill, discussed in 1987 and 1988 when the moralization of politics appeared to be at a peak, ran out of parliamentary time before a vote was put (Millns and Sheldon 1998). The only way in which this pattern could have been altered would have been for the Government to allocate time to ensure a bill was voted on. The fact that this never happened suggests that although, in abstract terms, moralism may have appeared attractive to many MPs, the propensity for this to translate into the government's enacting a political program based on moralized precepts was exaggerated by those commentators who believed Britain was witnessing the emergence of a "Moral Majority." On sexuality at least, as Martin Durham's study of the Thatcher administration during the 1980s makes clear, there was reluctance on the part of the government to commit to policies and laws to "remoralize" society. The defense of "family values" and of sexual propriety was only half-heartedly embraced at this time (1991).

Although it is undoubtedly the case that a great deal of rhetorical support was offered to a moralistic agenda at certain moments, very few examples of policy or legal developments based on this agenda can be found. It may be that the very few examples that were pursued—for example, the Child Support Act

(CSA), which mandated that "absent fathers," those who were divorced or separated from the biological mothers of their children, must pay maintenance for their children—succeeded because they promised a saving in welfare expenditure. It has been argued that the CSA proposal, which did enter the statute books and has remained there since, was primarily an economic policy justified in the language of "family values," whereas restricting abortion would not save the State money (Jackson et al. 1993). Although the CSA does constitute an example where the law was changed, it should be noted, however, that it "hit sticky ground" almost immediately (Rowbotham 1997:553) and has been dogged by problems and controversy ever since. In regard to abortion, as Durham argues, it is clearly not the case that moralism seriously threatened the legal status quo. The antiabortion campaign was "not part of a Thatcherite offensive but, on the contrary, was an attempt to force Thatcherism to move in a direction it was plainly unwilling to go" (1991:38). Even at the high point of the "moralization" of politics, the terms of the 1967 act proved for the government preferable to more restrictive laws. A medically justified defense against the criminal act of an "offence against the person" was endorsed, rather than a legal framework that restricted access to abortion on moralized grounds.

The 1990 Reform

As noted in Chapter 1, there was further parliamentary debate about abortion in 1990; it was during this debate that the claim that women suffer from a Postabortion Syndrome first appeared in this arena. It is important to note that a key difference this time, compared with previous abortion bills, was that the government allocated time for debate. It did so to ensure that an amendment was passed that would specify a time limit on abortion in the statute and thus finally resolve the issue that had formed the main focus for debate through the 1980s. Parliament, as a result, did amend the Abortion Act through a bill that became Section 37 of the Human Fertilisation and Embryology Act, an act that deals mainly with the regulation of embryo research and the provision of infertility treatment. After a very protracted debate and series of votes, the proposal by the Conservative MP Geoffrey Howe was accepted, which specified a limit for legal abortion of twenty-four weeks with exceptions where the life of the woman was at risk or where there was "substantial risk of serious abnormality" in the fetus.

In practice, the new amendment changed little (Sheldon 1997). The number of abortions carried out after 24 weeks, for reasons other than fetal abnormality, was tiny. In 1989, the year before the act was amended, only twenty-two were performed after twenty-four weeks, and, of these, eighteen were for fetal abnormality and four to save the women's life (Mihill 1990). In fact, ever since the 1967 Act was passed, the vast majority of abortions have been performed in the first fourteen weeks of pregnancy. In political terms, however, the 1990 debate was highly significant. It signaled a clear intention to put an end to debate about the Abortion Act in Parliament. As Kenneth Clarke, then Secretary of State for Health, told the House of Commons: "this is a suitable opportunity for the House to have a day at the end of which it can come to a conclusion, which should last a long time, on the time limits and future operation of the 1967 Act" (Millns and Sheldon 1998:15). This was taken as a "direct warning to anti-abortionist MPs not to use the private members' bill procedure again to bring about changes" (Wintour 1990).

It seems that, although there was never much prospect that antiabortion politicians would have succeeded in getting the changes they wanted passed, many politicians considered it preferable to find a way to avoid spending any more time debating their proposals. It is important to note, however, that it was more a dislike of debating abortion further than support for women's rights that made it possible for agreement to be reached on amendment of the 1967 Act, and thus put an end to debate about it.

In the process of amending the Abortion Act, one "prochoice" amendment was put forward that sought to allow abortion on request up to twelve weeks of pregnancy (from Conservative MP Emma Nicholson). This amendment, which was, in prochoice terms, very moderate, was notably not selected for debate. Although Parliament could accept a law that allowed legal abortion up to twenty-four weeks where two doctors agreed to it, it would not even debate a bill that gave legal recognition to the woman as the sole decision maker in abortion up to twelve weeks. In the actual debate, the vast majority of those speaking in favor of the twenty-four-week limit did not discuss women's rights. Rather, women's access to legal abortion was defended by presenting them as deserving of sympathy, in terms that Hadley has described as the "awfulisation" of abortion, where abortion is portrayed as an evil, but a necessary evil (1997:7). Abortion was justified on the grounds that abortion is, for women, a "tragedy" (V. Bottomley MP; Hansard 1990:182), "a decision women agonise about . . . that is never reached lightly" (Mahon MP; Hansard 1990:236), "a difficult and traumatic decision" and "not a legitimate form of contraception . . . a desperate measure for desperate situations" (Primarolo MP; Hansard 1990:246–7), and it was argued that those who are concerned about women's well-being should look for "ways of removing the trauma and stress that is suffered by all women who have to endure an abortion" (Doran MP; Hansard 1990:214). Alternatively, women's need for abortion was justified through an appeal to their desire to be good mothers: "it is because mothers are concerned about the quality of life for their whole families that they have abortions" (Gordon MP; Hansard 1990:209).

The dominant argument made, however, did not refer to women at all. Rather it emphasized that medical opinion was the arbiter of the issue, and once the law was in line with this opinion, there was no more need for debate.

As Frank Doran MP put it, "We need to establish a principle that is related to the best medical practices. We should not have to debate the matter year in, year out but should place our trust in medical practitioners and give them a legal framework within which they can operate and which the public can understand" (Sheldon 1997:104). Many participants in the debate inside and outside Parliament pointed out that the twenty-four-week limit should be supported because it was the one that gynecologists and the medical profession preferred. An editorial in *The Guardian*, one of the United Kingdom's leading daily newspapers, articulated this case for this approach particularly clearly:

> The vote to bring down the upper time limit for most abortion . . . displayed a cool pragmatism in the face of hysterical emotion and marches in step with the vast body of public opinion. . . . The legal premise that abortion could take place until 28 weeks' gestation . . . has simply been overtaken by the march of science. . . . Most medical opinion now agrees that an infant is capable of sustaining independent life at 24 weeks, and in practice the vast majority of abortions already take place within that limit. . . . So reducing the limit to 24 weeks is a sensible acknowledgement in law of current reality already acknowledged in practice. (1990)

The terms of fetal "right to life" are decided, in this approach, through scientific advance and medical opinion. This right is granted at the point where science makes survival outside the woman's uterus possible. Legal abortion is pragmatically accepted, but the question of women's rights and the right of bodily autonomy are not an issue.

For most British politicians, the legality of abortion had become established by the early 1990s as beyond question, but with the terms of its provision based not on support for choice but on medicalized grounds, with women deserving of sympathy but not rights. The effect of such agreement on abortion has been, since 1990, to almost entirely silence further debate about the issue in Parliament. Insofar as debate has taken place subsequently, it has been through early day motions and adjournment debates that have little import in relation to the statute and constitute no more than a symbolic measure. The content of such measures is also significant in relation to the difficulties faced by abortion opponents, in that issues that lie only on the fringes of abortion provision have been highlighted, such as whether fetuses aborted at late stages in gestation feel pain, "sex selection" abortion, and abortion where the fetus has Down's Syndrome, a chromosomal disorder. Such issues are considered contentious and controversial (Jackson 2000). But they relate to only a very small proportion of abortions carried out or requested, suggesting that the question of whether most abortions are accepted as legally justified has been resolved. This outcome of debate about the law has been considered important for activity and argument on the issue in Britain more broadly. As legal scholar Sally

Sheldon notes, "whatever disagreement or struggle there is regarding abortion [in Britain] . . . has become increasingly muted. . . . it appears a status quo with regard to the regulation of abortion services has been established, and those who continue to kick against it—be they pro- or anti-choice activists—are cast as marginal extremists" (Sheldon 1997:2).

In sum, moralized argument that presents fetal life as centrally "at stake" in abortion has failed to influence the outcome of legal debate in Parliament. Antiabortion arguments have not so much been defeated by a prochoice viewpoint, however, as circumvented. Claims for fetal rights have not been debated in Parliament and a clear conclusion reached, but have been avoided and sidelined. The effect is that legal abortion has been accepted by most of those involved in parliamentary debate in Britain, but on highly pragmatic grounds. The outcome, above all, is a political consensus that debate on abortion is undesirable.

The Courts

Abortion opponents have also attempted to contest abortion law in British courts. This contest has often focused on men who want to prevent their wives or partners from terminating pregnancies, who in Britain (and in the United States) have usually been supported financially by one of the major antiabortion organizations. Organizations that oppose abortion have, in fact, had an ambivalent relationship with such cases. As Phyllis Bowman of the SPUC argued during one such case, "SPUC has at no time supported the concept of father's rights; once we concede that a man has rights to stop an abortion so he has to be given rights to demand that a pregnant wife or girlfriend must have an abortion" (Birth Control Trust 1997). But presumably since men involved in such cases have often attempted to contend that the fetus, not just the putative father, has legal rights, antiabortion organizations have decided to support them (Nolan 1998). In the course of such cases in Britain, it has again been apparent that abortion opponents can gain only minimal support for moralized claims. The case for recognizing a fetal "right to life" in law has been tested and dismissed. It has also been clarified that putative fathers have no right to stop a wife or partner from aborting a pregnancy.

All three of these points were clarified in the first reported case that went to the courts in Britain, in May 1978. William Paton brought a case against the abortion provider British Pregnancy Advisory Service. His estranged wife was granted the necessary certification from two doctors in response to her request for a termination but did not tell her husband. He then sought an injunction to prevent the abortion from going ahead without his consent. The court found against his claim for the right to prevent the abortion. It was found that the fetus had no independent rights under the law until born, and the father had no right to prevent an abortion (Fox 1998). The significance of medical discretion in the eyes of the law was made clear in the judge's comment that "it would be quite impossible for the courts . . . to supervise the operation of the 1967 Act. The great social responsibility is firmly placed by the law, on the shoulders of the medical profession." In his famous concluding remark, he stated it would be a "foolish judge" who would seek to "interfere with the discretion of doctors acting under the 1967 Act" (Sheldon 1997:88).

That the fetus has no rights in law was reiterated in the high-profile case *C v. S,* brought in 1987 by Robert Carver, then president of the Pro-Life Group at Oxford University. Carver brought a case funded by the SPUC to prevent his former girlfriend, a twenty-one-year-old woman also studying at Oxford, from having an abortion. Carver did not attempt to argue that he had paternal rights but that first, he had the right to prevent the abortion on behalf of the unborn child itself suing as "next friend," and that second, he was seeking to prevent an illegal abortion on the grounds that the gestational age of the fetus (between eighteen and twenty-one weeks) meant it was capable of being "born alive." Thus, he argued, abortion would be unlawful under the Infant Life Preservation Act of 1929, which prohibits the "destruction of a child" that is deemed "capable of being born alive." The first claim was summarily dismissed following *Paton,* on the grounds that the fetus was not a person at law. It was the second claim that became the focus for the case. The decisive issue became whether the fetus was viable and therefore whether a crime would be committed under the 1929 Act, and the outcome was decided by evidence on this issue. The judge found against Carver on this ground, and the Court of Appeal, which dismissed his case, found likewise (Fox 1998).

In the course of this case, the importance of medical opinion was again strongly emphasized. The issue became what medical evidence indicated regarding the chances of fetuses at different gestational stages being "born alive" (a theme which, as I discussed above, also dominated parliamentary discussion from the late 1980s on). The question of the legality of abortion thus came to rest on a decision about the point at which medical science considers a fetus to be "alive." In effect, the issue of personhood under the law came to be decided by the extent of biological development of the fetus and of medical advance. The court found that it had to study the evidence of "medical men, all of high reputation" and assess "truly remarkable developments in medical science" (Sheldon 1997:88). The authority to determine "when life begins" and thus whether the fetus deserves legal protection was considered to rest with medical opinion. Implicitly, moral claims for either fetuses or women were deemed of little significance.

Stephen Hone brought the most recent case of this type in 2001. He launched a legal action to try to stop his ex-girlfriend from having an abortion. No attempt was made to argue for fetal rights since she was twelve weeks pregnant and thus well within the legal time limit for abortion. He first went to the High Court, and the case was made that the clinic that was to carry out the abortion had contravened the terms of the 1967 Abortion Act. His solicitor argued that only one doctor, not two, was consulted, and that no questions were asked about the woman's mental and physical health and why she wanted an abortion. The procedures taken by the clinic were described by his solicitor as "gravely deficient" (Taylor 2001). However, the judge adjourned the case at this point and argued that the clinic should be able to give representations. The clinic then did so and gave an undertaking that the judge described as "highly responsible and helpful"—that if the woman were to return to the clinic it would not rely on the certificate originally signed by the doctor who had seen her. In the meantime, however, the woman concerned had an abortion at another clinic.

The law is very clear on how abortion should be considered in the courtroom. Abortion, where doctors consider it permissible, is not subject to debate or consideration. The fetus does not have legal rights, and neither do men as putative fathers. Medicalized law has offered, therefore, a considerable degree of protection to women seeking abortion when they face claims for the father's or fetal rights. As Fox has argued, "despite the many valid reasons why women oppose the medicalisation of abortion, one positive side effect has been the ease with which it means third-party claims can be ruled out." However, the terms on which claims for rights for fetuses, or men, have been set aside have "allowed the courts to sidestep any reference to the woman's position or her procreative liberty" (Fox 1998:205). Just as medicalization of the law has shielded legal discussion of abortion from moralized claims for fetuses, so it has meant that discussion of women's moral claims for reproductive autonomy have also been circumvented.

In ruling against claims for fetal or paternal rights, the courts have only been implementing the law as it stands. Judges appear to have been able to do so without much difficulty. It has been clear that they consider they can make such decisions without reference to moral issues; as the judges in the *Paton* case stated, they would apply the law "free from emotion or predilection" (Sheldon 1997:88). In *C v. S,* the judge agreed with this approach, adding that "sociological, moral and profound religious aspects" of the issue were not relevant (Fox 1998:205). A medicalized law has clearly de-moralized the abortion issue in the British courtroom, leaving as the only issue for debate the time at which the fetus can be "born alive," an issue that has also been deemed a medical matter.

DIFFUSION

Given this failure of the argument for the need to legally protect the life of the "unborn child" in Britain, it is perhaps not surprising to find that other modes of argument, including the PAS claim, emerged. This claim first emerged in the British Parliament in the 1990 debates. But it had appeared in other contexts in Britain earlier and, as Chapter 4 illustrates, was continually articulated through the 1990s. The process through which British abortion opponents came to argue for PAS is an interesting one. The claim did not emerge in Britain independently; it emerged through a process that has been termed "diffusion" (Best 2001), as it moved from its country of origin, the United States, to Britain. How did this process occur?

One mechanism can be categorized as "relational" diffusion (McAdam and Rucht 1993:59), that is, direct contact between American claimsmakers and their British counterparts. At the end of the 1980s, a number of speaking engagements were organized in Britain by the Society for the Protection of Unborn Children that featured prominent American PAS claimsmakers. In 1985 Olivia Gans, the director of the organization American Victims of Abortion, spoke at a SPUC conference in Britain. Two years later British Victims of Abortion (BVA) was set up by the SPUC (Bowman 1996:xv). In 1988 Gans again visited Britain at the invitation of the SPUC and toured the country, "sharing from her own abortion experience, and speaking on the research into damage resulting from abortion" (Bowman 1996:v). In the same year, antiabortion MPs with links to Life and the SPUC invited Vincent Rue to speak at the House of Commons. During his visit he also spoke to other British audiences and is reported to have asserted that "'post-abortion trauma' does exist, and that it is a variant of post-traumatic stress disorder, similar to that experienced by Vietnam veterans" (Birth Control Trust 1989).

British abortion opponents' use of literature written by American proponents of PAS has also contributed to the diffusion of this claim. As part of the Rawlinson Commission in 1994, discussed in detail in Chapter 4, BVA was invited to give evidence about the psychological effects of abortion. It submitted as references a number of leaflets and reports from U.S. PAS claimsmakers.[1] BVA also distributes literature written by Americans,[2] and Life's literature has clearly been influenced by Rue's putative diagnostic criteria for PAS. A briefing paper written for Life by Dr. Michael Jarmulowicz describes PAS as a form of PTSD and emphasizes the importance of the "defence mechanism. . . . denial" to explain "why the condition is difficult to recognise and diagnose" (Jarmulowicz 1992:9). The use of Rue's comparison between PTSD and women's psychological response to abortion appears throughout Life's literature.

The influence of their American counterparts has also shaped the activities of antiabortion organizations in Britain. As well as BVA, which borrows from American Victims of Abortion, an organization named Project Rachel had been initiated to encourage Catholic priests to "get involved in recognising the syndrome [PAS]." This project borrows from the long-standing U.S. initiative Rachel's Vineyard, the name given to a Catholic and evangelical therapeutic project in the United States (Vogel 1999). Terry Waitling, who set up the project in Britain, explained: "We often use evidence from America because people there tend to be more open about their feelings, and the pro-abortionists quote experience from there too" (Moorhead 1989). This adoption of American approaches has also led British antiabortionists to attempt to use the issue of the psychological effects of abortion to effect legal change, as Chapter 4 discusses in more detail.

British proponents of PAS have therefore looked to the United States for a source of ideas and authority. If medicalized claims have their origin in the United States, what gave rise to such arguments in the country of their origin? Why did abortion opponents in North America develop the PAS claim? What is its context in the United States and how does this context compare with that in Britain?

ABORTION IN THE UNITED STATES

There may seem to be more differences than similarities when comparing the context for the PAS claim in the United States with that in Britain. Abortion opponents were politically marginalized in Britain, but in the United States, PAS came to prominence in the abortion debate during the Reagan presidency, when antiabortion organizations enjoyed unprecedented political patronage and support. As I detail in Chapter 4, the argument that abortion harmed women psychologically had its greatest visibility in the United States between 1987 and 1989. It was during this time that the then Surgeon General, C. Everett Koop, undertook an inquiry, at the behest of President Reagan, into the health effects of abortion. As a result of this support for the claim, the issue of the "psychological effects of abortion" became very visible as an aspect of the abortion debate in the United States.

The abortion issue has, in general, been positioned very differently in U.S. and British politics, and in the United States, abortion opponents have enjoyed far greater success in encouraging its politicization. A number of studies have investigated the emergence of the Moral Majority and the related political phenomenon of the Moral Right or New Christian Right in the United States (Francome 1984; Bruce 1988; Leibman and Wuthnow 1983; Somerville 2000), an influential force in politics for which opposition to legal abortion was a key theme. I will argue, however, that despite the tendency toward the politicization of abortion in the United States, the emergence of health-based claims against abortion represent, as in Britain, a response to the limitations and difficulties presented by the core claims made by abortion opponents.

As Wilmoth (1992) has argued, the context for the Koop inquiry in 1987 was a "stalemate" in abortion politics. Proposals for restrictive legal measures were not making headway in Congress, and therefore a new strategy was developed, in which a medicalized argument against abortion was intended to play a greater role. The White House considered it more likely that others would support antiabortion measures if they avoided the issue of whether abortion should be legal or not, and focused instead on other questions. Among the proposals put forward by White House staff were measures to transfer funds away from organizations that support or provide abortion to those involved with adoption; to end tax deductions for medical expenses associated with abortion; to veto every bill that authorized federal spending on abortion; and to direct the Surgeon General to promote the argument that abortion is associated with health risks. In the end, the last of these options was chosen, on the grounds that it would be most likely to command public support (although as I discuss below, it is also the case that measures to restrict state spending on abortion have been successfully promoted by abortion opponents). While people might support legal abortion but dislike it, thus considering abortion the lesser of two evils, their views could be tipped toward opposition to abortion if abortion, like smoking, came to be associated with significant risks to health (Wilcox et al. 1998).

U.S. abortion opponents thus came to frame their arguments in terms of health in the mid-1980s because claims that abortion should be legally restricted on moral grounds had not succeeded. David Reardon has more recently explained, for example, why he believes it is important for "prolife forces" to emphasize the negative psychological effects of abortion: "While efforts to educate the public about the unborn's humanity may help to motivate pro-lifers, such efforts will have no effect on those who support abortion. . . . the only way to reach them is for us, too, to focus on the woman" (1996:ix). The outcome of the debate about the psychological effects of abortion is detailed in Chapter 4. In the remainder of this chapter I discuss further the context for the PAS claim in the United States. Why did abortion become so politicized? How did the legal framework on abortion develop, and how have antiabortion claimsmakers responded?

POLITICIZING ABORTION

Two connected features of the abortion issue in the United States are relevant to its intense politicization. The first is the way in which abortion law was reformed. Whereas in Britain the law was reformed by Parliament, in the United States it was reformed by decisions made by the Supreme Court in the 1973 cases *Roe v. Wade* and *Doe v. Bolton*. The rationale for reforming the law was made, inevitably, in terms of rights, because the reference point for the Supreme Court is a written constitution framed in terms of rights. This meant that the U.S. abortion debate has been very clearly focused from the start on a polarized debate that sets women's rights against those of the fetus. Kim Lane

Scheppele maintains that by making abortion a constitutional question, "gradualist or compromise solutions" were eliminated (1996:23), and, according to Glendon (1987), it is the absence of a "compromise solution" on abortion and the existence instead of a constitutionally protected "right to abortion" that marks out U.S. from other law. The political question, of what rights women should have, has in this way been placed center stage. The way in which abortion was legalized in the United States thus tended toward encouraging, from the ouset, what legal scholar Laurence Tribe (1990) has termed the "clash of absolutes," a politicized contest about the rights of women versus those of the fetus. By contrast, decisions made by parliaments do not necessarily deal in rights—as detailed above, the decision made by the British Parliament clearly avoided doing so—and this legal framework, therefore, tends, unlike that in the United States, to encourage a depoliticized acceptance of the law.

Making abortion into a political question has also relied upon the existence of a second factor, a particular kind of social movement, resulting from distinctive features of American culture. A numerically sizable and well-organized "Moral Majority" developed in the United States, which viewed legal abortion as an exemplar of what was wrong with society. An equivalent movement that might have led to pressure being exerted on politicians did not come into existence in Britain, or at least insofar as it existed, it was far smaller and less influential. In the United States, politicians have been pressured into making abortion an issue that they act upon in a way that has not been the case in Britain, indicated by the extent of activity in the former society, which dramatically outstrips that in the latter. By 1998, over 1,000 bills about abortion had been introduced by members of the U.S. Congress (Wilcox et al. 1998), compared with the relatively limited British debate described above. This chapter now briefly discusses these two features of the construction of the abortion issue in the United States.

Competing Rights

Some laws passed before 1973 were similar to the "causalist" kind of law adopted in Britain. Termed "reform" laws, such regulations provided for abortion in particular states on health-based grounds, but left in place the laws that criminalized abortion. However, rulings made in 1973 by the Supreme Court changed the face of the debate about the law in the United States entirely. Through *Roe v. Wade* and in *Doe v. Bolton,* the Court established that the decision to have an abortion was a private one to be made by a woman in consultation with her doctors, in which the state could only legitimately interfere in the later stages of pregnancy. The Court in *Roe* found that

This right of privacy, whether it be founded in the Fourteenth Amendment's concept of personal liberty and the restrictions upon state action as we feel it is, or as the District Court determined in the Ninth Amendment's reservation of rights to the people, is broad enough to encompass a woman's decision whether or not to terminate her pregnancy. (*Roe v. Wade,* 153; Walbert and Butler 1973)

During the first three months of pregnancy, the Court argued, the state had no grounds upon which it could interfere with a woman's decision, and it could only do so legitimately in the second three months in order to protect the health of the woman. In the last three months of pregnancy, the state could restrict or prohibit abortion, by ruling that the fetus had interests that needed to be protected, but even at this point such interference could not take place where abortion was judged necessary to preserve a woman's life or health. Through this ruling, all laws in individual states that restricted abortion— whether they criminalized abortion or reformed the law to make abortion legal on the basis of exceptions—were deemed unconstitutional and thus invalid.

The difference between this approach to the legalization of abortion and that adopted in Britain is striking. According to the Supreme Court, legal abortion is justified as an aspect of moral precepts—freedom and privacy—a justification entirely absent from the British parliamentary debate in 1967 (and absent in any significant sense from the British debate since). As I discuss in Chapter 5, justification of abortion on the grounds of protecting women's health was present in the Court's discussion. However, a health-based rationale for abortion was put forward only as an *explanation* for why abortion might be sought, not as a *prerequisite* for its legal availability. Why was such an approach adopted in the United States? A number of explanations have been offered, which can only be discussed briefly here.

Davies contends that "Americans involved in these changes came to argue . . . in ways radically different from their British and West European counterparts, in part because of the nature of the American Constitution" (1992:103). As noted above, a court, rather than a parliament, was looked to to rule on abortion, in line with the Constitution and its values. This inevitably meant that those involved in arguing for change appealed to different precepts, compared with those appealing to a body of politicians accountable to an electorate (see Simms and Hindel 1971; Sheldon 1997; and Latham 2002 for accounts of the arguments and tactics adopted by the lobby for abortion law reform in Britain). In addition to this, framing arguments in moralistic terms made sense to Americans arguing for the legalization of abortion, in a way that was not the case for those arguing for legal change in Britain. As Davies argues, appeal to values of "freedom and righteousness" has been a long-standing aspect of American public discourse (1992:115), and this aspect of culture encouraged those who wanted to change the law to frame their arguments in moralistic terms.

There were also, however, specific issues shaping the abortion debate before

1973 in the United States, which also encouraged this way of framing claims. First, as Chapter 5 details, there was a difference in the way in which U.S. medical opinion viewed abortion compared with that in Britain. In both societies, support for a liberal view on abortion was current in psychiatry by the mid-1960s. In Britain, however, other medical professionals, most importantly those represented by the Royal College of Obstetricians and Gynaecologists and the British Medical Association, remained very opposed to liberal provision of abortion, whereas their U.S. equivalents were supportive of it and indeed, by the early 1970s, were prominent advocates for it. This contrast can be explained in part by the differences in prior developments in the regulatory framework on abortion and their implications for medical practice.

Second, and more important, perhaps, is the influence of claims for women's rights in the United States at the time of abortion law reform. The reform process in Britain was not influenced by claimsmakers arguing for women's rights; the framing of abortion as a women's rights issue did not emerge prominently until *after* abortion had been made legal (Simms and Hindel 1971; Sheldon 1997; Latham 2002). And, it has been argued, even then feminism had a relatively marginal influence on the abortion debate in Britain. Davies notes, for example, the absence of "women-centered" arguments about abortion in British political debate and argues that "feminist pressure to make abortion on demand a woman's right . . . has lacked political clout, and the ineffectiveness of feminist resistance to changes in the time limit after which abortion may not be carried out has revealed the impotence of the women's movement in Britain" (1992:125). By contrast, the women's movement was well established in the United States before the Supreme Court rulings. Feminist claimsmakers had a direct influence over the process of abortion law reform and interacted with others arguing for abortion law reform. Their case for women's rights had a broader cultural resonance by this time (Luker 1984), and the construction of abortion as a "women's rights issue" has pertained subsequently.

The "Moral Right": Politicizing Competing Rights

Whichever of these factors was dominant, the outcome was a law with no inherent tendency to de-moralize the abortion issue but which, to the contrary, encourages the contest over the morality of the procedure. But the prominence of the issue in American politics following its legalization cannot be considered inevitable. Other rights-based decisions have not generated the same degree of contest. The fact that the abortion issue has engendered the political response that it has since 1973 relates also to the emergence of a sizable social movement that exerted pressure on politicians. While *Roe v. Wade* acted as a focus for this movement and encouraged its development, its existence is based on broader features of American society and culture.

The debate following *Roe v. Wade* was the result of powerful cultural forces in the United States distinct to that society: a movement arguing for the "secular assertion of rights and liberties in the Constitution," which has tended toward support for legal abortion; and "waves of popular moral fervour rooted in religion that have impelled states and sometimes federal legislators to try to control private individual conduct by law" (Davies 1992:116). The tendency to support religious ideas expressed as "moral fervour" in the United States implies that some U.S. citizens define themselves centrally through reference to their religious belief, far more so than British people.

The fact that Americans are more religious than Britons has been noted by Jenkins (1992) and by Bruce (1988), who states that in 1988, about 60 percent of Americans claimed church membership and stated that they regularly attend church, compared with 17 percent of Britons who stated they were members of a church, with only 11 percent regularly attending. According to Somerville (2000), a 1989 survey found that 90 percent of Americans believe in a personal God, compared with 31 percent of British people; that 79 percent of Americans report gaining comfort from their religion, compared with 46 percent of Britons; and that Americans attend weekly church at twice the rate of the British. It has been argued that, in general, the explanation for this strong religious affiliation lies in the centrality of religion to the formation of Americans' identity (Davies 1992). At a national level, identification with the ideals of the Constitution creates a tie that binds all people together as "American." The United States has also been characterized, however, as a society comprising a "melting pot" of ethnic groups, in contrast to the relatively homogeneous societies of Western Europe, and as one with powerful trends toward individuation. In other words, it has been viewed as a society lacking in the kinds of broader affiliations and ties that bind that have pertained elsewhere, such as those generated by labor movements (important for Britons, certainly in the past), which are not overtly religious. Thus, broader connections between people have tended to be expressed through religious identification in America in a way that is not the case in Britain or in most European counties.

The religions that have been influential in opposition to abortion are Roman Catholicism and fundamentalist Protestantism. According to Davies, in the United States these religions have more affiliates and "grassroot strength" than they do in any Western country, with the exception of Ireland (1992:129). At the outset, opposition to *Roe v. Wade* was rooted in and organized through the Catholic Church (prior to the 1973 ruling, opposition to abortion had been dominated by the Catholic Church; Somerville 2000), and the existence of "grassroots support" for religious beliefs is indicated by its ability to mobilize people. The National Right to Life Committee (NRLC), formed following the *Roe v. Wade* ruling, was estimated to have 13 million members in 1981, and a study of the NRLC in the late 1970s found that 70 percent of its members were Catholic. The Conference of Catholic Bishops also organized very actively against abortion and has commanded considerable resources. A network of churches, priests, and churchgoers could be mobilized in opposition to measures to make abortion legal, to form a ready-made national movement, to promote the antiabortion cause nationwide through "every state Catholic conference, every Catholic diocese and every Catholic parish" (Francome 1984:187). Consequently in the mid-1970s, support for a campaign for a constitutional amendment to protect the life of the "unborn child" could draw on a budget of $43.9 million for antiabortion activities, which, according to Tribe (1990), had a clear effect on politics. The emergence of abortion as an election issue in 1976 came as a result of Catholic campaigning, although at this point it was not a big issue in the presidential campaign.

The abortion issue was also made prominent through the 1970s by the activities of other religious groupings, of which the most important was fundamentalist Protestants. The emergence of a joint effort based on common ground between traditionally anti-Catholic southern evangelical Protestants and the Catholic Church has been considered an "unlikely alliance" (Somerville 2000:112; see also Rowbotham 1997), and the tensions between these two dimensions of opposition to abortion have been discussed elsewhere (Francome 1984; Bruce 1988). The internal instability of an alliance built on contradictory foundations, including sharply contrasting views about issues such as welfare payments, has been noted (Hadley 1994). However, claimsmaking by both aspects of church-based opposition to abortion did mean that the abortion issue acquired a dynamic that was absent in Britain.

The emergence of a movement for which *abortion* was a central concern suggests, however, that the politicization of abortion was assisted by a more specific dynamic than the general religiosity of the population. The peculiar aspect of American society at this time was, as Bruce has argued, the substantial "new market" created over the 1960s and 1970s for the claims of those emphasizing moral decline. It appeared to a significant number of Americans that the existing structures and centers of power were giving way—America was becoming "unglued"—as ideas and ways of life that were perceived as immoral were viewed as being in the ascendancy, particularly those associated with women's social role and the domestic division of labor (Simpson 1983). Such developments threatened the displacement of beliefs, symbols, and patterns of behavior that fundamentalist Protestants and many Catholics held dear. In response, taking a stand and doing something to combat the apparently pervasive moral decay made sense to many.

It was not only the fact that *Roe v. Wade* made abortion a protected right that mattered for these religious forces, however. According to Petchesky (1990), this was perceived as an exemplar of the broader problem, namely the perceived "de-moralization" of society through dramatic changes made to women's position in the family. It is important to note, however, that growing concern about these issues was not voiced primarily by men and in fact encompassed large numbers of women on the ground. Moralized opposition to abortion, as well as activism on other moralized issues connected to the family, has been described as the "other women's movement" (Somerville 2000). The rooting of such opposition in the perceived importance of family life, for women who formed and joined antiabortion organizations, is a central finding of Luker's study of abortion politics (1984). According to Somerville, "probably the most outstanding feature of this movement [against abortion and the ERA] was that its rank and file members were overwhelmingly women" (2000:111).

A religiously oriented, grass-roots movement therefore existed in the United States that sought to defend the family and strongly opposed abortion. Through the 1970s and into the 1980s, its political influence grew and was encouraged to do so, and this was reflected in the position on abortion taken by the Republican Party's program, a process recounted in detail elsewhere (Bruce 1988; Liebman and Wuthnow 1983). A position, first adopted by the Republican Party in 1976, argued for "a more hospitable environment for family life" and advocated "a position on abortion that values human life." In 1980 this party's platform affirmed Republican "support for a constitutional amendment to restore protection of the right to life for unborn children" and stated in 1984 and 1998 that "The unborn child has a fundamental individual right to life which cannot be infringed. We therefore reaffirm our support for a human life amendment" (Hall 1992). In clear contrast to British politics, abortion emerged as an overtly moralized political issue.

It has been argued that the political influence of abortion opponents was not simply a result of the sizable number of votes that antiabortion politicians could be expected to gain, however, but that it was also the result of another factor—the structure of political life in the United States. First, the highly centralized political system in Britain has tended to restrict debate to the arena of Parliament (the only place where laws are made) and thus reduce the extent of debate and opportunities for challenging laws. The decentralization of U.S. political life, by contrast, gives greater scope for debate, through state-based legislatures, for example.

Second, the strongly organized system of national political parties in Britain tends against individual MPs becoming subject to pressure from moralistic campaigners. In contrast, "The lack of party discipline in American politics is a major incentive for pressure groups and social movements to become electorally active," whereas in Britain "there is little point in trying to replace a pro-abortion candidate of any party with an anti-abortion candidate" (Davies 1992:74). If this did happen, the national party would step in and replace the candidate, or exert pressure on them to drop the nonparty line. This has made

American politicians vulnerable to pressure from lobbying in a way that British MPs are not and has made members of state legislatures that have responsibility for "moral" legislation potentially subject to such pressure.

Third, MPs in Britain have found that electors vote for the party and its program, rather than on single issues, a fact made clear when attempts have been made by abortion opponents to mobilize against individual MPs (to little effect) and by the very poor results obtained when "single issue" candidates stand in elections. In the United States, however, politicians are far more susceptible to localized pressures, in a society where there is less affiliation with national parties and more localized and sectional interests dominate (Davies 1992).

LEGAL DEBATES

Highly organized campaigning on the part of abortion opponents has, therefore, been an influential facet of political life in the United States in a way that is not the case in Britain. MPs have been subject to lobbying at the time of votes on parliamentary bills, and some attempts have been made in general elections to publicize the stance of candidates on abortion, but neither strategy has been greatly significant. In the United States, by contrast, individual politicians have made opposition to abortion a hallmark of their views and have been highly active on the issue. But what has been the outcome of the politicization of abortion in the United States? More specifically, how have abortion opponents fared in their encouragement of challenges to *Roe v. Wade*? The account below discusses these questions through consideration of some legal debates from 1973 up to the mid-1990s.

WHAT HAPPENED TO THE "RIGHT TO LIFE"?

Following *Roe v. Wade,* the first aim of abortion opponents was an all or nothing solution to reverse this ruling (Tribe 1990:144). The success of abortion opponents in gaining political support for this aim is demonstrated by the adoption, in 1976, of an antiabortion position in the platform of the Republican Party. Rhetorical commitment to overturning *Roe v. Wade* continued into the 1980s, and under Ronald Reagan this project gained the backing of the White House. Reagan stated, "I strongly believe that the rights of the unborn child must be protected in a civilized and humane society. Therefore as President, I will ask Congress to pass a constitutional amendment to protect the rights of all innocent human life" (Francome 1984:199). Two days after he was inaugurated as president, Reagan met with Dr. Willke, then president of the

NRLC and other antiabortion leaders in the Oval Office, making clear the political influence of the "Moral Right" (Tribe 1990).

Such political support for the "right to life," however, never came close to being translated into a serious threat to the 1973 rulings (and this is still the case). Antiabortion politicians proposed that the Constitution be amended to protect fetal life. Proposals used a variety of terms to define the point at which the unborn should become a bearer of rights—some deemed the fetus a person at the moment of fertilization, at conception and at other points in biological development, and exceptions were proposed in cases, for example, where the woman has been raped (Wilcox et al. 1998)—but none got far. In fact it rapidly became apparent that amending the Constitution to protect fetal life was not a strategy that would succeed. This was highlighted in the 1970s, in response to motions proposed by antiabortion Senators Helms and Hatch.

Senator Jesse Helms first proposed a "right to life" motion, which defined the rights of a person as protected from the moment of conception, but in 1976 the Senate voted by forty-seven votes to forty to kill the motion (Francome 1984:189). Other politicians opposed to abortion recognized early on that this would be the likely outcome. On the basis that the Helms motion was unlikely to gain sufficient support in the Senate to move forward (an assessment shared by many conservatives), Senator Orrin Hatch put forward a different, more pragmatic measure. This proposal would not have amended the Constitution so as to deem the fetus a bearer of rights, but would have returned deciding power about abortion law to individual states. After amendment, it read simply: "A right to abortion is not secured by this Constitution." In this motion, therefore, the moralized case against abortion was less overt. Its supporters hoped that this formulation of why *Roe* should be overturned would appear more moderate and that it would appeal to anti-big government sentiment as well as to opposition to abortion.

This amendment got farther than Helms's proposal, but it also failed to get sufficient votes to progress, receiving fifty votes when sixty-seven were needed. Perhaps it is for this reason that since 1983, when the Hatch proposal was eventually voted on, no serious attempt to amend the Constitution has been made. After this point, "Even the most ardent pro-life members of Congress," argue Wilcox et al., "ceased anything more than token efforts at securing passage of legislation that would tip the policy balance in a significant fashion" (1998:7). The retreat from attempting to secure constitutional protection for the "right to life" in part reflected the procedural difficulties of doing so (passage of a constitutional amendment requires support from two-thirds of each chamber of the Congress, and then the amendment has to be passed by the states through ratification by three-quarters of the fifty states, a very complex and lengthy procedure). However, it also reflected the fact that there is a great deal of difference between politicians offering rhetorical support for antiabortion views and securing support for practical measures to outlaw abortion.

Wilcox et al. (1998) argue that from this point, up to a Supreme Court ruling of 1989 (discussed below), "it appeared as though a truce had been called within Congress" on the question of the "right to life" versus "the right to choose," and the 1973 ruling had been accepted. Even after the 1989 ruling, which was supportive of some restrictions on abortion, the question of a constitutional amendment has not been seriously revisited as a viable strategy. A measure was introduced in Congress in the early 1990s that would have declared a fetus to be a person, but this constituted little more than a token gesture. It was clear this measure was never going to be seriously considered. Similarly, in 1995 a Right to Life Act was introduced, which directed that "the right to life guaranteed by the Constitution is vested in each human being at fertilization." This proposal was not debated.

Abortion Funding

Proposals for "right to life" amendments to the Constitution, therefore, did not get far. However, other kinds of restrictive measures did go a long way (and have continued to), and it is notable that those that have been successful have avoided framing opposition to abortion in terms of the defense of the right to life. Rather, they successfully opposed abortion by using other frames of argument, resulting in other kinds of legislation.

In Congress, restricting access to abortion by curtailing funding has proved to be a successful antiabortion measure. Before 1976, one-third of abortions performed in the United States were funded by Medicaid. In that year Henry Hyde introduced the famous eponymous measure that sought to ban all such funding. The Hyde Amendment was passed in the House of Representatives in 1976. In 1977 it was reenacted, and it passed that year with no exceptions. At first the Senate rejected the measure, but it was then accepted when an amendment was added to allow for exceptions where the woman's life would be endangered. The Hyde amendment then passed in both houses as an amendment to an appropriations bill, which stated: "None of the funds contained in this Act shall be used to perform abortions except where the life of the mother would be endangered if the fetus were carried to term" (Hadley 1994:103). Women, therefore, were denied Medicaid funding for abortion except where a woman's life was in danger. In effect this meant that the law considered that women had the right to choose abortion, but that there was no obligation by the state to fund it.

This issue came to the attention of the Supreme Court in a 1980 case, *Harris v. McRae,* brought as a challenge to the ban on Medicaid funding. The Court upheld *Roe v. Wade* and strongly defended the idea of the right to abortion. It found, however, by a vote of five to four, that there was no obligation by the government or states to fund abortions (Kaplan and Tong 1994). The Court found that no state could use federal funds to pay for abortions other than to save a woman's life (although it argued that, if the state so wished, it could use nonfederal funds for abortion). Tribe (1990) has drawn attention to the significance of this ruling, in pointing out that during the years following *Roe,* states with antiabortion legislatures would enact restrictions that would ultimately be invalidated by the Supreme Court. The Court, up to 1989, stated time and time again the importance of the 1973 finding. The only "real exceptions to this rule," argues Tribe, were "decisions in which a majority of the Supreme Court upheld government restrictions to provide needy women with money or public services to cover the expense of childbirth but not to fund the less expensive choice of abortion" (1990:15). This was the area where the "greatest impact" was made following the defeat of the "right to life" amendment, as the question of public funding for abortion became the primary battleground. It was how abortion opponents made gains, since it was clear that direct restrictions on *Roe*—those that attempted to overturn the right to abortion—would be rejected.

The issue of funding has, following the approach taken by the Hyde Amendment, formed a constant focus for debate since the mid-1970s. Other kinds of funding bans followed, including the Treasury-Postal Services Bill, which prohibited coverage for abortion services in the Federal Employees Benefits Program, and a similar approach was taken in prohibiting coverage for abortion in insurance programs for Department of Defense employees. Some such Hyde-type amendments include exceptions (for example, where the pregnancy results from rape or incest), but others do not. The "Mexico City" policy introduced by the Reagan administration, effective since 1985, prevents funding through U.S. family planning aid to programs in other countries, even where abortion provision through those programs is funded by non-U.S. money. It is also notable that the same administration drew up new regulations for the Title X family planning program in 1987, under which any group providing abortion counseling or referral would be denied funding (a measure known as the "gag rule"). All organizations in receipt of Title X financing would be required to separate out programs funded federally and those that were not. This measure led to a great deal of legal debate and was opposed as unconstitutional in a number of states. Courts in Colorado and New York came to different views about it (the former declaring the regulation unconstitutional and the latter supporting it). The matter was finally decided through a Supreme court ruling, *Rust v. Sullivan,* in 1991, which found in favor of the proposal that abortion counseling could not be funded by the state.

It could (and has) been argued that in practical terms, the effect of Hyde-type measures is as problematic for women who seek abortions as measures that support the "right to life." What is the point of a guaranteed right that is made impossible to exercise? Those who support abortion should be very critical of the approach taken by the Supreme Court, some contend. The Court cannot be seen as "women centered" in its decision making when the legal doctrine of privacy protects the right to make a choice but provides for a right that cannot be exercized. Had the Medicaid rulings gone the other way, it would have laid the foundation for a "women-favored" abortion policy. As it was, states and the federal government were relieved of any pressure to provide abortion services (Stetson 1996; see also Himmelweit 1980 and Solinger 2002 for this kind of critique of the idea of choice), and, in practice, women are poorly served by American policy on abortion. The effects of the Hyde Amendment specifically on abortion funding have certainly been dramatic. Abortions financed by Medicaid had fallen by 99 percent by 1979 (although it is notable that this did not prevent an increase in the number of abortions performed, which rose through the 1970s and stabilized between 1980 and 1990; Wilcox et al. 1998).

However, in relation to the subject matter of this book, the difference between a Hyde-type measure and those that uphold the "right to life" is important, in that the success of the former and the failure of the latter draw attention to the problems abortion opponents have faced in gaining support for measures that restrict abortion on moralized grounds. Political support for the Hyde Amendment, and other such subsequent measures, can be understood as a way of dealing with the difficulties that the abortion issue poses for politicians; through voting for funding restrictions, politicians can be seen to dislike abortion without presenting themselves as opponents of the idea of choice as a matter of principle. It has been considered that this framing of restrictions on abortion has gained support through appealing to sentiment not (or not only) supportive of fetal rights. The Hyde Amendment was first proposed at a time when welfare spending was emerging as a high-profile political problem, and support for it was indicative of this development. It was not so much opposition to abortion on moral grounds, but support for cutting spending, that enabled the Hyde Amendment to succeed (Tribe 1990). It is arguable that this has continued to be the case subsequently. Restrictions on funding are clearly important, but their success suggests that it was already apparent by the 1970s that abortion opponents could not find a way to confront the argument for the legality of abortion by arguing for the "rights of the unborn."

State Legislation

Abortion opponents have also influenced legal debate at the state level. In 1990 alone, there were 465 abortion-related bills presented to state legislatures (Hadley 1994:104). Activity in this arena was encouraged first by the defeat of the Hatch Amendment in 1983, and this trajectory was further encouraged by Supreme Court rulings in 1989 and 1992. Before the late 1980s, as noted above, Supreme Court rulings had generally offered uncompromising support to the "right to choose." In 1976, the Court voted six to three in *Danforth v. Planned Parenthood* that a husband could not veto his wife's request for an abortion. In 1976 and 1979, it overthrew attempts to restrict the rights of under-eighteens to abortion. In 1979, the Court declared void a Pennsylvania law that required a physician to try to protect the life of a fetus if he thought it could survive. The only restrictive measure supported was, as discussed above, that states and federal government were not obliged to fund abortions.

In the 1980s, the situation appeared set to change since, under President Reagan, it was considered very likely there would be justices appointed to the Court known to have conservative views on abortion. Other than amending the Constitution, this was the strategy that abortion opponents hoped might succeed in overturning the *Roe* ruling. Having been politically significant in Reagan's victory, antiabortion forces hoped they were in a position to exert pressure on the presidency to change the makeup of the Court. And indeed, "President Reagan, who believed as they did, carried out the right to life plan to change the face of the federal judiciary" (Tribe 1990:17). He appointed those who were "prolife" to both the Federal bench and to the Supreme Court. If this had not been the case, according to Tribe, it may have been that the judgments in subsequent cases would have followed the earlier pattern. As it was, they constitute an interesting development in the regulation of abortion. Outright rejection of restrictions was abandoned, and the pattern of previous rulings was, therefore, interrupted. But the terms on which restrictions on the "right to choose" were set out were not, in fact, as restrictive as many had expected them to be, and their main effect was to further encourage activity at the state level.

The first ruling was in 1989, when the Supreme Court ruled on *Webster v. Reproductive Health Services,* a case that concerned a Missouri law that restricted abortion even where the woman would be funding it herself. It was considered likely by groups on both sides of the abortion debate that the *Webster* case might overrule *Roe* and jeopardize legal abortion. There was furious activity around this case; more than 300 organizations using 120 lawyers drafted 31 friends-of-the-court briefs for the prochoice side, and 46 briefs were submitted by organizations opposed to abortion. President Reagan's administration was directly involved, as his Justice Department offered a Solicitor General's brief calling for *Roe* to be overturned, an action that for the first time ever directly involved a president in a debate on a Supreme Court decision (Tribe 1990).

The fact that the justices could not agree on a single majority position has been noted (Studlar and Tatalovich 1996; Tribe 1990). Although the Court voted to uphold the regulations, it could not agree on a single opinion or piece of reasoning in the majority, resulting in a "badly splintered" Court (Tribe 1990:210). Four judges argued in favor of the Missouri law and four against, and those in favor made different arguments as to why the regulations could be upheld, including the argument that *Roe* should be overruled altogether. The vote that was decisive, however, was that of Justice O'Connor, which found that regulations that specified certain conditions must pertain if an abortion were to be lawful. All aspects of the Missouri law were therefore upheld. The Court found that public hospitals or other tax-supported facilities may not be used to perform abortions that are not necessary to save the woman's life; that public employees may not assist an abortion that is not necessary to save the woman's life; and that tests of fetal viability should be performed from twenty weeks' pregnancy (Kaplan and Tong 1994). The decision ended the idea that women enjoyed an absolute constitutional right to abortion and has generally been viewed as a serious setback for advocates of the right to choose. As Woliver argues, "The decision expanded the ability of the state and territorial governments to place obstacles in the way of women seeking abortion services" (1996:5). Tribe contends that "the constitutional tide turned in 1989 for state regulation of abortion. After years of striking down state restrictions on abortion, the Court finally upheld one" (1990:24).

This shift in approach was confirmed in decisions made in 1990, in *Hodgson v. Minnesota* and in *Ohio v. Akron Center for Reproductive Health,* both cases that concerned minors' access to abortion, and both of which found that parental consent was needed. The effect of these decisions was to encourage the antiabortion movement to adopt a more moderate, and rather contradictory, strategy: "In one breath they had to claim that they sought only moderate restrictions, while in the next breath they had to admit that they continued to believe that all abortion is murder" (Tribe 1990:178). The Court's approach, and that of abortion opponents, was pushed farther in the same direction in 1992 by *Casey v. Planned Parenthood of Pennsylvania.*

This case concerned a restrictive law dating from 1989, passed by the court in Pennsylvania in the wake of the *Webster* ruling, which required, among other things, spousal notification and a twenty-four-hour waiting period before an abortion could be legally performed. In its consideration of this law, the Supreme Court chose, to the surprise of some, to strongly restate the case that the right to choose abortion is protected by the Constitution. The Court upheld the idea of abortion as a right that cannot be limited by the Constitution (Stetson 1996) but also emphasized in particular that the ability to control fertility is central to women's ability to control their lives, thus drawing directly on the language used by supporters of women's equality. "The ability of women to participate equally in the economic and social life of the Nation has been facilitated by their ability to control their reproductive lives," stated the Court (Kissling and Shannon 1998:149). However, it also revised the clear ban on intrusion by the state into pregnancy decisions (in *Roe* such intrusions were outlawed altogether during the first trimester) and argued instead that the state could legitimately enact rules and regulations.

Some particular restrictions that were at issue are discussed in more detail in the following chapter. In brief the central argument made, which has had a great deal of significance in shaping the abortion debate since, was that while women have the *ultimate* right to make the decision on abortion, that does not provide "a right to be insulated from all others in doing so." The state can "show its concern for the life of the unborn" without placing an "undue burden" in the way of women. In particular, the argument was made that states can encourage counseling in abortion, and that the state "may enact rules and regulations designed to encourage [the woman] to know that there are philosophic and social arguments of great weight that can be brought to bear in favor of continuing a pregnancy" (Kissling and Shannon 1998:154). Thus states must not prohibit abortion, but they are free to establish policies that are considered to fit with the case made in *Casey:* that they do not constitute an "undue burden" on the woman's right to choose. This has made the issue of such regulations a major focus of activity and argument, subsequently leading to regulations that vary a great deal between different states.

The debate since *Roe v. Wade* as a whole does not, therefore, suggest clear gains for supporters of the right to life (although it is certainly far less than ideal from the perspective of supporters of legal abortion). In the legal arena, moralized opposition to abortion, which seeks to enact laws that defend the "right to life" of the fetus, has failed to make headway. The idea that the abortion debate is now about the right to life versus the right to choose, or indeed that it has for some time been about this clash of rights, has consequently been disputed by some. This representation of the abortion issue has been represented as a "phoney war" (Toner 2001), and it has been argued that the question for some time has been the extent and nature of restrictions, rather than the legality of abortion per se.

DEBATE IN THE LAST DECADE

The abortion debate in the United States, up to the mid-1990s, therefore, contrasts clearly with that in Britain. In Britain the issue became less and less debated, whereas the U.S. debate remained a constant feature of social life. The issue, of the law at least, came to be resolved in Britain but remained a focus for contest in the United States, and over the decade this pattern in these two countries has continued.

The abortion debate has become increasingly muted in Britain (Lee and Jackson 2002). The current new Labour administration has made it very clear it is hostile to parliamentary debate about the abortion issue, and in particular is entirely opposed to new Labour being associated with holding a position on the issue (to the disappointment of those who considered that this government would be supportive of the idea of women's choice in abortion). In

October 1996, in the period just before the general election when it was first elected, the Labour Party came under fire from the Roman Catholic Church, when the Church published its official briefing on how Catholics should vote (Combe 1996). The Scottish Catholic Cardinal, Cardinal Winning, made comments to the media on the issue and condemned "Christian politicians" in the Labour Party, and the future Prime Minister Tony Blair in particular, because they had "consistently avoided condemning abortion." In response, Blair reportedly "told friends" he was "personally opposed to abortion" but stated that he strongly disagreed with attempts by anyone to turn abortion into a political issue and that "I intend to do everything in my power to keep abortion out of party politics" (Wastell et al. 1996). According to media comment, then spokeswoman on women's issues for the Labour Party, Janet Anderson, indicated at this point there would be "virtual silence" from new Labour regarding the issue of women's need for abortion, when she refused to provide any comment about it (Bennett 1996).

In the United States, in contrast, there has continued to be a massive amount of legal and political activity at the state level in particular, provoking continued debate about the regulation of abortion. Discussing more recent U.S. debates about abortion laws, however, Wilcox et al. argue that the clear issue at stake in legal debates has not been the legality of abortion per se but "policies that would affect access to abortion or policies to encourage or discourage abortions" (1998:16). Since the mid-1990s, this has come to include more debate about funding for abortions; debate about mandatory delays between consultation with an abortion provider and provision of the procedure (usually twenty-four hours); the question of whether the right to protest outside clinics is protected through the right to free speech; and particularly the issue of minors' access to abortion.

In addition, there has been major debate about so-called partial birth abortion, relating to a particular technique used in the United States for abortions carried out at later gestation stages. It is notable that on this issue, however, the Supreme Court chose, in its 2000 ruling in *Stenberg v. Cahart,* to strike down a Nebraska ban on this abortion method, finding this ban to be an unconstitutional violation of *Roe v. Wade.* Subsequently, similar bans have been successfully challenged in many states (Center for Reproductive Law and Policy 2003). Measures that make parental notification a requirement for abortion for minors have, in contrast, gained support. Wilcox et al. (1998) argue that this may be because people who tolerate abortion in general have concerns about young women having access to it; opinion polls show majority support for parental notification among the general population.

It has been considered the case that with the election of George W. Bush in 2002, the situation will alter. The president is known for his antiabortion views, and thus more extensive restrictions of abortion will develop as a result, some suggest. This is an outcome made more likely by the fact that there is a

Republican majority in both houses of Congress. And, from the outset, Bush has made it clear he is a supporter of the "prolife" view. His rhetoric has made this very apparent. And he has ensured that antiabortion policies have been implemented in the international arena, for example, by the cutting of U.S. funding by his administration for overseas family planning programs.

This measure is noteworthy, however, in that it contrasts with measures that he has given his support to domestically. He has made "prolife" language very prominent in his speech; for example, in the period just before the thirtieth anniversary of *Roe v. Wade,* he declared that January 19 be designated National Sanctity of Life Day, to "reaffirm the value of human life and renew our dedication to ensuring that every American as access to life, liberty, and the pursuit of happiness," yet he has been relatively guarded in his policy and legal proposals. In promoting measures that would give fetuses "access to life," namely those that prevent women from having abortions, Bush has been careful so far. In his speech about January 19, for example, he focused his comments about legal measures on "passing laws requiring parental notification and waiting periods for minors" (that is, those that conform with the direction already established) but made no other reference to restrictive measures (National Right to Life Committee 2003).

There has been a lot of debate about what will happen when a new judge is appointed to the Supreme Court; it has been argued that the current administration will try its hardest to make sure a new judge is antiabortion and thus encourage the overturning of *Roe.* But given the difficulties this issue generated for the previous Republican president, the incumbent's father, and the political context since September 11, with the issues this raises, it is arguable that such dramatic measures will not materialize. It is also notable that all six Democrats who had announced by January 2003 their candidacy to run for president in 2004 publicly gave their support to a prochoice position on the thirtieth anniversary of *Roe.* Although this does indicate that abortion remains significant in American politics (although perhaps for reasons different from those of the past; it is arguable that abortion remains so rather by default, because it is now more difficult than ever for U.S. politicians to show voters how they differ from each other, thus making the abortion issue stand out), it does not indicate that profound alterations in the pattern of debate and its outcome so far are by any means predictable.

REFRAMING OPPOSITION TO ABORTION

The emergence in the 1980s of arguments that medicalize the abortion problem, through the claim that abortion damages women psychologically, can be situated as one response to the legal context described so far. How this claim has fared is the subject of the next chapter. But it should be noted that this is by no means the only example of the medicalization of the antiabortion argument. Other medicalized claims against abortion have also emerged.

The claim that women who have abortions are placed at increased risk of developing breast cancer has gained significant visibility in the United States (Simon 2002; *Newsweek* 2001). This claim has attracted media attention, particularly since it has become the subject of legal debate. In 2001, *USA Today* reported that at least eleven states were considering legislation that would require abortion providers to inform women requesting abortion that they would place themselves at increased risk of developing breast cancer (Kaiser Daily Reproductive Health Report 2001a). In March 2002, in California and North Dakota, claimants in separate cases brought against abortion providers argued they were not warned by the providers of the risk of breast cancer that abortion allegedly entails, and that they should have been warned about it. Both cases were dismissed by the judge, primarily on the basis of evidence from the National Cancer Institute, and the prolife groups involved were ordered to pay costs. (A case centering on this claim was brought in Australia prior to those cases brought in the United States, and this legal action was championed by antiabortion claimsmakers in the United States (Ertelt 2001c).)

This claim about the problem of abortion first emerged in the United States in the early 1990s. It was reported in 1993 that the argument that there was a link between abortion and breast cancer was a result of "anti-abortion activists seizing on science to further their political goals" and that an endocrinologist named Joel Brind was the key individual who had developed this argument and publicized it among organizations opposed to abortion (Goodstein 1993:A03). Brind has subsequently been very active in making claims about a link between abortion and breast cancer. His article was published in the *Journal of Epidemiology and Community Health* in 1996 and became the subject of much debate. He has also promoted the claim through his involvement with the Coalition on Abortion/Breast Cancer, an organization established to publicize this alleged health risk of abortion, and the Breast Cancer Prevention Institute, founded by Brind, which promotes the idea that breast cancer is best prevented by encouraging women to continue pregnancies rather than have abortions (Ertelt 2001b).

The claim that there is an abortion/breast cancer link has emerged in Britain too. Joel Brind's article in the *Journal of Epidemiology and Community Health* was debated in the British press, when abortion providers and scientists involved with British organizations that research and treat cancer disputed his arguments (Hall 1996; Dillner 1997). Brind's research findings were also evaluated by the Royal College of Obstetricians and Gynaecologists (RCOG) as part of the development of a guideline for abortion providers, published by the College in 2000. Brind's study was included for evaluation with others, and the RCOG found that on balance, studies were inconclusive and did not provide clear evidence that there is a link between abortion and breast cancer. Nonetheless, the idea that there is such a link became the subject of media debate; and the fact that the RCOG had included Brind's study in its evaluation was claimed by U.S. abortion opponents to provide justification for their support for the proposition that abortion and breast cancer are linked (Ertelt 2001a).

British antiabortion organizations have adopted Brind's claims. It was noted in 1994 that such arguments were being put forward by Life (Birth Control Trust 1994a). At the time of writing, visitors to Life's website can read the "latest research on breast cancer." A study is available which was commissioned by Life and launched publicly in Britain, with comments from Joel Brind. The new research, it is suggested, can assist women and those who aim to improve their health, by enabling them "to know all the facts" and "make an informed choice" if they are considering terminating a pregnancy. In a letter to *The Guardian* newspaper, Jack Scarisbrick, the chairman of Life, argued, with reference to this research, for the need for "major progress in prevention, diagnosis and treatment of what is now the commonest form of cancer" and stated that "horrifyingly large numbers of women could develop the disease . . . as a result of abortions that they have already had" and that "women have a right to be warned" about the damage abortion can allegedly do to them (2001a). In 2000 he argued that this alleged threat to women's health must be taken more seriously: "What this amounts to is hundreds of women are dying every year because of abortions. . . . Doctors are inflicting this on women" (Rice 2000).

The problems presented by moralized antiabortion claims can also explain why abortion opponents have prioritized other issues. Promoting opposition to cloning techniques in particular has become a central task of U.S. and British abortion opponents. In Britain, members of organizations opposed to abortion now describe themselves as "anticloning activists" and the "anticloning lobby," and campaigning on this issue has almost replaced that on abortion (Meek 2002). In their comments on this issue, moralized rhetoric has been very apparent. The Pro-Life Alliance, established initially to field candidates in elections to promote opposition to abortion, brought a British High Court case in 2002 that claimed, successfully, that the law the government was intending to use to ban human reproductive cloning (the Human Fertilisation and Embryology Act) would not in fact do so (the case was subsequently appealed, however, at which point the Pro-Life Alliance lost its case). Explaining its decision to bring the action, the Alliance explained that it opposes cloning because it involves "the deliberate creation and destruction of human life" (Rosenberg 2002). Jack Scarisbrick defended opposition to therapeutic as well as reproductive cloning, on the grounds of "commitment to the principle that the utmost respect is due to human life at all stages . . . this is the foundation stone of justice and hence civilization" (2001b). It may be that abortion opponents believe there will be resonance for moralized claims against cloning, where there is little for opposition to abortion framed in these terms.

For the reasons discussed above, in Britain, the problems of moralized argument against abortion have been more starkly posed than in the United States. Abortion has been framed explicitly in law as a medical question, has not become politicized, and enjoys a high degree of pragmatic acceptance. Overall medical authority, rather than moral imperative, has proved decisive in arguments over abortion. The abortion debate has been far more politicized and visible in the United States. It is marked out in this society by its relentless character. Yet the outcome of the debate about the law in this society indicates that moralized claims against abortion have not translated into the legal measures their proponents had hoped for here. Access to abortion has undoubtedly been compromised in many states in the United States. But ultimately American society has shown itself to be unsympathetic to claims that construe abortion as a procedure that should be deemed simply legally unacceptable on moralized grounds. Although the movement opposed to abortion has, therefore, been able to encourage the politicization of abortion in the United States, it has gained far less than it might have hoped to. In both Britain and the United States, although the legal framework has not ceded complete authority to women (in neither society do women have the "right to choose abortion" without legal constraint), it is also apparent that the claim that the fetus has a right to life has made very little headway.

In this context, the medicalized argument against abortion emerged. The potential advantage of the PAS claim is that abortion opponents could make gains by problematizing abortion in terms of a well-established cultural premise. The construction of abortion as an experience that is a health risk for women could appear to resonate with trends in contemporary society to present many aspects of human experience as medical problems. How far has this potential advantage been realized? In what ways has the PAS claim influenced debate and legal and policy developments about abortion?

4

Debating Postabortion Syndrome

Has the Postabortion Syndrome claim gained wider resonance? In what ways did the response differ in Britain and the United States? To discuss these issues, this chapter draws on media reports and public documents in which the PAS claim has appeared and been debated. I give an account of the key moments and aspects of the PAS debate, first in the United States, and then in Britain, and through this account assess the extent to which the PAS claim can be considered successful, in terms of the objectives of the anti-abortion movement. I also draw attention to the actors who have played a prominent and important role in the debate about PAS and highlight the counterclaims that they have made.

THE AMERICAN DEBATE

The PAS claim has been the subject of public debate since the late 1980s in the United States. Its public profile, as the previous chapter noted, was highest between 1987 and 1989, as a result of the inquiry into the health effects of abortion by then U.S. Surgeon General, C. Everett Koop. Since this point, the claim has reappeared continually as part of the U.S. abortion debate. What the discussion below indicates, however, is that although abortion opponents have continued to press their case and have consistently made their claim visible, they have, so far, been relatively unsuccessful in convincing others of its merit. The claim has been very visible at times, but in its effects, for abortion law and policy, it has not enabled abortion opponents to gain much ground. Overall, as the following discussion shows, the main problem that proponents of the claim have encountered is counterclaims that there is no scientific evidence to support PAS. In all instances from the late 1980s on, when the PAS claim has been made, others—often representatives of psychiatric, psychological, or medical organizations, and prochoice campaigners—have been able to strongly dispute the idea that abortion poses a significant risk to women's mental health.

THE KOOP INQUIRY

The Koop inquiry began as an investigation by the Surgeon General and his staff and took a year and a half to complete. This involved staff in several agencies of the Public Health Service evaluating 250 pieces of research, as well as meetings and discussion "with a variety of groups representing pro-life, pro-choice, and professional perspectives" (Wilmoth 1992:2).[1] A significant amount of time, energy, and resources was therefore spent by government officials investigating the issue of the health effects of abortion.

Given that Koop was known for his opposition to legal abortion (with Francis A. Schaeffer he coauthored *Whatever Happened to the Human Race?*, published in 1979, in which he argued that legal abortion has led to "the devaluation and destruction of innocent human lives on a massive scale"), many assumed that the inquiry results would emphasize the deleterious health consequences of the procedure. The terms of the abortion debate, in which the moral dimensions of abortion remained subject to continual contest, would then be resolved in favor of abortion opponents, by merit of official acceptance that abortion was a problem because of its effects upon women's health.

However, the inquiry was interesting because this was not its outcome. The issue of the physical health effects of abortion proved fairly uncontentious; evidence indicated that abortion is a relatively safe medical procedure in this respect. But the Koop inquiry did not find evidence to support the PAS claim either. It led instead to further struggle over abortion, and, as the account of this contest that follows makes clear, overall it was those who support legal abortion whose arguments in many instances were considered more credible. They made the case that there is a lack of scientific evidence to support the idea that abortion causes serious psychiatric problems, and these claims proved more influential in the subsequent debate. Their claims, that women are not frequently subject to negative feelings that are severe enough to constitute evidence that abortion makes women mentally ill, proved most convincing to others. It is noteworthy, therefore, that even though abortion opponents were relatively powerful politically at this point, this proved insufficient to allow them to win out, in the face of evidence against their arguments about the psychological effects of abortion. It is also notable that in the United States, those who disagreed with the PAS claim on the basis that it is not supported by scientific evidence played a very visible part in the debate.

Counterclaims

The Koop report was completed in January 1989, but it was not made public immediately. Instead Koop sent a letter to President Reagan, saying that there was insufficient evidence about the psychological effects of abortion to draw conclusions, and that research in this area was flawed. It may have been that the problem for Koop, and Reagan, was that since the inquiry had not found much clear evidence to support those who oppose abortion, it was considered to be a problem for its results to be made public. But, apparently against Koop's wishes, his letter to Reagan was then released to the press and public debate about the psychological effects of abortion ensued. There were different foci for these debates, beginning with what was in Koop's letter, but what is noticeable about each is that it was claims that questioned or disputed PAS which came to prominence.

The first debate was about Koop's letter. One issue that caught the interest of journalists was Koop's insistence that the 250 studies his staff reviewed "do not support the premise that abortion does or does not cause or contribute to psychological problems" (McCarthy 1989:F02). Koop's finding, it was reported, was that "the scientific studies do not provide conclusive data about the health effects of abortion on women" (Holden 1989:730). His assessment of the information given by those whom he spoke to for the inquiry was that "we have two groups of people saying very honestly and very sincerely different things" (Madigan 1989:1) and that "the available scientific evidence . . . simply cannot support either the preconceived beliefs of those pro-life or those pro-choice" (Holden 1989:730). It seems that, regardless of his own views on abortion, Koop had decided he did not want to be associated with conclusions that would aid either side in the abortion debate. Koop later stated, explaining his decision to conduct the inquiry as he did and not make its findings public, that "My position [on abortion] is well known to everybody in this country. I'm opposed to it. But I also took an oath to uphold the law of the land. That's why I walk a tightrope and why I prepared the report as I did" (Okie 1989:A03). According to the *Washington Post,* Koop later argued: "I didn't release the report because I didn't think it was proper to release a report that had no substance to it. . . . It would have raised expectations of some and aroused ire of others. It could have been torn apart scientifically and statistically by anyone with a proper background" (Specter 1989:A01).

However, in a context where, given the administration's antiabortion political stance, it had been expected that the Koop inquiry would lead to gains for opponents of abortion, some viewed this outcome as a clear setback for them. Koop's decision not to make his inquiry's findings public, and his emphasis in his letter on the lack of conclusive evidence about the psychological effects of abortion, were taken to be an outcome more favorable to supporters of legal abortion. "Those who favor abortion will jump up and down with joy and really beat the drums," said John Wilke of the National Right to Life Committee. The National Organization for Women and the Planned Parenthood Federation of America reportedly "hailed the surgeon general's objectivity," and Patricia Ireland, of the National Organization for Women, said that she was pleased that Koop's "professional judgement was not clouded by partisan politics" (Tinsley 1989:A5-2). It was also the case that the views of those who opposed the PAS claim, on the grounds that there was no evidence to support it, were given prominence in reporting on the issue at this time. Brian Wilcox of the American Psychological Association, who contributed a literature review to the Koop study, was quoted in the prestigious journal *Science* in February 1989. He argued: "[A]lthough we searched and searched and searched, there was no evidence at all for the existence of the 'postabortion syndrome' claimed by some right-to-life groups" (Holden 1989:730). In line with Wilcox's argument against PAS, the article was subtitled "Right-to-lifers fail to get hoped-for evidence to reverse Roe v. Wade when the Supreme Court reconsiders the issue this spring" (referring to the upcoming *Webster* case, discussed in the previous chapter). Other reports covered comments from APA spokespeople in a similar manner. The *Chicago Tribune* titled an article on the Koop inquiry "Study shoots down 'abortion syndrome,'" on the basis of a comment from an APA spokesman that, after having reviewed more than 100 studies of women who had had abortions for the APA's contribution to the inquiry, it was found that "'there is no evidence' for PAS" (Kotulak and Van 1989:7).

The debate did not stop there. Once the content of his letter had become public, it was only a matter of time before Koop's whole report was too. His report was finally released at a hearing of the Human Resources and Intergovernmental Relations Subcommittee, a subcommittee of the Committee on Government Operations of the House of Representatives, held on March 16, 1989.[2] This hearing was not originally planned as part of the Koop inquiry but was perhaps motivated by frustration at the lack of clarity in the debate about the psychological effects of abortion. In his introduction to the hearing, the chairman, Ted Weiss, noted that advocates on all sides of the issue were "disappointed" by Koop's decision not to release his report and that "Some experts believe that the medical evidence is, in fact, very clear" (House Committee on Government Operations 1989:2). The hearing itself did not draw any conclusions or make suggestions with regard to abortion law or policy. However, it did generate comment in the media about PAS.

According to some media accounts about the hearing, and the full content of the Koop report, the report had failed to draw a definite conclusion about the psychological effects of abortion. The *Washington Post* stated that the report found that "specialists agree that some women suffer severe, sometimes delayed, emotional reaction to an abortion, but they disagree about how often this occurs" and concluded that "most of the approximately 250 studies on the subject are flawed" and called for further research (Okie 1989:A03). Other commentaries also reiterated Koop's finding that studies about the psychological effects of abortion were flawed but also made it clear that Koop had

viewed his inquiry's findings as counter to what abortion opponents had expected them to be. It was reported that he told the hearing, with reference to
evidence submitted to the inquiry from this quarter, that although there was
"no doubt about the fact that some people have severe psychological effects after abortion . . . anecdotes do not make good scientific material" (Leary 1989).
In some reporting, the views of opponents of the PAS claim who gave evidence
to the Koop inquiry again achieved prominence. For example, Nancy Adler
from the APA was quoted in *Time* magazine as claiming that "abortion inflicts
no particular psychological damage on women," in an article titled "A Setback
for Pro-Life Forces." Adler, the article stated, "pointed out that despite the
millions of women who have undergone the procedure since the landmark ruling *Roe v. Wade* . . . there has been no accompanying rise in mental illness"
(Thompson 1989:A5-2).

In the months following the hearing, debate about PAS continued in a similar vein. In December 1989, a statement included as part of a report about the
work of the House committee chaired by Weiss was reported in the media. It
was said to be highly critical of the way the Reagan government "chose not to
report to the public clear evidence of the relative safety of abortion" and included material from meetings between Koop and those who provided him
with evidence for this inquiry, at which he "stated in those meetings that legal abortion was safer than pregnancy and childbirth and posed no public
health risks to women's mental or physical health." Koop, it was reported, had
"expressed concerns to antiabortion advocates" about the poor quality of the
research evidence they had offered, in the hope that the final report would
"support their battle to restrict abortions" (Associated Press 1989:1). The
Washington Post described the committee's report as a "harsh report . . . [which]
criticized the former surgeon general . . . for withholding last January a long-
awaited study on the medical and psychological impact of abortion even
though he reached many conclusions that could have been published" (Specter
1989:A01).

On balance it seems that this whole episode in the debate about the relationship between abortion and mental illness was, therefore, a boon to abortion rights supporters and a setback for proponents of PAS. Writing about the
Koop enquiry in 1995, David Reardon, proponent of the link between abortion and mental ill health, commented scathingly that Koop "ducked the as-
signment" and that the "pro-abortion media twisted Koop's non-report into a
claim that no dangers to abortion could be found." Reardon makes it clear that
the Koop inquiry was a disappointment for those who believe abortion to be
a cause of mental ill health. He claims that, in the aftermath of the Koop inquiry, "distortions" of the evidence about the psychological effects of abortion
continue, since in "medical journals . . . pro-abortion researchers frequently
cite the Surgeon General's letter as an 'authoritative review.' . . . Dr. Koop con-

tinues to be haunted by the whole affair, facing the sporadic denouncements of conservatives who believe he 'betrayed' the cause" (Reardon 1995:7).

Counterclaims Continued

The overall effect of the Koop inquiry, ironically, appeared therefore to favor those who support abortion more than it did its opponents. In the years immediately following it, it is notable that those who had made claims disputing PAS appeared able to capitalize on this advantage. Reporting continued to draw attention to their evidence. But it did so because opinion formers who were important in the debate about the Koop inquiry generated still more evidence that abortion does not cause mental illness, and thus they were able to maintain the issue's visibility, but this time on their terms.

In 1990, there was a significant amount of debate of this kind. In April of that year, for example, following a study carried out by the American Psychological Association, it was reported the APA had found that "severe negative reactions after abortions are rare and can best be understood in the framework of coping with a normal life stress" (Brotman 1990:4). Counterclaims from PAS critics also appeared in important publications. An article, often quoted subsequently, by psychologists associated with the American Psychological Association and other scientific organizations, appeared in the journal *Science,* also in 1990. It stated: "A review of methodologically sound studies of the psychological responses of U.S. women after they obtained legal, nonrestrictive abortions indicates that distress is generally greatest before abortion and that the incidence of severe negative responses is low." The article also noted that C. Everett Koop did in fact testify at the congressional hearing that the chance of the development of significant psychological problems after abortion was "miniscule from a public health perspective" (Adler et al. 1990:41). In May 1990, comments made by "a panel of leading psychiatrists" at the American Psychiatric Association's annual meeting also made the news. The panel argued that "government restrictions on abortion are far more likely to cause women lasting harm than the procedure itself would," and that Association officials "absolutely reject the definition [PAS], on the basis there is no evidence at all to support it" (Specter 1990:A03).

The American Medical Association (AMA) did not give evidence to the Koop inquiry, but published an article on the subject in its journal in 1992. This article, by Nada Stotland of the American Psychiatric Association, is titled "The Myth of the Abortion Trauma Syndrome" and has been a reference point in subsequent reporting on PAS (Vogt 1992; Boodman 1992). It begins: "This is an article about a medical syndrome that does not exist" and suggests that the only evidence in support of the claim that there is such a syndrome is to be found in a "small number of papers and books based on anecdotal evidence and stressing negative effects . . . presented and published under religious auspices and in the nonspeciality literature." Stotland (1992) claimed that, although women may experience abortion as a loss and thus feel sad afterward, a feeling is "not equivalent to a disease," and that negative feelings should always be distinguished from psychiatric illness. The journal carried a further article in 1992 submitted by the AMA's Council on Scientific Affairs that reported:

> Until the 1960s, many assumed that serious emotional problems following induced abortion were common. In 1989, after reviewing more than 250 studies of the emotional aftermath of abortion, Surgeon General C. Everett Koop concluded that the data were "insufficient . . . to support the premise that abortion does or does not produce a post-abortion syndrome." He noted, however, that emotional problems resulting from abortion are "miniscule from a public health perspective." (Council on Scientific Affairs, American Medical Association 1992)

The Koop inquiry did not, then, lead to an outcome that provided the basis for abortion opponents to decisively move forward their campaign against legal abortion, on the grounds that abortion damages women's health. Perhaps the most important factor in ensuring the failure of the claim to bring about this degree of success for PAS claimsmakers was the opposition to the claim put forward, most notably by the American Psychological Association, but also by representatives of other important scientific organizations. Following this intense debate about PAS, the claim reappeared in the United States throughout the 1990s. After the Koop inquiry, although the political debate at the federal level about the health consequences of abortion appeared to have ended, the public and political debate continued at the state level.

BACK TO THE STATES

As the previous chapter discussed, throughout the 1980s, legal cases centering on modifications or restrictions in the way in which the *Roe v. Wade* ruling had framed the abortion decision, brought in particular states, were heard by the Supreme Court. It has been argued that these cases were the result of the fact that lobbying for the passing of abortion legislation at a state level became a relatively more important part of the strategy of the American antiabortion movement at this time. Abortion rights advocates Kissling and Shannon contend that this approach was clearly apparent from 1983, since from this point the antiabortion movement prioritized "testing the limits and narrowing the scope of *Roe*, principally through restrictive measures passed by state legislatures" (1998:147). The Court generally rejected restrictive modifications during this time, however, and it was not until 1989, in *Webster*, that it seemed that the Court had moved to become more accepting of the idea that individual states could modify the *Roe* holding.

In relation to state-level regulations about abortion provision, the issue of the health effects of abortion featured as part of this debate. In this respect, the debate focused on what information women need to be given if they are to be considered "informed" when they give their consent for an abortion to be performed. Up until the early 1990s, the Court found that many proposed requirements about "informed consent" were against the spirit of *Roe*. In *City of Akron v. Akron Center for Reproductive Health* (1983), for example, the Court struck down a municipal ordinance that set precise standards for physicians about information women need to be provided with (for example, about fetal development, the negative physical and emotional effects of abortion, and agencies that assist with childbirth and care of children). The Court found that the ordinance's informed consent language was not intended to inform a woman about her choice, but rather had the purpose of dissuading her from proceeding with an abortion (Eller 1996:100). In 1989, in *Thornburgh v. American College of Physicians,* the Court struck down a Pennsylvania statute that required physicians to inform women of "detrimental physical and psychological effects" of abortion. The Court found that the statute would be likely to "increase the patient's anxiety, and intrude upon the physician's exercise of proper professional judgement." The opinion authored by Justice Blackmun condemned the proposed statute in no uncertain terms, finding that the sections compelling abortion providers to give women materials produced by the state, which described the fetus and discussed alternatives to abortion, to be "an outright attempt to wedge the Commonwealth's message discouraging abortion into the privacy of the informed consent dialogue between the woman and physician" and "may serve only to confuse and punish her and to heighten her anxiety" (Eller 1996:658).

There was a shift in approach from this point on, however. Legislation passed in Missouri and Pennsylvania stated, among other requirements, that women seeking abortion should be informed of the medical and psychological risks of abortion in order for it to be legally considered the case that they had given their consent for the procedure to take place (Wilmoth 1992:3–4). The Pennsylvania regulations were the subject of the 1992 Supreme Court ruling *Planned Parenthood of Southeastern Pennsylvania v. Casey,* which, as Chapter 3 noted, found that state laws could burden, but not "unduly burden," a woman's abortion decision. In addition to the provisions discussed previously, the Court also decided to uphold the provision in the Pennsylvania law that required a twenty-four-hour waiting period, and the provision of certain information to a woman considering abortion. It was stated that the attending doctor must "orally describe the commonly employed abortion procedures, the medical risks associated with each, and the possible detrimental psychological effects of abortion" (Center for Reproductive Law and Policy 1999a). The statute also required that the physician inform the woman of the "probable gestational age of the unborn child"; inform her of the availability of material published by the state, which described the fetus; provide information concerning medical assistance for childbirth; and provide listed resources that would be available if the woman chose to give birth to the child. The Court stated:

> In attempting to ensure that a woman apprehend the full consequences of her decision, the State furthers the legitimate purpose of reducing the risk that a woman may elect an abortion, only to discover later, with devastating psychological consequences, that her decision was not fully informed. If the information the State requires to be made available to the woman is truthful and not misleading, the requirement may be permissible. (Eller 1996:662)

It was argued that, although a woman's right to make the abortion decision is paramount, this is not "a right to be insulated from all others in doing so." The only Pennsylvania provision the Court rejected was the requirement that married women inform their husbands when they intend to seek an abortion (Blanchard 1994:36). The Court found, however, that the physician did not have to comply with the informed consent provisions "if he or she can demonstrate by a preponderance of the evidence that he or she reasonably believed that furnishing the information would have resulted in a severely adverse effect on the physical or mental health of the patient" (Eller 1996:663).

These legal developments do indicate that the question of the health effects of abortion had come to be considered important in the regulation of abortion by the early 1990s. A woman's right to choose an abortion had come to be considered one that did not pertain in isolation from the question of what kind of information states should provide about its health effects. This may indicate that claims that medicalize abortion had had an effect for the law by this time, but I now argue that this effect has not been to clearly endorse the PAS claim. I suggest that developments in the law suggest that overall, while choosing an abortion has come to be considered an act that a woman should perform in awareness of its risks, those who have aimed to make abortion providers emphasize to women that the risks are great have not managed to make the law reflect their aims. While abortion opponents have, in some states, managed to encourage the development of a legal framework that is more restrictive than that implied by *Roe,* at the same time, they have not managed to generate laws that clearly reflect the PAS claim.

Informed Consent Regulations

Since 1992, there has been a huge amount of legal activity and debate regarding the amount and nature of the information women need to be provided with, if "informed consent" is to be achieved, and the extent to which physicians have to comply with state mandates that they provide information. By 1997, according to legal scholar Kathy Seward Northern (1998), twenty-seven states had passed laws that make performing an abortion conditional upon obtaining the woman's informed consent. Such statutes are specific to abortion; they operate in addition to provisions for informed consent that apply to all medical procedures.

In their specifics, such statutes sometimes comprise very brief specifications about what a woman must be told before she can be considered to have consented to the performance of an abortion. For example, the law in Connecticut stated (in 1999) that prior to an abortion, a woman must receive information including an oral explanation of the procedure and a description of the discomforts and risks from a "qualified counselor." The woman must sign a consent form that describes the "nature and consequences of the procedure which shall be used" (NARAL 1999:32). But others, sometimes termed "Women's Right to Know" statutes and usually promoted by opponents of abortion, are far more detailed and restrictive.[3] Where laws of this kind have been passed, they have been continually subject to debate, with opinion divided between those who are prochoice and oppose them, and those who are opposed to abortion and support such laws. Prochoice advocates have often challenged laws of this kind in the courts. They have argued in particular that they compel physicians to provide inaccurate information. In opposition to Michigan's informed consent rules, for example, Julie Kay, an attorney for the Center for Reproductive Law and Policy (CRLP), argued the law was unconstitutional because "it forces physicians to provide medically inaccurate, misleading and harmful information to women seeking abortions or face criminal penalties." Kay claimed that medical experts have testified that the information in the materials that the law specifies must be given to women is inaccurate, "including exaggerated descriptions of fetal development and portrayal of women's emotional reactions to abortion as primarily negative, even though only a minority has such feelings. . . . Ambiguous provisions about how to secure informed consent create a trap for providers because even those who make good faith efforts to meet the law's requirements will be at risk of violating the law" (Center for Reproductive Law and Policy 1999b).

Decisions about what "informed consent" is deemed to entail, and what kind of laws a state should pass, thus appear to be related to the extent to which claimsmakers involved in the abortion debate have influenced the process of making the law.[4] As Northern argues, while purporting to protect informed choice, some statutes are rather intended to dissuade a woman from going through with an abortion, reflecting the opinions of abortion opponents. She suggests that "a number of these statutes appear to have been enacted to protect the unborn child from what the legislature perceives as the ill-considered action of the mother and the coercive conduct of the abortion provider"

(1998:541). Russo and Denious (1998), who support legal abortion, have also suggested that opposition to abortion underpins many such laws. They argue that their aim is to place special burdens on physicians who perform abortions, by creating a framework that goes beyond the usual liability for medical malpractice and places particular financial and other detrimental legal penalties on such physicians. Abortion opponents have made it clear that their strategy does indeed include lobbying for particular kinds of informed consent laws. David Reardon argues: "In *Planned Parenthood v. Casey*, the Supreme Court approved state-mandated informed consent requirements for abortion which are intended to protect the rights of the women as patients. Following this lead, pro-life organizations in several states have successfully lobbied for regulations. . . . This is a positive development and should continue" (1996a:67). But to what extent do these laws suggest that those who have medicalized the abortion problem have achieved their goals? In particular, to what extent has the PAS claim gained ground through them?

The first point to make is that, overall, there are significant differences between states, and in some states abortion opponents feel their cause has moved forward through "informed consent" rules. In Virginia in February 2001 an "informed consent bill" was passed, for example. The CRLP criticized the bill for placing "another burden on poor and rural women" who would have to travel to neighboring states with less restrictive laws when seeking abortion. Antiabortion politicians were reportedly very pleased, however, since according to the *Richmond Times-Dispatch* they had tried for twenty-two years to get such legislation passed (Kaiser Daily Reproductive Health Report 2001b). But even where these laws are passed the result in practice may not, according to some, turn out to be what abortion opponents hope for. In Arkansas, a "Woman's Right to Know" Act was signed into law in February 2001. An antiabortion advocate from Arkansas Right to Life claimed that, as a result of the law, "It will no longer be business as usual. . . . This law will undoubtedly save some women and children from suffering the tragedy of legal abortion." The terms of the law were, however, modified from those that had originally been proposed (for example, criminal penalties for physicians found to have violated its requirements were removed). As a result, a Planned Parenthood of Arkansas representative argued in the *Arkansas Democrat-Gazette* that the new law had been made "absolutely ineffective" and would not alter "past practice" of doctors, which was to provide women with information they need (Kaiser Daily Reproductive Health Report 2001c). Abortion opponents were less successful still in Colorado in 2000. The *Denver Post* reported that a "Woman's Right to Know" bill, which had "fired up the emotional debate" about abortion, had failed, since 60 percent of Coloradans had voted against the measure in a ballot. Opponents of the bill had described it as an "invasion of privacy" (Kaiser Daily Reproductive Health Report 2000c). In Indiana, according to the *Chicago Tribune*, in March 2000 a judge in the district court struck down part of the state's law that required "face-to-face counseling" eighteen hours before an abortion. The judge's decision was claimed as "a victory for the women of Indiana" by the Center for Reproductive Law and Policy (Kaiser Daily Reproductive Health Report 2000a).

Evidence suggests, therefore, that abortion opponents have managed to lobby successfully for some restrictive rules in some states. But in others they have been defeated or have generated regulations whose bark is worse than their bite. What do we find when the particular aspects of these laws that make provisions for information about the mental health effects of abortion are considered? With regard to the claim that women need to be warned about the mental health of abortion before they can be considered to have given "informed consent," have abortion opponents managed to generate the kinds of regulations they want?

It seems that without exception, proposals of this kind have generated heated debate. A bill proposed in 1993 in Montana, by the Republican Senator Ethel Harding, an opponent of abortion, led to such a contest. The Montana *Billings Gazette* reported that Right to Life executive director Arlette Randash had argued in support of the bill, claiming that it would "protect Montana women from making an uninformed decision concerning an elective abortion, and many later deeply regretted their decision." Others arguing in support of the law were counselors offering a "Christian-based practice that deals with post-abortion problems and other disorders," who argued that "many women . . . suffer from a 'post-abortion syndrome' that can include profound depression." Arguing against the law, psychologist Anne Pincus said that "there is no such . . . syndrome" and that "several studies . . . showed increased self-esteem and reduced stress among women who have chosen an . . . abortion" (Kaiser Daily Report 1993c). The theme of whether there is evidence to support the claim that abortion leads to mental ill health, dominant in the debate about the Koop inquiry, thus also featured prominently in this example.

The outcome of this debate appears to be, as for the Koop inquiry, almost without exception in favor of those who oppose the PAS claim. In instances where it has been challenged in the courts, the inclusion of the particular provision that women should be informed of their possible risk of suffering from severe psychological problems after abortion has been defeated. Indeed, it should be noted that this outcome has been implied from the start. In 1992, although *Casey* did enable states to introduce informed consent rules, it firmly ruled out the evidence that there is a Postabortion Syndrome. Vincent Rue had testified at the trial for the defendant, in support of the Pennsylvania laws that had come to the attention of the Supreme Court. Rue's testimony that women suffered from PAS following abortion was found to be "devoid of . . . analytical force and scientific rigor." The judge argued that "his admitted personal opposition to abortion, even in cases of rape and incest, suggests a possible personal bias." Together with Rue's lack of "academic qualifications and scientific credentials possessed by plaintiffs' witnesses," this led the judge to find that his evidence was "not credible" (744 F.Supp. 1232 (E.D.Pa. 1990):1234). A similar outcome has resulted in subsequent instances, for example, when Elizabeth Karlin, of Planned Parenthood of Wisconsin, together with representatives of Summit Women's Health Organization, brought an action in 1997 against C. William Foust and others, to challenge a restrictive state law.

Foust was defendant in his official capacity as district attorney for Dane County. Karlin's case challenged the Wisconsin law regulating the process by which physicians obtain voluntary and informed consent of patients seeking abortion. According to one part of this law, enacted on May 6, 1996, women could only be deemed to have given informed consent for an abortion after being told of the medical risks associated with the particular abortion procedure that would be used. Under the law, the "risks" women were to be informed of included infection, psychological trauma, hemorrhage, endometritis, perforated uterus, incomplete abortion, failed abortion, danger to subsequent pregnancies, and infertility. The woman also had to be physically given printed materials, developed by the state Department of Health and Social Services, which included information about the medical and psychological risks associated with each common abortion procedure. Violation of the law incurred the payment of "damages arising out of the abortion, including damages for personal injury and emotional and psychological distress and punitive damages of not less than $1000 or more than $10,000." As the opinion by District Judge Barbara B. Crabb noted, the question at stake in the case was "whether the new law will make it so difficult for women in Wisconsin to exercise their constitutionally protected rights to obtain abortions as to constitute an 'undue burden' as articulated in *Planned Parenthood v. Casey.*"

Expert witnesses were called to give testimony in the case. On the question of psychological risks of abortion, Nada Stotland testified. Stotland, an authoritative figure in the American Psychiatric Association, testified as chief of psychiatry at the Illinois Masonic Medical Center in Chicago on behalf of the plaintiffs. She argued that there are no medically accepted risks of psychological trauma or injury associated with abortion, because there is no way to separate the circumstances surrounding a stressful pregnancy from the abortion procedure itself. Her evidence was accepted. Anne Speckhard also testified, in support of the new law, and argued that abortion itself leads to PTSD in some women. According to Speckhard, the "death event" involved in abortion is a potential "traumatic stressor" because it severs the psychological and physical "maternal-infant attachment bond" developed during pregnancy. As a result, a woman may suffer symptoms of PTSD following abortion. Speckhard testified that at least 20 percent of women who have had abortion suffer from this, and 40 to 45 percent experience some posttraumatic sequelae, such as guilt, grief, and shame. The judge found Speckhard's opinion that 20 percent of women who have abortions suffer from posttraumatic stress disorder to be "ludicrous." "If she were correct, approximately 4,000,000 women . . . would be suffering from the disorder. This would be a psychiatric epidemic of epic proportions that could hardly escape the notice of the nation's physicians." The judge therefore decided to disregard all of her testimony.

The evidence given by Stotland proved important in the final outcome of the case. Judge Crabb found "that psychological problems caused by abortion are not a major health problem," and, as a result of research carried out since 1989, the "better evidence tends to show that abortion does not lead to posttraumatic stress disorder in and of itself." The judge reached the conclusion that although he could not "say on the basis of the present record that there could never be a psychological injury from the fact of abortion," this does not mean that doctors have to warn women about postabortion trauma. In relation to the law in Wisconsin, the judge pointed out that although doctors are required to inform patients about the risk of psychological trauma, if they reasonably believe that no such risk exists and "discuss the risks on the basis of their medical training and experience, they have no legitimate fear of prosecution." This means that if the physician believes that no psychological trauma is associated with the abortion procedure to be used, "that is what the statute requires him or her to tell the patient." As a result, doctors can use their own judgment regarding what they tell a woman seeking abortion about its possible psychological effects. The judge drew the final conclusion that "the majority of Wisconsin's law is constitutional because most of the restrictions it imposes do not constitute undue burdens upon a woman's right to choose whether to continue or terminate her pregnancy." The existence of abortion-specific informed consent regulations, which are more extensive than those in place previously, was thus endorsed. However, it was clear that where such regulations mention the "psychological risks" of abortion, there is no need for doctors to inform women that there is a significant chance that they will suffer mental illness (all references at *Karlin v. Foust,* 975 F. Supp. 1177, W.D.Wis. 1997).

According to Northern (1998), in most instances the outcome of such a contest is along these lines; in many states where "Women's Right to Know" legislation is enacted, its excesses are in fact modified. She argues that this may be because in many courts, a "reasonable patient standard" applies. The view is taken that if, in the opinion of the physician, a woman indicates that she has already obtained sufficient information to consider her options, the physician or counselor need not provide any further nonmedical information. Thus even in instances where statutes require that information concerning fetal development, adoption, or child placement services and so on be made available to the patient, the patient is not required to read it.

It seems that antiabortion advocates have made a concerted effort to pursue the PAS claim at a state level, but with limited success in regard to its effects for law and policy. A general pattern of modifying the construction of abortion developed in *Roe,* through individual states introducing laws that in different ways restrict or limit the provision of abortion, has emerged. But including the PAS claim within such regulations, by mandating that information emphasizing the threat posed by abortion to women's mental health must be provided in the interests of women's health and rights, has been contested and frequently defeated. As with the Koop inquiry, counterclaims about evidence concerning the psychological effects of abortion have been visible and, where they have reached the courts, have decisively influenced the outcome of proceedings to the detriment of the PAS claim.

Civil Liability Laws

The PAS claim also entered the legal debate at the state level in another way. Abortion opponents have advocated that specific laws, sometimes termed "civil liability laws," are needed to make physicians who practice abortion liable for payment of damages, where it is alleged that abortion has harmed women's health. A conference held in August 1998, "Women at Risk," promoted such an approach. The literature for the conference explained that its aim was to give "victims of abortion an opportunity, for the first time, to come together to strengthen each other." It launched a new "public advocacy" organization, Women at Risk, an offshoot of David Reardon's Elliot Institute that "seeks to protect the health and safety of women by making abortion practitioners properly liable for abortion-related injuries." David Reardon argued that the conference could "revolutionize the whole abortion debate. They [Women At Risk] will give voice to those who have been hurt by abortion . . . . I can honestly say I have never been more excited." A resolution was passed at this conference calling upon Congress to amend the Civil Rights Act, to specifically provide for compensation claims to be made following abortion:

> To protect the constitutional and civil right of women to receive full disclosure of all the information that a reasonable patient might consider relevant to a decision to decline an abortion; and to provide women the opportunity to seek just compensation for violation of this civil right during the period of time between completion of the abortion and two years after they have recovered from any emotional disabilities that may impede prosecution of a claim. (Birth Control Trust 1998b)

At the time of writing, discussion of amending the Civil Rights Act in this way has not been taken up and pursued by others. At the state level, however, the attempt to make abortion providers liable for damages on the grounds that abortion has harmed a woman's health has had a legislative impact. The outcome has been characteristic of the effect of the PAS. In line with the evidence discussed so far, civil liability laws have occasionally been passed and have become a matter of debate in which the terms of such laws have been found to be highly problematic.

The main example to date of this kind of law was introduced in Louisiana when Act 825 was passed into law on August 1997. Louisiana already had a very detailed "Woman's Right to Know" law, but the new law made those who perform abortions additionally civilly liable under tort law for "any damage occasioned or precipitated by the abortion." Under this law, the signing of a consent form by the woman in accordance with the "Woman's Right to Know" law did not negate a cause of action under the new law, but only reduced the recovery of damages to some extent, where the content of the consent form the woman had signed had informed her of the risk of the type of injuries or loss from which she might later be seeking to recover. Liability on the part of the physician could last for ten years following the performance of an abortion (in contrast to state law for other malpractice claims, which places a three-year limit on filing claims and caps damages at $500,000). The argument that liability should last for this length of time was made partly on the basis of the claim that the psychological effects of abortion are "denied" and may only surface years later, a characteristic feature of the PAS claim.

The law was challenged on the day before it was to become effective, and the District Court of East Louisiana issued a temporary restraining order to prohibit its operation. A further hearing took place in 1998, when the court was asked to consider whether a preliminary injunction against the law would be issued. The court found that it was "baffled" as to why there should be a need for specific legal liability under tort law, and that "if defendants are concerned that women should be informed of risks in the area of psycho-stress following abortion, psychological side effects of abortion, post-abortion syndrome and psychological trauma associated with abortion, then shouldn't these concerns (alleged risks) be placed in the Woman's Right to Know Statute?" The court found in its conclusion that those challenging the act had met the legal tests for the issuance of a preliminary injunction enjoining the operation of the act, and their motion was granted. The court's justification was that the statute

> . . . presents a new battlefield—that is, unconstitutional regulation of abortion providers so as to directly strike at a women's right of choice. The statute has the purpose and effect of infringing and chilling the exercise of constitutionally protected rights of abortion providers and women seeking abortion. Such backhanded and subtle attempts that chip away at a vital component of a person's liberty will not be tolerated.

The liability provided for by the act was considered

> . . . unlimited, unpredictable and ambiguous in which no abortion provider can possibly operate. . . . [The Act] has the purpose and effect of placing a sub-

stantial obstacle in the path of a woman seeking an abortion . . . this court cannot ignore that the statute's invisible duty of care, unlimited liability and the
implication of the fetus as a person for civil damages indicate a purpose far more
reaching than mere informed consent. This statute appears to be a subtle, back-
handed attempt to burden a woman's choice to terminate her pregnancy. (all references at *Ifeanyi v. Foster,* Civil Action No. 97-2214, United States District
Court for the Eastern District of Louisiana, 981 F. Supp. 977; 1998)

It was thus made clear that, according to the court, this attempt to pursue the
PAS claim in relation to the law was not going to succeed.

This ruling has by no means brought an end to debate about the proposed
law in Louisiana; it has been debated each year since 1998 following decisions
in appeals courts, most recently in spring 2002. The 1998 ruling has been
challenged through arguments about which kind of court should have the authority to rule on whether the law is constitutional, and whether the state can
be held accountable for the terms of the law, since the state would never itself
sue an abortion provider and no lawsuit had ever been brought by a woman
herself. This protracted and peculiar legal wrangle suggests that there are determined proponents of the PAS claim in Louisiana, who can ensure that their
claims are debated in legal and political arenas. However, given the response
to the PAS claim to date, when it specifically has been debated and ruled on
in a court, and the fact that no cases have as yet been brought against abortion
providers, it seems unlikely that, even in Louisiana, the "civil liability" law
will achieve the effects intended by its proponents.

COUNSELING AND LITIGATION

The final aspect of activity related to the PAS claim in the United States that
I will discuss has focused on the provision of counseling. Organizations that
contend that abortion harms women psychologically promote their own version of abortion counseling, sometimes termed "crisis pregnancy counseling."
The development of such activities on the part of abortion opponents has been
viewed as an important aspect of the abortion debate since the 1980s, contex-
tualized by recognition among antiabortionists that enacting a "right-to-life"
amendment was not an option, and that there was a need to respond to prochoice criticism that they had no concern for pregnant women (Staggenborg
1991; Ginsburg 1989).

Estimates suggest there are over 3000 Crisis Pregnancy Centers (CPCs) offering such counseling in the United States. The National Right to Life Committee (NRLC) claims that CPCs have "from the inception of the pro-life
movement . . . been on the front lines of the fight to save unborn babies from
the horrors of abortion." They do so by providing "free services that center
around informing women about the true nature of their unborn children and

what is available to assist the women to carry their babies to term." More recently, "because of the growing awareness of the continuing trauma caused by abortion," CPCs have "added post-abortion recovery support, with counseling or support groups to help women recover from a past abortion" to their activities (Townsend n.d.). In its submission to the Koop inquiry, the NRLC emphasized this kind of activity and drew attention to the development of "many self-help groups and an entire post abortion counseling specialty," listing American Victims of Abortion (AVA), Women Exploited by Abortion (WEBA), Victims of Choice, Post Abortion Counseling and Education (PACE), and the Healing Vision Network as relevant organizations of this kind. The submission also suggested that a specialist literature had emerged in this area in the United States, and listed a number of books, including *Will I Cry Tomorrow?*, *Abortion and Healing: A Cry to be Whole,* and *Women Exploited: The Other Victims of Abortion,* written on the topic of "post-abortion healing" (National Right to Life Committee 1987:8).

Project Rachel was reported in 1990 to have programs in sixty Roman Catholic dioceses in America, "offering counseling to women troubled after abortion" (Brotman 1990:4). The Right to Life League established such centers under the directorship of PAS claimsmaker Teri Reisser (Connelly 1992). In 2001, around one and a half million copies of a newspaper insert titled "Hope and Healing," produced by the Elliot Institute, were circulated in the *Washington Post* and newspapers in California, Florida, North Carolina, and Illinois. Providing details of the symptoms of Postabortion Syndrome, and a questionnaire to complete to find out "if you are suffering from post-abortion stress," the supplement gives the telephone number for Project Rachel and encourages readers to "find a therapist who has experience and training specifically in the field of post-abortion counseling" (Elliot Institute 2001). CPC organizations host websites to publicize their work, encourage others to set up centers, and put forward their claims about the health risks of abortion to women considering terminating a pregnancy. One such site, Pregnancy Centers Online, advises that if abortion is being considered, "you need to know about the very real possibilities of risks and complications. . . . Such risks can and do include increased changes for breast cancer, psychological distress, and may other physical, medical and emotional problems." It links to the website for David Reardon's Elliot Institute and displays items such as a press release claiming, "Over 500,000 Women Affected by Post-Abortion Syndrome."

The merits of the kind of counseling offered by such organizations and their purpose in offering it have become the subject of debate, giving further visibility to the contest over the extent and nature of the psychological effects of abortion. This debate has sometimes focused on the claim that such centers mislead women and advertise their services (for example, in the Yellow Pages) in a misleading manner. Abortion rights groups have protested that "bogus 'abortion clinics' . . . draw women in through fraudulent advertising and give them anti-abortion counseling" (Braxton 1992:B3). In the late 1980s, some investigations and lawsuits were initiated by prochoice organizations, resulting in increased media attention and a congressional hearing about CPCs in 1991. The result was that advertising and other practices of CPCs were deemed legally problematic on the grounds that they were deceptive and fraudulent (CARAL 2001:3). More recent debate suggests that the extent of controversy about CPCs and the degree of support offered to them, like other dimensions of the response to the PAS claim, intersect with law and politics and thus vary between states, but overall the effect of this dimension of the PAS claim has been less successful than its proponents expected.

It has been argued that generally, as a result of the success of efforts made by prochoice campaigns regarding the way in which CPCs have advertised their services, there has been a shift in presentation of their work. CPCs have changed their names (for example, from New Life Crisis Pregnancy Centre to Pregnancy Care Center of Crescent City) to emphasize the idea of "care" rather than "crisis" and highlight the medical and social services they offer to women (CARAL 2001). In this form, state funding has been argued for and has sometimes been forthcoming, where those opposed to abortion have promoted the work of CPCs. In 1999, the Women and Children's Resources Act, introduced by antiabortion members of Congress, proposed that $85 million should be provided in federal grants to CPCs, and President George W. Bush proposed including CPCs as recipients of federal funding through the Faith-Based and Community Initiatives, which began with his administration (CARAL 2001: 18–19). In some states, CPCs have been successful in attracting public money for their activities. In Pennsylvania, CPCs receive half of all public money appropriated for reproductive health care for low-income and uninsured women (over $4 million a year), and the state of Missouri provides $1.2 million to fund "alternatives to abortion" in the state, $620,000 of which goes to organizations that promote CPCs.

However, CPCs have also been criticized by politicians with influence who are skeptical about the centers' promotion of their activities. In 2002, subpoenas issued by New York Attorney General Eliot Spitzer to CPCs in New York state became the subject of heated debate. Reports in the *Washington Times,* for example, focused on Spitzer's allegations that the centers may be "misrepresenting the nature of services they offered" and practicing medicine without a license, and the *New York Times* noted how Spitzer's legal actions had been criticized by politicians from other states, who were supportive of CPCs. In the end the subpoenas were withdrawn, on the basis of an agreement reached with CPCs about how they present their services.

Most significantly for the PAS claim, debate about the work of CPCs has also focused on their relationship to litigation. Organizations such as Project Rachel and Women at Risk attempt to encourage women who feel bad following abortion to blame the abortion provider and take legal action. David

Reardon has suggested that women should be encouraged to do so, since it will "propel post-abortion litigation" and lead women to "bring legal action against the abortionists who have injured them." He argues that one of the goals of the "pro-woman/pro-life strategy" is to make counseling "an important issue in abortion malpractice suits" (Reardon 1996:64).

A strategy that connects counseling with litigation has been promoted by Ted Amshoff, a member of a legal firm that "deals with cases involving abortion injuries." He claims, "Until legislation is passed to protect them, women can still seek justice one-on-one through the courts. You don't need politicians for justice. All you need are twelve people in a jury box" (Sobie 1998). The website for Priests for Life asks supporters to "encourage mothers who have been harmed by abortion to bring suits against the abortion industry" (Russo and Denious 1998:27). The particular group most associated with this strategy is Life Dynamics Inc., founded in 1992 by Mark Crutcher. A manual distributed by the group urged support for malpractice lawsuits "to protect women, but also to force abortionists out of business by driving up their insurance rates" (Northern 1998). Life Dynamics Inc.'s website promotes an Abortion Malpractice Litigation Campaign as the main activity of the organization.

The issue of litigation after abortion, encouraged through claims about the kind of counseling women need, has become a visible part of the abortion debate. Life Dynamics Inc. made the news from 1993 on, for example in a report for *Newsday* about its "lawsuit tactics," which explains to attorneys "how to argue in court that a woman experiencing depression or conflicts after her abortion has suffered emotional damages" and how to allege that abortion providers "do not obtain adequate informed consent from women who often experience post-abortion syndrome" (Kaiser Daily Report 1993b). At the end of 1993, *Eye on America,* broadcast by CBS, examined "the growing practice of suing abortion providers for malpractice." The program profiled one woman who successfully sued the doctor who performed her abortion for malpractice causing psychological damage, and commented that "anti-abortion activists . . . have launched a new campaign urging lawyers to sue abortion doctors for malpractice. . . . A campaign that's making doctors nervous." The program argued that what is disputed "is the idea that all women should be counseled for emotional trauma, the so-called postabortion syndrome, when the American Psychological Association says no such syndrome exists." It predicted that the debate in the future would revolve around whether litigation is a response to "real injuries" or "just another tactic to hound doctors" (Kaiser Daily Report 1993a).

This strategy has also been debated in the medical press in the United States. According to one article in *American Medical News,* claims against physicians who practice abortion have been filed with no intention of pursuing the claims, but which nonetheless results in a claims record against the physician concerned. Such tactics were described by the author of this article as "a real subtle form of mind games. . . . It's guerrilla-warfare tactics [which aim] to throw providers so off balance that they just decide to get out of the business" (Gianelli 1995:3). A *Washington Times* article reported in 2000 that antiabortion activists hope to bankrupt abortion providers by filing lawsuits regarding disclosure of information about the alleged risks of abortion. The article quotes a representative of Rachel's Vineyard, who claimed abortion can lead to "suicide, breast cancer, child abuse, infertility, depression and alcoholism" and that "there are millions of potential clients who can seek redress in the courts" (Kaiser Daily Reproductive Health Report 2000b).

What effect has this strategy had in relation to its stated aim? It has been argued that clinics and doctors have been "hit with a spate of lawsuits" that are eventually thrown out but may require the physician concerned to go through a long and costly court battle (Yeoman 2001). The *Washington Times* noted in 2000 that courts have awarded settlements in such medical negligence cases in the past, including a 1995 case against Planned Parenthood, which paid $80,000 to a plaintiff for emotional distress (Kaiser Daily Reproductive Health Report 2000b). But, especially when compared with the ever-increasing amount of litigation about pregnancy and childbirth in the United States generally, there does not seem to be much evidence that many women are suing, successfully at least, on these grounds. There are a few cases, such as those mentioned above, but it does not seem that a spate of litigation of this kind has emerged, and where cases are brought they can be successfully disputed.

One author, supportive of the notion that civil actions should be brought and physicians sued for malpractice by women said to be suffering from "post abortion psychological trauma," writes that there is little such case law, and what there is does not focus on "informed consent" but on whether damages are recoverable for the alleged injury (Eller 1996). According to Northern, although there are indications that abortion malpractice litigation is on the rise compared with the past, and this may stem from antiabortion advocates adopting a strategy through which they try to discourage doctors from providing abortion, this strategy may often be unlikely to succeed:

> Although the availability of punitive damages, and even the ability to tap a doctor's private assets, may appeal to [antiabortion] groups as effective harassment tools, the need to prove both contact and vitiation of consent (rather than simply lack of informed consent) will serve as substantial bars. Indeed, the courts may find it easier to dismiss unfounded battery claims on the pleadings—or to impose sanctions for frivolous claims. (1998:507)

Northern focuses here on the legal argument that an offense of battery was committed because the operation was performed without consent and contends that where this interpretation of consent is used by courts the litigious approach of abortion opponents is unlikely to succeed. This outcome may not be assumed, since, as Northern points out, some courts are interpreting the meaning of consent in a different way, using a higher standard of consent. In this instance, it is not required simply that there was sufficient consent to mean that the performance of an abortion is not battery, but rather that the physician acted in the patient's best interests, and ensured that the treatment provided led to the best outcome for the patient.

In this interpretation of consent, when applied to abortion, the responsibility of the physician is not simply to make sure the patient is aware of the possible risks of abortion. Rather, if the woman is to make autonomous decisions about her pregnancy, it is claimed, it is not sufficient that the state simply give her the freedom to do so by abolishing restrictive laws. It must also require that those health professionals with whom she interacts do everything possible to ensure that she makes the best possible decision for herself. Her autonomy is not, in this framework, only a product of freedom from state control; it also requires that professionals enable her to exercise her choices. Such an approach to consent, it is argued, requires that physicians (and potentially counselors or any other professionals the patient interacts with) should intend to discuss every possible factor that may pertain to a decision to undergo treatment, and may be negligent if they do not. According to Northern, this interpretation of consent might enable a woman to successfully bring a claim for negligence on the grounds that "a physician or crisis counselor unreasonably failed to provide information necessary to its [procreative autonomy] full and effective exercise" (1998:516). However, at the time of writing, it does not seem to be the case that the courts have been deluged with cases in which a woman claims she did not give her informed consent, according to this definition of it, and the court then finds it agrees with her.

In summary, in the United States, the PAS claim has been consistently the subject of visible debate and contest since its emergence in the early 1980s. Faced with often successful counterclaims that there is no scientific evidence that such a syndrome exists, the claim has not, however, achieved the policy and legislative effect the antiabortion movement hoped and expected that it would. "Women's Right to Know" laws, motivated by antiabortion sentiment, have been introduced in some states. The introduction of such legislation indicates that abortion opponents have found ways to pursue their case, in which abortion is problematized in medicalized terms. However, the component of such laws that refers to the relationship between abortion and mental ill health has only sometimes reflected the views of PAS claimants; its success has been limited, and gains have been made only in states with a strong tradition of opposition to abortion.

PAS claimsmakers have also attempted to gain legal recognition for the claim in regard to compensation, and in this aspect of the law too, the result, from the perspective of those who consider abortion a social problem because it damages women's mental health, has not been decisively in their favor. The attempt to gain legal recognition for the PAS claim appears to have had limited success in relation to litigation initiated by individuals who have brought malpractice suits. But even here, its effects do not amount to those envisaged possible by the proponents of the PAS claim.

POSTABORTION SYNDROME IN BRITAIN

The process of diffusion of the PAS claim from the United States to Britain was examined in the previous chapter. The adoption of the claim by abortion opponents in Britain suggests that they perceived that they could make gains by opposing abortion because of its mental health effects. What kind of debate has ensued about PAS in Britain? How far has the claim enabled the British antiabortion movement to influence the abortion debate? Has the attempt to construct abortion as a social problem on the grounds of its effect upon women's minds found support among those with influence in the British abortion debate? How has the debate compared with that in the United States?

THE RAWLINSON COMMISSION

The most significant attempt to promote the PAS claim in Britain took place in 1994, with the publication of the report of the Rawlinson Commission on the "physical and psycho-social effects of abortion on women." The Rawlinson Commission was headed by Lord Rawlinson of Ewell and administered by Christian Action Research and Education (CARE). Its stated aim was to carry out an investigation into the "physical and psycho-social effects of abortion," rather than to discuss the ethics of abortion. Its brief was therefore confined to an investigation of the effects of abortion on women's health (Rawlinson 1994:1). The thirty-four Rawlinson Commission members included representatives of the organizations Feminists Against Eugenics, Life, the SPUC, Doctors Who Respect Human Life, Labour Life, and CARE, and those members who were members of Parliament included the veteran antiabortion MP David Alton and Rev. Martyn Smith MP. It was reported that, at the press conference to launch the report, David Alton confirmed that "no members [of the Commission] were drawn from individuals or organisations with a pro-choice perspective" (Birth Control Trust 1994b), although some members of scientific and medical organizations did participate. What was the effect of the commission and its report for the British abortion debate? To what extent did those who gave evidence to it, that supported the PAS claim, gain broader support for their case? The Rawlinson Commission stands as an interesting contrast with the Koop inquiry. As I will now show, the debate about it was far less visible and influential than that in the United States in the late 1980s. This indicates the problems that have confronted PAS claimsmakers in Britain in their attempts to gain authority for the claim through means similar to those adopted in the United States, namely through endorsement by politicians.

Debating the Rawlinson Commission Report

It should be noted first that although Lord Rawlinson was a respected member of the British Parliament (he was a life member of the House of Lords and was the Attorney General under the Conservative Party administration during the 1980s), the commission was very different in its status from the Koop inquiry. Although Lord Rawlinson's chairmanship of the commission gave it some credibility, there was no governmental involvement in it at all. Where the Koop inquiry involved government officials at the highest level, the British Department of Health "did not feel it appropriate" to give evidence to the Rawlinson Commission, agreeing only to "respond to a specific question" that arose from evidence that was given (Birth Control Trust 1994b). Of the seven members of Parliament who were members of the Rawlinson Commission, none was close to the government or held a position in policymaking on health. The commission was therefore, in parliamentary terms, unofficial.

It is perhaps not surprising that, as a result, it generated a relatively low-key debate. Other than one response from the Royal College of Psychiatrists (RCP), no major scientific organizations responded to the commission's report. A representative of the RCP had given evidence to the commission, and in its press release about its findings, the Rawlinson Commission claimed that this evidence stated that there are "no psychiatric indications for abortion." The press release claimed that this "raises serious questions given that 91 per cent of abortions are carried out on the grounds of the mental health of the mother." The RCP subsequently issued a statement (the only public statement issued by a British medical association or college in the last ten years in direct response to the PAS claim) to say that this was an "inaccurate portrayal of the College's views on abortion" and to ask for a public retraction of the statement. The RCP also chose to restate its opinion, in terms similar to those used by the American Psychological and Psychiatric Association in the United States, that "There is no evidence of an increased risk of major psychiatric disorder or of long lasting psychological distress [following abortion]" (1994).

Another kind of counterclaim also emerged from this organization. The RCP stated that the risks to psychological health from the termination of pregnancy in the first trimester "are much less than the risks associated with proceeding with a pregnancy which is clearly harming the mother's mental health" (Royal College of Psychiatrists 1994). This claim, that it is unwanted childbearing, rather than abortion, that threatens mental health, was also made in comments from the RCP subsequently. In an interview, Margaret Oates of the RCP, who was the psychiatrist who gave evidence to the Rawlinson Commission, explained that she was "furious" about the press release. "What I actually told them is that having an unwanted baby is the biggest tragedy in the world but that you couldn't *guarantee* that a psychiatric condition would deteriorate if a woman didn't get an abortion," she argued. In the same article, Diana Mansour, director of a large contraceptive clinic in London, argued similarly that "You can be sure that there is far more trauma associated with continuing an unwanted pregnancy than terminating it" (Rogers 1994:6). Apart from this, however, the Commission did not elicit a response from medical or scientific bodies. In Britain the response of prochoice organizations was also quite different from that in the United States. Such organizations issued press releases in response to the publication of the report (National Abortion Campaign 1994; Pro-Choice Alliance 1994). But according to a report in the *Independent on Sunday,* the Commission itself "involved 25 prominent anti-abortionists. . . . and pro-choice experts refused to participate" (Lacey 1997:32).

There were a small number of articles in the press about the Commission's report, and the debate received far less media coverage compared with the aftermath of the Koop inquiry. These articles reported different aspects of the commission's findings. Insofar as they passed comment, the Commission's findings were sometimes endorsed rather than refuted, but it was also emphasized that the Commission was made up of antiabortion members. One article stated that an "inquiry panel, made up mainly of members opposed to abortion," had found "there are psychological effects on women, sometimes lasting for years, following an abortion" (Macdonald 1994). According to the *British Medical Journal* (1994:8), the report recommended that centers providing abortion "should initiate independent and long-term follow-up of those clients considered to be most at risk of emotional distress." A comment piece in the London *Evening Standard* (1994:11) highlighted the "traumatic" emotional consequences of abortion and criticized the "breezy attitude" of those who are prochoice who believe "abortion is no more traumatic than defrosting a fridge . . . or hoovering up after a messy party." The author applauded the Commission on the grounds that it would break a "taboo," permitting women to admit that they felt bad after abortion. The *Sunday Telegraph's* article on the subject drew attention to the publication of the report, noting that the Commission involved twenty-five prominent antiabortionists, and that the report contended that women can suffer long-term depression after abortion (Rogers 1994). The amount of coverage was small, however, compared with the U.S. coverage of the Koop inquiry. It seems that journalists in Britain did not perceive the publication of the report as of great significance.

PAS and British Abortion Law and Policy

The Rawlinson Commission made a number of recommendations about changes to abortion policies. Is there evidence that the kind of policies recommended have been adopted in Britain? One recommendation, similar to that proposed by PAS claimsmakers in the United States, was that the kind of information given to women considering abortion should be altered. The Rawlinson Commission report argued, with reference to evidence given by Life, BVA, and CCFL (Christians Caring for Life), that there was "credible evidence" that women were not given adequate information before abortion by abortion providers, in order to permit an "informed decision"; and that as a result women "experience regret afterwards at having made what they subsequently considered the wrong decision." The Commission urged the Department of Health to introduce policy that would require abortion providers to give "essential information as to the risk of physical and emotional consequences and stages of fetal development." The Rawlinson Commission report also argued that there was evidence that counseling before and after abortion, which was intended to reduce the "trauma" of abortion, was inadequate. The report stated that the Commission "would like to see the issue of both pre and post abortion counselling urgently addressed in order to minimise the distress experienced by women who have undergone abortion without adequate opportunity to address the emotional turmoil they are often experiencing."

In the years since the Rawlinson Commission, the Department of Health (DoH) and the British Royal College of Obstetricians and Gynaecologists (RCOG) have issued guidelines that make reference to the kind of information women requesting abortion should be given and provide guidance about counseling before and after abortion. The RCOG guideline is "evidence based": "Recommendations [in the guideline] were based on, and explicitly linked to, the evidence that supports them" (2000:13). Thus, the case made by the RCOG is presented as objective and scientific. The development and publication of the guideline were supported by funding from the U.K. government's Department of Health, and the members of the group that developed it represent the main medical organizations involved with the provision of abortion and contraception in Britain.

The guideline does make reference to the issue of counseling and the psychological effects of abortion. As media reporting following its publication noted, the guideline states: "Only a small minority of women experience any long term adverse psychological sequelae after abortion. . . . Early distress, although common, is usually a continuation of symptoms present before the abortion. Conversely, long-lasting, negative effects on both mothers and their children are reported where abortion has been denied" (Boseley 2000). The guideline recommends, on this basis, that counseling should be offered to women considering abortion, but that the guideline development group "favours the use of the term 'support' rather than 'counselling,'" and that "services should have access to counsellors . . . and should refer the minority of women who will require such specialist help" (Royal College of Obstetricians and Gynecologists 2000:32). Thus the guideline separates out the provision of psychological or psychiatric "counselling," which it suggests most women do not need, from "support," which it considers the responsibility of abortion providers to provide. After abortion, the guideline contends, "a small minority" of women "experience long term post abortion distress," and "further counselling" should be made available for them (2000:60). The Rawlinson Commission report can, therefore, perhaps be considered to have influenced the case made in the guideline, insofar as it was deemed necessary to address the issue of whether counseling is needed after abortion. However, if this is a response to the PAS claim, it is implicit and rejects, on the grounds of available evidence, the idea that abortion leads to significant psychological problems.

Guidelines from the Department of Health, termed Required Standard Operating Principles (RSOPs), were most recently issued in 1999. Clinics outside of the National Health Service in Britain are legally obliged to abide by the terms of these procedures and, given that around 50 percent of abortions carried out in Britain are performed in such clinics, RSOPs constitute an important aspect of the regulation of abortion provision. A section of the Principles is titled "Advice/Consent/Counselling." It does not mention counseling after abortion. It does provide specifications for counseling before abortion, which state that counseling must be available, but that certain women rather than all women might benefit from it, such as women "who are having difficulty in coping emotionally," those "with a history of psychiatric illness," or those whom the "partner, family or employer is possibly coercing into having an abortion" (1999a:11). Thus the DoH does not consider all women in need of counseling and does not seem to consider mental health problems after abortion a major problem.

In regard to information provision and counseling, the Rawlinson Commission report also recommended that "clinics be required to make information available about local and national *independent* counsellors and counselling agencies who offer post-abortion counselling" (emphasis in the original), and that such organizations be "encouraged and official grants be provided for training courses to be made available to lay post-abortion counsellors to cope with the increasing demand" (Rawlinson 1994:18). The DoH and RCOG guidelines do specify that certain information should be provided for women. The RSOPs state that "literature on alternatives to abortion—for instance adoption and motherhood—from sources independent of the clinic for women who decide to continue with the pregnancy" should be available (Department of Health 1999a:10). The RCOG states that verbal advice "must be supported by accurate, impartial information which the woman considering abortion can understand and may take away and read." The kind of information women need to be given is about physical risks, such as blood loss or anesthetic complications. "Short term emotional distress" is also mentioned, as is "psychological sequelae," listed as "Long term effects of abortion (which are rare or unproven)." Women are to be informed that "abortion is safer than continuing a pregnancy to term and that complications are uncommon" (2000:26). Neither guideline, therefore, requires abortion providers to provide the kind of information recommended by the Rawlinson Commission report. Applications to the Department of Health, for funding for "crisis pregnancy counselling," have, in fact, been rejected (Caldwell 2000).

A final noteworthy recommendation in the Rawlinson Commission report related to the way the statute regulating abortion in Britain is interpreted by doctors. As Chapter 3 made clear, British abortion law differs from U.S. law in that, at all stages of a pregnancy, abortion can be performed legally only if two doctors agree "in good faith" that the woman requesting the procedure meets one of the medical grounds set out in the law. One of these grounds states that an abortion is legal where the continuation of the pregnancy constitutes a "greater threat to the mental health" of the pregnant woman than if the pregnancy were terminated. Thus, if two doctors believe that a woman's mental health is less threatened by abortion than by childbirth, they can recommend an abortion.

British women who have abortions do so most frequently on these grounds. In 2000, for example, of a total of 183,391 grounds given by doctors for legal abortions, the mental health effect of continuing the pregnancy was mentioned 170,167 times (Office for National Statistics 2000:8). The mental health ground for abortion has regularly been problematized by abortion opponents, on the grounds that doctors are interpreting its meaning so broadly that the law is being flouted. The notion of a threat to mental health, they contend, should comprise psychiatric evidence that mental illness will result if an abortion is not performed. (By contrast, many British doctors define a threat to mental ill health as a woman feeling "stressed" by her pregnancy (Paintin 1998:17).) This issue was taken up in the Rawlinson Commission report recommendations, which state that "the Department of Health should ensure compliance with the Abortion Act (1967) and the Human Fertilisation Act (1990) [sic] by regular inspections, or spot checks, of the grounds given for abortions, in order to ascertain whether mental health grounds . . . are genuine and can be substantiated, or do not comply with the legislation and should be challenged" (1994:17). However, no such checks have been introduced, and since 1994, the number of abortions legally permitted on mental health grounds continued to rise.

The Rawlinson Commission can therefore be considered to have failed to influence the development of policy and the practice of abortion in Britain, certainly in the direction intended by the opponents of abortion. Policy-makers have considered the issue of the mental health effects of abortion and have drawn the conclusion that there is no evidence that such effects are a health risk, thus implicitly refuting the PAS claim. If anything, they have considered that the extent and severity of negative feelings after abortion have been overestimated in the past and that the need for counseling for this reason has been overstated. Doctors appear to consider unwanted pregnancy a greater threat to mental health than abortion, if the number of abortions performed on mental health grounds is taken as evidence of this viewpoint.

. . . AND STILL THEY WEEP

Since 1994, there have been a number of other attempts to draw attention to the putative problem of PAS. One such attempt, which did achieve some sympathetic coverage in the British press, was the publication of *. . . And Still They Weep: Personal Stories of Abortion.* This was a collection of accounts from women who have had abortions, who were associated with British Victims of Abortion (BVA); their stories were intended to "introduce the signs and symptoms of Post Abortion Syndrome" (Bowman 1996:ix). Some local newspapers covered sympathetically the case made in the book. Papers published in towns where women working for BVA lived, whose stories were detailed in the book, reported the PAS claim without criticizing it. The *Northern Echo* reported on the launch of the book, explaining that "Women in the North East who have undergone abortion are telling their stories of anguish in a new book which claims they were denied permission to grieve" (Marsh 1997:6). The *Evening Gazette,* published in Middlesborough, reported the story of "Emma," in an article titled "Women who weep for their 'lost' babies" (Armstrong 1997). The local paper in Canterbury reported the "harrowing experiences" of local resident Kathy Bone, who "began having terrible nightmares and panic attacks which lasted for two or three years," which she eventually discovered through counseling were caused by her abortion (Lampert 1997:17).

The response in national papers was not extensive and reflected the general approach of the paper that reported the story. The *Daily Mail,* known for its conservative stance on "moral issues," reported, in an article titled "Women haunted for life by their abortions," that "Psychologists have identified a mental disorder known as Post Abortion Syndrome, symptoms of which can include violence towards children, sleeplessness, eating disorders and alcoholism" (West 1997). The liberal broadsheet the *Independent on Sunday* also reported on the story, but, by contrast, drew attention to prochoice groups' criticism of the PAS claim and argued that "the increasing temperature of the debate will only have added to the torment of women who are deciding whether or not to go ahead with an abortion" (Thorpe 1996:3). A further story in the *Independent on Sunday* referred to the book and asked, "Does abortion really ruin your life?" It argued that "In the vast majority of cases of legal, early abortion, the answer is no" and referred to the work of Nancy Russo, a U.S. psychologist prominent in the debate about PAS, who found through her research that "abortion itself had no independent effect" on the mental health of women who terminated pregnancies and that "there is no relationship of depression to abortion." Russo, it was reported, also argued that not having an abortion in the case of accidental pregnancies is even more likely to cause future problems. The publication of . . . *And Still They Weep* did, then, achieve some visibility for the PAS claim, and in some instances media reports did not contest the claim. However, although women's personal stories of their experiences have met with some sympathy on the part of journalists, "counseling services" offered by antiabortion groups have not.

COUNSELING

In Britain, as in the United States, antiabortion organizations fund and staff crisis pregnancy counseling centers. They offer women counseling before abortion, to warn them of the alleged health risks of the procedure, and afterward to help them deal with the effects of Postabortion Syndrome. Such counseling has become the subject of media reports, which in general have been unfavorable to the activities of PAS claimsmakers.

One journalist who, feigning pregnancy, visited a counseling center run by Life wrote critically that the counselor she saw "starts off in a non-direction . . . but the end of her first sentence gives the lie to its beginning. . . . I hear about the guilt of 'post-abortion syndrome,' the scarring that 'many women suffer.' . . . how I will have to bear the secret alone for the rest of my life. . . . [A leaflet] tells me how 'abortion violates women'" (Wynn Jones 1997:11). A report in 1995 for the *Independent on Sunday,* by a journalist visiting an abortion clinic, argued critically that antiabortion "sidewalk counsellors" outside the clinic were on a "crusade" to dissuade women from having an abortion, by handing out leaflets on "PAS, post-abortion syndrome" that were intended to "deter women from going ahead with their terminations. Sexual dysfunction, nightmares, inability to sustain intimate relationships, suicidal impulses, they are told, could all be in store for them" (Glass 1995:3). Another journalist reported in 1997 how, having pretended to be pregnant and visited a counseling center run by an antiabortion group, "Pro-life's trump card is vicious:

abortion is devastating and you can *never* escape the scars of guilt and shame" (Aitkenhead 1997:17).

In 1999, a number of national newspapers reported critically on antiabortion counseling centers. *The Mirror* sent a reporter to centers in a number of British cities and titled the resultant article "Exposed: Scandal of the Pregnancy 'Advisers.'" At one such center, run by Life, the article reported that the journalist was "handed leaflets telling her: 'When you have an abortion you feel you have been raped and your baby killed'" (Cummins and Jacques 1999:22–23). *The Guardian* reported that women were being "scared off having abortions" by such centers and quoted the consultant gynecologist at one of London's target hospitals, who described the information given to women by such centers as "absolute garbage" (Carter 1999). In 2001, the *Sunday Express* accused such centers of "duping pregnant girls." It drew attention to "a growing number of bogus abortion centres which act as fronts for fanatical pro-life groups" (Johnston 2001). In the same year, the women's magazine *Marie Claire* published an exposé of a "nationwide chain" of centers, "a front for a fanatical pro-life organisation" which "peddled propaganda," such as "in 85 per cent of cases [abortion] causes severe psychological trauma" (Reid 2001:145–147).

LITIGATION

British abortion opponents, like their U.S. counterparts, argue that women should sue doctors following abortion on the grounds that they received inadequate information about the health risks of abortion. In 2001, it was reported that at an "interfaith conference on abortion," a speaker argued that under European legislation on human rights, women could sue doctors who terminate pregnancies. It was claimed that Article 10 of the European Human Rights Convention states that information should not be withheld from patients, and that, on this basis, women could sue where they were not "informed" about the alleged risks of abortion. It was argued that Britain was "internationally isolated" in its stance regarding information, since British law places the onus on doctors to decide what information should be given. The claim was made that many women suffered from PAS and should be able to claim where they were not warned of the risk (Twiston Davies 2001:3). The argument that women should seek compensation for harm allegedly caused by abortion was made from the mid 1990s, but to date it appears to have gained little visibility, and insofar as it has, it has been contested by medical organizations.

In 1998, Life announced that it was setting up a "help line" for women to call. April of that year saw the thirtieth anniversary of the implementation of the 1967 Abortion Act, and Life used this occasion to publicize this "new service" for women. The initiative was reported in the *Independent* and *Daily Telegraph* newspapers. Jack Scarisbrick claimed that a growing body of medical evidence showed that abortions left women at "vastly increased risk of conditions including cancer, infertility and increased incidence of later miscarriages as well as psychiatric illness." He said, "We want women who have suffered either physical or mental trauma as a result of abortion to contact us. We will encourage them to take the doctors responsible to court." The move was opposed immediately by the British Medical Association on the basis that "Evidence of the type which Life is using for these claims does not exist. As long as the abortion is approved according to the criteria of the 1967 Act, including the fact that the mother has fully consented then it would be very difficult to bring a case of this nature" (Birth Control Trust 1998a). Subsequently, the "help line" has not made the news in Britain.

There does not appear to have been much litigation related to the issue of negative feelings following abortion, and what there has been has been even less successful than that in the United States. One case was reported in 1999. A forty-two-year-old woman said she had been diagnosed with posttraumatic stress disorder, following an abortion performed two years previously at a clinic run by the abortion provider Marie Stopes International, and her lawyer issued High Court proceedings against the clinic and two of its doctors. He claimed, "Post abortion trauma is a recognised syndrome and doctors should bear it in mind in approaching and advising a woman whether to have an abortion. Every doctor should consider it and no consideration was given here. Given my client's age and profile, she was a classic case of risk." The case was described as "ground-breaking" and, it was claimed, could pave the way for other claims (Gordon 1999). However, this case did not make it to court. In 2001, it was reported that that a "mother of six who believes abortion is murder" was suing Marie Stopes International "for failing to give her adequate counselling before she terminated a pregnancy." This case did make the High Court, and the woman concerned testified that she was "so mentally traumatised after undergoing an abortion . . . that she felt compelled to have another baby" (Laville 2001). In the end, however, the woman withdrew her action and costs were awarded against her by the court.

Overall, the PAS claim has, therefore, been less successful in Britain than in the United States. Debate about PAS has been much less visible in Britain, and where the claim has been publicized in the media, coverage has been relatively small-scale. It has provided some endorsement of the claim, but insofar as the claim has been taken into account in debate about abortion law and policy, it has been to elicit rejections of the idea that abortion causes mental ill health from those who are influential in policy-making on abortion.

As Chapter 3 showed, the medical profession is at the heart of debate about and regulation of abortion in Britain. Given this context, influencing medical bodies is a crucial task for those with an interest in abortion. PAS claimants, however, have failed to do this. It seems that the British medical profession, in the main, has chosen not to respond directly to the PAS claim. Insofar as medical opinion has responded to the idea that abortion harms women psychologically, it has cited evidence that abortion does not constitute a major risk of this kind to underpin its recommendations regarding information provision and counseling and has claimed that unwanted pregnancy and childbearing are a greater threat to mental health, and that it is this, not abortion, that is the cause for concern for psychiatry.

In contrast to scientific and medical bodies in the United States, the most striking feature of the response to the PAS claim from the British medical profession is therefore its absence. The argument that abortion constitutes a social problem on the grounds of its alleged serious psychological effects has not generated a direct response from medical bodies with an interest in abortion. Other than the RCP's response to the Rawlinson Commission, no statements or research findings that directly mention the claim have been issued by scientific or medical bodies. The citation index Medline cites a number of articles and commentaries about "Post-Abortion Syndrome," but all are to be found in American and Canadian medical journals. Whereas the *Journal of the American Medical Association* has published a debate about the issue, no equivalent articles appear in the *British Medical Journal*. The only exception to this trend is a response to the PAS claim given during the debate about the Alton Bill in 1988. As part of the debate about the bill, some antiabortion MPs made reference to "post-abortion syndrome." As sociologist Maureen McNeil has pointed out, in response, some doctors made it clear that they did not believe PAS was a credible way to talk about women's postabortion psychological state. Respected British gynecologist Wendy Savage argued: "Post-abortion trauma is another condition dreamt up in the US and flown over here to add weight to the [antiabortion] argument. Studies of women (including one I did myself) do not show that long term regret after legal abortion is at all common" (McNeil 1991:158).

Four main points emerge from the story of PAS in the United States and Britain overall. First, PAS claimsmakers have met with considerable active resistance. Medicalized opposition to abortion has been disputed as strongly as the moralized antiabortion argument. Claimants for PAS have found it difficult to use the cultural resource of the "Syndrome Society" to gain acceptance of their case. In contrast to many other examples, where claims have been made that certain groups of people should be considered victims of posttraumatic stress, PAS has been subject to a determined process of counterclaiming. The claim that women who have abortions should be considered victims has met with a high degree of skepticism. The argument has been made that whether there is a Postabortion Syndrome must be tested by scientific evidence, based on a clear definition of what this alleged mental illness comprises.

Second, the main way in which debate about PAS has been framed is in terms of whether or not there is scientific evidence that abortion leads to mental ill health. In their counterclaims, those opposing PAS have contended that the best available evidence attests to the safety of abortion in this regard. Those making counterclaims have successfully presented this research as the best available evidence. As psychologists from the American Psychological Association argued of the Koop inquiry, "Koop's failure to draw the conclusions expected by the White House might be due in part to the efforts by psychologists to argue an accurate accounting of the relevant research" (Wilcox et al. 1998:21). A key aspect of successful claims for victims, that they suffer from an unrecognized problem that must be taken seriously, which has been insufficiently researched or considered, has thus been disputed, on the grounds that much available evidence is available to attest that abortion does not lead to mental ill health. Indeed, as the following chapter discusses, it is where women continue pregnancies that the real risk to mental health has been considered to exist.

This points, third, to the crucial role that some institutions have played in disputing the PAS claim. In the United States in particular, the public role of scientific and medical opinion overall has been to contest, rather than endorse, the claim. Mainstream medical, psychiatric, and psychological opinion has, in this instance, acted to counter claims that emphasize risk to mental health. Arguments that dispute PAS have been very visible in the United States, as part of the high-profile debate that emerged from the Koop inquiry. In Britain, although PAS has not become the focus for as much public debate, it has nonetheless been contested. And where other claimsmakers have contested PAS (for example, prochoice organizations in the United States and Britain), they have drawn heavily on the kind of arguments made by such organizations. The argument that there is no scientific evidence for PAS has proved a powerful and decisive resource for supporters of the right to choose.

However, not all institutions have responded in this way. This leads to a fourth point: that the claim has had a greater degree of success in influencing debate about law and policy in United States than in Britain. The differences in the story of the claim in these two societies can largely be explained by differential response to PAS in the realm of politics. In the United States, some politicians, at the national and local levels, endorsèd the claim and have thus ensured that it has become part of the abortion debate, and that it has some effect on the evolution of law and policy. Insofar as PAS has achieved a high degree of prominence in the media, as well as a limited legislative effect, this has resulted from the significant political support offered to claimants. Support for the PAS claim given by the Reagan administration in particular proved vital in transforming the claim into a publicly debated issue. The Koop inquiry utilized state resources, involved senior officials and members of the U.S. political establishment, elicited a response from key organizations and individuals with expert knowledge about the psychological effects of abortion, and led to a number of articles and commentaries in the American media. This aspect of the PAS claim has been almost entirely absent in Britain, where the claim has been consequently far less visible and has had a minimal effect on abortion law and policy.

In the following chapters, I discuss in more detail why the PAS claim met with the response it did. Why, in relation to the example of abortion, did the process of counterclaiming discussed above emerge? How has the issue of pregnancy and its outcomes in the United States and Britain been constructed, so as to lead to this outcome? In particular, why did medical and scientific organizations oppose the PAS claim? I turn now to examine further these limits to the PAS claim.

5

Pregnancy and Mental
Health in the
United States and Britain

A notable aspect of the story of the Postabortion Syndrome claim—perhaps the most interesting aspect of it—is that those with authority in medicine, psychiatry, and psychology have strongly *contested* it, a response that contrasts with other instances where experiences have been deemed traumatic, as detailed in Chapter 2. Where the trend toward the medicalization of experience has become generally dominant, in this instance it has been strongly argued that it is inaccurate and unhelpful to present the experience of women who have abortions in terms of mental illness. This chapter considers whether such claims, prominent in the debate about PAS, reflect trends toward the *demedicalization* of abortion. Was the contest about PAS a result of the dominance of a construction of abortion, in which the issue of whether women should be able to have one had come to be considered a clearly nonmedical question? Was it that women's state of mind following abortion had come to be deemed a matter that does not pertain significantly to the legitimacy of abortion? Had the issue of whether and how abortion should be regulated become separated from the issue of how pregnancy and its outcome make women feel?

Through consideration of the history of and background to the contest about PAS, I draw the conclusion that this has not been the case, and that the emergence of the claim that abortion is relatively risk-free in regard to mental illness reflects less a trend toward demedicalization than the *reorientation of medical concerns*. Abortion, as a result of this process, has remained constructed as a health issue. But its effects have come to be considered *relative to other possible outcomes of pregnancy*. I now turn to examine in detail the development of claims that have been prominent in the contest about PAS to show how this is the case.

THE PSYCHOLOGICAL EFFECTS OF ABORTION

Whenever the PAS claim has been made, its opponents have made a key counterclaim, that the majority of studies have found that abortion does not result in long-term, negative effects for women's mental health. Abortion does not cause mental illness, it has been strongly argued, and the available scientific evidence indicates that the idea of a psychiatric syndrome following abortion lacks foundation. Those opposing PAS have been able to refer to a large body of research to back up this counterclaim. In its submission to the Koop enquiry, for example, the American Psychological Association (APA) argued that its members had conducted research on the "psychological sequelae of abortion" and referred to papers published in 1971, 1975, 1976, 1979, 1980, 1981, 1984, and 1985 about this subject (American Psychological Association 1987:2). According to Michael B. Bracken, professor of obstetrics and gynaecology at Yale University and opponent of the PAS claim, since the 1960s there have been several thousand reports published on this topic, "arguably making abortion the most widely studied of all medical procedures" (1989:letters page).

This suggests that prior to the issue of the psychological effects of abortion becoming a visible aspect of the abortion debate during the 1980s, the terms of the main counterclaim to PAS were already well established. This issue had already become important, if less visible, because it had already featured in debates in psychiatry and psychology. And the outcome of these debates was the emergence of a dominant view that abortion and mental illness are not significantly connected. The terms of the main counterclaim made in the debate about PAS from the 1980s on were, therefore, predicated on a field of research and discussion that already existed by the time this claim emerged. How did this area of discussion emerge within science and medicine? Why did the issue of women's feelings after abortion become a matter for scientific investigation?

An Emerging Debate

For the first half of the twentieth century there was, in fact, very little published about this issue in the relevant literature. According to Potts et al. (1977), in both the United States and Britain abortion was not considered a legitimate or respectable issue for those involved in medicine to consider and was infrequently discussed by them. Insofar as claims did appear in the medical press, they presented abortion as a pathogen, likely to cause mental illness. Zimmerman (1981) argues, however, that by the mid-1950s there was evidence that this situation was beginning to change. Studies of the psychological and emotional effects of abortion began to accumulate. Published investigations about this issue usually consisted of doctors' clinical reports and often concluded that abortion inevitably caused trauma, posing a severe threat to psychological health. But some examples contested this view and presented evidence that disputed the dominant view (Sarvis and Rodman 1974).

The book *Therapeutic Abortion,* for example, first published in 1954, carried competing arguments from U.S. psychiatrists. The very title is interesting, in that it indicates that the subject matter for debate was abortion carried out legally by doctors where, according to the vast majority of state statutes at the time, abortion could be performed if the woman's life was considered at risk (the term "therapeutic abortion" is thus used in distinction to criminal "back-street" abortion). That a book was published on this subject indicates that the number of such therapeutic abortions was considered sufficient to merit discussion and that others should be encouraged to consider the issues they posed. This suggests that the prior medical consensus about abortion, in which it was considered immoral and rightly illegal in the vast majority of instances (Luker 1984; Linders 1998), had begun to fracture, which in part took the form of a dispute about the psychological effects of the procedure.

The prevailing attitude of the day was expressed by Dunbar, who argued that "the experience of abortion inevitably arouses an "unconscious sense of guilt," which he termed "post abortion hangover." Wilson, in an approach that prefigures the subsequent PAS claim, claimed similarly that women who undergo abortion are "traumatized by the act to such a degree that the memory becomes a potential factor in [their] future behavior." In contrast, however, psychiatry professor Theodore Lidz claimed that the dangers of abortion have been "overaccentuated," and that many women who have abortions experience "little disturbance" and "great relief." For Mandy also, psychiatrists often issue "exaggerated" and "frightening" warnings about the "frequency with which serious depressions may follow abortion," and "no attempt has been made to gather data on the thousands of women who had one or more induced abortions without suffering any ill effects" (Sarvis and Rodman 1974:107). In Britain, disagreements were also apparent. According to Ferris, evidence was "wildly conflicting" in discussion within the medical and psychiatric press (1966:118). Thus the psychiatrist Sim argued strongly that abortion tended to precipitate mental illness, whereas other psychiatrists tended toward considering abortion a form of psychological relief, rather than source of illness (Hordern 1971).

Differences of opinion were expressed in the literature from this point, up until the late 1960s, as changes occurred in the legal status of abortion. (In the United States, states began reforms in their local statutes around the same time as the law was reformed in Britain.) The overall picture at this time has been described as "rather confused and contradictory" (Sarvis and Rodman 1974:112). A summary of research literature on the subject from 1935 to 1964 by Simon and Senturia, subsequently considered to be the most comprehensive overview of published opinion from this time, concluded that "Deeply held personal convictions frequently seem to outweigh the importance of data. . . . In the papers reviewed the findings and conclusions range from the suggestion that psychiatric illness almost always is the outcome of therapeutic abortion to its virtual absence as a post-abortion complication" (Sarvis and Rodman 1974:112).

A New Consensus

As the debate about PAS indicates, by the mid-1980s, this lack of a consensus regarding the psychological aftermath of abortion in psychiatry, psychology, and medicine had been resolved in favor of those who disputed the idea that abortion results in mental illness. Claims made in the literature in the period in which this outcome was reached are dominated by one main theme: that those who claim that abortion has negative psychological effects base their argument on unscientific, anecdotal evidence. If arguments are to be made about the mental health effects of abortion, it was increasingly claimed, they must be based on science and evidence.

By the late 1960s in the United States, concern was increasingly expressed about the lack of "research-based evidence for a definitive answer," and several discussions of the issue "forcefully pointed out the contrast between the weak research data and the dogmatic positions taken on abortion" (Sarvis and Rodman 1974:105). Writing of studies from this time, the psychologists Illsley and Hall note that the opinion had become "widespread" that "past research in this field has been inadequate in scope, faulty in methodology, unsystematically organized, and in general motivated and directed towards problems posed by ideological rather than scientific considerations" (American Psychological Association 1987:5). According to Brewer, British psychiatrists in the late 1960s and 1970s viewed with caution the reports from the United States of the 1950s that emphasized the negative effects of abortion. Brewer claims that "British psychiatrists on the whole were not impressed with the alleged psychiatric dangers of abortion" and considered it necessary to carry out better designed studies (1978:2).

In the main, over the late 1960s and early 1970s, commentaries in both societies problematized reports from the past, which found that abortion inevitably causes mental illness, claiming they were based on small, anecdotal samples (Zimmerman 1981). Such studies were compared unfavorably with those adopting what was considered superior methodology. In this light, one study from the 1950s was widely discussed as the first exemplar of good research. This study, by the Swedish psychiatrist Ekblad, was praised because the sample of 470 Swedish women who underwent legal abortion in 1949–50 was larger than those in previous research. The research made an attempt to control for causality between abortion and postabortion psychological states, because Ekblad took into account variables that might have had an effect on a woman's feelings after abortion: including personality type, age, intellectual level, new pregnancy after abortion, previous pregnancies, influence of other people on the women's request for abortion, and relationship with male partner (Zimmerman 1981).

As well as criticizing past reports, studies accumulated in which the argument for the need for sound methodology was repeatedly made. In the United States, a burgeoning literature of this kind emerged through the late 1960s and 1970s. One bibliography lists 108 studies that appeared mainly in the 1970s, the majority of which are North American, and at least one of which was published in each of the major medical and psychiatric journals (Winter 1988). Criticisms made in such studies were that the assessment of women's mental state was often made through "clinical judgments," with almost no use made of "standardized procedures." A study by psychologist Henry David, a figure prominent in the subsequent debate about PAS, thus begins with the observation that the professional literature is "replete with clinical observations and assumptions about psychological aspects of abortion, but systematic studies are few and far between." David argued that the immense literature on the subject relied on "personal impressions" and that there was a "near total lack" of empirical studies (1972:61). Psychologist Nancy Adler, also prominent in the PAS debates, wrote in 1975 that studies of the after-effects of abortion were "based on insufficient evidence, and the conclusions reached were frequently slanted by the authors' own beliefs about abortion" (1975:446). It was claimed in particular that, because of the unscientific approach that had been taken, psychological problems that might be evident in women after abortion were mistakenly assumed to be the direct result of abortion. This perceived possible mistake in the attribution of cause and effect meant that the need to address the issue of causality between abortion and psychological difficulties women might have following abortion was emphasized, and the use of control groups or comparison groups was advocated (Zimmerman 1981:67). Adler argued that, however, by the early 1970s more attention had been paid to methodology, and that "there has been a shift away from the previously common view that abortion would frequently precipitate severe negative reactions" (1975:446).

In the British literature similar concerns were expressed. Studies from the years before the legalization of abortion were considered mainly irrelevant because of "often unacceptable methodological approaches" (Brewer 1976:1), and it was argued that the first significant British study of the psychological sequelae of abortion was published in 1966 (Lask 1975:173), because this was the first time a study was designed in such a way that its results could be considered scientific. Greer et al. justified their study of 360 British women carried out in 1971 and 1972 on the grounds that comment on the issue is "all too often [informed by] emotional rather than factual considerations" and that there is a "paucity of detailed, systematic data about the psychological and so-

cial sequelae of abortion" (1976:74). Their discussion emphasized the importance of paying attention to methods used to recruit participants and to the
scientific validity of the scales and measures chosen to assess women's feelings
and psychological responses. Brewer's study of women conducted over a fifteen-
month period in 1975 and 1976 emphasized the lack of precise figures from
existing studies of "post-abortion psychosis." Thus his data on 1,333,000
women were collected by twenty-one psychiatrists (a very large sample), and
Brewer highlighted that in the study, the kinds of symptoms to be looked for
were clearly defined ("a serious disorder requiring admission and manifesting
delusions and/or hallucinations, or gross overactivity") and that the partici-
pating psychiatrists were asked to record whether women had been admitted
to their care previously with such symptoms (1977). The size of the sample
and the design of the study have led this research to be subsequently referred
to as reliable, and its finding, that such symptoms were present in 0.3 women
per 1,000 who had had an abortion compared with 1.7 per 1,000 after delivery of a baby, has been referred to in many discussions since the study was
published.

Through the 1970s, the old orthodoxy was therefore undermined. A view
was emerging in which abortion was seen as having some negative effects for
some women, but only in the same way that other experiences might.
Women's negative feelings after abortion, by the mid-1970s, had come to be
increasingly considered "no more severe and possibly less severe than other
psychological states which women commonly experience." The U.S. psychiatrist Stephen Fleck thus argued that abortion was like other medical procedures, in that "every surgical operation, every inroad on a person's body, has
psychological elements or sequelae which may leave psychological scars"
(Sarvis and Rodman 1974:105).

Since the 1970s the issue of the need for watertight methodology has continued to feature strongly where the issue is discussed. For example, a 1995
report about a British study carried out by the Royal College of Obstetricians
and Gynaecologists and the Royal College of General Practitioners emphasized
that facets of its design were methodologically sound (Gilchrist et al. 1995).
The findings of the study, that abortion did not increase the risk of psychiatric
symptoms, were said to be valid because of the large sample of women used.
Other studies have been given approval for similar methodological reasons.
Use of a recognized test for psychological response is often mentioned as an
important aspect of a study design, and, significantly, the importance of dis-
tinguishing clearly between negative feelings and psychiatric problems has
also been frequently emphasized. In other instances, as I have argued, the idea
that there is a "continuum" of negative feelings, where negative emotional
states blur into medical conditions, has been *infrequently* criticized. By contrast, the effects of abortion have been subject to the demand for a rigorous ap-

proach on the part of researchers, and the argument has been made that negative feelings and mental illness must be clearly distinguished.

Women "at Risk"

Another kind of claim has also emerged, however. Although the notion that abortion does not constitute a psychological hazard in general has maintained its presence in the literature, studies have not presented abortion as always benign. Rather, concern has been expressed about how certain groups of women have come to be deemed "at risk" of emotional problems following abortion.

Claims regarding this issue first came to prominence in the mid-1970s. The argument that the negative psychological effects of abortion were less widespread and serious than previously thought "brought expressions of concern that perhaps the extent of abortion-related psychological distress was being underestimated" (Zimmerman 1981:68). Some researchers were concerned that they were not paying enough attention to the differences between women in their psychological response to abortion. It was argued that, although most women did not suffer psychologically following abortion, more needed to be known about factors leading to a negative psychological response in those who did report negative feelings. Some research became oriented toward studying "risk factors" in abortion, where the aim was to find out why some women had a psychological response to abortion that was different from that of others, or, as the American Psychological Association put it following the legalization of abortion in the United States: "investigations [were] designed to examine under what particular conditions women [were] more likely to respond positively or negatively to abortion" (1987:4). Looking back on research from this time, Dagg noted that the trend toward the liberalization of access to abortion had had an important effect on research, encouraging a move away from emphasizing the possible complications of the procedure and measuring their extent and severity, to use of "a model in which research examines the psychological sequelae and antecedents that affect a woman who seeks an abortion" (1991: 579). In other words, a focus developed that claimed to pay attention to the particular reasons why those women who did experience psychological sequelae did so.

One of the first studies to adopt this approach was carried out by Payne et al. (1976). It drew attention to differential levels of feelings of guilt at six weeks after abortion. Women who had been ambivalent about abortion and women with negative cultural or religious attitudes toward abortion were more likely to feel guilty than other women. Women with a poor relationship with their mothers were found to be more angry than other women following abortion, and women in unstable relationships were more depressed. The presence of social support systems was found in other research to have a positive effect upon how a woman felt after abortion (Brown and Harris 1978). A British study that was intended to build on existing research findings that abortion is generally psychologically benign or beneficial attempted to "identify those patients particularly at risk for such [negative] sequelae" (Lask 1975:173), and found that although "many patients clearly benefited from the termination," certain women were "at risk," such as those who already had children, had been deserted by their partner, or had previously had psychiatric illness. Sachdev drew mainly on U.S. reports to provide a more extensive list of variables that he thought influenced the psychological outcome of abortion: the woman's age, marital status, religion, attitude toward abortion and motherhood, circumstances of and reaction to her pregnancy, relationship with her sexual partner, parity, preexisting psychiatric conditions or morbid personality, gestational age, and concurrent sterilization (Sachdev 1981:63). In 1981, Zimmerman summarized the view held by U.S. researchers as "the growing recognition . . . that, while the psychological consequences of abortion are not nearly as serious and painful as previously thought, they emerge from a broader and more complex psychosocial process" (Zimmerman 1981:66). Thus, in addition to studying the woman and her emotional-psychological status, studies also examined the nature of her interpersonal relationships and social situation.

An overview of research carried out by psychiatrists Zolese and Blacker and published in 1992 restated the need for this approach, concluding that the emphasis for research should be upon certain groups who are "especially at risk from adverse psychological sequelae." These included those with previous psychiatric history, younger women, those with poor social support or previous pregnancies, and those who belonged to sociocultural groups antagonistic to abortion (1992:742). More recently, women who aborted a pregnancy on grounds of fetal abnormality have also been designated particularly "at risk" (Donnai and Harris 1981; Dagg 1991). The psychiatrist Ian Brockington writes approvingly of studies that have assessed factors that increase or decrease risk of negative psychological effects, such as those studies that assessed emotional states following abortion in adolescents, in women who had late terminations, and in women with religious convictions, and those studies that considered whether there were differential reactions according to the abortion method used (1996:89). The representation of abortion that appears in many advice books and leaflets written by medical professionals for women considering abortion reflects this approach. Thus Haslam writes, in an advice book for women who are considering abortion, "there is a sub-group of women who are less likely to have such an untroubled aftermath to their terminations" and lists women who have later abortions, multiple terminations or pre-existing psychiatric problems, and women who are adolescents, who lack support at home, or who have abortions for medical or genetic reasons as possibly "at risk" (1996:225).

In summary, by the time the PAS claim emerged (and indeed, the more general process of the expansion of PTSD claims), the medical field of "the psychological effects of abortion" was already well established. In this field it has been claimed in particular, arguably *in contrast* with the trend later emergent in claimsmaking about victims of PTSD, that careful distinctions needed to be made between negative feelings and mental illnesses. The point has also strongly made that the issue of causality, between abortion and women's feelings afterward, needs to be clearly addressed. This field has, as a result, comprised a body of research and opinion in which abortion has been construed as generally unthreatening to mental health, but with certain groups of women "at risk." In this light, it seems unsurprising that PAS claimants faced difficulties. It was perhaps to be predicted that, insofar as they could find resonance for PAS, it would relate only to a small number of women, those already deemed "at risk," but that a representation of women as generally likely to be traumatized by abortion would not get very far.

DEMEDICALIZATION?

The developments in scientific opinion about abortion described above have a context, however. The form of the argument that has been made, as the above discussion illustrated, has centered on what constitutes good research. But the new field of research that emerged in the late 1950s and has developed since, in which this argument has been made, was not the product of simple curiosity or academic interest. The claim that better research needed to be carried out has constituted, more or less explicitly, a rejection of the idea that abortion was generally unacceptable and has signaled an increasing openness to the possibility that it should be accepted, certainly in law and policy, as a necessary, justifiable medical procedure.

I now turn to examine some reasons why abortion came to be viewed in this way, as a legitimate procedure that should be permitted by regulatory frameworks. I discuss some reasons why, from the point of view of psychology, psychiatry, and medicine, abortion came to be viewed as a procedure a woman should be able to choose to have. What has it meant to claim that women should be able to choose to have an abortion? What is support for this idea, for medical and scientific opinion, constituted in? As the following discussion shows, such support for the idea of choice does not constitute an argument in which medical considerations are considered irrelevant. It is not the case, simply, that the matter of whether a pregnancy is ended, or not, has come to be viewed as a political issue—a question of women's rights—rather than a medical one. Rather, the issue of choice has been articulated by making a comparison between the medical effects of abortion, compared with continued pregnancies.

I make this case by considering the way in which a relationship between continued pregnancies and mental illness emerged in medical and scientific opinion, a process that has run in tandem with debates about the psychological effects of abortion. I argue that this relationship, which in itself can be considered an aspect of the medicalization of pregnancy, has constituted an important part of the reasons why medical opinion became and continues to be supportive of the idea that abortion should be socially accepted and legally available. I discuss this issue in regard to debates in Britain and the United States and highlight the differences between the two. I draw attention to some different ways in which, in Britain and in the United States, ideas developed in psychiatry and psychology have acted to legitimize abortion by problematizing the mental health effects of continued pregnancies. In doing so, I show how the issue of choice has featured differently in claims made in these two societies, drawing attention in particular to some reasons why support for the concept in a way that is more overtly political featured more in United States than in Britain. I show that in both societies, however, a key issue for medical opinion has been concern with the mental health effects of alternatives to abortion, and it is this that can help account for why such opinion has tended to make claims opposed to PAS.

Continued Pregnancies and Mental Illness

In debates about Postabortion Syndrome, as the previous chapter noted, PAS was disputed directly on the grounds of lack of evidence. An additional counterclaim, however, disputed it indirectly by claiming that *continued pregnancies* posed the real threat to women's mental health. For example, the Rawlinson Commission report (1994) stated that those who gave evidence that the psychological effects of abortion were not a major health problem drew attention to the psychological effects of pregnancy and childbirth. Representing the Royal College of Psychiatrists, Dr. Margaret Oates gave evidence that she considered childbirth to be the biggest risk to the mental health of a woman, and that psychological problems resulting from abortion were few in comparison. British psychiatrist Colin Brewer stated that "his own study . . . showed that abortion results in less risk of psychological consequences than does pregnancy" (Rawlinson 1994:11).

Such counterclaims, as well as those that attest to the psychological safety of abortion, constitute a change of opinion. Mainstream medical opinion in Britain up until even the mid-1960s represented continued pregnancy as almost always psychologically desirable for women. In 1966, the Royal College of Obstetricians and Gynaecologists published a report titled *Legalised Abortion: Report of the Council of the RCOG,* in which it argued that "There are few women, no matter how desperate they may be to find themselves with an unwanted pregnancy, who do not have regrets at losing it." The report went on to suggest that these feelings of regret were a "fundamental reaction, governed by maternal instinct . . . mollified if the woman realises the abortion was essential to her life but if the indication for the termination of pregnancy was flimsy and fleeting she may suffer from a sense of guilt for the rest of her life. The incidence of *serious* permanent psychiatric sequelae is variously reported as being between 9 and 59 per cent" (Simms and Hindel 1971:52; Ferris 1966:118). By contrast medical bodies in the United States were, for reasons I discuss later on, by the 1960s, advocates of abortion law reform. However, this position constituted a major shift from that held previously.

Luker (1984), in her ground-breaking study of the abortion problem in the United States, describes the medical profession as the first "Right to Life" movement and traces the central role played by physicians' organizations in moving abortion's place in the law from one governed by no statute laws at the start of the nineteenth century to a procedure regulated by the criminal law in every state in the union 100 years later. Luker contends that the most clearly identifiable aspect of the process through which change in the legal status of abortion came about was the work of a "visible interest group agitating for more restrictive abortion laws . . . composed of elite or 'regular' physicians, which actively petitioned state legislatures to pass anti-abortion laws" (1984:15). The new laws advocated by doctors were harsh (and very similar to those in Britain): abortion was forbidden at any stage of pregnancy except to save a woman's life, and not only the person who carried out the abortion, but in most states the woman herself faced the prospect of criminal prosecution. The reasons for the development of these laws, advocated by doctors, have been discussed in detail by Luker and others (Mohr 1978; Linders 1998), but in part, as Linders points out, they were based on the idea that "in the United States, abortion was construed as a direct violation of motherhood" (1998: 498). Doctors and their organizations in the United States defended such laws until the 1940s. According to Alan Guttmacher, one of the most prominent advocates of legal abortion through the 1960s and 1970s, his experience of the 1920s and 1930s was that "obstetricians and gynaecologists were the most conservative medical group in regard to abortion" (1973:65). Their aim was to keep the incidence of abortion as low as possible, and they did not consider the legal framework to be a problem.

Psychiatry has taken, in general, a more liberal approach to abortion provision than gynecology (or general medicine). According to Hordern this difference of opinion is a reflection of the contrasting roles that different professionals have played in providing abortion. Psychiatrists, since they play no actual role in performing abortion procedures, have tended to have "less compunction about recommending termination," whereas the gynecologist "takes part in the actual physical process" and thus is likely to find the issue of abortion "more disturbing" (1971:23). Luker (1984) makes a rather different case, that opposition to abortion by doctors on moral grounds in the

United States was a means through which the authority of medical profession was established. This argument would suggest that the view that abortion is ethically problematic has a particular historical and social context, and does not relate only to the fact that gynecologists perform abortions. Whichever explanation of the difference in approach is correct, psychiatrists (and psychologists), unlike gynecologists and other members of the medical profession, justified the performance of abortion earlier and more frequently than their colleagues.

Nonetheless, as noted above, it was still the case that until the 1950s, psychiatrists often considered abortion likely to cause psychological problems for women, and they viewed continued pregnancy favorably. Psychiatric opinion was often deemed to provide evidence that abortion would harm women, on the grounds that ending pregnancy violates the appropriate or "natural" role of women in society. For example, Bolter argued of such opinion in the United States:

> Despite protests to the contrary, we know women's main role here on earth is to conceive, deliver, and raise children. Despite all other sublimated types of activities, this is still their primary role. When this function is interfered with, we see all sorts of emotional disorders. . . . This is not just textbook theory, as those who practice psychiatry know very well (Sarvis and Rodman 1974:103).

Galdston argued similarly, in 1958:

> . . . from the psychiatrist's viewpoint the strivings that animate the female can best be understood in terms of the functioning of the uterus. The uterus is the main rationale of the *biological female*, and this is not new or novel, but is very ancient knowledge. . . . Drawing upon my experience I would summate the major psychological effects in three terms: frustration, hostility, and guilt. . . . I would subsume abortion as a form of sterility associated with profound biological and socio-economic pathology (Sarvis and Rodman 1974:104, emphasis in the original).

According to Zimmerman, such views were based on the framework of Freudian psychology, dominant in psychiatry in the United States at the time, where a rejection of the wish for motherhood was considered to be an indicator of abnormal psychological adjustment, which led to mental disturbance (1981:66).

In Britain, Freudian concepts were less influential, but accounts of psychiatric opinion from the time indicate that abortion was, as in the United States, considered problematic by some psychiatrists. Journalist Paul Ferris (1966), author of a widely referenced account of abortion in Britain before the law was reformed, commented that some psychiatrists at this time gave abortionists the "legal loophole" they needed for an abortion to be performed legally, by deeming continued pregnancy in women requesting abortion to be a risk to life and health, and thus legal under the existing statute and case law (an issue discussed in more detail below). This practice was strongly attacked explicitly by some, however, of whom Dr. Myre Sim, a psychiatrist from Birmingham, was the most prominent (Hordern 1971; Francome 1984; Ferris 1966). He claimed, in articles published in the medical press through the 1950s and 1960s, that psychiatrists were under pressure to justify legal abortion on psychiatric grounds (to argue that abortion should be legal because it was necessary to prevent the psychiatric illness caused by unwanted pregnancy) but that through such a demand, "psychiatrists are expected to disregard the clinical facts in order to satisfy a desire for a social reform . . . [abortion] cannot be to prevent mental illness, for abortion is not a prophylactic against psychosis but rather a precipitant" (Ferris 1966:90).

The debate about PAS suggests, however, that, as far as *majority* medical and psychiatric opinion is concerned, by the 1980s this issue had come to be resolved in favor of those who consider alternatives to abortion a possible cause of mental health problems. The idea that continuing a pregnancy is almost always better, from the point of view of its effects on women's mental health, than having an abortion had become strongly rejected in medical opinion. The claim that that childbearing is always psychologically desirable had come to be considered highly questionable.

The influence of such ideas about the potentially detrimental effects of continued pregnancy for women's mental health is, in fact, identifiable in debates about the law in the late 1960s. By this point, an association between some continued pregnancies and mental health problems had been established. In Britain, the wording of the new statute passed in 1967 makes this very clear. As Chapter 3 discussed, abortion was made legal on explicitly medicalized grounds. Most significant of these grounds was the provision that abortion could be legally performed where two doctors agree in good faith that the *continuation* of the pregnancy represents a *greater threat* to the physical or *mental health* of the woman than if the pregnancy is terminated. To put it another way, in the terms of the 1967 Abortion Act, bearing a child was constructed as a potentially greater risk to a woman's mind (and body) than having an abortion (the circumstances in which this was the case were to be decided by two doctors through consideration of the grounds for abortion set out in the Abortion Act), and abortion was made legal on this basis.

In Britain, there was no suggestion that a woman should be able to have an abortion because it was her right. Although the rationale for legal access to abortion set out in the United States in *Roe v. Wade* made abortion a woman's right, here, too, the claim that the alternative to abortion was risky for a woman's mind clearly affected this Supreme Court ruling. Although, in contrast to Britain, medical testimony that a woman's mind may be harmed by continuing a pregnancy was not construed a *requirement* for legal abortion, the idea that unwanted childbearing was a mental health problem was discussed as a *justification* for the change in the law. Justice Blackmun, author of the key justification for the ruling, thus explained the decision to consider the "right of privacy . . . broad enough to encompass a woman's decision whether or not to terminate her pregnancy" through reference to the "psychological harm" caused by unwanted pregnancy, the "distress of an unwanted child," and "the difficulties of bringing an unwanted child into a family" (Schneider and Vinovskis 1980:xix). Argued Blackmun:

> Maternity, or additional offspring, may force upon the woman a distressful life and future. Psychological harm may be imminent. Mental and physical health may be taxed by child care. There is also the distress, for all concerned, associated with the unwanted child, and there is the problem of bringing a child into a family already unable, psychologically and otherwise, to care for it. . . . All these are factors the woman and her responsible physician necessarily will consider in consultation.

These claims about continued pregnancies suggest that ideas about why women should be able to have legal abortion were connected with concern about the psychological effects of its alternatives. Ideas about this aspect of the outcome of pregnancies had come to be included as part of the regulatory framework for abortion. The discussion that follows shows in more detail how and why this construction of the justification for abortion emerged and has developed subsequently, in turn providing increasing support, on medicalized grounds, for legal abortion.

BRITAIN

The 1967 Abortion Act, as noted above, states that a pregnancy can be terminated if two doctors agree that continuing it could represent a greater threat to the (physical and) mental health of the woman than if the pregnancy were terminated. This indicates that, by 1967, the idea that carrying a pregnancy to term was a "mental health problem" was already important, to the extent that it became recognized in law as a key plank of the new legislation. How and why did the mental health effects of continuing a pregnancy become considered grounds for abortion in Britain? In what sense, by this time, was doing so considered possibly more problematic than abortion, and for what reasons?

The Psychiatric Exception

One specific development, a legal case, has been considered important in paving the way for including mental health as a ground for abortion in Britain in 1967 (Simms and Hindel 1971; Francome 1984; Hordern 1971; Ferris 1969). This case, which came to court in 1938, centered on the actions of

Dr. Aleck Bourne, and its significance has been considered to be that it made clear that a woman's mental state could be considered as important as her physical state in assessing the merits of abortion requests. It was important because it led to the recognition by the law of the "psychiatric exception" for abortion.

Bourne had been charged with committing a criminal offense, after performing an abortion on a 14-year-old girl who had become pregnant after being raped by soldiers. The girl was first denied an abortion, but after Dr. Bourne observed her for eight days he considered her to be in dire need of termination of pregnancy. He found she underwent "complete breakdown. . . . This decided me at once that she had to be relieved of her pregnancy" (Simms and Hindel 1971:70). In order to generate discussion of the issue in the courts, Bourne deliberately provoked the police into arresting him, by alerting them to the fact that he had performed the abortion. He was acquitted without charge, and in the ruling the judge, Justice McNaughten, argued that it was legal to terminate a pregnancy to safeguard a woman's mental health and prevent her from becoming "a physical and mental wreck" (Simms and Hindel 1971:13). In his summing up, the judge stated that too narrow a view must not be taken of the words to "save the life" of the woman, the only ground for abortion specified in the statute law (Francome 1984:70).

Bourne was not the first doctor to argue publicly that continuation of a pregnancy could threaten a woman's mental health, that it could be as damaging, if not more, to a woman's health for a pregnancy to be continued as to be ended. As early as 1926, a consultant at the Charing Cross Hospital had argued at the British Medical Association annual meeting that doctors must consider whether they have the right "to insist that a woman shall pass through an ordeal she is unwilling to face" (Simms and Hindel 1971:68). However, following Bourne, the greater degree of legal recognition of this idea meant that grounds for legal abortion could be interpreted as a severe threat to *mental health,* not just to a woman's *life.* Whereas before Bourne, an abortion could be preformed where a psychiatrist attested that the women's life was at risk because she may commit suicide if the pregnancy were not ended, after Bourne the additional argument could be made that the risk of her becoming a "mental wreck" was sufficient. According to Cohan, through the Bourne judgment, "by adding the term, mental, to physical, the concept of the lawful abortion was expanded by the judges" (1986:37).

This judgment did not result in large numbers of doctors prepared to perform abortions on this basis. The medical profession remained dominantly antiabortion, and the procedure remained a criminal offense according to statute law. Between the Bourne judgment and the passing of the 1967 Abortion Act, it has been estimated that the number of abortions performed legally remained a small proportion of the total—one estimate suggests that 100,000–150,000 criminal abortions were performed annually, against a total of 10,000 legal procedures (Greenwood and Young 1976). However, where doctors were prepared to perform abortions on medical grounds, they could use the judgment as the justification for doing so. Insofar as the practice of legal abortion took place before 1967, it was, therefore, done on this basis, and as negative attitudes toward abortion lessened after the Second World War, abortion was more frequently performed to assist women's mental health.

The psychiatrist Hordern (1971) notes in his account of abortion before 1967, for example, that some gynecologists were prepared to use the precedent of the Bourne judgment to abort women where a psychiatrist would express the opinion that the continuation of the pregnancy would be deleterious to the mental health of the woman. He claims that, by the time the law was amended in 1967, evidence suggested that 90 percent of abortions legally performed in Britain were carried out on psychiatric grounds, and that psychiatrists in Britain "had developed a flexible attitude towards termination of pregnancy." This constituted a significant change from practice before Bourne and even through the 1940s, where psychiatric grounds for abortion were generally restricted to the possibility of severe or irreversible psychosis or imminent danger of suicide (Hordern 1971:80). Ferris argued in 1969 that "the scope for legal abortion can be seen to have grown enormously since the Bourne case. . . . 'Socio-economic factors' and 'social stress' can be taken to mean almost anything," he stated (1969:92). Simms and Hindel note than between 1958 and 1967, the number of therapeutic abortions carried out in the NHS hospitals in England and Wales rose from 1,600 to 9,700 per year (1971:49), and Hordern explains that in these cases, the indication for abortion would frequently be psychiatric—that continuation of the pregnancy was a mental health risk (1971:5).

The fact that abortion was legally available on this basis before the 1967 Abortion Act was passed does not detract from the significance of this statute. Despite the Bourne judgment, there was much confusion about the law, and a general climate of opposition to abortion within medicine remained. Many doctors would not perform abortions, because a lower court ruled on the Bourne case and did not, therefore, overturn the statute under which abortion was still criminalized. Nonetheless the Bourne judgment and the practice it made legitimate did mean that before 1967, the idea and practice of abortion on the grounds that pregnancy was a threat to mental health, and that continued pregnancy could be considered a significant mental health risk, had some currency.

Changing Constructions of "Mental Health"

The Bourne judgment facilitated the provision of legal abortion through the "psychiatric exception," but the propensity of psychiatrists to testify that it should be provided for this reason was encouraged by broader developments. One of these was changes in the understanding of health and illness, which encouraged acceptance of the idea that continuing a pregnancy could be considered a problem not only because of its effects for physical health, but also because of its relationship to the woman's state of mind.

According to Boyle, during the second half of the twentieth century an accepted system of thought emerged in Britain that allowed the incorporation of a wide range of behaviors and psychological experiences into the notion of health. Previously, the idea of psychiatric grounds as a justification for legal or medical intervention tended to be viewed as little more than an excuse for wrongdoing (Boyle 1997:17). However, by the 1950s, this perception had shifted, and certainly by the time the Mental Health Act was passed in 1959 it was clear that a new cultural norm had emerged, in which there was "widening [of] the range of behaviour and experiences that were seen as falling within the remit of 'mental ill-health.' . . . in the 1960s, a much broader interpretation of 'psychological harm' could be made without it appearing, at least to the majority, that the boundaries of medicine were being breached" (Boyle 1997:18). By the time the 1967 Abortion Act was passed there was, therefore, already a legal framework and cultural norm in place in which "physical and mental health held identical status as medical reasons for abortion; it was simply that different factors needed to be taken into account in judging whether these reasons were present in a particular case" (Boyle 1997:65). Before 1967, psychiatrists could rely on their professional status to justify their authorization of abortion—as Ferris pointed out, "the power to mould it [the law] springs from the psychiatrist's freedom of judgement. He is the one who has been able to say, 'I think this woman's mental health will break down if she is forced to have this child'" (1969:88). But greater acceptance in general of the problem of mental ill health, broadly defined, gave them legitimacy in doing so.

This broad definition of health, in particular the elasticity of the concept of mental health, according to Chriss (1999), is not confined to British society. He argues that this approach to health was characteristic of industrialized societies in the post–Second World War period. He contends that, impelled by the establishment of the World Health Organization in the 1940s and its definition of health, in which health is defined as "a state of complete physical and social well-being and not merely the absence of disease or infirmity," the medical and health professions came to consider that areas of life that previously fell outside their remit should be included within it. In order to assist in the development of "a state of complete physical and social well-being," it was not enough simply to be concerned with a limited range of physical illnesses. Thus medical practice was extended to include "not only the clinic and the hospital, but also the home, churches, schools, prisons, business, and government" (Chriss 1999:7–8). The effect of this ethos in relation to pregnancy, in the United States as well as Britain, was also to encourage the idea that pregnancy and childbearing could be considered "mental health" problems.

Unwanted Children and Mental Health

A third factor, which expressed a broadened definition of health and illness, was the growing perception that "unwanted childbearing" was a significant problem. In particular, the idea that certain women who bore children would prove unable to care for them properly had emerged as an important concern, and this was expressed in relation to mothers' mental ill health. This idea was evident in parliamentary debate about the bill that became the 1967 Abortion Act.

Supporters of abortion law reform, while agreeing that motherhood was ideally the desirable end to pregnancy, made it clear that in some circumstances this was not the case. According to David Owen, then Labour Member of Parliament for Plymouth, abortion was legitimate for the woman "in total misery" who "could be precipitated into a depression deep and lasting. What happens to that woman when she gets depressed? She is incapable of looking after those children, so she retires into a shell of herself and loses all feeling, all drive and affection" (Sheldon 1997:21). This approach is more apparent in the following comment, from Dr. John Dunwoody (Labour MP for Falmouth and Camborne): "My belief is that in many cases today where we have over-large families the mother is so broken down physically and emotionally with the continual bearing of children that it becomes quite impossible for her to fulfil her real function, her worthwhile function as a mother" (Sheldon 1997:21). Abortion was construed as an option for a certain type of woman. She was already a mother, but was also "worn down" physically and emotionally and so could not cope with another child sufficiently well to be a good mother. Articulated in Parliament by proponents of abortion law reform, this argument about the problem of childbearing had significant currency in medical and particularly psychiatric opinion.

Within medical opinion, as discussed above, the majority was still opposed to law reform in the mid-1960s. Among psychiatrists, however, the acceptance of abortion on such mental health grounds was fairly widespread by the 1960s, and abortion was openly advocated on this basis. For example, Professor Anderson, a leading English psychiatrist, claimed that "termination was often indicated in asthenic women with a poor reaction to stress, the so-called 'worn-out mothers'" (Hordern 1971:81). Writing of psychiatry in the 1960s, Hordern, himself a psychiatrist, argued that abortion was not only justified because of the problem unwanted pregnancy represented for women, but also because of its effects on the child to be born. Many psychiatrists, he claimed, agreed with abortion because "from the standpoint of the unwanted child . . .

[there is] the overwhelming handicap of being born unwelcome into a hostile and rejecting environment. These factors make the average psychiatrist favour therapeutic termination of unwanted pregnancies and made him eager to reform the law to this end" (Hordern 1971:24). Psychiatrists considered the law prohibiting abortion to be a problem because it reflected "insufficient concern for the welfare of the child" and lack of interest in the "sociological effect of bringing unwanted children into the world in bad physical circumstances—an action that was illogical in view of the acknowledged contribution of bad homes to delinquency" (Hordern 1971:126).

In 1966, the first "authoritative general statement of British psychiatric opinion" appeared when the "Memorandum on Therapeutic Abortion" was published by the Royal Medico-Psychological Association in the *British Journal of Psychiatry*. It stated that therapeutic abortion should be legal and argued that if, after taking into account medical, psychiatric, and all social circumstances, "a psychiatrist should form the opinion that the mental health of the mother and the whole family would be promoted by termination, then it should be lawful for him to recommend it." According to Hordern, Professor Ferguson Roger explained the thinking behind this recommendation in an article published in 1966 in the *American Journal of Psychiatry*. This article considered whether it could ever be in the interests of the child to be destroyed before birth. Roger concluded that, although it ran in contradiction to traditional religious thinking, this was the case because "as a result of an abortion not being carried out, the child might not be able to enjoy the health and happiness to which it was entitled" (Hordern 1971:28). Support for the viewpoint put forward in the memorandum was clear when 300 senior psychiatrists in Britain were circulated with questions regarding abortion law reform. Of the first 100 replies, 24 thought that abortion should be freely available to all women, 56 that indications for abortion should be based on evaluation including the mother's social circumstances, and 16 that existing case law (the Bourne judgment that allowed for abortion on mental health grounds) should be included in the statute.

By the 1960s, British psychiatrists had, therefore, come to claim that unwanted childbearing was a mental health problem. The effects of unwanted children were viewed, in the main, as adverse to both mother and child. "They contrast strikingly," argued one psychiatrist, "with the results of therapeutic abortion, which are usually excellent, especially where abortion is performed early in pregnancy" (Hordern 1971:55). For women, unwanted pregnancy was considered a burden that would impair their ability to mother the resulting child. "A depressive state with anxiety is much the commonest response to an unwanted pregnancy; the symptoms may be severe and, as in all depressive illnesses, there is a risk of suicide," argued Hordern (ibid:57). For the child, as the "maternal attachment" thesis of John Bowlby was considered to have demonstrated, unwanted children in such circumstances faced severe difficulties. One psychiatrist drew the conclusion that the "lack of affection and emotional security . . . can have the most deleterious psychological consequences. Better perhaps not to be born than to come unwanted into a world where there is no assurance of affection" (Hordern 1971:60).

Mental Health and Childbearing since the 1970s

The three factors discussed above were all important in informing the development of regulations relating to abortion provision in Britain, in which abortion was justified in relation to the mental health effects of continued pregnancies. How has this problem been discussed subsequently? First, the construction of unwanted pregnancy as a problem, framed in terms of its mental health effects, has pertained. In 1982, writing in the *British Journal of Clinical Psychology,* Handy noted that the psychological effects of unwanted pregnancy have been the subject of much discussion since the early 1970s. Studies have addressed this issue by comparing effects of denied abortion resulting in unwanted childbirth with abortion for women and their children; Handy (1982) refers to such studies published in 1970, 1971, 1974, and 1976. Overall investigations of this kind have found that "the psychological and social consequences of refused abortion are frequently more serious than the consequences of abortion," since the health of mothers of unwanted children suffers, as does the development of their children. Urquart and Templeton, influential members of the RCOG, wrote in 1991 that whereas the evidence attesting to the psychological safety of abortion was abundant and definitive, the effects of unwanted pregnancy were a cause for concern. They note that fears that the widespread availability and use of abortion might lead to emotional problems "have not been borne out by studies either in this country or the USA." They note also, however, that unwanted childbirth "may have a detrimental effect on the mother's mental health, and also on the emotional, social and intellectual development of children born after a refused abortion request" (1991:396).

Second, the effects for children have been increasingly emphasized, on the grounds that child development is impaired when a child is not planned for and wanted. Delinquency, criminal behavior, and alcoholism are considered to be problems that result from children being born in such circumstances (Handy 1982:39). For psychiatrist Colin Brewer unwanted childbearing, unlike abortion, could lead to psychiatric problems for women, and "apart from the effects of unwanted childbirth on the mother, we must not forget the effects on her family." He argued that abortion should be welcomed for its role in preventing mental illness and social problems: "It is said that as many as a third of all births are not really wanted, which means that abortion is probably a valuable prophylactic agent" (1976:1). Psychiatrist Ian Brockington's claims typify those made by proponents of the problem of unwanted child-bearing. An advocate of the argument that mental illness in mothers generally is a very serious social problem, he argues that "[puerperal psychosis] is not the only mental illness that complicates pregnancy. Much commoner, and arguably more serious in their effects, are depression and mother-infant relationship disorders. These may be more common and severe after unwanted pregnancy" (1996:85).

It may be that such ideas about the relative problems of the mental health effects of abortion, and those of unwanted pregnancy, partly explain why abortion has become more and more accessible to British women on mental health grounds. The ground for abortion under which a pregnancy can be legally terminated in Britain, where two doctors agree that continuing the pregnancy represents a threat to the woman's health, has turned out to be by far the most commonly used since 1967. A report from the Office for National Statistics that reviewed abortions from 1974 to 1980 found that 86 percent were performed for this reason (Haslam 1996). Over 98 percent of the abortions currently carried out in England and Wales are done on such health grounds (Royal College of Obstetricians and Gynaecologists 2000:10).

In part, the relatively greater threat to physical health posed by childbirth, as compared with early abortion, has allowed doctors to judge just about any first trimester abortion legal. As the medical doctor David Haslam has argued of the characteristic approach of medical judgment, since the vast majority of women who request abortions do so in the first ten weeks of pregnancy, it can be argued that in all cases where the woman is in good health, continuing a pregnancy is more risky than having an abortion: "[S]tatistically at least, almost any woman requesting an early termination of pregnancy will have good grounds under existing law for this to be carried out" (1996:78). The concept of "risk to a woman's mental health" that is considered to be posed by continuing an unwanted pregnancy has also encouraged the provision of abortion. As the renowned gynecologist David Paintin has argued, "the Act can be interpreted so that abortion can be provided virtually on request" because of the mental health clause (1998:17). The way in which the Abortion Act is now interpreted in Britain is undoubtedly different from the interpretation envisaged by those who advocated legal reform in 1967. At that time, it was a minority of doctors who broadly interpreted the "threat to mental health" posed by unwanted pregnancy, and most in the medical profession were opposed to extending the grounds for legal abortion. However, it may be that the perception that it is important to avoid unwanted childbearing, already articulated at that time, has become a far more commonplace assumption, and it is this which facilitates the current provision of abortion to British women on such mental health grounds.

THE UNITED STATES

In the United States, the construction of continued pregnancy as a mental health issue is not central to the legal regulation of the procedure in the way it is in Britain. However, this does not mean that the idea that abortion can be justified on mental health grounds has not been important. As I detail below, it is arguable that the case for abortion on the grounds of the "psychiatric exception," in the context of the legal framework in the United States, played a crucial role in generating the demand for the decriminalization of abortion and the repeal of restrictive laws. From the 1960s, the case for abortion on mental health grounds was, as in Britain, also increasingly argued through reference to the problem of continued pregnancies from the mental health point of view and has played an important role in legitimizing abortion ever since.

The Psychiatric Exception

As in Britain, the idea that continued pregnancy constitutes a psychiatric risk was used as an indication for abortion before its legalization in the United States, although there was little consensus about how this ground should be defined. Obstetrician Alan Guttmacher, a leader of the later campaign for legal abortion in the 1960s, noted that in the 1920s the accepted view within the medical profession was that therapeutic abortion should be performed very rarely and avoided if at all possible, and that in his experience, psychiatric grounds were almost nonexistent. The only possible justifications for abortion at that time, put forward during Guttmacher's medical education, involved "threats of dysfunction in three organs, the heart, the lung and the kidney." "No medical sanction" where he was taught medicine "was then given to abortion on socio-economic or psychological grounds" (1973:63). Other accounts suggest that abortion was available on psychiatric grounds, but that it was considered necessary to define the psychiatric indication very strictly. For example, in 1929 one commentary stated that possible psychiatric indications for abortion included preexisting psychosis, schizophrenia, recurrent psychosis, severe anxiety and depressions, which could be used to determine the cases in which abortion was, or was not, appropriate (Sarvis and Rodman 1974:77). Discussion of the issue in the *Journal of the American Medical Association* and the *American Journal of Obstetrics and Gynaecology,* however, indicated that that some physicians assumed that abortions were acceptable to preserve not only the life, but the health, of the woman, including her mental health (Luker 1984:47).

Before the 1940s, there was little pressure to bring such differential and inconsistent views about the grounds for abortion to a head. Insofar as psychiatric grounds were considered to pertain, it is clear that they were still secondary to the dominant rationale for legal abortion at that time, which was the threat a continued pregnancy might pose to a woman's physical health. According to Shaw, even in the mid-1940s, there were still forty-four separate diseases and conditions listed as indications for therapeutic abortion in the New York Lying-in Hospital (1969:66). From the 1940s, however, psychiatrists were increasingly called upon to authorize abortion on medical grounds; to verify that the women's life would be placed at risk if the pregnancy were not terminated. According to most accounts, the main basis for this propensity for psychiatric risk to become relatively more important was the reduction in indications for abortion on physical grounds. As medicine improved, very swiftly after the Second World War, the physical risk posed by childbirth became more and more remote, and, Shaw argues, by the late 1960s had "faded to vanishing point" (Shaw 1969:67). By this time, therapy and cures existed for many conditions that previously would have posed a serious risk to the life of the pregnant woman had her pregnancy continued. Thus a strictly medical argument as to why abortion should be carried out on this basis was difficult to make. Insofar as physicians were prepared to consider abortion requests, therefore, they came to look to psychiatry to attest to the risks that continuing a pregnancy represented.

Writing of the 1960s, one commentator argued that thousands of legal abortions were performed each year, and that "Since medical advances have made it possible for women with almost any kind of physical illness to survive pregnancy and childbirth, the only way that abortions can be legally justified as 'necessary to preserve life' is on psychiatric grounds" (Schwartz 1973:141). Fleck claimed similarly that as medical and surgical care had advanced, indications for abortion on this basis became rare. Demand for abortion continued, however, "and the usual statutory requirements that the life of the woman must be threatened before an abortion . . . have brought to the fore the contingency of self-destructive behavior induced by the pregnant state as an 'indication' for abortion" (1973:184).

The practice of psychiatrists authorizing legal abortion in this way had important effects for the process of abortion law reform in the United States. The provision of legal abortion in practice was very similar to that in Britain, but with the notable difference that there was no equivalent of the Bourne ruling to justify this provision legally. It remained the case that abortion was *illegal* unless the woman's life was considered at risk, yet in reality abortion was provided on broadly defined psychiatric grounds. Both those opposed to and those sympathetic to abortion criticized this situation, but a common point made was that there was a problematic disparity between law and practice. According to Luker, "the improvements in medical and obstetrical care [in the 1950s and 1960s] therefore planted the seeds of a crisis within the medical profession" (1984:55).

This emergent crisis had important effects for the development of the regulation of access to abortion. It led first to the development of "various approval systems" in individual hospitals, of which the "therapeutic abortion committee," pioneered in 1945 by Alan Guttmacher, became the most popular (Sarvis and Rodman 1974:37). Such committees were staffed by varying numbers of medical personnel, often an obstetrician and a psychiatrist among others, in an attempt to generate consensus and agreement about accepted grounds for abortion, and in particular to smooth over tensions between psychiatrists and others. Luker (1984) argues, however, that these measures in effect delayed confronting the problem, rather than resolving it. Many who have commented on the practice of such committees through the 1950s and 1960s have noted that hospitals adopted widely varying interpretations of law, leading to the establishment of separate therapeutic abortion policies and procedures in each. Some took a liberal approach. For example, a 1959 study based on a questionnaire to the chiefs of obstetrical service in twenty-nine hospitals in the San Francisco and Los Angeles areas found that physicians were prepared to authorize and perform abortion on medical grounds that stretched far beyond those justified by the therapeutic exception of the threat to life allowed under California law (Sarvis and Rodman 1974:36). One hospital had defined the ground of threat to mental health in terms that included only "overtly psychotic or highly suicidal" patients to begin with, but which later moved to adopt a different view of mental health, as "a disorder of thinking, feeling or behaviour producing a breakdown in living so that the individual cannot deal with reality or cannot function in dealing with daily problems of living" (Sarvis and Rodman 1974:43). In other cases, hospitals would only authorize a small number of requests, by requiring a unanimous vote from all committee members, and there are many accounts of the numbers of abortions performed in hospitals falling dramatically after such a committee was established.

Supporters of abortion provision criticized this situation as discriminatory and claimed that it was a way of making sure abortion did not become normalized. It was described as a "smokescreen behind which sexual discrimination flourishes" (Sarvis and Rodman 1974:37). Even for those who did not support abortion, however, the obvious lack of agreement across medicine and psychiatry about the grounds for abortion generated discomfort. The perception that the situation was problematic, and could not continue, was acute among those who were most at the "coal face" of the problem—psychiatrists. Whether opposed to or supportive of abortion, there was a shared view that psychiatry was being discredited as a result of the situation that had emerged. The psychiatrist Richard Schwartz, for example, wrote angrily that since "there are no guidelines indicating whether the risk of suicide has to be 100, 50, or 1 per cent" in order for abortion to be justified, in practice the psychiatrist was reliant on his own views in making a recommendation, rather than on an agreed medical definition. Schwartz argued that four different groups of psychiatrists had developed, one that would have nothing to do with abortion, on grounds that society should decide whether abortion should be permitted or not, rather than "evade the decision" by delegating to psychiatrists; a second that refused to participate, but on religious or moral grounds; a third that considered the situation "hypocritical and unfair" but consulted with women because they considered that not to do so would be unethical, and therefore would reluctantly authorize abortions; and a fourth that believed abortion to be very necessary for women and would "authorize abortions in cases where they believe the risk of suicide is minimal or nonexistent" (1973:142–3).

The division between law and practice was thus perceived as a great problem, and, as Sarvis and Rodman noted of the late 1960s, "Whatever the abortion statute says and whatever practices have evolved, the split between the law and practice has become an outstanding feature of the abortion controversy" (1974:28). Luker (1984) argues that at the center of this controversy was a breakdown in the consensus about abortion. Its past status as an illegal procedure was held together by agreement within the medical profession that abortion was morally unjustifiable other than in very rare, medically defined circumstances. As long as abortion remained viewed this way, it remained hidden from public debate or contest. Questioning the extent of the medical dangers of abortion constituted a powerful impulse to fracture this consensus and drive abortion into the realm of public debate.

For psychiatry and medicine specifically, the tension between law and practice arguably pushed those involved in these professions in a reformist direction, in a way that was not evident in Britain. The absence of a "legal loophole" such as the Bourne ruling meant that the contradiction between the legal status of abortion and its provision on mental health grounds was starkly posed, and it may be that this impelled medical and psychiatric organizations to involve themselves in arguments for legal reform. For example, Niswander, a doctor prominent in debates about law reform in the United States, argued that before its legalization, psychiatrists were "at the forefront of the fight to expand grounds for legal abortion." Schwartz claims that "ordinary" psychiatrists, not just the leaders of their professional organizations, had come to adopt "a liberal position in the [abortion] debate, favouring repeal of traditional, restrictive abortion laws" (1973:139).

The proposals for law reform took a number of forms. Some involved in medicine and psychiatry gave their support to the proposal from the American Law Institute for a Model Penal Code, first drawn up in 1959. This code, much like the law passed in 1967 in Britain, rested on the idea that

A licensed physician is justified in terminating a pregnancy if he believes there is substantial risk that continuance of the pregnancy would gravely impair the physical or mental health of the mother, or that the child would be born with grave physical or mental defect, or that the pregnancy resulted from rape, incest, or other felonious intercourse. (Sarvis and Rodman 1974:40–1)

This kind of approach to law reform was taken up in a number of states in the late 1960s, which passed "reform laws," in which while abortion remained criminalized, the law protected physicians providing it where they did so on medical grounds. For some, however, the approach of "repeal laws" passed at the same time in other states, through which abortion was removed from the criminal law altogether, was far preferable. For example, according to Schwartz some psychiatrists argued that reform, rather than repeal, "in many ways perpetuated the difficulties that existed previously." Since there were very few physical conditions that were made worse by continuing a pregnancy, repeal laws had to rely on the mental health exception and, he claimed, would perpetuate the problem for psychiatry, because judging whether pregnancy was a threat to mental health was "more nebulous" than the idea of a risk of suicide posed by pregnancy (1973:144). Schwartz's conclusion was to argue for "abortion on request," leaving the decision to the woman (1973:144).

In 1969, the American Psychiatric Association indicated that psychiatry had officially come to support repeal, not just reform, when it adopted the following resolution, which appeared in the *American Journal of Psychiatry* in 1970: "A decision to perform an abortion should be regarded as strictly a medical decision and a medical responsibility. It should be removed entirely from the jurisdiction of the criminal law. . . . A medical decision to perform an abortion is based on the careful and informed judgements of the physician and the patient" (Schwartz 1973:168). By the time *Roe v. Wade* was judged in the Supreme Court, it was therefore *already* the case that psychiatric opinion considered the provision of legal abortion necessary and that the issue should be considered a medical, rather than criminal, matter, to be decided on by the woman and a doctor, and argued this publicly. In 1969, the American Psychological Association adopted a resolution stating that "termination of unwanted pregnancies is clearly a mental health and child welfare issue" and advocating that "termination of pregnancy be considered a civil right of the pregnant woman, to be handled as other medical and surgical procedures in consultation with her physicians, and to be considered legal if performed by a licensed physician in a licensed medical facility" (American Psychological Association 1987). Unlike in Britain, most significantly, medical organizations also advocated the decriminalization of abortion laws by this time; those adopting this position included the American College of Obstetricians and Gynecologists, the American Medical Association, the American Medical Women's Association, and the American Public Health Association (Sarvis and Rodman 1974:10). According to Niswander, by the late 1960s many physicians in the United States recommended legal abortion, which indicated the "changing philosophy over the past two decades." They, he claimed, together with "other influential groups of citizens such as lawyers, psychologists and social workers," were arguing that the law should change "in order to take into account factors other than the 'life' of the pregnant patient" (1973:217).

Some even took a more radical view; they made the case for demedicalizing the grounds for abortion in law. Like Schwartz, who argued for women being able to choose abortion, Alan Guttmacher came to the conclusion that abortion on request was "the only way to truly democratize legal abortion" in 1969, after forty-seven years of involvement with abortion provision. Important to his shift in opinion was the increasing use of the psychiatric exception (over 90 percent of abortions performed legally in California in 1968 were carried out on this ground), and this, he claimed, placed psychiatrists in the "untenable position of being an authority in socio-economics." Better simply to align the law and reality, in which women request abortion on such grounds, and leave behind the idea that medical grounds in any form should be necessary for its legal performance (1973:70). As my previous discussion of the *Roe v. Wade* ruling suggested, however, this approach was not the one that came to be clearly dominant, although it is important that in contrast to Britain, where the link between support for legal abortion and the issue of rights was not overtly apparent at all, it was far more clearly articulated in the United States.

The effect of the emergence of forthright support on the part of psychiatrists and other doctors for removing abortion from the criminal law in the United States is, therefore, an interesting one in regard to the differential outcome of abortion law reform here compared with Britain. As Chapter 3 noted, the far greater reference to the issue of rights in the legal framework in the United States compared with Britain relates to both the contrasting legal and political traditions in these two countries and the greater influence of feminist claims for women's rights in the United States. But it is also arguable that the differences in the internal pressures on psychiatry and medicine discussed above are important too. They led to the development of a clear difference in views about abortion law reform from this quarter in these two countries, with important consequences for it. In Britain, doctors were prepared to consider at most the creation of medically authorized exceptions to the illegality of abortion, and many opposed even this kind of reform in the late 1960s. In the United States, in part because of the factors discussed above, some doctors became publicly identified with a far more radical kind of reform. The emergence of this approach to abortion law on the part of psychiatry and medicine can therefore be considered to have shaped, as well as to have been shaped by, the far greater degree to which considering abortion as a question of women's rights came to pertain in the United States. There was far less contradiction between this idea and medical attitudes in this society as compared with Britain.

Changing Constructions of "Mental Health"

The growing use of the psychiatric exception to authorize abortion in the years before *Roe v. Wade,* which eventually led many American psychiatrists and doctors to support radical reform of the abortion law, was not, however, only impelled by the declining importance of the risk to physical health posed by pregnancy. As in Britain, in the United States the perceived importance of improving mental health informed medical opinion. As Sarvis and Rodman note of the 1960s, "A broader definition of health and therapy" had emerged, and, along with medical advances in controlling many physical diseases, this explained why "so-called psychiatric indications" had increased relative to medical indications for abortion. They point out that health had come to mean, for many involved in health care, not simply the absence of physical illness, but an expanded concept of the healthy person. Thus, "despite the elimination of traditional reasons for abortion in cases of heart disease, some kidney disorders, tuberculosis, and some neurologic diseases, a woman and physicians may still be aware of the difficulty of caring for the child and the attendant threats to health. Thus new reasons for abortion have arisen" (1974:71).

The inclusion of pregnancy as an aspect of psychiatric interest in "the healthy person" can be considered part of the redefinition of the remit of American psychiatry and psychology at this time. As Ellen Herman's fascinating study of this issue notes, following the Second World War American psychiatrists and psychologists moved to concern themselves with aspects of life previously considered outside of their realm of expertise. "The agony of the desperately ill" no longer needed to be their only preoccupation, she writes, and they could "set their sights on the normal anxieties of ordinary people." She argues that in this context, clinicians "pledged themselves to careers as architects of social as well as personal change" (1995:238). And this included changing sexual and reproductive behavior.

The importance of this development, according to Herman, was not only that family life and personal experience became the subject of psychological and psychiatric interest but that there was a rapid institutionalization of this development. There was "the swift acceptance by federal government of an unprecedented responsibility for the mental and emotional well-being of the entire U.S. population," argues Herman. Mental health, and the prevention of mental ill health, was cast as a national, public concern. The passage of the National Mental Health Act of 1946 was notable in particular, as this indicated that "the mental health of ordinary citizens would become a consequential public policy issue in its own right . . . federal legislation, in turn, provided the infrastructure necessary to support community-oriented psychology and psychiatry during the 1950s and 1960s" (Herman 1995:240). First called the National Neuropsychiatric Institute Act, the replacement of the reference to neuropsychiatry with "mental health" exemplified the shift from concern with extreme illnesses among those with psychiatric conditions, to forms of behavior and aspects of the daily life of the "normal" population. By the early 1960s, psychiatric activity was defined as "all social, psychological, and biological activity affecting the mental health of the populace . . . including programs for fostering social change, resolution of social problems, political involvement, community organization planning, and clinical psychiatric practice" (Herman 1995:255).

Herman notes, instructively, that one critic in the discussion of the new legislation argued that a trajectory that would include "all problems of life and
living" in the practice of medicine might be problematic. This was a lone
voice, however, which was overwhelmed by support for dealing with and improving the population's mental health (Herman 1995:246). The new legislation laid the basis for the National Institute of Mental Health (NIMH),
formally established in 1949, which has as its founding goal not just the prevention of mental ill health but also the promotion of mental health. The
abundant funds offered to psychological professionals by NIMH through the
1950s and 1960s ensured the expansion of the field of treatment and prevention of mental illness and the promotion of mental health. Psychology and psychiatry were thus promoted as socially responsible enterprises with a key remit
within society, that of solving social problems by improving mental health.
The profession's expertise was defined not only in terms of the narrow remit
of treating long-defined mental illness, but now in relation to social improve-
ment and social change.

Unwanted Children as a Social Problem

In this context, the effects of pregnancy upon women's minds and the broader
issue of child development within the family came under the auspices of U.S.
psychiatry and psychology. It is not surprising therefore that from the 1950s,
the psychiatric exception for abortion became not only more accepted but also
more broadly defined. The notion that a woman's *life* was at risk if the pregnancy continued had shifted to mean that some psychiatrists would attest to
such a risk where they considered that her mental health, broadly defined,
would be damaged by having a baby. Niswander notes that two psychiatrists
writing in 1965, Rosenberg and Silver, argued that when a psychiatrist recommended a therapeutic abortion, "he is likely to be considering the socio-
economic factors at least as much as the psychiatric indications" (1973:209).
Claims about the mental health consequences of unwanted pregnancy and
unwanted children became increasingly visible in the psychiatric and medical
literature during the 1960s and 1970s, as part of this new interest in mental
health. The psychiatrist Stephen Fleck, for example, a forthright advocate of
"abortion on request," claimed in 1973 that there was "no more important issue" for society in general and psychiatry in particular "than the prevention of
unwanted offspring." "In the sense of literally aborting unwanted pregnancies," he argued, "abortion remains an important stopgap for the psychiatrist's
general proposition that unwanted parenthood is undesirable for the mental
health of both parent and child. A significant decrease in the incidence of psychiatric illness might be accomplished if unwanted parenthood were prevented" (1973:193). Similarly, claimed Schwartz, it was not abortion that was
the problem, from the psychiatric point of view, but unwanted childbearing.
Where abortion was not a cause of mental ill health, unwanted childbearing

was, and, as a result of the harm it caused to women's minds, the latter was an important source of social problems. The unwanted children born as a result, he claimed, "are likely to receive inadequate care during their early, formative years, and, as a result, often become vulnerable to psychiatric disorders" (1973:140).

Such problematization of unwanted childbearing drew attention to the mental health problems for women, but, as in Britain, the often more prominent claim concerned the effects upon the child, and the deleterious impact on society more generally, resulting from children born unwanted. "Psychiatrists generally agree that the single most important cause of mental disorders is inadequate parental care during the formative years," argued Schwartz. While the notion that unwanted children are more likely prone to develop psychiatric disorders than those born wanted had "never been tested," he argued, when "planned pregnancy" becomes the norm, the proportion of "unloved and inadequately reared children would decrease," leading to a "decrease [in the] incidence of psychiatric disorders." In turn, social problems would be resolved. With reference to the work of psychiatrist Karl Menninger, it was claimed that "the unwanted child becomes the undesirable citizen, the willing cannon fodder for wars of hate and prejudice" (Schwartz 1973:158). Hence the legalization of abortion would contribute greatly to alleviating "many of our most serious social problems," including overpopulation, poverty, and behavioral disorders. As in Britain, the psychiatric case for abortion, relative to unwanted childbearing, has continued since abortion was made legal. For example, in 1991, psychiatrist Paul Dagg claimed that "Many women denied abortion show ongoing resentment that may last for years, while children born when the abortion is denied have numerous, broadly based difficulties in social, interpersonal, and occupational functions that last at least into early adulthood" (1991:578).

Well before the claim for PAS emerged, therefore, in both the United States and Britain a consensus had been established within psychiatry, psychology and medicine that continuing a pregnancy constituted a relatively greater threat to women's mental health than abortion. The argument for the psychiatric exception indicates that this justification for abortion has a long history. Its role in shaping claims regarding the legal status of abortion in the United States and Britain is different and leads to contrasting effects in relation to legal reform. In both societies, however, the notion that abortion can be justified on mental health grounds has become increasingly influential. Changing perceptions of the meaning of mental health have been important in informing the growing influence of this view since the 1960s, but so too have claims in which the psychological effects of unwanted childbearing are emphasized. Claims that construct alternatives to abortion as problematic on mental health grounds have not only been made about unwanted pregnancy, however. Motherhood in general, it has been increasingly claimed, is a mental health issue, and it is to this issue that I now turn.

A BRIEF HISTORY OF POSTPARTUM DEPRESSION

By the 1970s, some comment on the psychological effects of abortion claimed that abortion compares favorably with not just unwanted childbearing but motherhood altogether. Fleck argued in 1970, for example, that postpartum blues "are a well known, almost universal occurrence known to all [obstetricians] as typical depressive stress manifestations to the end of pregnancy and the beginning of nursing tasks, whereas post-abortion reactions of the same type have been observed to be brief and mild" (Sarvis and Rodman 1974:105). He also argued that delivering a child can result in major psychiatric disturbance in one or two cases per 1,000 women, "while no such major psychiatric complications have been reported as a clear consequence of abortion" (Fleck 1973:184). Schwartz claimed similarly that the "low risk of psychiatric problems following *abortion* must be contrasted with a relatively high frequency of psychosis following *childbirth*" (emphasis in the original) and noted that in the United States there were 4,000 cases of postpartum psychosis requiring hospitalisation each year (1973:151). David and Friedman referred to the same figure of 4,000 "documented postpartum psychoses requiring hospitalisation in the United States per year" and no evidence of similar responses to abortion. "Whereas 'postpartum blues' are well known as typical depressive stress reactions to the end of pregnancy," they argued, "'postabortion blues' have been observed to be generally brief and mild" (1973:315).

Such comparisons between the experiences of abortion and motherhood draw on a field of psychiatry and psychology, emergent from the 1960s on, in which the association between motherhood generally and mental illness became the focus for research and discussion. As the comments above suggest, this field includes research and discussion of "postpartum blues" and "postpartum psychosis." At its center, however, has come to be a concept that is now highly visible in British and American societies, namely postpartum depression (termed postnatal depression in Britain). For the sake of clarity, from this point on I will use the acronym PND to refer to this concept as discussed in both countries.

A New Illness

According to most accounts of the concept, PND is a relatively recent addition to psychiatry. Before the 1950s, the term was not widely used. Psychiatrists had often noted the development of very atypical, extreme forms of behavior in some women after childbirth for some time—a condition known as postpartum psychosis, according to many accounts apparently first identified in ancient Greece, and discussed extensively by some psychiatrists in the nineteenth century—but there was little discussion of a more general connection between motherhood and mental illness.

Katharina Dalton, author of a widely referenced text on PND, contends that puerperal psychosis (psychosis related to pregnancy) and postpartum psychosis were recognized before the 1950s, but these illnesses were not a subject of major interest or research. She writes that mothers with psychosis after childbirth "showed the same diverse presentations as other men and women in the psychiatric wards" and "tended to be treated in the same way." It was widely accepted, therefore, that a very small proportion of women developed very extreme symptoms of mental illness after childbirth, but this was not situated as part of a larger field of general mental illness resulting from giving birth. In addition, according to Dalton, it was also considered that a very mild kind of psychological disturbance affected a large number of women who had given birth. Termed the "baby blues," such mental disturbance had been recognized by midwives well before the 1950s, but this phenomenon was not considered to be related to mental illness and was not of interest to psychiatrists. Other accounts also note that before the 1950s, the "baby blues" were a commonly discussed side effect of giving birth. However, this experience was envisaged as a common and accepted aspect of motherhood and was not considered a major cause for concern (Stein 1982). In sum, "Until the mid 1960s, there was little interest in this subject. . . . Puerperal psychosis was recognised. . . . [at] the other extreme there was the blues" (Dalton and Holton 2001:5).

During the 1960s, however, motherhood began to be taken more seriously by psychiatry as a cause of mental ill health. According to psychiatrist Ian Brockington, author of a number of key texts and articles on mental illness and motherhood, there were "crude" descriptions of what came to be termed PND in the psychiatric literature of the 1950s. But the seminal paper was written by the psychiatrist Pitt in 1968, in which he argued for a distinct category of "postnatal depressions" (Murray and Cooper 1997:x). Pitt's study found notoriety because he deemed a larger proportion of women to be suffering from illness than had previously been identified. According to his study, "depressive neurosis" was present in 10 percent of women, and their symptoms were different from those in women with psychosis—they did not suffer from "delusions or hallucinations," as did psychotic women, but "were suffering from an unusual degree of depression which was disabling" (Priest 1978:7). In particular, the significance of Pitt's study has been considered to be that only two of his twenty-seven interviewees were found to have "the classical picture of depressive illness," and he therefore decided to describe the kinds of feelings and forms of behavior described by the mothers he studied as "atypical" and worthy of the title "postnatal depression" (Kumar 1982:103). According to Kumar, this is the classic study of postnatal depression and laid the basis for future work in positing a incidence rate of 11 percent for neurotic depression within six weeks of delivery, against which others have subsequently measured their findings (Kumar 1982:94).

From this point interest in PND increased. Whereas before the 1960s psychiatry had been primarily interested in psychosis following childbirth, which was considered to be a rare and serious form of mental illness, a new interest emerged in what appeared to be more common, and less serious, difficulties. Dalton writes that she conducted another of the first studies that brought about recognition of the illness, in which she found that 7 percent of mothers developed depression severe enough to require medical treatment. These findings were published in the *British Journal of Psychiatry* in 1971, and "Psychiatrists and psychologists suddenly appreciated the vast amount of ill health that was suffered by new mothers which was much more severe than the blues, yet without the confusions, delusions or hallucinations of women with psychosis" (Dalton and Holton 2001:6). Pitt noted in 1978 that while psychiatric interest in mental illness in pregnant women and women who have given birth was, in one sense, "nothing new," since there is a long tradition "wherein psychiatrists have been intrigued by women who break down at the time of childbearing," it had come to receive "more attention" on the part of psychiatry, and an interest in illnesses of "a less disturbed type" was growing (Priest 1978:1).

Experiences and forms of behavior in mothers that had previously not been investigated by psychiatry thus came to feature in a field of research termed, from the late 1960s on, "motherhood and mental illness." From this point, research and discussion about the new category PND—its causes, its symptoms, and whether there are particular risk factors for its development—have come to feature prominently in the psychiatric literature. Interest in the connection between motherhood and mental illness has expanded rapidly, and by the time the PAS claim emerged as a contested concept in the early 1980s, the idea that this reproductive choice was a cause of mental illness was well established in psychiatry.

A New Specialism

A measure of the development of psychiatric interest in PND is indicated by the emergence of the subject of motherhood and mental illness as a particular field of psychiatric research and clinical work, involving a dedicated group of psychiatrists. In 1980, a conference organized by the University of Manchester Department of Psychiatry resulted in the foundation of the Marcé Society (Brockington and Kumar 1982). The main aim of the society at the outset was to "focus long overdue attention on the heart rending syndrome of postpartum psychosis" (Brockington 1996:viii), but it has subsequently come to "provide a forum for exchange of information and ideas between professionals concerned with the welfare of women and their families around the time of childbirth," with the problem of PND at the center of its work (Marcé Society, Australasian Branch 1998).

Motherhood and Mental Illness, a key psychiatric text published in 1982, was written following the Manchester conference to draw attention to the "growing body of research into the psychopathology of reproduction" and "serve as a platform for more coherent research." Chapters in the book indicate that the issue of mental illness and its relationship to motherhood had emerged by this time as a significant area of interest for psychiatrists on both sides of the Atlantic. Senior psychiatrists from universities and hospitals in Manchester, Edinburgh, London, and Kent in Britain, and Stanford and Iowa in the United States, contributed chapters on psychiatric disorders that were considered to result from giving birth. In the years following the conference, the notion that motherhood can make women mentally ill became further consolidated within psychiatry, and Post Natal Depression in particular came to be considered to be specific illness that results from giving birth.

It was in the 1980s and 1990s that this field of research expanded most rapidly. In a book published in 1980 recounting twenty-five women's experiences of PND, the author referred to Pitt's study, but argued that there was, at that time, very little else published on psychiatric problems connected with childbearing and contended that the "milder forms of postnatal depression" have hardly been studied at all by psychiatry (Welburn 1980). If this representation was correct in 1980, the picture a decade later had changed significantly. Between 1980 and 1990, over 100 studies of "postnatal psychological illness" were published in key medical and psychiatric journals. The focus varied from severe psychiatric illness to clinical depression, the "maternity blues," and more recently the impact of maternal depression upon the family (Nicolson 1998:27). Most recently still the effect of childbirth upon men, including the possibility that they, as well as women, might suffer from PND, and its effects upon the development of children, have featured particularly prominently in the psychiatric literature (Welford 2002).

In 1997, the editors of a collection of essays on the subject authored by eighteen psychiatrists and psychologists from universities in Britain and the United States could write: "Postpartum depression is relatively common and easily identified" (Murray and Cooper 1997:ix), suggesting that the illness was considered an important and well-researched problem. The following extracts from factsheets published for new mothers by the leading psychiatric bodies in the United States and Britain make clear that motherhood is considered to pose a significant mental health risk to women:

Postnatal Depression (now often referred to as "PND") means becoming depressed after having a baby. Sometimes this is easy to explain—the baby is unwanted or abnormal. Mostly, though, the depression makes no obvious sense: "I was so looking forward to having this baby, and now I feel utterly miserable. What's the matter with me?" "The labour went beautifully—much better than I expected, and everyone's been marvellous, especially Jim. So why aren't I over the moon?" "I was so afraid there'd be something wrong with her, but she's perfect. So why aren't I enjoying her? Perhaps I'm not cut out to be a mother?"

These women are not ungrateful or unmotherly: they are experiencing one of the most common complications of childbirth, from which too many women still suffer unnecessarily in silence—Post-Natal Depression. (Royal College of Psychiatrists 1997)

Postpartum depression is caused by changes in hormones and can run in families. . . . About one in 10 new mothers experience some degree of postpartum depression. These complications usually occur within just days after delivery, and can occur even a year later. These symptoms include:
Sluggishness
Fatigue
Exhaustion
Feelings of hopelessness or depression
Disturbances with appetite and sleep
Confusion
Uncontrollable crying
Lack of interest in the baby
Fear of harming the baby or oneself
Mood swings—highs and lows. (American Psychiatric Association 2001)

The features of PND, it is claimed, are that it is very common (one in ten is the statistic most commonly given to represent the proportion of mothers who have the illness), that it has a broad range of symptoms, usually set out in the kind of list above, and that it can be treated by counseling or antidepressant drugs. These features of PND now appear regularly in articles published in medical and psychiatric journals. For example, in 1998, the *British Medical Journal* published "Postnatal Depression," an article authored by two professors from the Department of Psychology at Reading University, England. Its summary points include the statements: "Postnatal depression affects 10% of women in the weeks immediately postpartum"; "Postnatal depression is commonly missed by primary care teams despite the fact that simple reliable detection procedures have been developed"; and "The treatment of choice in most cases of postnatal depression is counselling, which can be effectively delivered by health visitors" (Cooper and Murray 1998:1884). Motherhood had come to be considered a risky enterprise in regard to mental health.

The Status of PND

A further measure of the identification of PND as an important problem is the discussion surrounding its status in the *Diagnostic and Statistical Manual of Mental Disorders* (DSM) and the *International Classification of Diseases* (ICD). Neither postpartum blues nor postpartum psychosis is included in either manual as a specific category of illness. "Neither the severity or duration of the blues passes the threshold for a psychiatric disorder," writes American psychiatrist Michael O'Hara (1997:4). Indeed, the construction of the "blues" as a psychological state relies centrally on the idea that its symptoms do not last long and that they constitute an unpleasant experience but are nothing very serious. Postpartum psychosis, by contrast, is defined in psychiatry by its severity and the fact that it persists for a long time. Its symptoms are defined in the familiar terms of long-established categories of mental illnesses: "mania," "depression," or "psychosis." According to DSM IV, if episodes of these illnesses occur within four weeks of childbirth, the woman can be diagnosed as suffering from postpartum onset of psychosis. Thus a link with childbirth and the development of severe mental illness can be posited. However, the illness is considered similar to that which can occur outside the postpartum period (O'Hara 1997:5).

Postpartum depression, by contrast, is included as a specific category of illness—this took place with the publication of DSM IV. Its diagnosis required "that a woman be experiencing dysphoric mood along with several other symptoms such as sleep, appetite or psychomotor disturbance; fatigue; excessive guilt; and suicidal thoughts" (O'Hara 1997:5). Thus, as I discuss further in the following chapter, PND has come to be considered by psychiatry to be an illness that does not have the characteristic features of "normal" depression. Its distinction from regular depression is given by the requirement that "a woman be experiencing dysphoric mood along with several other symptoms" (O'Hara 1997:5).

It is significant that, unlike other instances in which women's state of mind and its relation to the reproductive process, or women's biology, have become the subject of psychiatric interest and been conceptualized in terms of illness or disease, there appears to have been relatively little debate about this way of defining women's state of mind or behaviors following childbirth. The number of critics of the concept of PND is small (Nicolson 1998), and interestingly, some of those who have popularized this term who argue that there is too little recognition of this illness are also among the foremost critics of the medicalization of childbirth in regard to obstetric practice. Many aspects of the medicalization of pregnancy and childbirth have been subject to thoroughgoing criticism, for example, the historical process by which a largely male obstetrics profession took over from midwives and in doing so reinvented pregnancy as an illness, or the increasing medical management of pregnancy through growing rates of Caesarean section (Johanson et al. 2002). But the notion that there should be a specific diagnostic category, through which a particular type of depression in mothers is recognized, has not been subject to very much dispute. This contrasts with the debate around PAS and with the 1980s struggle over whether Premenstrual Syndrome (PMS) should be included in the DSM (Figert 1996). As yet, there has been relatively little argument over whether PND, as opposed to PMS, makes sense as a specific category of illness, on grounds that compare the relative effects of the menstrual cycle and becoming a mother.

Indeed, insofar as criticism has been made regarding the DSM and the ICD, it has mainly emanated from psychiatrists and centered on the claim that those responsible for the content of the diagnostic manuals have been *too reluctant* to recognize motherhood as a cause of a specific sort of mental illness and have not gone far enough in giving official recognition to the psychiatric consequences of giving birth. Some psychiatrists who are enthusiastic proponents of the social problem of mental illness in mothers have written scathingly about the perceived reluctance on the part of psychiatry to officially recognize the link between giving birth and pathological states. For example, the subsuming of "puerperal psychosis" under broader classifications has been criticized. Ian Brockington writes that ICD and the DSM have a "stranglehold" on the ideas of psychiatrists and have profoundly influenced clinical practice to its detriment in relation to mothers (1996). For Brockington, the legacy of the Kraepelinian definition of psychoses (that used in the DSM) has meant that developments in diagnosis "have been frozen" and have acted to prevent the recognition of "puerperal psychosis" as a distinct disorder.

In DSM IV, there is a section on postpartum psychosis in its chapter on mood disorders (which, as noted above, suggests that mood disorders or psychosis can be defined as postpartum disorders if they occur within four weeks of childbirth). Brockington considers this to be inadequate, and he is even more scathing about the ICD, which recommends against psychiatrists' recording "puerperal psychosis" exclusively in their returns to official bodies (for example, the U.K. Department of Health) where they diagnose mental illness in mothers. Although the ICD does include a paragraph on puerperal psychosis specifically, it recommends that this should be recorded alongside other diagnoses, stating: "Most experts in this field are of the opinion that a clinical picture of puerperal psychosis is so rarely (if ever) reliably distinguishable from affective disorder or schizophrenia that a special category is not justified" (1996:207). Brockington writes approvingly of those psychiatrists who have diagnosed puerperal psychosis specifically, doing so "in ignorance or defiance" of what the ICD recommends, since this has meant that the illness comes to be listed in official statistics. He concludes that the influence of the ICD and the DSM in relation to puerperal psychosis has been "adverse." "The concept has been eclipsed by numerically more important but vaguely conceived entities. . . . The absence of the *imprimatur* of the World Health Organization and the American Psychiatric Association has depressed research and the provision of services" (1996:208-9).

Whether or not WHO and the APA are considered reticent in their approach to promoting the idea of a relationship between motherhood and mental illness, it is not the case that they have often been criticized for going too far in this direction. Rather, as the following chapter shows, the notion that more must be done to highlight the mental illness that motherhood can cause has dominated the discussion as the concept PND in particular has become established and is widely used and accepted both within psychiatry and beyond it.

This chapter has demonstrated that well in advance of the PAS claim, medical and particularly psychiatric opinion came to emphasize that abortion should be legally available and justified its provision. The notion that abortion is a cause of psychological problems has been contested for a long time on the grounds that this relationship is not scientifically verifiable for most women. Claims that emphasize the psychological safety of abortion emerged, however, not as a clear result of the demedicalization of abortion but in the context of changes in the construction of pregnancy and its outcomes more broadly. The justification of legal abortion in regard to mental health comprises a set of interrelated claims about the outcomes of pregnancy and their effects on women's minds. The context for such claims has been a growing interest in the effects for mental health of women bearing unwanted children, and the relationship between mental health and motherhood more generally.

The PAS claim emerges against this background, suggesting that this claim ran against the grain of medical and psychiatric conceptualizations of pregnancy dominant by the early 1980s. In the debate about PAS the issue of whether abortion is or is not a mental health problem was clearly linked to a set of questions about the legal status of abortion, as Chapter 4 described. But the issue of the social acceptability and legal status of abortion was not only about abortion; it had already come to be related to constructions of the health effects of the alternatives to it. The development of these constructions of reproduction as a mental health issue have, therefore, had a very important effect for the abortion debate. They have meant that claims that abortion damages women's mental health have been contested in two ways; both *directly* through counterclaims that there is no scientific evidence of a Postabortion Syndrome and *indirectly,* through competition from claims that continuing a pregnancy can pose a significant threat to women's mental health. The idea that abortion damages women's mental health has been refuted, and, at the same time, the alternatives have been constructed as a mental health problem, and this has been important to the notion that abortion should be considered legally as a matter of choice. I now go on to show how this latter construction of the problem of the outcomes of pregnancy has gained significant visibility and support subsequent to the emergence of the PAS claim.

6

Motherhood as an Ordeal

The previous chapter argued that the contest over PAS has been informed in part by claims that continuing a pregnancy can pose a greater risk to women's mental health than abortion. It showed how this claim emerged and developed from the 1960s on. And it highlighted how, over the 1980s and 1990s (the point at which the PAS claim was the subject of pointed public debate), one aspect of the debate about the relationship between pregnancy outcomes and mental illness became more and more prevalent within psychiatry. While claims that there was a relationship between continued pregnancies generally and mental illness were articulated at this time, discussion about *motherhood and mental illness* became particularly marked as a theme. The category of mental illness postnatal depression developed to become an important concept for psychiatry, the visibility of which in the psychiatric debate increased significantly over this time.

Discussion of this concept has by no means remained confined to psychiatry, however. The problem of depression in mothers has become the subject of a much wider public debate, and claims about this problem provide an interesting counterpoint to those that have been made about abortion. Debate about the psychological effects of abortion has been characterized by contest, with abortion opponents accused of exaggerating the extent and seriousness of the problem. Becoming and being a mother, in contrast, has come to be represented in a very different way.

In the popular media, for example, there is very little argument about the idea that depression in mothers is more serious and widespread than many considered it to be, and that too little is done about it. "Majority of depressed mothers go untreated," stated a recent British article, which drew attention to celebrities who suffered from PND, including the late Princess Diana and model Jerry Hall, and noted that the World Health Organisation claims that by 2020, "major depression, of which post-natal depression is a sub-group, will be the second highest cause of death and disability in the world" (Womack 2002). "The shocking statistic . . . that fewer than a quarter of mums have their post-natal depression diagnosed, is a prime example of how the Health

Service neglects new mothers," contends Dr. Rosemary, in a typical piece in a British newspaper's health advice column (2002:40). "Many practitioners tend not to pick up on postpartum depression," argued an American newspaper's woman's pages article about the need for ob-gyns to do more to diagnose depression in women generally, and after childbirth in particular (Condor 1996).

The experience of celebrity mothers has become a particular means through which this problem has gained visibility. Marie Osmond is one American celebrity who "spoke out" about suffering from PPD. Her account of her experience was published as *Behind the Smile: My Journey Out of Postpartum Depression* in 2001, following a TV interview where the author "went public" about her own experience on *Oprah* and *Larry King Live*. In Britain, TV personality Zoe Ball has become the latest celebrity to publicize the emotional problems she experienced following the birth of her son. Ball's comment to the press, that she "felt like walking out on her baby," was applauded as a helpful contribution to raising awareness about the problem of PND in Britain. The experiences of other high-profile British mothers who have been diagnosed with PND, including the celebrity Esther Ranzen and a number of soap opera stars, have also been discussed on television and in newspapers, and often feature in advice books for women about motherhood.

There are some differences in the way in which the mental health risks of motherhood are explained in the two societies, but as these examples show, in both the United States and Britain PND has come to be represented as an important mental health problem. This chapter examines the arguments of the different claimsmakers who have contributed to this representation of the mothers' mental state. Its main focus is the way that the concept PND, first owned by psychiatry, has come to be shared by others. It draws attention to how the concept has developed in different domains (including health policy and practice, advice books for pregnant women and new mothers, and feminist commentary) and shows how these different domains have overlapped and acted together in a claimsmaking process through which motherhood and mental illness have become linked. The overall burden of my argument is that the claim that motherhood is an ordeal—expressed through the concept of PND—has, unlike PAS, found a great deal of cultural support and has been subject to very limited contest.

PSYCHIATRY AND POSTNATAL DEPRESSION

The previous chapter argued that in the late 1960s, PND emerged as a psychiatric concept and subsequently became the subject of a great deal of research and debate in this arena. How does psychiatry now define PND? Key issues, in line with a conventional medical approach, are identification of its symptoms and causes. But on both counts psychiatry has often, in fact, generated findings characterized by uncertainty. An interesting feature of this issue is that although, as suggested above, there is a widespread representation of PND as a defined condition, with many sufferers who need to be treated, this representation coexists with an ongoing debate within psychiatry about the key features that might designate it as an illness. The following discussion draws attention to these debates and indicates how psychiatry has developed means through which it can, nonetheless, give coherence to the concept of PND.

Symptoms

Since the concept of Postnatal Depression was first named in the 1960s, there have been numerous attempts to define what characterizes it, but substantial difficulties appear to have confronted psychiatrists attempting to do so. British psychiatrist R. Kumar, coeditor of the influential text *Motherhood and Mental Illness,* asked in 1982, on the basis of a review of the research literature then existing, "Is there really such a thing as postnatal depression? . . . What is not at all clear . . . is when postnatal depression becomes ordinary depression on the time scale after delivery, and whether there are any special clinical or other features which distinguish postnatal depression from episodes of depression" (Kumar 1982:106–7). In the mid-1980s one specialist in PND explained, "There is no generally accepted definition, no diagnostic test and none of the symptoms is specific to this disorder" (Comport 1987:15–16). Fourteen years following Kumar's statement on the problems of defining what is specific about depression in mothers, the psychiatrist Ian Brockington wrote of PND, "One must examine with scepticism, the scientific value of this concept. Depression after childbirth is clinically very similar to any other depression" (1996:170). The difficulties in defining PND that have emerged relate, as these comments suggest, to disputes about whether a specific sort of depression is evident in women who have given birth.

Despite a large number of studies, no clear resolution has been found that has allowed PND to be clearly identified as a specific kind of illness. "Significant questions have been raised that consider whether PPD is a distinct entity from nonpuerperal major depression," state Evins and Theofrastous (1997: 241). A study published recently in the *British Medical Journal* that made the news on both sides of the Atlantic also drew attention to this problem (Evans et al. 2001). According to its authors, despite concern about postnatal depression, "in reality, more British women are depressed during pregnancy than after giving birth" (O'Neil 2001). It was also reported that in any case the idea of PND existing as a specific syndrome "is a popular myth" that has "entered public consciousness as a sort of condition somehow separate from the rest of depression" (Kaiser Daily Reproductive Health Report 2001d).

An interesting aspect of PND is that a definition of it has developed, however, which coexists with these debates about it. While there is, on the one hand, ongoing debate about exactly what defines PND, at the same time a definition in psychiatry of what "counts" as PND has emerged. This is a definition in which the illness is defined by positing its symptoms as midway in their severity between two other forms of psychological disturbance in mothers. Considered to be most severe in its symptoms is postpartum psychosis. The other end of the spectrum, considered insufficiently severe to count as mental illness (although increasingly represented as a "risk factor" and often discussed as a "psychiatric complication" of childbirth), is the "baby blues." U.S. PPD specialist Michael O'Hara has summarized this argument emergent from psychiatry as a "custom" within the literature which "distinguish[es] three phenomena: postpartum blues, postpartum psychosis and postpartum depression" (1997:4). Evins and Theofrastous, adopting this custom, contend: "Postpartum depression is classified separately from two other postpartum psychiatric disorders: maternity or postpartum blues and postpartum psychosis. . . . the blues is considered a transient, normal sequela of childbirth. . . . In contrast. . . . Psychosis is associated with a family history of bipolar disorder" (1997:241).

Postnatal depression is thus constructed in substantial part through claiming it is not "only" the blues, but neither is it a very severe form of mental illness. It is less serious than psychosis, which is distinguishable because its key symptom is delusion, but its symptoms are worse and longer-lasting than those of the "blues"; thus whereas "postpartum blues almost always go away in a few days," postnatal depression "lasts longer and is more intense" (American College of Obstetricians and Gynecologists n.d.).

Causes

The question of what causes PND also appears to be open to question in the psychiatric literature. From the outset the possibility that there is a causal link between the development of depression and giving birth has been a key focus for research. The term *postnatal depression* clearly suggests such a link, but as Brockington has argued:

> . . . the concept of "post-natal depression" does not emerge from 30 years of research with much scientific credit. If postpartum psychosis is excluded, there is only modest evidence of an association between depression and the puerperium. It has not been demonstrated that depression is more common after childbirth than at other times among the female reproductive period. (1996:173)

Studies of women's feelings and forms of behavior after childbirth, as compared with before, have indicated a "specific association" between childbirth and "the blues" and with the development of psychosis, yet O'Hara argues that psychiatric studies have not clearly demonstrated an association between depression and childbirth. He notes that studies (for example, the first carried out in Oxford, England in 1988, another in Iowa published in 1990, a second in the United States in 1990, and a further study in the Midlands in England published in 1993) in fact found no significant difference in prevalence rates of depression for childbearing and nonchildbearing women and argues as a result that "there is no elevation in the risk for non-psychotic depression associated with childbearing" (1997:9).

Research has investigated whether women are more or less depressed at different times following birth. The psychiatrist Nott did not find any association between childbirth and the timing of the onset of depression. O'Hara found through his research that 69 percent of "depressions" occurring after childbirth began within three weeks of the woman giving birth, but those used as a control group "had depressions that occurred within the same time frame."

In contrast, Kumar and Robson have suggested there is a link between childbirth and depression, highlighting their finding that more than three times as many new cases of depression were evident in women who had given birth three months previously than at six months and at one year. O'Hara has argued, however, that one of the reasons for findings that link childbirth and the onset of depression may be that where childbirth is used as the "anchor" for the interview, women identify that their symptoms began following the birth of child. Thus he suggests that the timing of the onset of depression is "difficult to determine," and there may be "judgement biases by both subjects and investigators" at work (O'Hara 1997:10). Perhaps not surprisingly, following their discussion of the findings of research about PPD, Evins and Theofrastous conclude (inconclusively), "It is possible that PPD represents a heterogeneous group of depressive disorders of which some are specific to the postpartum period" (1997:242).

Unlike some other examples of medicalization, the concept of PND does not always posit a clear relationship with biological factors and symptoms in the women concerned. American commentaries more than British ones tend to place emphasis on the biological causes of the illness. The illness is "caused by changes in hormones and can run in families," states the American Psychiatric Association (2001). According to O'Hara, "hormonal factors have been thought to play an important etiological role in postpartum depression" (1997:14). In contrast, British psychiatrists Cooper and Murray state that "there is little evidence for biological aetiology; antenatal personal and social factors are more relevant" (1998:1884). Bewley argues similarly, "A definitive cause of such depression has not been found and, although research has sought a relationship between the development of depression and hormonal imbalances, this has not been convincing" (2000:32).

One of the most determined advocates of the idea of a biological basis for PND is Katharina Dalton, who is also an advocate of the recognition of Pre-

menstrual Syndrome as a hormonally caused disease. In her book, first published in 1980, she advised that "special types of drugs" should be prescribed,
as opposed to the usual medical treatment for depression, to deal with the hormonal changes that explain the particular symptoms of PND (Kumar
1982:111). This biological approach, however, has been criticized by most
British authorities. For example, Kumar argues that Dalton's view does not
have the backing of controlled clinical investigations and hopes that the measures she advocates (such as regular injections of progesterone) will not be generally adopted (Kumar 1982:112). "Probably there isn't a single cause, but a
number of different stresses," argues the Royal College of Psychiatrists. The
College continues: "It seems likely that PND is related to the huge hormone
changes which take place at the time of birth, but this evidence is still lacking. . . . no real differences have been found in the hormone changes of women
who do and do not get PND" (Royal College of Psychiatrists 1997).

The absence of evidence for a clear biological cause of the illness has resulted
in the dominance of an inclusive approach to identifying the origins of the illness. Many personal and social factors have been muted and discussed in the literature, so as to make PND an illness that is most often understood to be
multicausal. The British authority John Cox argues that although there is "substantial support" for the idea that biological changes cause illness in mothers,
"the interaction between biological, psychological and social factors is extremely complex," and that factors, including a woman's hostile relationship
with her own mother, claimed to be important in some psychoanalytic approaches, and "social factors," defined as marital status, number of children, and
the circumstances surrounding the birth, may all be relevant (1986:36–9).

A Population of Patients

It has been argued, as a result of the evidence summarized above, that there is
little agreement within psychiatry on what PND is, how to treat it, and how
to avoid it, and arguments in the literature about the nature of postnatal mental disturbances have been described as "endless" (Comport 1987:15). Psychologist Paula Nicolson contends that "almost none of the scientific papers
set out a clear operational definition of PND" (1998:28). One aspect of the
psychiatric discussion of PND stands out for its clarity, however, namely confidence in being able to define a population of patients. The concept has acquired coherence particularly through the development of tests to identify
women who can be considered depressed postnatally; "What counts [for psy-
chiatry] is that there are effective screening instruments," argues Nicolson
(1998:27). Despite the uncertainty about what defines PND, there is, as a result, certainty that many women suffer from it. This is one of the most notable
features of the construction of the problem of PND within psychiatry; if psychiatry is unclear about how and whether to define women's feelings follow-

ing birth as a specific form of illness, there is a great deal of enthusiasm for generating a means through which the numbers who are ill can be specified.

According to O'Hara, in the 1980s, studies conducted in Britain and North America "converged to suggest that the prevalence of postpartum depression . . . was between 8% and 15%" (1997:5). In 1982 Kumar wrote, "Half a million births each year allied to an incidence of about 10% for postnatal depression add up to a substantial potential problem" (1982:113). Ian Brockington argues, "Post natal depression can affect anything between 3 and 20 per cent of women after childbirth. . . . Rates of recurrence in subsequent pregnancies vary between 10 and 35 per cent" (Aiken 2000:129). The claim that appears most frequently in the psychiatric literature on PND is that 10 percent of mothers have the illness. The American Psychiatric Association insists that "About one in 10 new mothers experience some degree of postpartum depression" (2001). "How common is it?" asks a fact sheet from the British Royal College of Psychiatrists. "Very!" it replies. "Again and again it has been found that no less than one in 10 women suffer depression after childbirth" (1997). In Britain a figure of 10 percent would mean that, given there are 680,000 live births per year, 68,000 women experience PND annually (Hehir 2001b), and in the United States 400,000 of the approximately 4 million women who give birth would have PPD per year.

Critical to the ability of psychiatry to argue with confidence that a large number of women have PND has been the development of "screening instruments" through which those who have the illness are identified. The most important of these is the Edinburgh Postnatal Depression Scale (EPDS). The scale was developed in 1987 by psychiatrists in Edinburgh for use in primary care (Brockington 1996:173). It has been the development of the EPDS that has been crucial in impelling more and more research and debate about PND, as the scale is tested and verified in different populations of women. The scale has spread rapidly through psychiatry worldwide, to become influential in many countries. It has been translated into Dutch and Icelandic (Brockington 1996:175) used in other countries, including Portugal (Areias et al. 1996), North America (Reighard et al. 1995), Italy (Benvenutia 1999), the Punjab (Clifford et al. 1999), and Australia (Matthey et al. 2001), and among Japanese women giving birth in England (Yoshida et al. 1997).

The scale is based on a series of ten statements with four possible responses relating to mood and feelings. Responses to each of the statements are rated on a scale of zero to three, with the former constituting an absence of symptoms, the latter maximum severity. A score of fourteen or more out of a maximum of thirty indicates that the mother may be depressed. Statements include: I have been able to laugh and see the funny side of things; I have felt worried and anxious for no good reason; Things have been getting on top of me; I have felt sad or miserable; and I have been so unhappy that I have been crying. The significance of EPDS is that it has made it possible to establish

PND as a particular kind of illness, distinct from "regular" depression. The issue of defining symptoms and causes can be set aside, since evidence for the existence of the illness is found through use of the scale.

One particular claim made in favor of the EPDS is that it allows the concept of PND to be made "real" for women, and it is viewed as important to encourage the idea that mental illness in mothers is a real illness. Brockington argues, for example, that the concept poses the danger of "insinuating that there is a homogenous disorder which can be investigated and treated as if it had a single cause." However, he contends, the term has value, since it has "legitimised maternal depression in the minds of the public. . . . It has aroused concern about an important public health problem" (1996:173; Aiken 2000:120). A similar approach is taken by the RCP, which claims that it is to women's advantage to be able to think of their experiences in terms of illness. "It helps many a mother to be told 'You've got PND'. At least she knows her enemy. She can be reassured that she is not a freak of a bad mother, and that many others are in the same boat" (Royal College of Psychiatrists 1997).

This aspect of the psychiatric concept of PND distinguishes it clearly from understandings of the psychological effects of abortion. Where it has been considered by most, beyond abortion opponents, to contest the idea that ending a pregnancy makes women ill, it has come to be viewed as helpful to draw attention to the psychological difficulties associated with becoming a mother, by representing them as a specific kind of illness. It is perhaps testimony to the very peculiar character of current U.S. and British culture that this idea (that it helps women to be told they have a specific kind of illness) has gained this degree of authority. The notion that it can be of benefit to make fixed and defined what might otherwise be considered a more temporary experience has become almost common sense. As I now discuss, it is this idea that has significant resonance beyond psychiatry. As Nicolson has argued, with reference to the work of the sociologist Thurtle, "PND has become a 'folk concept' relating to any psychological difficulty after childbirth" (1998:25). This concept has become a widely accepted way of defining and understanding the feelings and experiences of mothers, and in what follows I discuss where and how this has come to be the case.

ADVICE LITERATURE

The idea that it is helpful for women for PND to become more widely recognized has appeared in claimsmaking about mothers' problems in advice books and literature written for pregnant women and new mothers. In many such books, such as the U.S. "pregnancy bible," *What to Expect When You're Expecting,* discussion of PPD appears alongside that about breast-feeding and baby care generally. But most strikingly, the visibility of PND has increased through a burgeoning body of advice literature about this issue specifically. An early British book of this kind is *Post Natal Depression* by Vivienne Welburn (1980), but most such literature dates from the late 1980s and 1990s.

The over-riding message of these advice books is that there is a far greater need for recognition of the problem of PND. It is vital, these books argue, that women come to understand as quickly as possible that their problems are symptomatic of the fact that they are ill. Some, through their titles, make it clear they intend to encourage women to identify their problems in a medical framework. The authors of the U.S. books *The New Mother Syndrome: Coping with Postpartum Stress and Depression* and *This Isn't What I Expected: Recognizing and Recovering from Depression and Anxiety After Childbirth* invite women to think of their problems in this way. Another approach is to present scathing assessments of health professionals' interaction with mothers for failing to allow this to take place. The author of one book on PPD argues that the medical community has "trivialized PPD" (Huysman 1998:sleeve). This book includes a chapter on the "medical disregard" of PPD and ends with a dire warning of its consequences, in a chapter titled "Mothers Who Killed." Linda Sebastian (1998) discusses why health professionals, in her opinion, are so often unprepared to discuss and treat PPD. It is made clear in this way that it is considered important for PND to be taken far more seriously as a medical problem by doctors. In doing so more women can come to realize that this illness explains their problems, and they can be given treatment.

A common feature of this literature is for the case to be made that PND is a very serious problem and therefore needs greater recognition and visibility. Some books use personal accounts, which graphically describe the problems the author experienced, to do so. *Sleepless Days: One Woman's Journey Through Postpartum Depression* describes the author Susan Kushner Resnick's "descent into a type of depression seldom discussed and little known" (2001:sleeve). *A Mother's Tears, Understanding the Mood Swings that Follow Childbirth* is by Dr. Arlene M. Huysman, both a medical doctor and PPD "survivor." The use of the term "survivor" is common to some such books—shown by its use in titles such as *Surviving the Baby Blues* by psychotherapist Jane Feinmann and Cara Aiken's *Surviving Post-Natal Depression*—which also emphasizes the seriousness of the problem by representing motherhood as an experience women can, with help, "survive."

The most common means through which the seriousness of the problem is emphasized by drawing attention to the numbers of women who are depressed when they become mothers. Kleinman and Davis Raskin (1994), authors of one advice book on PPD, thus state that approximately 400,000 American women suffer from the illness annually. Linda Sebastian writes that "few [mothers] anticipate having postpartum depression or anxiety, yet 400,000 women suffer from it annually. In fact it's the most common complication of pregnancy" (1998 sleeve). The size of the problem is also emphasized, however, through the claim that many more women than these figures suggest have this illness. In doing so, the feelings and experiences of very large numbers of women are turned into "symptoms," evidence that they too are suffering from the illness PND.

What to Expect When You're Expecting claims in its 2002 edition that between 60 and 80 percent of new mothers suffer from "some form of baby blues or depression." It is notable that, when it was first published in 1984, the figure quoted was 50 percent, and the section of the book about PPD was half the size it is in the most recent version (Huget 2002:HE01). Jane Feinman argues in her book about PND, "No one knows exactly how prevalent post natal depression is. Official statistics put it at one in ten women, but these are 30 year old 'guesstimates'" (1997:12). There are grounds to believe that far more mothers are mentally ill than this figure suggests, she claims, since following the revelation by the late Princess Diana during a television interview in Britain, that she found herself depressed after the birth of her son William, "thousands of women identified with her descriptions and jammed the switchboards asking for help [from the Association for Post Natal Illness]" (1997:12). Price claims similarly that while "strict psychiatric criteria" produce a proportion of mothers with PND of 15–20 percent, "If those criteria are relaxed a little to include more transient disturbances the rate rises to 30–40 per cent" (1988:134). Welford contends that although psychiatric textbooks put the figure of women who suffer from PND at 10–15 percent, "if you include in your definition of postnatal depression all post-childbirth distress and misery, including the more shortlived forms, it's probable that the majority of mothers recognize many of the symptoms" (2002:2). Curham, with reference to Pitt's seminal paper on PND, argues that although he found that 10 percent of his sample of mothers were depressed, the actual incidence of postnatal depression "may be as high as 20 per cent" and that "as many as 90 per cent of new mothers experience some feelings of depression after the birth" (2000:36).

In these accounts, there is a significant modification of the three-part definition of the mother's mental states characteristic of psychiatry. All become variations of a single illness. Thus Roan, author of the U.S. manual *Postpartum Depression: Every Woman's Guide to Diagnosis, Treatment and Prevention,* claims, "It's no wonder that as many as 80 per cent of new mothers experience a period of depression popularly known as 'the baby blues.' While many women recover in a matter of weeks, others find blues changing into a mild, moderate or even severe depression sometimes lasting for months!" (1998:sleeve). Welford (2002) argues that there are three different forms of "postnatal distress": the blues, PND, and psychosis. Through this approach, PND becomes normalized—it is represented as common, in one form or another, to all mothers.

Emphasis on the diffuseness of the symptoms of PND also allows it to be normalized very easily. Cara Aiken states:

[C]ommon symptoms include depression, fatigue, sleeping difficulties, feelings of guilt (not fulfilling expectations of motherhood), feelings of inadequacy, loss of appetite, irritability, acute anxiety, fear of being alone with the baby, fear for the baby's well-being, fear of 'cot death,' fear about own physical and mental health, clinging to someone for constant support, hostility towards partner or loved ones, unexplained tearfulness, loss of enjoyment and inability to laugh, not coping, panic attacks, feelings of isolation, lack of confidence, bad memory, night sweats, unexplained fear about everything, suicidal tendencies, temptation to injure the child, loss of libido, low self esteem/self image, numbness, paranoia, constant physical ailments, obsessive behavioural patterns, the fear of further pregnancies and of PND, lack of bonding with the baby, false self-expectations, inability to concentrate, utter despair, feeling trapped, lack of enthusiasm. (2000:12–13)

It is notable that there are very few examples where advice available for women departs from this approach. For example, websites that seek to advise mothers about their experiences make similar claims. "With mild to moderate depression you may have a hard time sleeping," says the U.S. Women's Health Advisor website. It continues, "You may also feel: Tired, Discouraged, Irritable, Forgetful, Tearful. With more severe depression you may also: Feel confused, restless, anxious, guilty or worthless, lose your appetite, have rapid changes in your mood, lose interest in your baby, and have thoughts of death or suicide" (n.d.). In a particularly clear example of the tendency to turn women's feelings into evidence of a defined medical problem, the BBC Health Online website explains, "Postnatal depression is a very distressing condition with many symptoms. . . . Postnatal depression is an illness like any other. Ask for help just as you would if you had broken your leg" (n.d.).

CAMPAIGNS

A related development of the 1980s and 1990s has been claimsmaking by organizations that intend overtly to raise awareness and generate greater recognition of PND. The main such specialist organization in Britain is the Association for Post-Natal Illness (APNI), which was established in 1979. In the United States, Postpartum Support International (PSI) was established in 1987, and its founding aim is to "increase awareness among public and professional communities" (n.d.) about PPD and anxiety disorders affecting mothers. Other organizations with similar aims are the National Childbirth Trust in Britain, and Depression After Delivery, Inc., and The Postpartum Resource Center of New York in the United States.

Claimsmaking by such organizations centrally involves normalization of PND; claims in which differentiation between "normal" women and those who are "ill" is elided. One way this happens—as in advice books—is through claimsmakers contending that large numbers of women have PND. The Association for Post Natal Illness explains that its work is essential since such illness affects "between 70 000 and 100 000 women and their babies in the U.K. every year" (n.d.), more than the 10 percent of women that psychiatrists suggest. The idea of a "hidden epidemic" or a population of women "suffering in silence" is often invoked to show how more women than is commonly believed are depressed. The APNI labels PND the "silent epidemic," on the grounds that many women who suffer from it are never diagnosed or treated and thus are not counted in the statistics. The Postpartum Resource Center contends similarly that although it is estimated that 10–20 percent of new mothers experience postpartum depression, "we suspect that this number is greater since many cases go unreported" (undated).

Where psychiatry has made a distinction between the "blues" and PND through reference to longevity and severity of negative feelings, the tendency in such accounts is for this distinction to become thoroughly blurred. "Concept slippage" between these different categories frequently takes place. A common representation of women's experience when they have a baby is to discuss the differences between different kinds of "postnatal illness" as a matter of degree. The Postpartum Resource Center thus explains that PPD is a "general term used to describe a wide range of emotional disorders a woman can experience after the birth of her child. Three types of disorders are generally recognized: The Baby Blues, Postpartum Depression, and Postpartum Psychosis" (n.d.). A campaign by PSI exemplifies the way in which concept slippage functions in claims about PND. At the time of writing, PSI is encouraging support for "new federal legislation concerning postpartum health" through Bill 2380, introduced into the House of Representatives, named in honor of Melanie Stokes:

> Chicago native, Melanie Stokes was a successful pharmaceutical sales manager and loving wife of Dr. Sam Stokes. However, for Melanie, no title was more important than that of mother. Melanie believed motherhood was her life mission and fiercely wanted a daughter of her own. This dream came true on February 23, 2001 with the birth of her daughter, Sommer Skyy. Unfortunately, with the birth of her daughter, Melanie entered into a battle for her life with a devastating mood disorder known as postpartum psychosis. Despite a valiant fight against postpartum psychosis, which included being hospitalised a total of three times, Melanie jumped to her death from a 12-story [sic] window ledge on June 11, 2001. . . . Melanie was not alone in her pain and depression. Each year over 400,000 women suffer from postpartum mood changes. Nearly 80 percent of new mothers experience a common form of depression after delivery, known as "baby blues." . . . As was seen recently in the case of Andrea Yates of Houston, Texas who drowned her five children, postpartum depression and psychosis can have a dire impact on one's family and society in general. (Postpartum Support International 2001)

In this account, the problem of PPD is typified through reference to an example of a woman whose life ended tragically and who was diagnosed as suffering from psychosis. However, her experience is then linked to others suffering from PPD (400,000 women) and those who experience the "baby blues" (the vast majority of mothers).

PPD is also typified above through reference to the high-profile case of Andrea Yates. Indeed, in much debate about the Andrea Yates case, her act of drowning her five children was discussed as an extreme manifestation of the common mental illness PPD. The experience of Emily Sampino, coexecutive director of Postpartum Resource Center of New York, for example, who it was reported often cried uncontrollably, had panic attacks of "overconcern," and felt like she was "going crazy" for ten months after giving birth, was used to illustrate the widespread problem brought to light by the death of Yates' children (Burby 2001). The organizers of a major conference on women's health in 2002 publicized their event by connecting the Yates case with the "common problem" of psychiatric disorders in pregnancy and postpartum. In this construction of the problem, the significant percentage of women who are considered to suffer from PPD are represented as being at risk of very serious problems—possibly even killing their children—and greater intervention by health professionals in relation to new mothers' mental health is consequently encouraged.

It is notable that there has been little dispute of this approach. The Andrea Yates murder trial provoked a highly visible debate about how the law should consider those who commit murder, but are deemed insane by psychiatric testimony. There was, understandably, much concern expressed about the possibility that she would face the death penalty, or would be imprisoned for a substantial amount of time. The case also provoked a wider discussion, however, about motherhood and its effects, as it became a hook for commentaries that raised the problem of PPD. "Eighty percent of all mothers experience the baby blues; one in ten new mothers develop . . . a full blown clinical depression, and one in 1,000 develop psychosis," said one commentator, who concluded that "despite 40 years of feminism . . . we still refuse to release our notions of what motherhood means," but that it is high time to stop denying that motherhood can be bad for women's health (Slater 2001).

HEALTH POLICY AND PRACTICE

As noted above, claimsmakers often represent PND as insufficiently recognized by health professionals. Yet since the mid-1990s particularly, evidence suggests that the mental health of new mothers, in contrast to these claims, has featured more and more as a problem in health policy agendas and in the practice of relevant health professionals. Those involved in designing and implementing interventions directed toward mothers have proved themselves very keen to draw attention to the psychological problems mothers experience and to advocate that more should be done to identify and treat PND. If Chapter 4 showed how proponents of PAS experienced considerable difficulties in finding ways to make abortion policy and the practice of abortion provision reflect their claim, the discussion that follows suggests that claims about the problem of PND have generated a more sympathetic response.

In Britain, over the past five years in particular, PND has come to increasing prominence, as part of the broader trend to define social problems in relation to mental ill health. *Health of the Nation,* published by in the early 1990s by the then Conservative Party government, identified mental ill health in general as a key social problem that health policy should address, and for the first time set targets, in particular the reduction of the suicide rate. The policy, however, had little consequence since no means of achieving the target was specified and resources were not provided (Fitzpatrick 2001). This gap has been filled more recently, under the new Labour government elected in 1997, through the setting of new targets and the allocation of resources that are intended to allow them to be met. As Chapter 2 discussed, recent policy documents from the U.K. Department of Health (DoH) emphasize that mental health is a major problem. Mental ill health is considered "so common that one in six people of working age have a mental health problem" at any one time, "most often anxiety or depression." Its causes are very broadly defined and include poverty, poor education, unemployment, major life events such as bereavement, and poor parenting. Within this agenda, postnatal depression has been highlighted as a central, growing problem, and new mothers have been targeted as a group in need of greater attention. Women's mental health in general also has been paid more attention. "Recent government policies have raised the profile of women and families with regard to mental health issues," notes Gerrard (2000:1), and as part of this too, PND has become the focus for new interventions.

This has taken place as government policy has encouraged health professionals, primarily health visitors and midwives but also GPs, to place more and more emphasis on measures that can identify women with PND and encourage them to obtain treatment. In 1998, a government document, *Supporting Families,* suggested that midwives and health visitors should be able to assess the quality of relationships between woman and their partners, assess if factors are present that might contribute to PND, and if so encourage the woman to seek help (Gerrard 2000:1). In 2000 Julia Drown, chair of the Maternity Services Group in the British Parliament, indicated that making sure health professionals provide more "support for new mothers" to alleviate PND is an important part of government policy on maternity services. Health visitors particularly, Department of Health policy states, are "at the forefront for early identification of mental illness in mothers, their partners and children" (1999c).

In the United States, claims that emphasize the need for health professionals to do more to diagnose and treat depression in general, and PPD in particular, are also very evident. As the previous chapter suggested, improving mental health emerged as a public policy goal in the United States in the post–Second World War period, but, more recently, tackling mental illness as a whole, and depression in particular, have become a clear priority in health policy. The National Institute of Mental Health (NIMH) claims that, in confronting the problem of mental illness, "the stakes for our nation are high" since "mental disorders represent four of the ten leading causes of disability" (1999). Mental illness is also represented as a problem of major proportions by the current Surgeon General, who claims that agendas for improving public health have neglected mental illness, which affects nearly one in five Americans in any year, "yet continue too frequently to be spoken of in whispers and shame" (Sacher 2001:Preface). Mood disorders, including depression, "take a monumental toll in human suffering," he contends, and affect the lives of women in particular (Sacher 2001:226). Major initiatives from government bodies that emphasize the need for more to be done about depression date from an earlier point, however. The DART program described briefly in Chapter 2 was launched by the NIMH in 1986, and in 1993 the Department of Health and Human Services gave its support to a new set of guidelines developed for the Public Health Service that urged family doctors and other health professionals to make active efforts to detect depression and encourage patients to seek treatment.

Claims that construe women as especially at risk of depression, together with most other forms of mental illness, feature prominently in policy documents about the problem. Nineteen million Americans, or one in ten adults, experience depression each year, states the NIMH, but twice as many women as men experience it (2000). The causes remain unclear, the Institute contends, but they include reproductive, hormonal, and genetic factors, together with the effects of abuse, oppression, and personality characteristics. Active identification of the illness by health professionals and its treatment are essential, it is claimed. Encouraged by such attention to the problem of mental illness in women, bodies of health professionals including obstetricians and family doctors have become active in promoting the need to recognize and treat PPD. The American College of Obstetricians and Gynecologists claims that PPD is far too rarely recognized, and that obn-gyns must "pay attention to the mental health of our pregnant patients, as well as to the physical aspects of pregnancy" (2002). The College advocates that physicians identify women at risk from PPD during pregnancy and following delivery, by asking their patients "about their mood and adjustment to motherhood," and suggests physicians use the Edinburgh Postnatal Depression Scale, "to identify patients suspected of having significant depression" (2002).

How does the concept of PND function within such policy agendas? What are key ways in which the problem of mental illness in mothers is constructed in this domain? The following discussion suggests, first, that there is a clear diffusion of the central plank of the concept as developed by psychiatry—the merit of screening to identify patients—to this domain. Second, a related aspect of PND in health policy is the way the problem is linked to the broader social problem of parenting. Mental illness in mothers is problematized and professional intervention advocated and promoted as helpful, in relation to the problem of interactions between parents and their children.

Identification

In both Britain and the United States, claims that health professionals need to become more proactive in identifying PND are frequently made. "Postpartum Depression is the most under-diagnosed obstetrical complication in America," claims Dr. Diana Dell, ob-gyn at Duke University Medical School, describing the position on the issue taken by the American College of Obstetricians and Gynecologists (Morris 2000). Writing on a website for American obstetricians and gynecologists, Leopold et al. note that "despite the recent growth in publicity, postpartum depression is still all too often unrecognised or cavalierly dismissed." They write to encourage primary care physicians to do more, and claim, "as with other common complications of pregnancy, physicians must remember that all women are at risk" (n.d.). Similar criticisms are made by British health professionals' organizations. "Some doctors and Health Visitors are good at spotting PND, because they know about it and look out for it," explains the Royal College of Psychiatrists, "but others overlook or ignore it, or say, wrongly 'Oh, that's just the Baby Blues'" (2001). According to Hehir (2001b), articles published in medical journals have argued that family doctors need to do more about identifying and treating PND and have criticized them for constantly failing to identify PND, or recognize it for what it is. In 22 to 25 percent of cases, it is claimed, they underestimate the existence of depression. Health visitors and nurses who specialize in family health have also become subject to criticism of their approach, on the grounds that they too are failing to diagnose PND in 75 percent of cases.

Problematization of current practice, in which health professionals are deemed too cavalier about the problem of PND, serves to emphasize that the health professional's role is crucial in identifying the illness. The notion that health professionals must interact with pregnant women in a way that avoids trivializing their negative feelings and instead looks out actively for PND is commonplace. Advocacy of the need for health professionals to do more is also emphasized by drawing attention to the lack of self-diagnosis by women and a consequent lack of preparedness to seek help on their part. The problem, according to an article in the *British Journal of General Practice,* is that only one-third of women who were identified by researchers as having PND believed themselves to be suffering from it, and over 80 percent had not reported their symptoms to any health professional (Whitton et al. 1996). The disparity between women's own perceptions of what is "wrong" with them and the need to diagnose their feelings and behavior as PND appears frequently in discussions of the problem.

In Britain, the ability to identify PND has become more and more prominent in discussions of the role of the health visitor particularly. The Community Practitioners' and Health Visitors' Association (CPHVA) published *Postnatal Depression and Maternal Mental Health, a Public Health Priority* in 2001 and has established a Postnatal Depression and Maternal Mental Health Network for its members, "to support practice and service development in what the Association recognises is a key area of practice for our members" (CPVHA 2002:143). New initiatives and services have been developed in many areas of Britain, funded through government programs that are intended to improve mental health, within which a key aspect of contact with women is extensive use of the Edinburgh Postnatal Depression Scale (EPDS), to identify women at risk and ensure they are offered treatment, particularly counseling (Hehir 2001b).

The use of the EPDS has, in fact, become a matter of dispute in Britain. According to the National Screening Committee (NCS), a body responsible for advising government health ministers in Britain on screening policies, the EPDS falls far short of the criteria considered necessary by the NCS for use at a national level. The scale, claims the NCS, is inaccurate because women's responses to the questions that they are asked can be scored in varying ways, meaning that where one health professional finds signs of PND another may not; it is not always acceptable to postnatal women, and some decline to answer the questions because they find them intrusive; and there is little evidence of "value for money" resulting from its use. While noting these findings, however, the CPHVA contends that health visitors should continue using the scale. The EPDS "provides a useful framework for assessing common symptoms affecting depressed mothers" and "remains a useful tool" for health visitors to use, claims the Association. Continuing the "explosion of local activity" by spotting PND through use of the scale, developing new strategies and care pathways through which mothers can come into contact with health visitors more regularly, and treating it through "innovative means such as baby massage," are considered to be the priority despite the criticisms by the NCS (CPHVA 2002:143). The U.S. National Institute of Mental Health also advocates the use of the scale. A special meeting to discuss PPD, involving the NIMH Division of Services and Intervention Research, and Office of Women's Mental Health, discussed how PPD should be identified and found that the EPDS was a "well-established, reliable and valid measure" that could be used by primary physicians, pediatricians, and obstetricians to identify PPD (National Institute of Mental Health 2001b).

Treatment

PND is also represented as a condition that can be treated through medical intervention; most often counseling or drugs. A significant amount of research about PND comprises studies of treatment options, a dimension of the concept that increases its visibility significantly. New treatments are usually first discussed in the medical press, but are then often reported and discussed in the popular media, also contributing to the visibility of PND. In 1996, it was reported in the United States and Britain that a study published in *The Lancet* conducted by British doctors in London and Salisbury had found that mothers who wear a skin patch delivering a small dose of the hormone estrogen each day could be relieved of the condition (Fletcher 1996; Gilbert 1996). According to researchers from Manchester, writing first in the *British Medical Journal,* "Prozac is effective in overcoming post natal blues, but a course of skilled counselling is just as successful" (Fletcher 1997). "Baby massage" carried out by mothers has been promoted as a helpful practice by Vivette Glover, professor of perinatal psychobiology and director of the Fetal and Neonatal Stress Group (Glover 2001; BBC News Online 1999b).

In the United States it is more frequently advocated in health policy that drugs be prescribed to treat PPD than in Britain. This area is subject to dispute, and it has been claimed that more emphasis should be given to counseling. The "aggressive treatment" of women with drugs has been criticized by American psychiatrist Michael O'Hara, who contends that "brief, nonpharmacological interventions may be equally effective" (Morris 2000). Diane Sandford, psychologist and president of the Women's Healthcare Partnership and author of an advice book on PPD maintains that doctors are too quick to prescribe drugs and should instead offer psychotherapy (Morris 2000). In Britain, the dominant form of treatment that has emerged is based on a counseling model that involves interaction between mothers and health professionals. Women diagnosed with PND through use of the EPDS are offered "listening visits," for example, from health visitors. According to Bewley, health visitors trained in using the EPDS and in "nondirective counselling skills" now play a crucial role in spotting and treating PND. Research, it is argued, shows that mental health is improved by having a close friend to talk to. But since motherhood, it is claimed, "can bring isolation, particularly where extended families living close by are no longer the norm," counseling has become a key aspect of health visitors' work, particularly that which uses the Rogerian principles of "genuineness, empathy and non-possessive warmth" (Bewley 2000:34). Other national bodies of health care professionals also claim that interaction between mothers and health professionals is essential in the treatment of PND. The Royal College of Nursing thus advocates that "Practical help and a listening ear are instrumental in the support of newly delivered women and are significant in the prevention and detection of postnatal depression" (Bewley 2000:34).

PND and Parenting

Claims that represent PND as insufficiently recognized appear, therefore, to have generated a response in health policy and practice. The idea that intervention to detect and treat PND is an essential part of health professionals' work is given added weight in another way, too—through reference to the problem of parenting. The trend toward constructing parents as being in need of professional and expert advice and intervention if they are to "parent" effectively has been considered to be a marked feature of contemporary British and American societies (Hardyment 1995; Furedi 2001), and this trend is reflected in the way the concept of PND has developed in health policy. The claim that it is helpful for mothers if the problem of PND is emphasized and taken seriously is given added weight through reference to this well-established social problem.

A claim central to health policy that emphasizes treatment of PND links depression in mothers to inadequate child development, especially in boys, leading allegedly to problems in later childhood and possibly adult life (Macdonald and Todd 1998; Cooper 2001; Murray 2001). "The real concern for those working in public health," states a briefing for British health visitors, "is the growing body of research highlighting the potential long term effects of maternal depression on children and families." These effects, it is claimed, include delay in children's cognitive and social development, and that children of depressed mothers are more likely to have behavioral problems and to be abused (Adams 2002:263). According to one summary of the literature, "The negative effects of PND on the infant appear to happen very early in life. . . . The behavioural effects are long lasting, especially in boys from lower socioeconomic classes" (Shakespeare 2002). According to Gerrard, nurses in Britain need to be clear that PND matters because it is not just a "woman's problem," but has "ramifications for the family and society" (2000:1). The problem, Gerrard continues, is the impact on the child because depressed mothers cannot parent effectively, which in turn leads to social problems. She also draws attention to the effects on "boys from lower socio-economic classes" who are "most vulnerable" and are most likely to have socially damaging behavioral problems if their mothers were depressed (2000:7).

Claims made for the importance of British schemes established to treat PND, such as "Brief Encounters" in London, draw attention to the perceived link between improving the quality of parenting and the treatment of PND. In this scheme, health visitors "identify areas where problems in relationships were leading to problems with parenting," including evidence of PND (Bewley 2000:34). Claimsmaking that connects PND and the problem of parenting is taken one stage farther in the claim that the negative effects of maternal depression for the child begin in the womb. In a paper presented at a conference for health visitors, it was argued by one British authority on child development that "maternal mood can have a direct effect on the fetus" and that women who are depressed during pregnancy are likely to bear children with significant behavioral problems, particularly those who give birth to boys. Not only mothers with PND but also those depressed during pregnancy must be treated, it was claimed (Glover 2001:14).

The problem of depressed mothers' parenting, in clear contrast with their experiences after abortion, is also very much highlighted in the United States. A publication from the American Psychological Association problematizes depression in adults in relation to its effects for children (one of a number of books on this subject). PPD is a serious problem, its editors claim, because "many of the symptoms of depression are incompatible with good parenting" (Goodman and Gotlib 2002:4). The "most alarming consequence [of PPD] is the mother's inability to bond with and nurture her child," says another U.S. commentator who claims that more needs to be done to treat PPD, on the basis that "studies show that infants of depressed mothers are slower to interact with people and objects." Poor motor skills, trouble regulating their emotions, and poor cognitive abilities are consequences of not treating PPD, and a "cycle of depression" can develop, in which babies of mothers who were depressed are at risk of being depressed themselves throughout life (Morris 2000). In 2002, in a summit on early childhood development, the current president's wife, Laura Bush, announced a new initiative in parent education, a magazine produced by the Departments of Agriculture, Education, and Health and Human Services titled *Healthy Start, Grow Smart.* The magazine discusses the effects of PPD for child development and emphasizes the importance of mothers seeking treatment to prevent poor mother/child interactions (together with the need for safe car seats and breast-feeding) (Nelson 2002).

Linking treatment of PND with the problem of parenting is also reflected in the way in which endorsement is given to the importance of the work of health professionals in development of the parenting skills of fathers. The domain of PND has expanded to include men as well as women. This makes for another notable contrast with PAS. Abortion opponents' claims that men can be traumatized by their partners' abortion have gained little visibility beyond their ranks. Yet claims that draw attention to the importance of health professionals not "missing out" men when responding to the problem of PND feature prominently in literature for health professionals (Curham 2000; Gerrard 2000). According to Gerrard, writing in a monograph for British nurses, fathers must be included in discussion and policy about the problem of PND, and she states that 10 percent of fathers experience mental health problems. "Targeted support from health professionals" for fathers, especially in the first weeks after a baby is born, is critical, states this commentator (2000:7).

The need to include men in support and treatment for PND has been promoted by key institutions. In 1999, the U.K. government launched a guidebook aimed at men whose partners were expecting a baby or who had recently given birth. Titled *The Bounty Guide to Fatherhood,* its aim was to "challenge traditional views about fatherhood" and encourage men to become more involved in parenting. According to the pamphlet, the problem of PND was one reason why men needed to do so. Men often feel ignored by maternity services, states the booklet, but "when dads are well-informed, mothers typically have shorter labours and need less pain relief, successful breastfeeding is more likely and post-natal depression less likely" (BBC News Online 1999c). It is not only the case, it is claimed, that fathers need professional support to reduce the problem of PND for their partners. Fathers Direct, the charity commissioned by the U.K. government to write *The Bounty Guide to Fatherhood,* claims that in addition to postnatal depression in one in ten women, postnatal depression in men is a significant and unrecognized problem. "Between three and 10 per cent of new fathers become depressed," this organization claims (BBC News Online 1999d). The problem of postnatal depression in men has been promoted by other organizations too, as part of their argument that poor health among men is not taken seriously enough. Men's Health Forum made the news at the time of the launch of *The Bounty Guide to Fatherhood,* when it claimed that up to 10 percent of men suffer from depression following the birth of their baby. The Forum said that it "wants to see the subject of male depression discussed at ante-natal classes so that men know what they are suffering from if they develop the condition" (BBC News Online 1999e).

Domain expansion is also evident where PND has been linked to claims from those who contend that child abuse is a major social problem. The problem of PND is emphasized even more dramatically in claims made in relation to this issue, and the need for professional intervention to treat PND is further endorsed as a result. In 2000, Britain's most important child protection organization, the National Society for the Protection of Children (NSPCC), launched a highly publicized campaign, featuring posters and TV advertisements that pictured, for example, a happy mother or father with their small baby, with the comment, "That night he felt like slamming her against the cot" or, "Later she wanted to hold a pillow over his face." The campaign claimed to be supporting "stressed partners at risk of abusing their babies" who were suffering from PND, which contributed to the likelihood of a parent harming his or her child. The NSPCC, it was reported, wanted better antenatal advice for new parents, and lessons about family life to be taught to schoolchildren (BBC News Online 2000).

The NSPCC's argument was welcomed by the U.K. government, and the

NSPCC campaign was considered important in that it offered further support to parenting classes offered since the late 1990s to parents that in part aim to reduce the incidence of child abuse. Indeed, the link between PND and child abuse has been given institutional support in other ways in Britain. Claims regarding the need for listening visits by health visitors have been justified on similar grounds, even when a woman says she does not want or need such intervention, "to determine whether the non-compliance represents a potential or actual child protection concern" (Hehir 2001b).

FEMINISM AND POSTNATAL DEPRESSION

A final arena for claimsmaking about PND is feminism. This arena has been considered important for some time. Pitt, who coined the term PND, noted in 1985 that "the emotional disorders of the puerperium, along with many other aspects of obstetrics, are rapidly becoming feminist issues" (1985:148). Claims made in advice books and campaigns discussed above are closely related to this field of discussion about PND, since many who have authored or contributed to books and who are active in campaigning for greater awareness of the problem would describe themselves as feminist. However, feminism can be considered separately, since PND often appears in broader discussions about women and their problems, written from an explicitly feminist perspective.

Some feminists, such as Ann Oakley, have written about women's problems for many decades and have discussed PND in their work. More recently—particularly since the late 1990s—other feminists have come to write about motherhood too. Prominent titles of this kind are Naomi Wolf's *Misconceptions, Truth, Lies and the Unexpected on the Journey to Motherhood* (2001), widely promoted in Britain as well as the United States, *Life After Birth* by British feminist writer Kate Figes (1998), and Susan Maushart's *The Mask of Motherhood* (1999). This is an arena deserving of attention in a book of this kind, because it is from feminism that it might be expected that there would be most dispute with psychiatry about its conceptualization of women's problems. As noted in the Introduction, feminists have often made claims critical of medicalization, particularly with regard to pregnancy. The interaction between the concept of PND as developed by psychiatry and claims emanating from these sources is interesting, however, in that feminist claims have come to tend to reinforce, rather than run counter to, those developed by psychiatry.

Is Medicalization a Problem?

A feminist approach to pregnancy and birth was defined, in the 1970s at least, by its claim that the medical profession colonized these events at the expense of women. Although obstetrics and gynecology have been construed as the main problem in this regard, it is also the case that psychiatry has been criticized for pathologizing women through its claims about the relationship between mental illness and reproduction (Oakley 1992; Showalter 1987). According to Showalter, for example, whose work has acted as a reference for some feminist discussion of PND, psychiatry's conception of pregnancy, childbirth, and their effects on women's minds has been highly problematic. She argues that because there was considered to be a "synthetic connection" between the brain and the uterus, mental illness in women was naturalized. Victorian psychiatry was disturbed by women who became psychotic following birth, since such behavior seemed to "violate all of Victorian culture's most deeply treasured ideal of feminine propriety and maternal love" (1987:58), and considered such behavior to be the result of biological change, a reflection of the weakening of women's minds as result of childbirth. This viewpoint attracted criticism from Showalter and other feminists, both for its practical implications in the kind of "treatment" given to women, but more broadly for its construction of women's response to childbirth as disease. A case has been made that rather than being pathological, such a response could be considered a product of social conditions. Showalter suggests, however, that even though symptoms of psychosis and infanticide were associated with women who were the poorest, because women's behavior was pathologized by psychiatry, any connection was consequently ignored.

This basic point, that the danger of medicalization is that it represents social problems as medical ones, has featured in arguments about PND. The claim that has been made, however, is not so much that the concept of PND avoids discussion of poverty, but that it avoids discussion of the general problem of being a mother in contemporary society. A feminist critic of the medicalization of childbirth, Sheila Kitzinger, has thus argued that through PND women can be "forced to explain the distress they experience at the way in which society is treating them by reference to their glands" and claims that, in fact, "depression, anxiety, numbing exhaustion, pervading guilt and a shattering loss of self esteem" are better understood as an "occupational hazard" of being a mother in Western cultures (1988:1). Renowned British feminist Ann Oakley has described PND as "a pseudo-scientific tag for the description and ideological transformation of maternal discontent" (Comport 1987:21). The burden of this point is that negative feelings in mothers do not indicate mental illness caused by raging hormones. In this approach "postnatal depression" is nothing more than a label for the unavoidable psychological distress generated by a society that overburdens women, and mothers in particular, in manifold ways.

Feminist counterclaims in which the concept of PND is criticized have remained relatively marginal, however, or, perhaps more accurately, most such claimsmakers, especially those writing more recently, have proved able to accommodate and endorse the concept of PND. Claims made by those arguing from a woman-centered perspective suggest that it has proved possible for the concept of PND to be shared with psychiatry, with PND represented in a way that is not perceived to pathologize women, as shown by the following discussion, of what I suggest can be considered a new narrative of women's problems.

A New Narrative of Women's Problems

It could be argued that to suggest that the problematization of motherhood by feminists is a "new narrative" overstates the case. There has been a very long-standing discussion, for example, of the problem for women of incorporating the responsibilities of motherhood into their lives. Hochschild famously brought this problem to light, with regard to the issue of mothers' work outside and outside the home, in her book *The Second Shift,* but arguably this problem has been a theme for feminists for a much longer time. Feminist discussions in the late nineteenth century and early twentieth century of the "woman problem," through to the work of Simone de Beauvoir, related to this problem in that they examined the relationship between the public and private spheres for women's lives and drew attention to how this relationship denied women freedoms they needed to be equal to men.

The point of suggesting there is now a "new narrative" is not, therefore, to suggest it is new for feminists to write about the problem of motherhood. But recent accounts are distinctive in that the problem is described, far more overtly than previously, through reference to women's emotions. Recent feminist work is striking in the attention it pays to the experience of being a mother, and the feelings generated by the experience, for the author concerned in particular and, by extension, for women generally. This is not to say that issues that featured previously in feminist work about motherhood (for example, the need for better child-care provision) are absent. But there is a new kind of demand made. This is for a *shift in culture,* to generate a public discourse that has the emotional difficulties of the experience of motherhood at its center.

Feminist work about motherhood now often thus demands recognition in the public realm for the feelings and emotional experiences of mothers. Kate Figes writes, "The turmoil of new motherhood is still a taboo subject. . . . It is almost as if there is a conspiracy of silence surrounding the transition to motherhood" (1998:3); breaking this silence is her aim. Naomi Wolf contends: "Only by listening to the full spectrum of stories that women confess to one another, including stories that cultural reasons dictate we must not speak out loud, can the taboo against voicing our fears and bowdlerizing our experience be broken" (2001:8). Susan Maushart complains of the "collective denial about the chaos that is motherhood in contemporary society," a problem she describes as "the mask of silence." Her claim is that "we owe it not only to our own mental health but to the very future of the species to take motherhood seriously, to strip off the masks we have been wearing, and to see with clear eyes and speak with open voices about the realities we experience" (1999:xxi).

In these claims, the feminist project is couched in overtly therapeutic terms. It is through speaking of experience and demanding that others listen to women's feelings that change comes about. Indeed, a key complaint is that society is organized through a conspiracy of silence with regard to the mother's experiences (a phrase that is common to much recent feminist work about the problem) and that central to making change is to make women's emotional experience public. The problem of the public realm is defined by the refusal to listen to what women say about their experiences. Figes contends, in this vein, that the problem is one of being "trapped in silence . . . when things get rough, because of the fear of being labelled 'selfish', 'immature', or 'not fit to be a mother'" (1998:245). This is a key theme in Wolf's arguments too. She claims that an important freedom women are denied is the ability to talk publicly about their experiences. She thus describes her experience at seven months into her pregnancy, in the following way: "I longed for something tangible that could reflect or give voice to those moments of otherworldliness I experienced. I wanted some acknowledgement of what I sometimes saw as the sacredness of my state" (2001:85). Claims for the beatification of the pregnant state are less frequent, however, than those for recognition of the psychological pain and suffering that becoming a mother entails.

For Maushart, therefore, "At least part of the problem is that our society propagates a ridiculously positive myth of pregnancy" (1999:53). The strongest forces that constrain women, she argues, are those that "minimize the difficulties we face, insisting that motherhood is no big deal after all" (1999:36). Wolf writes scathingly of books that present motherhood in positive terms and that, in her view, do not talk enough about women's negative feelings. *What to Expect When You're Expecting* is attacked on this basis, for what Wolf considers its problematic reluctance to make it clear to women that motherhood is an ordeal. What is most distressing "is not the prospect of a woman hearing about some of the tougher aspects of labour and delivery . . . but, rather, the psychic cost to the mother-to-be of literature that is determined to focus on happy talk and sentimentality" (2001:3). Figes's book is written as an attack on the "taboos surrounding new motherhood," and she explain's that her aim is to "emphasize the positive aspects of motherhood" but also "be honest" by telling about the negative ones. If by doing so, her book prevents "the births of unwanted children, because women have their suspicions confirmed that motherhood is not for them, then I am proud of that," she says (1998:viii).

With regard to each aspect of pregnancy and motherhood recounted in such books—from getting pregnant, to being pregnant, giving birth, going to work or staying at home with children, and interactions with male partners—claims are made that it is necessary to "tell the truth" and "break the silence" in order to make others aware of women's negative feelings and experiences. It is easy to see, in this approach, why the problem of PND appeals. It can give legitimacy and weight to claims that it is negative emotions that feature centrally in women's experience as mothers, and which are currently unrecognized. The problem of PND, in its most diffuse form, provides a means through which these feminist writers can make the claim that motherhood is a far greater ordeal than is currently recognized.

For Figes, PND thus "hovers in the huge chasm between [the] two extremes of mild 'baby blues' and psychosis" (1998:41). She argues strongly that PND is not something that is experienced by just a few women but is, in fact, the common experience: "It [PND] is a sliding scale, starting with the 'baby blues' affecting 80 per cent of women, and ending with puerperal psychosis. . . . The vast majority of women sit somewhere on this scale" (1998:40). She states: "The medically defined symptoms of postnatal depression are all-encompassing: tearfulness, irritability, feelings of despondency and inadequacy, self-reproach, excessive anxiety and sleep disturbances. It is hard to find a new mother who does not suffer from some or all of these" (1998:24). The claim that culture needs to change and give more recognition to these negative feelings that all mothers have is articulated by claiming that medical professionals need to do more to diagnose this illness. Naomi Wolf states, therefore, that PPD may start at any time during the first year after the birth of the baby, and that "Postpartum depression affects 400,000 mothers per year in the USA. . . . This is the data that few practitioners give us when warning us gently about the 'baby blues'" (2001:185). She contends that the situation is far better in Britain than in the United States, since in the former, "new mothers are routinely screened for PPD," whereas no such policy is implemented in the United States, "which has the highest postpartum depression rate in the industrialized world" (2001:186). Wolf does not make clear how it is known that the United States has the highest rate, in the absence of screening programs for the illness. Nevertheless, she refers approvingly to the argument made by Kleinman and Davis Raskin in their book on PPD, that American women face a huge problem, in that they often "fall through the cracks" in the system, and that "if a woman turns to her OB-GYN for help, she is likely to hear that she is merely 'going through a period of adjustment'" (2001:186–7).

The approach taken by those who are in other ways critical of medicalization thus appears, in the case of PND, to encourage the far greater use of this medical label, rather than contest it. Claimsmaking in the feminist domain points to an interesting contrast between abortion and motherhood. Where in the former example, there have been clear demands that lines be drawn between feelings and illness states, that the effects of abortion on women's minds be placed in context and not exaggerated, and that the experience of women who experience no negative feelings after abortion be highlighted, no such counterweight is evident where motherhood is concerned.

This narrative has achieved a high degree of visibility. This is not to say that criticism of the case for a culture shift, to a culture in which the ordeal of motherhood is given prominence, has attracted no criticism. It has been argued by one columnist in a major British newspaper that there is a trend, "for women of a certain type to enter into parenting expecting an apocalypse . . . this has become the only fashionable approach; those women who look forward to the whole business are considered stupid, retrograde and unaware that a sadistic joke is being played on them" (Knight 2001:4). Another has claimed that such books "display a growing incontinence in their desire to disseminate the detail of their reproductive selves" (Sarler 2001), and that there is a problematic propensity for middle class working women, with "nanny, cleaner, nice house and two cars" to complain about the stress of their lives (Marcus 2002). One reviewer in the *Washington Post* noted that Wolf's book had been considered "self indulgent, poorly written and is accused of letting the side down through self-obsession" (Warner 2001:T10). The feminist journalist Katha Pollitt (1999), with reference to Wolf, has also criticized what she views as a wider tendency for feminists to write about their own experience and draw general conclusions from it. Much media response has been supportive, however. As Figes notes herself, "The taboos surrounding new motherhood are beginning to crumble slowly," and points out that where once journalists were used rarely if ever to write about the negative aspects of new motherhood, they now do so regularly (1998:x). It is certainly the case that articles drawing attention to the problems of motherhood have become commonplace, with articles titled, "The truth about life after birth," "Mother's ruin," and "Motherhood and the big lie," drawing on feminists' claims to articulate further the problem of the perceived lack of recognition of the ordeal of motherhood.

PREGNANCY AND CHILDBIRTH

The process of claimsmaking with regard to motherhood thus contrasts clearly with that for abortion. The observation that there is a clear differentiation between these two processes is given further weight when debates about other aspects of women's experiences of pregnancy and its outcomes are considered. It is not only motherhood that is presented as a psychological ordeal, with claims that emphasize the need for greater recognition of this problem achieving visibility and resonance. Earlier stages on the path to motherhood, in particular giving birth, have also been problematized in similar terms. An interesting feature of the process of claimsmaking in this instance is that the time between psychiatrists discussing these problems, and their appearance in other domains, has been markedly shorter than that for PND. If the visibility of PND incrementally increased over more than four decades, mental health problems linked to childbirth gained visibility far more rapidly once psychiatry defined them, and the distinction between the different domains where motherhood and mental ill health have become linked is more blurred.

Childbirth and PTSD

Experiences considered traumatic and therefore a cause of mental illness, as discussed briefly in Chapter 2, now include giving birth. Whereas medical and scientific opinion, in the United States in particular, has rejected the claim that abortion can lead to a form of PTSD, in contrast the claim that childbirth can do so has been advocated. Published studies by psychiatrists, psychologists, and other health professionals argue that PTSD is an insufficiently recognized outcome of childbirth for some women and claim more must be done to deal with it, and these claims have been endorsed and publicized by other opinion formers. Although it has less of a profile than war, violence, or sexual abuse as a traumatic experience, birth has thus been established as a cause of PTSD.

The discussion of this issue in the medical literature began in the mid-1990s. In 1994, as part of a feature on PTSD, *Nursing Times* carried an article, subsequently cited in many other publications, which argued the case for "acknowledging the psychological trauma that can result from childbirth" (Ralph and Alexander 1994). Authored by a lecturer in midwifery, and a tutor for the British organization the National Childbirth Trust, the article contended that although health professionals may not associate PTSD with a "natural, everyday incident like childbirth," many women may in fact suffer from the syndrome after giving birth, and the "value of undertaking a form of postnatal debriefing similar to that used to prevent PTSD should be urgently investigated." Labor for women, it was claimed, can be considered a stressor capable of leading to PTSD since while "normal" in that it is very common, it is not "usual" for those women experiencing it. Thus, where the symptoms of PTSD are present, giving birth can be viewed as their cause, and PTSD diagnosed. They suggested, further, that if including labor as a PTSD stressor were problematic, then the condition might be called Postnatal Stress Disorder and be considered a specific mental illness in its own right. Writing in 1995, Ballard, Stanley, and Brockington, psychiatrists at the University of Birmingham, conducted a study to investigate this problem further and found that, "As confirmed by other reports, the prevalence of PTSD associated with childbirth is a matter of concern" (1995).

These studies made reference to a 1993 article by counselor Janet Menage in which the author argued that her study confirmed "a connection between obstetric and gynaecological procedures and the development of post-traumatic stress disorder" (1993:226), and in which a similarity between obstetrical/gynecological experience and "sexual violence and other causes of PTSD," proposed previously by other researchers, was suggested. Women in her study,

Menage argued, experienced childbirth and other obstetrical procedures as "violation" and their psychological responses could be legitimately compared to those of Vietnam War veterans and women who had been raped.

In the late 1990s, further studies relating childbirth to PTSD were published and became a subject of discussion in the media. Consultant psychiatrist Fiona Blake, from the John Radcliffe Hospital in Oxford, has been prominently associated with promoting the idea that childbirth leads to PTSD. Her argument, as detailed in Chapter 2, was reported in the medical and popular press in 1996 and 1998. In the latter year, it was reported that many hospitals in Britain were setting up midwife-run services to help women recover from giving birth. Such sessions offer "individual listening," and women are either counseled by the midwife or referred to other mental health professionals. The rationale for such services is that woman giving birth are at risk of developing PTSD; according to Dr. Blake, this experience can leave women with something similar to the mental illness suffered by those who have been involved in disasters. She has seen women "who are chronically ill as a result of a difficult birth. It can ruin their lives" (Moore 1998).

The claim that PTSD can follow childbirth is by no means restricted to Britain. Research reports from many countries have appeared in psychiatric and medical journals. In *Primary Care Update for OB/GYNS,* published in the United States, researchers from the Department of Psychiatry at the University of Illinois discussed the problem of the development of a range of mental illnesses—depression, bipolar mood disorder, schizophrenia, panic disorders, obsessive compulsive disorders, eating disorders, and PTSD—in women during pregnancy. It was noted that "traumatic labor and delivery experiences may . . . be associated with PTSD" and that "pregnancy, labor and delivery may exacerbate PTSD in some women" (Miller and Shah 1999). The journal of the American College of Obstetricians and Gynecologists has also reported on "post-traumatic stress disorder and pregnancy complications" (Seng et al. 2001). In these articles, research from a number of other countries was cited, including that mentioned above published in the British publication *Nursing Times,* an article in the *Journal of the Canadian Medical Association,* and one by the Scandinavian Psychiatric Association.

Psychiatrists and other medical professionals from Australia, Singapore, Sweden, Canada, and Germany have also published on the subject. According to Creedy at al. (2000), at the Faculty of Health and Nursing at Griffith University in Australia, PTSD following childbirth is a poorly recognized phenomenon that is more prevalent than is currently considered to be the case. Ayers and Pickering argue in *Birth* magazine that it is necessary to "increase awareness about the disorder" since "at least 1.5 per cent women may develop chronic posttraumatic stress disorder as a result of childbirth" (2001). Using the DSM IV definition of PTSD, Swedish researchers found that 1.7 percent of women had PTSD after giving birth (Wijma et al. 1997). German researchers found that "PTSD can develop after a traumatic delivery with long-term negative consequences for the health and mental condition of the mother" (Pantlen and Rohde 2001). American researchers Kruckman and Smith drew on research published in the *Australian and New Zealand Journal of Psychiatry* to argue that some interventions during birth "leave a mother susceptible to grieving, posttraumatic distress, and depression" and noted that much research has found that "conditions surrounding the birthing process" are risk factors for the development of post-partum depression, as well as PTSD (1998).

The representation of birth as a potentially traumatic experience has been publicized in the media—for example an article about postpartum depression, described as a "salad-bar of symptoms," typically including "depression, anxiety and chest-pounding panic attacks that can mimic a heart attack," maintained that women who give birth were also "at risk for post-traumatic disorder, the syndrome made famous by Vietnam vets" (Goodnow 2000). As with PND, its visibility is linked to its endorsement in other arenas. Advice books on PND also discuss the trauma of birth and some, such as U.S. author Lynn Masden's *Rebounding from Childbirth* (1994), make the case for "birth trauma" being viewed as a specific type of PTSD. Kate Figes (1998) says that PTSD "can follow anything such as a car crash, violent crime, an experience of war or an earthquake and symptoms include nightmares, insomnia, excessive irritability, anxiety and repeated recollections of the event. . . . Many women have similar symptoms after birth." Citing research by Janet Menage, Figes explains that women who have given birth "were found to be suffering from post-traumatic stress disorder, with scores [in a psychiatric test] similar to those of eighty-nine Vietnam veterans who had completed the same questionnaire" (1998:32-3). Sheila Kitzinger, who disputes PND for pathologizing motherhood, nonetheless endorses the idea that birth leads to PTSD in some women arguing, "After the Vietnam War soldiers on both sides who had not suffered any physical injury often became distressed. . . . The same thing can happen after a birth. . . . [A woman] may feel as if she has been raped. . . . This can happen even with so-called 'normal' birth" (n.d.).

Psychotherapist Jane Feinmann, author of *Surviving the Baby Blues,* writes that a "sizeable minority of women, probably one in a hundred or more" suffer from PTSD after childbirth. She says that "the experience is similar to that first described by Vietnam War Veterans. . . . Some women are so depressed that they cannot contemplate even having a smear test, sex, a future vaginal delivery, or even another pregnancy" (1997:50). Ian Brockington, in a chapter he contributed to a book for mothers written by PND "survivor" Cara Aiken, states that at least twenty different psychiatric disorders can occur in the postpartum period, one of which is "stress reactions," including PTSD. He argues that the pain and trauma of childbirth should not be underestimated, and that even with modern obstetrics, women are at risk of suffering from PTSD after they give birth. On the basis of his clinical experience, claims Brockington, the stress of childbirth can have long-lasting effects and may even result in women developing another kind of mental illness, a pathological fear of childbirth he calls "tokophobia" (Aiken 2000:118), a claim repeated before and since (Royal College of Psychiatrists 1999; Hofberg and Brockingon 2000; Hill 2001; Moore 2002:40). The notion that health professionals need to provide much more extensive help for women who have given birth is frequently advocated in such literature. Feinmann, for example, refers approvingly to the argument made by psychologist Sarah Clement, who states that postnatal "listening visits" should be used by health visitors to provide "psychological debriefing" so that women can "talk through" their experience of giving birth and thus prevent "feelings of post-traumatic stress" following childbirth (1997:78).

In health policy, the link between birth and PTSD is also endorsed. The Maternity Care Working Party, a British group whose members include the National Society for the Prevention of Cruelty to Children, the Royal College of General Practitioners, the Royal College of Midwives, the Royal College of Nursing, and the Royal College of Obstetricians and Gynaecologists, notes that mothers may experience PND and PTSD. The proportion experiencing the former, the Working Party states, is 10-15 percent, whereas the number experiencing the latter is not known, but greater support for mothers is needed (Maternity Care Working Party 2001). Medical bodies' policy documents urge their members to take this problem seriously. The American College of Obstetricians and Gynecologists (ACOG) has advocated that its members be aware of this problem since the mid 1990s, and has made efforts to bring it to public attention. In a press briefing following the September 11 terrorist attacks, the ACOG claimed that the Andrea Yates case had brought necessary attention to the problem of both PPD and PTSD related to birth. In the light of September 11, it was claimed, further vigilance was needed since pregnant women and women who had given birth were, because of the effects of these attacks, at even greater risk of developing both conditions (American College of Obstetricians and Gynecologists 2001).

The conclusion this chapter points to is that the psychological and psychiatric problems associated with having a child, rather than avoiding doing so, have over recent years gained more and more visibility. Claims that mental illness, in the form of PND and PTSD, is a significant problem for mothers have been generally endorsed. In Britain and the United States to date no body of opinion has emerged to contest the evidence presented to substantiate claims regarding the negative effects of pregnancy for women's mental health. Such claims have resonated, or at least appeared beyond question, in a way that claims about the negative psychological effects of abortion have not.

The concept of PND is the most developed construction of this kind. An interesting aspect of the claims made to draw attention to this problem is that unresolved difficulties for psychiatry about how to explain and define PND have come to coexist in their claims with the widespread use of the concept to capture and express the idea that motherhood is an ordeal. These difficulties coexist with the emergence of agreement that it is important for mothers' feelings and behavior to be discussed in these terms. This agreement is key to the construction of PND as a concept and as an accepted problem. It means that discussion of motherhood in specialist medical and psychiatric journals, self-help books for women authored by experts and women themselves, texts authored by feminist commentators, and health policy documents include claims that emphasize the risk of PND. While the language used in these texts varies—that written for an audience of psychiatrists of course adopts a style and tone different from that of advice leaflets from Depression After Delivery—taken together, they indicate that claims that associate motherhood and mental ill health have gathered pace. The relatively greater speed at which claims for PTSD following birth, compared with PND, have gained visibility and support suggests there is a significant dynamic to the construction of motherhood and its aftermath as a cause of mental illness.

7

Reexamining the Issues

So far, this book has examined claims about the outcomes of reproductive choices, made in the context of the "Syndrome Society." This is a context in which, as Chapter 2 explained, human experience tends to be increasingly explained and understood in medicalized terms. This chapter also showed how the medicalization of human experience is reflected clearly in the fact that more people than ever are now considered to be suffering from a greater range of definable mental illnesses. Other chapters have shown that claims about women's experience of abortion, and of becoming a mother, have emerged in this context, and I have discussed how claimsmakers involved in debates about these experiences have used ideas and themes typical of the "Syndrome Society" to make their case.

But the evidence discussed in the previous pages suggests that they have done so to contrasting effect. The idea that there is an association between abortion, and women suffering from a specific form of mental illness afterward, Postabortion Syndrome, has been greatly contested. It stands as an example where there have been clear limits to the extent to which medicalization has taken place. Childbirth and women's experience afterward, in contrast, have come to be more strongly viewed as experiences that are connected with the development of the mental illnesses PND and PTSD. There has been, therefore, a process at work that I have termed the *selective medicalization* of reproduction. This final chapter will look again at some issues this raises. In particular I will consider further how we might explain and understand this process and how we might assess its consequences.

SELECTIVE MEDICALIZATION

Previous chapters have made it very clear that there has been a great deal of debate about whether there is a Postabortion Syndrome. The context of the "Syndrome Society" (together with one in which moralized antiabortion claims have failed to win support for measures that would strongly limit the legality of abortion) meant it made sense for those opposed to abortion to frame the abortion problem in medicalized terms. But as it has turned out, abortion opponents who have made this claim have not managed, to date, to generate much support for it. As my account of the debate about PAS has shown, beyond the organized antiabortion movement, very few have argued that it is accurate to represent the effects of abortion on women's minds in this way, or that it helps women to do so. What conclusions can be drawn from this? What might it tell us about the reasons why there are sometimes limits to the medicalization of problems?

First, when the PAS claim has become visible, and has acted to influence the abortion debate, why has this been the case? Comparing the response to this claim in the United States and Britain helps answer this question. Insofar as PAS has gained significant visibility and has influenced debates about abortion, it has done so in the former society. Its profile and influence have been greater in the United States than in Britain. This difference in the response to PAS in the two societies has emerged largely as a result of the greater extent to which some American politicians have offered support to PAS claimsmakers and their proposals. But this arguably draws attention less to the success of this *specific* framing of the abortion problem than to the general propensity for some politicians in the United States to lend support to many proposals advocated by opponents of abortion. Beyond such political support, however, there are no significant arenas where the PAS claim has found resonance in either country.

Most importantly, as I have discussed in detail, claims that have emerged from science and medicine have acted to strongly constrain the efficacy of the PAS claim. The debate over PAS, as a result, is an example where claims framed in medical language that emerged *outside* the scientific and medical profession have been strongly contested by those *within* it. In both the United States and Britain, when the PAS claim has been made, arguments based on the findings of scientific research have dominated the content of counterclaims—although in the United States, people associated with science and medicine have played a more public claimsmaking role than in Britain. Rebuttal of PAS, when it has become the subject of public debate, which draws on such scientific evidence, has proved very effective. Even where the PAS claim gained most support, in the United States during the Reagan administration, it has proved impossible for the advocates of the claim to trump this medical imperative. Such counterclaims have since reappeared to discredit the PAS claim time and time again in American debates and have set the terms for discussion in Britain.

The effect of these counterclaims has not been, however, to *demedicalize* the issue. A demedicalized construction of abortion would arguably lead to a situation in which the matter of a woman's mental health would be construed as being of no great significance for abortion law and policy. The only issue would be individual choice, with the abortion provider or medical professional deemed to bear little responsibility for women's feelings after abortion, as long as the woman concerned consented to end her pregnancy. As Chapter 4 showed, this has not happened either in the United States or in Britain. But the evidence I have discussed also indicates that the form in which abortion remains medicalized is one in which this choice is constructed as "low risk" with regard to mental health, and as clearly justified on these grounds. For the purposes of this book, this is the most significant feature of the contemporary abortion debate. In both the United States and Britain—although more explicitly in the latter—it is a procedure that has gained more and more legitimacy on mental health grounds.

The importance for PAS claimants of opposition from science and medicine to their arguments conforms with findings from some other studies of the limits to medicalization. Although, as the Introduction argued, endorsement from the medical profession is not *always* necessary for a problem to be medicalized, evidence does suggest that the support of some sympathetic, credible professionals is usually required. There are instances where it has proved possible to medicalize a problem to a significant degree without this support, and sometimes even despite opposition or ambivalence on the part of established medical and scientific opinion. (It has been argued this is the case, for example, with alcoholism and myalgic encephalomyelitis.) But as Conrad and Potter (2000) explain, in instances where claims have been made that a particular condition should be understood as a medical problem, where the primary advocates have been lay interests without the support of some medical professionals, such claims have proved likely to encounter difficulties.

The effects of continued pregnancies for women's mental health have been the subject of a great deal of research too, some of which has been explicitly connected to the abortion debate. Research about unwanted pregnancies that are continued has tended to legitimize abortion, by indicating that there is a greater risk of mental disturbance in women where such pregnancies end in birth than when they are aborted. As Chapter 5 suggested, this research has also resulted in some claims that have represented the birth of unwanted children as a problem because this is a cause of social problems. Being born unwanted, it has been argued, leads to the development of psychiatric problems, which in turn are the cause of antisocial and criminal behavior, and therefore allowing women to end unwanted pregnancies can help alleviate such social problems. Thus some claims about abortion, in which abortion is justified in relation to its mental health effects, have also contributed to medicalization in another way. These claims have medicalized social problems, through relating their development to psychiatric problems among unwanted children. Abortion has, through this argument, become legitimized in part on the grounds that bearing a child that is planned for and wanted is not only best for the mother, but that it is best for society in general. This holds for both Britain and the United States.

Overall, however, the medicalization of abortion, with regard to its effects on women's minds, has been relatively constrained. An association between what is good for women, and the encouragement of greater recognition of PAS, the point at the heart of this representation of the abortion problem, has not gained much ground. To put it another way, the representation of women typical of claims about the problem of PAS, in which they are portrayed as victims who have not made their own decisions about having an abortion, has not been well received. PAS, as a form of contest of the idea that women who have abortions choose to do so, has so far proved unable to disrupt this idea, certainly to the extent of successfully contesting the legal provision of abortion. It may be that a connection between freedom of the individual and opting to have an abortion has remained culturally resonant. As Conrad and Schneider have noted, the "value of individual liberty may limit to a certain extent, extreme medicalization. . . . Freedom of choice may indeed counter medicalizing tendencies" (1980:78), and this observation seems to be borne out in the case of PAS. It is arguable that as long as there is a cultural affiliation with the idea of individual choice in relation to abortion, it is unlikely that abortion opponents will find they have the resources to medicalize the abortion problem to the extent to which they hope they can. As long as claims against abortion are viewed as antichoice, then they are unlikely to gain much ground.

There is also another way of explaining the phenomenon of the constraints to the efficacy of the PAS claim. This explanation would suggest that the connection between opting to have an abortion, and its outcomes for how women feel, has remained constructed in a relatively fluid way. The idea that there is a predetermined relationship between a woman's actions when she makes the decision to have an abortion and the effects that decision will have for how she will feel afterward has not become the dominant one. Instead, the relationship between action and outcome is viewed as relatively variable and contingent. Whether a woman experiences negative feelings after abortion is considered dependent on all sorts of factors that may pertain when she makes her decision, and which may change afterward. Insofar as it is considered the case, therefore, that this action is likely to lead to predictable mental health problems, this is only deemed to hold for certain groups of women; those who have been represented as more at risk of experiencing negative feelings than women generally. But the relationship between choosing abortion and its psychological effects has not been *objectified in general*. Most importantly, it has not been the case that abortion has come to be defined as a cause of mental illness through the emergence of a relevant psychiatric diagnostic category, or through the use of an existing one. In both the United States and Britain, abortion is constructed as an experience that has no clear relationship to the emergence of mental illness, and this holds for all women.

This explanation draws attention to an important aspect of the way that the experiences of abortion and of becoming a mother have come to be constructed differently. In the latter case compared with the former, there has been a greater degree of objectification of the relationship between the experience—giving birth and becoming a mother—and women's subsequent mental state. The relationship between becoming a mother and women's state of mind has been framed in a way in which one is viewed as fairly directly related to the other. The claims examined in Chapter 6—for example, that many women suffer from a form of PTSD following childbirth, or that a greater number of mothers than is often suggested suffer from PND—illustrate this point. Event and outcome have come to be viewed as quite clearly related. Through the representation of women's state of mind in the form of specified categories of mental illness, PTSD and PND, the connection between experience and its effects has become fixed. In this sense, in contrast to the example of abortion, much claimsmaking about the problems of the experience of motherhood strongly reflects themes characteristic of the "Syndrome Society."

The visibility of and resonance for this representation of the effects of becoming a mother is, of course, relative to the past. Motherhood is clearly not generally represented as most likely very depressing for most women, and birth and its aftermath are not consistently portrayed as an inevitably traumatic ordeal. In both British and U.S. cultures, the birth of a baby is still considered to be an event women often look forward to with excitement and can find to be a joyous experience, and motherhood remains connected with ideas about self-fulfillment and pleasure for women (and their male partners). But the emergence of a more visible representation of the experiences of pregnancy, birth, and becoming a mother as causes of defined states of mental illness is an important development. It suggests that, although both abortion and continued pregnancies have remained linked to debates about the development of mental illness, the stronger dynamic is toward problematizing reproductive choices where the latter option is chosen. This is perhaps the most important finding that emerges from this study—that there is a now a quite powerful tendency in British and American cultures to represent motherhood as an ordeal and, in particular, as an experience that is linked to the development of mental illness. I will now offer some further observations about the objectification of the psychological effects of becoming a mother and make some critical comments about this process.

THE EFFECTS OF SCIENTIFIC CLAIMS

The most obvious component of the objectification of the relationship between becoming a mother and the development of mental illness has taken place in the way that psychiatry and medicine have offered support to this understanding of it (in clear contrast with abortion). This experience, as Chapters 5 and 6 described, has been researched by psychiatrists in regard to its mental health effects, and it has been argued that women who become mothers do experience symptoms characteristic of definable mental illnesses and that they are more likely experience these conditions than women who have abortions. For example, women who give birth have been found to be more likely to experience psychosis than those who have abortions. In either case the numbers affected are very small, but postpartum psychosis has been established as a mental illness that, while rare, occurs more frequently than psychosis following abortion. Depression, too, it has been argued, is more prevalent in women who become mothers than in women who have an abortion. While psychiatry is unclear about how to explain it, a minority of mothers have been identified as likely to be depressed in the months after childbirth.

It is arguable that to some degree, the mental illnesses that have come to be associated with motherhood in this way are "objective," at least in the sense that they do seem to recur in different societies and different historical contexts. Puerperal psychosis and postpartum psychosis, in particular, stand as examples of mental illnesses of this kind. And it can also be argued that it is not problematic—indeed it may be very helpful for those women who are affected by these conditions—to think of their experience in this way, as evidence that they are suffering from very real illnesses. To the limited extent that severe forms of mental disruption afflict women who have given birth, it would surely be inhumane and highly problematic not to think of the women concerned as ill. It is only right, for example, to think that Andrea Yates (the Texan women who killed all of her children, whose case I discussed in the previous chapter) should be viewed in this way. She, and women like her, should be provided with appropriate medical treatment, not sent to jail.

But this having been said, it could be considered that there are, in fact, significant differences between these scientific "facts of the matter" and what might flow from them, and the public representations of the relationship between motherhood and mental illness described in Chapter 6 and their consequences. Although it could be argued that, in a limited sense, it is to women's advantage that it is accepted that becoming a mother can make women ill, the way in which the connection between the one and other has developed more recently arguably constitutes more a burden for women than a boon. To make this problem clear, I will compare again the arguments that have been made about abortion and becoming a mother.

In the abortion debate there has been a clear insistence from science and medicine that conceptual lines be drawn between mental illness and women's feelings—feeling bad or down is not the same as a psychiatric condition, it has been argued. The effect of this argument has been to keep distinctions between the two in very clear view, with important consequences. Although those who have argued for these distinctions may not have always made this explicit, it has meant that women's experience, and what women are considered in need of as a result, have been constructed in a particular (and from this author's perspective, very positive) way.

It has been argued that a small proportion of women experience very negative and problematic feelings following abortion and may therefore benefit from some sort of medical treatment. These women may require something more than just everyday life (counseling or drug treatment, for example) if they are to "get over" their experience. But most women, it has been argued, do not suffer from feelings so serious or long-lasting as to qualify as illness. Insofar as most women experience negative feelings, they will likely be transient and will change as life moves on. This, it has been explained, is why it makes no sense to call such women ill. And this representation of women's state of mind carries with it an important notion, the idea that the best form of "treatment" for most women will be life itself and women's interactions with it. This will, for most women, do the trick and make them better. Hence, in this representation of the relationship between an event and its aftermath, it is implied that experience is mutable and open to transformation. Experience may change as life moves on, as we interact with new events and episodes. The attraction of this way of thinking about experience is that people (in this instance, women) are viewed in a way that can be considered forward-looking, as relatively active in relation to their own futures.

But for motherhood, the arguments have been different. There is still, as Chapter 6 explained, a distinction drawn about the way that the mental state of women following childbirth is best thought of, with a line drawn between depression and "the blues." The negative feelings of most new mothers are transient, it is argued, but for a minority of women these feelings last longer and are thus more serious. They constitute a form of mental illness and mean that the women concerned will need some form of medical treatment. This distinction, however, is now more and more frequently broken down in claims about mothers' mental state. In contrast with abortion, the dividing line between women who will "cope" because they will find ways to deal with their feelings and will "get over" them, and those who will not and will thus require some form of special intervention and treatment, has become increasingly blurred.

This is most clearly the case in claims made by those outside psychiatry. As I have already detailed, it is frequently claimed that many (perhaps most) women suffer from PND and that far more women are in fact in need of some kind of medical treatment than those who are provided with it. But the dividing line between depression and "the blues" is also less clearly upheld by science and medicine too. Psychiatry still makes this distinction formally but appears reluctant to place it at the center of its public representations of women's problems. Thus, although psychiatry could make it very clear that the 10 percent of mothers it considers likely to be depressed in the time after childbirth are a minority, and that most mothers will need no special assistance or support (they will be able to "cope"), it has tended instead to blur the differences between depressed mothers and the rest. "The blues" have thus become construed a "risk factor" for depression, and psychiatry has helped popularize and institutionalize vigilance about this state of mind. For example, through its active advocacy of the use of its scale, the EPDS, psychiatry has helped encourage the process of breaking down boundaries between different mental states, and has helped raise awareness among women themselves that they are potential victims of PND and may require assistance from health professionals as a result.

The same process is evident for birth. At the extreme, women who give birth have been compared to both Vietnam War veterans and victims of rape. This is a claim that is not characteristic of psychiatry. But even if psychiatry has not argued for this particular comparison, the concept of Postnatal Stress Disorder, defined as a form of PTSD, has not been contested either. It has not been argued that representing childbirth as a cause of a specific form of mental illness may be a misrepresentation of the feelings a woman experiences when she is delivered of a child and an exaggeration of the severity and long-term importance of these feelings for her future life. In contrast, it has been advocated by psychiatry that childbirth can be usefully thought of in this way, as a specific stressor that can give rise to a definable state of mental illness, with important implications for a women's future.

In this sense, whereas medicine may now be more sensitive to accusations about the overmedicalization of childbirth with regard to obstetrics (although perhaps more in Britain than in the United States), psychiatry paradoxically seems rather less aware of problems that may occur through arguing that childbirth is a cause of PTSD (and now also "tokophobia"). There is little doubt that those who argue the case for greater recognition of the trauma of giving birth intend to help women. The argument that women who give birth quite often suffer from PTSD afterward is made with the best possible intentions. But it could, of course, be argued that in the same way that obstetrics can routinize the experience of birth for women to their detriment, through treating them as "bodies" rather than active participants, a similar problem can occur if childbirth is viewed as a cause of PTSD.

Feelings of being out of control when in labor and delivery are first generalized. This discounts the fact that many women continue to experience the physicality of childbirth and the fact that their baby is the result of it as greatly exhilarating, but it is notable that this representation of childbirth now has a relatively low profile. Second, these feelings, especially if they pertain after childbirth, are represented as possibly symptomatic of the presence of a long-lasting, serious illness. In Chapter 2, I discussed how the concept of PTSD generally expresses a perception in which human experience in the present and an event in the past come to be entirely bound up one with the other. The stressor event for PTSD thus comes to be one that scars for life. The idea that the concept of Postnatal Stress Disorder communicates is just the same, that the event and aftermath are connected in a predicable, definable, and highly damaging way. Women, it is argued, can be scarred for life by their experience of childbirth, and thus it makes sense to view childbirth as a potential stressor event for PTSD. But surely this approach should be questioned. Undoubtedly some women do have terrible experiences when they give birth, but nonetheless the notion that a diagnosis of PTSD and postbirth counseling to treat it are the right response may be a very problematic one. It may derogate the possibility that women can simply come to later experience this traumatic event differently, as life moves on, and, in addition, arguably a diagnosis of PTSD may make this outcome less, not more, likely.

My own mother, for example, would have been a good candidate for being diagnosed with PTSD following the birth of my brother. Her labor was extremely long and arduous, conducted in the "old-fashioned way" (this was in mid-1960s Britain), in which women were discouraged from moving around, and their legs were held by stirrups to assist the obstetrician getting a clear view. After over twenty-five hours, the baby was eventually delivered with forceps, leaving my mother badly torn as well as exhausted and demoralized, with a very battered and bruised baby to show for her ordeal. Without doubt this experience affected her very significantly for the following year or so. But it is also interesting that she went on to have a further child (a birth that she always describes as a "great relief." "All my worries disappeared the minute the baby was born," she recounts.). And, while her bad memories have never left her (she can describe her childbirth trauma blow-by-blow to this day), this does not mean she has failed to "cope." Indeed this description would be entirely untrue.

Perhaps my mother is just a particularly stoic woman. I think, more likely, she just did what most women can, which is to find her own way to cope, and to do so very successfully (this is not, by the way, to be taken to mean that the way her first baby was delivered was by any stretch of the imagination ideal). And it does not seem at all clear to me that she would have benefited from a psychiatric diagnosis and trauma counseling; indeed this may have made her less able to cope than she showed herself able to do. All these years later, however, the argument would be made that there could be merit in doing so. But my point is that such an approach can be criticized for medicalizing childbirth just as much as other ways of doing so can be. Its effects, in policies that advocate that since women are likely at risk of PTSD after childbirth they may well benefit from psychological debriefing by a professional counselor following it, can be viewed as just as routinizing and impersonal as obstetrics has ever been.

This all suggests there may be grounds for being wary of psychiatry's rather enthusiastic promotion of the problem of mothers' mental illness, in the way it has now come to be defined. Its objectification of the relationship between becoming a mother and the development of mental illness has come to hold for far more women than would have been the case in the past, and it makes sense to ask questions about whether this really helps women. There is another aspect to the objectification of mental illness in mothers too, however, and it is to this issue that I now turn.

NEW PROBLEMS FOR WOMEN?

A distinctive feature of current representations of motherhood as an ordeal, as Chapter 6 explained, is how different domains of opinion have worked together. In clear contrast with abortion, claims originating from *within* psychiatry that relate becoming a mother with the development of mental illnesses have been extended and made far more visible by claimsmakers *outside* psychiatry. Social actors from different domains have come to share ownership of the relevant psychiatric concepts. Unlike for abortion, feminists and those who are concerned with women's health have, in particular, encouraged medicalization in this case. Claims that encourage the social recognition of the mental illnesses associated with becoming a mother have, thus, come to the fore, and claimsmakers of various kinds have argued that others should encourage women to identify themselves as suffering from these illnesses.

As noted previously, a particularly commonplace representation of mental illness in mothers is that the problem is underrecognized. Its extent and severity are much greater than they were considered to be in the past, it is claimed, and they are a growing problem. Thus, the greater visibility of the problem of motherhood and mental illness is applauded as a positive development. It can be argued that through this kind of claim too, there is objectification of the relationship between the act of becoming a mother and women's subsequent experience of mental illness. In the articulation of why the problem is both more visible and is growing, another aspect of this process is evident.

For some, the increased profile of and awareness about the problem of mental illness in mothers constitute a belated and appropriate recognition of a problem that has always existed. Thus Daws explains, in her account of why PND is now more recognized than in the past, "Postnatal depression is not new, but decreased maternal and infant mortality has given us the space to notice it. When the struggle was to keep mothers and babies alive, survival was in itself a triumph and emotions perhaps took second place" (1996:11). It is not so much that there is a new problem, therefore, but that an always-existing one has come to be recognized. This kind of explanation is, however, less frequent than that which contends that changes in society have tended to make motherhood a more difficult experience than it might once have been.

Underpinning many claims about the reasons why mental illness in mothers has come to be more recognized are claims of various kinds that suggest that both childbirth and motherhood have come to be more difficult experiences for women now than in the past. Thus while some claims about the problem draw attention to causes that might be considered to have little historical dynamic (for example, the relationship between hormonal changes and the development of PND), other emphasize new social issues and suggest that these account for the emergence of a new problem. Figes states in this vein that, because of a lack of historical research, "we have no way of knowing whether rates of postnatal depression . . . have changed over time. . . . We can only presume that certain aspects of modern living make the transition to motherhood harder." She draws attention to women now being more likely to work and have interests they enjoy, thus giving them more to lose when they have a baby, and "the absence of an extended family nearby to help hold the baby [which] exacerbates the isolation a new mother can feel" (1998:45). Issues of this kind appear frequently in accounts of why there are more women with PND now than in the past.

The problem of the lack of nearby relatives who can assist with looking after babies and children is often highlighted. "It's not known whether postnatal depression was as common prior to the 1960s, when it was first identified," observes Feinmann, "but it may also be no coincidence that postnatal depression has come to prominence during a time of change in family life in Western countries" (1997:45). "The disintegration of the extended family means there are no helpful grannies, aunts and neighbours on hand," states one commentary on the subject. The author contends that the main source of support for a new mother is now usually the father, who "is even more clueless than the mother. . . . As a result, it is increasingly becoming commonplace for health first-time mothers to suffer the kind of prolonged post-natal exhaustion more in keeping with 19th century slum dwellers on their tenth pregnancy." This, it is argued, accounts for the greater incidence of PND (Helgadottir 2000:16).

Curham argues similarly that, as with antenatal depression, "the breakdown of the extended family plays a significant role in the incidence of postnatal depression," and she compares modern Western societies with "more traditional societies" where the family helps more and takes more responsibility for looking after a new baby. She draws the conclusion that support from the family "needs to be replaced by other sources," namely professional help from health visitors and midwives, and support groups (2000:70). Wolf highlights similar issues, in angrier terms. "It is not the depressed new mother who is aberrant," she argues, "but her situation." She states that in many cultures, including that of the United States, until fairly recently, a new mother had support from family and community. In many non-Western societies, this still continues, she contends, but not in the United States: "Only in the developed world and only since the 1950s, with the advent of socially isolated suburb [and] the atomization of the extended family . . . has there been this expectation that one woman alone . . . must be able to do the primary work of caring for . . . a restless baby . . . mostly by herself" (2001:189). In this argument, the rise of the problem of depression is by-product in large part of these changes. Increasing geographical mobility and the consequent spatial distance between women and their relatives are in this way problematized.

The propensity for women in the both the United States and Britain to have children later in life than they once did is also pointed to as a factor. This is without doubt a very marked development in both societies. In Britain a decline in fertility among women in their early twenties is a long-term trend, evident since the mid-1960s. For women in their late twenties, the decline is more recent, dating from the late 1980s. In general, fertility rates for older women have increased over the same period of time. Women aged twenty-five to twenty-nine are still the most likely to give birth in Britain, but since 1992, those aged thirty to thirty-four have been more likely to give birth than those aged twenty to twenty-four. This crossover pattern, between women in their early twenties and women in their early thirties, is common to European countries. The outcome is that the mean age of mothers at first birth has risen consistently. In 1971 it was 24.0 years, in 1984 it was 27.0 and in 1999 it was 29.4. To put it another way, in 1976, 69 percent of live births were to women in their twenties, and 20 percent were to women in their thirties. By 1998, these figures had changed to 48 and 42 percent, respectively (Office for National Statistics 2001). In the United States too, postponement of childbearing is a notable trend in recent decades. As Abma and Peterson (1995), of the National Center for Health Statistics, explain, among women aged twenty to twenty-four, the percentage of childless women increased from 48 in 1960 to 67 in the 1990s. They explain that among women at the end of their childbearing years, aged forty to forty-four, the percentage of childless women rose from 9 in 1975 to 16 in 1993, suggesting that for some women delayed childbearing eventually results in not having children at all. (This is a phenomenon that has also become the subject of much discussion in Britain. There is an important difference in this respect between these two societies, however, in that childlessness throughout life is an experience almost exclusive to white women in the United States (Abma and Peterson 1995; Luker 1996), whereas in Britain the differentiation in this sense is far less marked.) It is important to note that in the United States, however, as in Britain, fertility among older women has increased; the fertility rate among women aged thirty to thirty-four increased from 61.9 to 87.4 from 1980 to 1998. In the age range of thirty-five to thirty-nine, it increased from 19.8 to 37.4, and for women aged forty to forty-four, from 3.9 to 7.3 (U.S. Census Bureau 2000). That is to say, although more women as a whole will remain childless throughout their lives, women in their thirties and forties are now more likely to give birth than in the past.

These changes can be viewed as a result of the fact that women see motherhood less as a natural destiny than as one aspect of their lives, which also include education and career. While this may be differently experienced by women who are more or less middle class (a factor that has been considered connected with the clear differences that pertain generally in the childbearing patterns of black and white women in the United States) (Luker 1996), overall, changing patterns of fertility are coincident with a greatly changing relationship between women's lives and the worlds of both education and work in both Britain and the United States. And in some accounts of mothers' mental illness this is taken to be a factor that can account for this growing problem. As a consequence of these changes, it is argued, women have higher expectations about what being a mother will be like, which can be dashed by reality. "Having children is being put off until career goals are attained and then, after years of independence and spontaneity, the joys of parenthood can come as a huge shock," claims Curham (2000:66). As Welford notes (although she criticizes this argument), some have argued that PND can, in this respect, be the result of "disappointed expectations." Childbirth, it has been claimed by some, has come be anticipated as "some sort of transcendental expectation. . . . That childbirth experiences can often fall short of such exaggerated expectations is a potent source of disappointment and sense of loss for such parents" (2002:23). In this approach, the opening up of opportunities for women in the world of work and in other respects becomes a double-edged sword, generating problems as much as gains.

Some also emphasize the related issue of changes in relationships between men and women. The central point in many such accounts is the contention that, in advance of having children, men and women now operate in a way that is very different from the past. They act as equals in their lives and in their relationships (both partners go to work, they share common expectations and experiences and divide domestic responsibilities between them). But with the birth of a child, it is argued, this all changes. Wolf argues this point particularly strongly. "All around me, it seemed, the baby's birth was cleaving couple after couple—once equals in roles and expectations—along the lines of the old traditional gender roles. . . . The baby's arrival acted as a crack, then a fissure, then an earthquake, that wrenched open the egalitarianism in the marriages of virtually every couple I knew" (2001:191). Rachel Cusk, whose novel *A Life's Work: On Becoming a Mother* is an account of her own experience, argues similarly that "after a child is born the lives of its mother and father diverge, so that where before they were living in a state of some equality, now they exist in a sort of feudal relation to each other." This phenomenon is evident, too, in her claim that parenthood now induces a "slide into deeper patriarchy" than was even the case in the past (2001:5).

The point here is that social changes with regard to education and work have the effect of transforming relationships between men and women, making the genders more similar to each other than at any previous point. But at the point when a child is born, this similarity ceases to pertain. The way in which the genders relate to and experience becoming parents is so different and so unlike their previous experience in common, that it results in psychological crises for women of a greatly significant order. Men, it is argued, continue their previous lives to a significant extent (and want to), whereas women do not do so. For example, their relationship with the labor market alters significantly, and, furthermore, they do not *want* their lives to stay the same.

Others also emphasize that PND is linked to changes in relationships between men and women, but in a different way. Welford points to research that found women with very supportive partners, who made significant modifications to their lives when they became fathers (so-called new men), were in fact *more prone* to depression than other women. The explanation for this, she suggests, may be that such women felt their partners "were accumulating debts they couldn't repay" (2002:26). The reality for women, of feeling "tired, stressed and unsexy and disillusioned" when they had had a baby, meant they felt guilty about what they could offer their partners and felt more depressed as a result. Whichever way it is viewed, however, it is considered that changes in gender relationships account in part for the increase in mental illness in mothers.

As my discussion so far has suggested, it is the issue of women's changed relationship to the world of work that is implied as the decisive question in many discussions the epidemic of PND. It is relevant to the issue of geographical mobility, delayed childbearing, and changes in the way men and women relate to each other. This point, about the effects of women's greater participation in the labor market, is often made explicitly. It is the fact that women now expect, are expected, to "have it all"—combine work and motherhood—that matters most. "Gone are the days when a woman's sole purpose in life was to have children and create the perfect home," says Curham. "One of the major changes in our society of recent times has been the role of women in the workplace. Many women work extremely hard to establish a career and enjoy the challenges and motivation that it provides. They are faced with a very difficult decision when they start a family" (2000:65). Either giving up work or returning to it after having a baby comes as a shock to the system and may account for high rates of PND, she believes. Figes says that "numerous women feel emotionally torn, demoralized and deeply guilty about going back to work when their children are young" (1998:51). "Growing numbers of women now expect to be able to work, pursue their career aspirations and have children. But few of us are prepared for the logistics of juggling the two responsibilities, or for the way that our priorities and attitudes towards working can change after the birth of a child," she contends, in her explanation of the problem (1998:71).

It is important to note, however, that in these accounts it is not just women who work having to do more when they become mothers (Hochschild's "double shift") that is at issue. It is not just the practical issue of combining career and motherhood that counts, and therefore making child care better and more available, to allow women to more easily do the two, is at best viewed as only a partial solution. Thus, with regard to work, "men and women . . . see things from completely different perspectives," states Wolf (2001:192). Even when a woman, because she has the financial resources, can have enough child care to allow her to go back to her previous occupation easily, the problem still pertains to her. Unlike a man, she cannot just carry on as before, but as a mother. "I needed to go back to work to feel attached to the real world again," explains Figes of her own experience, "but I found it almost impossible to leave my baby" (1998:71). It is the problem of the tensions between work and motherhood that is made central to many arguments about why there is more PND than ever before—this is the new problem for women, it is argued—but at the same time this development is viewed as one with no easy solution. As Cusk puts it, of mothers' experience of the difficulties of work, "When she is with them, she is not herself; when she is without them she is not herself; and so it is as difficult to leave your children as it is to stay with them" (2001:7).

In these different ways, the emergence of more mental illness than in the past is, therefore, objectified. It is represented as a development that relates in large part to real social changes. This is an explanation that has much power. It can certainly seem convincing, particularly in the face of the increasing number of accounts in which women describe their experience in just such terms. The issues discussed above are all very visible in cultural representations of women's lives now. For example, the genre of novels tagged "mummy lit," that have been published recently, clearly reflect these issues.

Take Allison Pearson's novel, *I Don't Know How She Does It* (2002), a best-seller on both sides of the Atlantic. This is a story about Kate Reddy, a high-flying London-based professional, with a nanny and a loving husband. Central to her narrative of her life is the problem of "juggling," how to manage both career and motherhood. But this is clearly not just a practical issue for Kate. Although she does experience a problem common to many working parents, the so-called time famine, that's not really her problem. It's that she (but not her husband) worries about not being able to make homemade mince pies for her daughter's school Christmas party, like a good mother should. It's that she (but not her husband) feels terrible when she is not there to put her baby son to bed, because of the pressures of work. "And they call this progress," she quips, about the changes in women's lives since the 1970s. But she loves her job, and at the start of the novel it seems clear she would never consider being a stay-at-home mum. But by the end, she and her husband have "moved up to Derbyshire, near my family, and bought a place on the edge of a market town with a view and a paddock." Happiness at last? "I was bored to the point of manslaughter," Kate recounts.

Similar themes appear in Helen Simpson's fiction. In one of her stories in her collection called *Hey Yeah Right, Get a Life* (2000), Nicola, a woman with

a successful career in London and four children, experiences problems just like
Kate Reddy's. "The most hurtful thing . . . was the assumption that because
she was successful at work she must have sacrificed her children; that her children must have suffered," explains Nicola. In another story by Simpson, Dorrie is a full-time mother of three. Once a successful professional, "nowadays
those few who continued to see Dorrie at all registered her as a gloomy, timid
woman who had grown rather fat and over-protective of her three infants." Her
husband tends to think this way too. And in her own heart, too, Dorrie agrees.
She knew she "had failed," she confesses to herself, about not feeling able to
combine work and motherhood. Sam, a central character in Jane Green's novel
Babyville, is a similarly depressed mother. Her husband doesn't understand her
problems either, and her anger with him gets her close to having an affair (Kate
Reddy nearly did this too). Sam decided not to go back to work after her son
was born, but swings between liking her situation and resenting her husband
massively. "At least you get away from it," she screams at him. "At least you
get out of this fucking house. I'm trapped here all day."

   In the "real world" it is clear that these representations of women's problems make sense to many people. It was striking, for example, that in Britain
in 2002 the Prime Minister's wife, Cherie Blair, found it easy to explain why
she had made a serious political *faux pas* in these terms. Mrs Blair had become
embroiled in what became known as Cheriegate—a major public discussion
about the fact that she had become involved in a house-buying deal to purchase a residence for her son who had just gone off to university, which as it
turned out was being brokered by a known swindler. Notwithstanding the issue of why this came to dominate political debate in Britain for nearly two
months, given she did not actually break any law, Mrs. Blair's account of what
had led her to buy property this way was notable. In a speech to Britain's media about the issue, she explained, on the verge of tears, her problems as a
woman trying to juggle her responsibilities as barrister and judge, and mother
of four. "I am not superwoman," she explained, as her eyes welled up. "Sometimes some of the balls get dropped." It was striking that one of Britain's most
successful, highly paid women, the wife of Britain's most powerful man, who
has access to as much paid help and, by most accounts, family support that she
could want, nonetheless explained her actions this way. It was also an account
that, in the view of most, "played well" with Britain's media, which had, up
to this point, ruthlessly turned her actions into a public scandal. This suggests
there is little doubt that the idea that women today face significant new problems has a great deal of cultural support.

REEXPLAINING THE ISSUES

Accounts of the problem of mental illness in mothers, which objectify it in relation to social changes, are commonplace and have gained cultural endorse-

ment. But despite their ubiquity, there are problems with these explanations. Without doubt, many very significant changes have taken place in women's lives over recent decades. But it could be argued that none of this explains convincingly why more women than ever before experience mental illness as a result of becoming mothers.

This problem is raised by the fact that the changes described above could be interpreted and experienced in another way altogether and could therefore lead to a quite different set of claims. These changes could, overall, be taken to mean that women are more equal to men than ever before and can make far more choices about how they want to live their lives. It could be argued that women are in fact far better off than they have been in the past. To make this point another way, surely few would argue (including those who have made claims about the growing problem of mental illness in mothers) that life *really was* better for women overall before these social changes occurred. Betty Friedan famously described the existence of the American woman in the 1950s in the following way, in the opening to her book, *The Feminine Mystique:* "As she made the beds, shopped for groceries, matched slipcover material, ate peanut butter sandwiches with her children, chauffered Cub Scouts and Brownies, lay beside her husband at night, she was afraid to ask even of herself the silent question: 'Is this it?'" (1963:13). This problem that "has no name," of a restrictive, stultifying existence for women that was centered on home and family, no longer typifies the experience of most. This does not, of course, mean that there are not other problems for women. But it is difficult for this author to accept that the kind of society that has emerged in the intervening decades is one that poses women with *more* problems and difficulties, or is even as out of step with what women need and want as society was in the 1950s.

This is not to say, by any means, that there are not important new tensions and difficulties in women's lives, and that these need not be addressed. More should certainly be done to make it easier for women to negotiate the tensions between working life, and motherhood, for example. Those who have argued that there is a pressing need for culture to change in both the United States and Britain to take far more seriously the need for maternity leave and proper child care to be provided for women make a compelling case (Hewlitt 2002; Dench et al. 2002). These issues need to be addressed in both societies, although it has been demonstrated that U.S. women currently get a worse deal in these respects than those in Britain (Luker 1996; Crittenden 2001; Hewlitt 2002). But notwithstanding these issues, it is not at all apparent that the changes in women's lives discussed above should have inevitably led to a representation of their effects as being so negative for women. There are, in particular, problems with the idea that the development of ever-increasing rates of mental illness in mothers can be read as a direct result of these changes.

Take the notion that problems result from the fact that the extended family has broken down and that women now lack family support as a result. The idea that motherhood is, as a result, more of an ordeal for women than in the past does not easily flow from this fact. If what is being discussed is increasing geographical mobility—the fact that more women (and men) than in the past move away from their place of birth to work and pursue other activities and thus live farther away from family members—it is arguable that this may make life less depressing for women, not more. It could be taken to mean that women have more freedom to shape their lives and futures and have more opportunities available to them. Insofar as women in the past did tend to continue living in their place of birth, with family nearby, it is debatable that this made their lives less fraught with problems than they are now.

The fact that women are now more likely to delay motherhood until later in their lives could similarly be taken as symptomatic of the fact that women have more control over their lives than in the past. The proposition that women on average are having their first child later in life than previously is clearly connected to their experiencing motherhood as an ordeal is questionable. Quite the opposite point could be made, that in doing so, women are more likely to have children when they feel ready for it, and this expresses the fact that they have more latitude to make choices about their lives. Interestingly, the idea that having children later is a problem for women has emerged in a context where having children "too early" has also become a major preoccupation for both U.S. and British cultures—the problematization of teenage pregnancy is very visible in both. This social problem is a very complex one (Luker 1994). But it is notable that as part of it, the idea often features that young mothers are a group considered especially at risk of developing PND (Social Exclusion Unit 1999), suggesting, at least, that unless we are to draw the conclusion that becoming a mother is inevitably depressing whenever women do it, there are important contradictions in the explanations on offer for the phenomenon.

Perhaps, above all, the idea that greater involvement in the world of work is related in a fairly direct way to women experiencing motherhood as an ordeal is a problematic one. As I have already argued, this is not to say that the difficulties associated with combining the two are not very real. But on the other hand, opportunities for women are now far greater than at any point in the past (although the author is very well aware of the fact that there are very significant distinctions to be made, that cannot be discussed here, in the extent to which this is true for women of different class and ethnic backgrounds). It is, therefore, hard to escape from drawing the conclusion that there must be more to what has changed than simply objective shifts in what women's lives are constituted in, if we are to account for both the way women experience motherhood as an ordeal and its representation in medicalized terms.

If there are difficulties with some accounts of the relationship between motherhood and mental illness, in which the "objective" changes in women's lives described above are highlighted, then perhaps the way these developments have coincided with another phenomenon can help clarify some issues. It may be that what is at issue is not that so much that women will inevitably experience problems when they strive to "have it all," but that the emergence of a context in which it appears possible for at least some women to try to do so has taken place alongside the development of a "child-centered" culture. My account of this issue will be necessarily brief, but I hope that it can help explain why the experience of becoming a mother has come be portrayed, and arguably often experienced, as an ordeal.

First, the idea that becoming a mother has assumed some sort of transcendental meaning in the way that was not the case in the past merits further comment in this regard. As discussed above, this notion has been raised in relation to women having children later in life than before. But it could be argued that what matters is not so much the age at which women have children, but what doing so constitutes in relation to other aspects of women's lives. It may be going a bit far to suggest that this experience has come to be perceived as one that will provide women with transcendental meaning, but it is arguable that the experience of parenthood has come to be perceived as one that can provide women (and men) with meaningful relationships and experiences that no other aspect of life appears to provide.

It is important to note, for example, that becoming a parent stands now as one of the few aspects of life that is assumed to both demand and provide commitment. People become parents in the United States and Britain in a context where other kinds of bonds between people have assumed a fragile and impermanent character. Most obviously, the fact that a child is "for life" stands in stark contrast to relationships between men and women, which are now often perceived to be, and are experienced, as impermanent, risky, and insecure. As the journalist Jennie Bristow has said of British culture, "making a commitment to anything—even one's lover—is viewed as potentially dangerous" (2002:15), and Hochschild has made the same point about the United States, through her discussion of the phenomenon of "cultural cooling" (1999).

"Commitment phobia" has emerged as a term widely used on both sides of the Atlantic to describe this phenomenon (Dafoe and Popenoe 2002). And the coincidence of the marriage contract being at the same time easier to end (thus arguably making marriage less of a "trap" and thus best avoided), but at the same time less popular than previously, has been situated as expressive of ihis trend. It has been demonstrated that when people do make the decision to commit (for example, to get married), they do so in the knowledge that their union may well not stand the test of time, and the advocacy of both prenuptial agreements and the need for wives to keep bank accounts separate from their husbands' have been situated as expression of the emergence of a more "realistic attitude" toward the likely longevity of relationships of this type (Bristow 2002). If accounts of this kind are right, it would perhaps come as no surprise that women, and men, do have heightened expectations about what parenthood can generally bring to their lives, and make developing their relationships with their children very central to them.

In her very informative contribution to the discussion of these issues, how-ever, Bristow also argues that expectations about we what might expect from personal relationships are not unique in this respect. In many spheres of life, a sense of insecurity prevails: "[W]e seem to live in a more uncertain world than ever before," she says. "From politics to personal relationships, from re-ligion to the world of work, the norms and traditions of the past no longer ap-ply" (2002:28). What is important, Bristow contends, is not just that old traditions and ways of interacting with other people have less purchase—there is much that could be criticized about them and in many ways the demise of the old is no bad thing—but that they "have not been replaced by any 'new' certainties.'" "In a sense," continues Bristow, "the only definitive thing that can be said about contemporary society is that everything seems to be up for grabs" (2002:29). There is, of course, a large literature about this subject, of the problem of the decline of old certainties and the absence of new ones. This issue has been discussed extensively and controversially, by scholars, including Lasch (1977, 1984) and, more recently, Sennett (1998), Hunter (2000), and Putnam (2000). But what matters for my purposes here is that a propensity to perceive and experience parenthood as not just one aspect of life among oth-ers that are equally fulfilling and important in other ways, but as the most im-portant and meaningful part of life, may be reflective of these complex social changes.

And this might explain, in particular, why there can be new difficulties for women when they give birth today. It is certainly clear that many women do, in today's child-centered culture, now put a great deal of effort into anticipat-ing and planning for childbirth and expend much emotional energy doing so. Although again, this may apply to some women more than others, from preg-nant women changing their behavior in ways that correspond with impera-tives from health promotion advice, to their making birth plans, being pregnant and anticipating the birth of a child have become activities that both demand more of women and engage them to a greater degree than in the past (Lee and Jackson 2002). Childbirth, as a result, has come to be an experience that is looked forward to (and worried about), from the confirmation of a preg-nancy on, in a way that may be more intense than was previously the case.

It may be that, as a result, *some* women (and their partners) do have partic-ular expectations about what their experience of childbirth will be like, and the reality, as a result, can be a difficult one for them. Many surveys have shown that, without doubt, some do experience childbirth as far worse—in particu-lar as more terrifying—than they expected it to be, and some accounts have shown also that many women feel let down themselves, and feel that they have let others down, when they experience it this way. Perhaps this reflects the fact that because giving birth, as part of the transition to parenthood, has come to be viewed in a way that imputes new significance and import to it, expecta-tions have been created that many women simply cannot live up to. Current experience certainly creates a very interesting paradox—which is also a very difficult one to resolve—in which childbirth is physically safer than ever before for both mother and child but is, arguably, also more of an ordeal. What constitutes best practice in the management of childbirth, in this context, has become the subject of a great deal of debate.

Another aspect of the "child-centered" culture is worth discussing here. They are many important accounts of the way in which both U.S. and British cultures have developed a dominant "child-centered" *ideology*. Some accounts show clearly how this is a long-term development, and they provide a very subtle and nuanced account of it. The American sociologist Sharon Hays, for example, details the "historical construction" of the ideology of "intensive mothering" in the United States over the past 400 years, in which the imperative to offer unconditional love to the child has been placed center-stage. Intensive mothering demands of women endless sacrifice for their children. Hays argues that a key problem for women is a deep-seated "cultural contradiction" between this imperative, on the one hand, and the values of the market—profit maximization and striving to reach the top at work—on the other. She contends this contradiction is now more pronounced than ever before: "the sacred character of the child is fully elaborated and articulated: nowhere does the language of impersonality, efficiency, and profit enter in" (1996:69). It is therefore understandable that, as Hays shows through her interviews with American mothers, that they, despite class differences, commonly experience tensions between demands of the public world and the private domain.

Ann Crittenden (2001) also provides a compelling historical account of the development of this fissure between the values of the public and private worlds, and draws attention to the problems created for women when they try to reconcile the two. Figes (1998), unlike most who draw attention to the growing problem of mental illness in mothers, also details the development of ideologies of the "good mother," in the twentieth century particularly, and shows how these ideologies have acted to stigmatize the working mother. Her discussion of this issue also describes how, as part of this development, experts issuing advice to mothers became a feature of society from the late nineteenth century on. Psychological theories about the maternal-child bond, and its importance for child development and, by extension, social development, featured centrally. The overall impact of the proliferation of such expert advice, Figes suggests, has been to make most women experience being both mothers and workers as a guilt-inducing phenomenon, an experience that is very clearly articulated by the mothers she interviewed. Other accounts, however, suggest that although the development of a child-centered ideology is a long-term trend, particular features of it have emerged more recently, and it is these that now make the problems of parenthood more intense than ever.

The issue of the way that expert advice to parents about how to care for their children has developed and changed over time is the subject of historian

Christina Hardyment's fascinating study *Perfect Parents* (1995). She begins her account with the year 1750, pointing the fact that advice-giving about child-rearing has a long history. Hardyment writes in a way that is very sensitive to how the content of such advice has changed, however. Her point about what characterizes the kind of advice given from the early 1980s to the mid-1990s is that it has placed the spotlight on parents in a way that was never the case before. It is the risk that the *parent* can pose to the child that has emerged as the key theme. For Hardyment, behind this new focus lies the fact that women are now more likely to work outside the home than ever before, and the fact that marriages are less likely to last than ever before. For many, she suggests, these trends have been taken to mean that children are now "at risk" emotionally and physically to a far greater degree than in the past, and as a result the development and issuing of advice to parents has become both more extensive, and more "risk aware."

One particularly interesting aspect of her account is in the way in which she draws attention to the place of expert advice about the importance of minimizing the risks to children's safety and well-being in recent advice developed for parents. These risks include hampered physical and/or emotional development if a baby is not breast-fed, is not read bedtime stories, is not cuddled enough, is left to cry at night (or, alternatively, allowed to sleep in the parents' bed), cot death and manifold health problems if babies and children are not given the right kind of diet. In sum, she claims, "We are now so bombarded with horror stories . . . pessimistically presented statistics, and hearsay that it would be easy to believe that we are bringing up our children in the most dangerous, degenerate, and perverted world since time began, rather than the healthiest quarter-century in human history" (1995:328)

The issue of the way in which the child "at risk" has become iconic in advice now issued to parents is at the center of Furedi's account of contemporary child-centered ideology too (2001, 2002a). He argues that, as a result, both American and British societies are now characterized by a style of child-rearing he calls "paranoid parenting" in which almost every aspect of parents' interactions with their children has come to be considered a cause of damage to their offspring, and thus parents are often engulfed by worry about these risks. Like Hardyment, he also details the way in which the world has come to be represented as more risky for children than ever before. But for Furedi, it is also the case—and this is the most significant issue for him—it is the behavior of *parents themselves* that has become construed as most risky for their children.

Parents are warned about how their behavior can negatively affect their child's development from the point of conception on. Furedi observes, for example, that pregnant women have become subject to unprecedented amounts of advice-giving and scrutiny. The issue of the way that pregnant women who drink large amounts of alcohol or take drugs has become a highly visible social problem is an obvious case in point, and their criminalization in the United States for doing so is notable (Jackson 2001). But this is only the extreme end of this development. As I implied above, just about everything pregnant women eat or drink and many aspects of their lifestyle have become subject to often contradictory warnings about the risks faced by the fetus as a result, and women are considered to be irresponsible and certainly uncaring if they do not take measures to reduce these alleged risks (Lee and Jackson 2002). From this point on, what the parent does has come to be considered the determining factor in how children develop; it is parental behavior that is represented as central to whether children thrive or fail: "Today, parenting has been transformed into an all-purpose independent variable that seems to explain everything about an infant's development," explains Furedi (2002a:59). This phenomenon is based in two now culturally dominant myths, he says, that of the "vulnerable child" and that of the "parent as God."

On the one hand, children are now represented as less resilient and less able to recover from anything from accidents to interactions with other children than ever before. And it is now also assumed that what parents do "has an overwhelming impact on a child's development" (Furedi 2002:58). These two myths are widely articulated in the form of advice given to parents about how they should interact with their children, and their ascendancy has ensured that it is widely considered the case that parents will fail, or at least perform worse than they might, without professional guidance. Giving advice of this kind has become an industry in both the United States and Britain, Furedi argues; parenting has become professionalized. But the result is a problematic one: "The more we complicate childrearing and the more we insist on inflating the tasks facing mothers and fathers, the more we ensure that paranoia will dominate the style of contemporary parenting," he concludes (2002:103).

Furedi (2001, 2002a) also shows how it is particularly striking in both the United States and Britain that this way of thinking has become institutionalized. In particular it has become central in political life, as the problem of parenting has become an all-purpose explanation for social problems within political agendas, and "doing something" about this problem has become a key policy objective in both societies. A dominant feature of the way in which institutions now represent social problems, and offer solutions for then, is to make the case that they will improve the quality of interactions between parents and children. A similar point is made by Wallwork Winik, in his discussion of what child-rearing has come to constitute in the United States. The matter has come to be far from a private one, he explains, to be debated by mom and dad, "after the kids have brushed their teeth and gone to bed." Instead, not only have mental health professionals, child-development experts, counsellors, researchers, authors, and radio call-in hosts all come to be participants in the process, ready to dispense advice and guidelines, "Even various arms of the federal government have weighed in with their estimations of

what's best for their smallest citizens" (2000:41). According to Furedi (2003)
this phenomenon can be understood in part at least as a by-product of the increasing erosion of other ways of understanding social problems. "Old-fashioned" ideas about problems of poverty, social divisions, and antisocial
behavior have lost their purchase or, perhaps more accurately, have been recast
as originating in the private realm of the family.

This phenomenon, of a highly institutionalized "child-centered" culture,
may also shed further light on the differences between the abortion issue and
that of becoming a mother, in particular on why the former is less uniformly
a concern for policymakers than the latter. The difference is obvious, really; it
rests in the fact that becoming a mother involves opting to take responsibility for raising a child, whereas abortion does not. In a culture where, as discussed above, the ability of parents to cope with the responsibilities of
parenthood has come to be considered often lacking, abortion would be less of
a concern than motherhood, certainly for those who are not prolife.

Other than in the minds of those who advocate that there is a Postabortion
Syndrome, women are mostly considered responsible enough to be able to
choose to end a pregnancy, and it is thus expected that they will, mostly, be
able to cope afterward. But once a child comes into the picture, the understanding changes. Whether a mother, or father, really can be expected to be
responsible for their child is viewed differently. It is only some women and
men who are very clearly deemed to be "irresponsible parents," for example,
deadbeat dads or crack-addicted mothers. But the ever-increasing amount of
advice-giving, support-offering, and policy-initiating that now surround parenting suggests that the degree of responsibility that all parents are considered able to take for their children's welfare has been at best called into
question, at worst diminished to a significant degree. An agenda has emerged
in which relationships between family members have, therefore, come to be
subject to an unprecedented amount of scrutiny and are influenced by a wide
range of forces external to them.

Perhaps one of the most interesting aspects of all of this, however, is that
agendas that represent parents as having a relatively diminished role in relation to ensuring their children's welfare often play out well. The claim that
providing support and advice to parents needs to be central to policy agendas,
because bringing up children is the "hardest and most important job in the
world," seems to frequently meet with the perceptions of parents themselves.
This is, of course, not always true. Like any aspect of culture, child-centered
imperatives will meet with differential degrees of acceptance. It is notable, for
example, that many descriptions of the ordeal of motherhood draw more on
the experience of middle-class women than on those who are working class.
And it may also be that aspects of this culture make sense to people differ-
entially, and pertain to a varying degree in different contexts. For example, the
notion that parents should be prevented from smacking their children is

accepted by some parents and rejected by others, and seems overall to have greater resonance in the United States than in Britain. This issue, of how and why people engage with this cultural trend in varying ways, is a fascinating and important issue. But for now I will nonetheless suggest that child-centeredness has become a powerful influence, from which few remain entirely immune.

As a result, the boundaries between the public and private have come to be eroded, and professional intervention in what were once considered private relationships has come to be considered more necessary than ever before. And in this context, it is perhaps not surprising to find that women's experience of pregnancy, birth, and motherhood can be one fraught with problems. It would be hard for women to find themselves unaffected by these child-centered imperatives. While many have not gone so far as to spend hours playing Mozart to their tummies, even the most critically minded pregnant woman must find it hard not to worry about whether she should have a glass of wine with dinner. And even the most sensible mother will likely worry about whether she spends enough time with her children and is doing all she can to influence them in the best way. It would be a very unusual mother indeed who found herself able to resist the pressures of the advice coming at her from all sides.

THE PROBLEM OF MEDICALIZATION

Yet there is an unanswered question. I have argued that it is the emergence of a child-centered culture that may explain why other social changes that might benefit women are not experienced in a positive way. This may account, at least to some extent, for why motherhood has come to be portrayed as, and is often experienced to be, a highly contradictory experience—as both an ordeal and a greatly fulfilling experience. But this still does not point in an unproblematic way to the conclusion that more mothers than ever before have mental illness.

It is a big jump from explaining how and why becoming a mother can be an ordeal to arguing that women who experience it in this way have defined psychiatric conditions. Some might argue that concepts like PND or Postnatal Stress Disorder just represent a short-hand description of this experience, and that it is harmless for them to exist as such. But in this author's view the use of these particular terms constitutes more than this—it is not just a description—and can have important consequences. The medicalization of experience is a serious step to take, and my final comments will address the issue of why this is the case, for mothers and for other people whose experience comes to be subject to explanation in a medicalized framework.

The fact that women's experience has come to be represented more in medicalized terms gives further weight to the idea detailed at the start of this book, that there is a powerful tendency to explain human experience in the medical idiom. As Chapter 2 argued, in the United States and Britain claims that emphasize that it is positive to recognize the problems of trauma, stress, addiction, and depression have become commonplace. Cultural support has been offered to the idea that it is helpful for the problems generated by significant life events and experiences to be explained and conceptualized in this way. The arguably now promiscuous use of medical labels to describe women's experience as mothers conforms to this pattern of claimsmaking.

But whether the issue is motherhood or other aspects of human experience, questions need to be asked about the effects of this development. The issue at stake is not so much whether medical research and science have or have not proved that we are more likely than ever to be mentally ill. Rather, it is about whether we consider it culturally positive for people to be encouraged to think about their problems in this way. Insofar as women (or men) do experience problems, does it help to understand them in terms of a medical label? Claims for the recognition of psychological suffering the through use of a medical label suggest that it does, but it is not immediately obvious why this should be the case. A number of possible objections could be raised in response to this culture, which are applicable when the focus for discussion is childbirth and its aftermath, or indeed other significant life events and experiences.

A first objection could be that representing problems of living as medical ones may have an effect, for us as individuals and as a culture, of narrowing down the frame of reference through which we understand our problems and may hamper us from thinking about them and how to resolve them in other ways. Elaine Showalter concluded, from her study of, among others, the conditions Chronic Fatigue Syndrome, Gulf War Syndrome, and Multiple Personality Syndrome, that these epidemics "have already gone on too long, and they continue to do damage: in distracting us from the real problems and crises of modern society [and] in undermining respect for evidence and truth" (1997:206). In relation to the subject area of this book, insofar as mothers (and fathers) do experience being parents in a problematic way, perhaps it would be more beneficial for us to concentrate on understanding better what the "crises of modern society" are that have made this the case, than calling this experience illness.

There is a further, related issue, the danger that people can become trapped by such medical labels. This is a problem that I alluded to above, in relation to the issue of fixing the connection between action and outcome. By objectifying experience as a cause of illness, a process is arguably unleashed in which people become more passive and less able to act in relation to their problems, and as a result become more likely to remain "ill." As Fitzpatrick has pointed out, "the net effect of the dramatic expansion in the range of psychiatric diagnosis is that, instead of conferring strength on the patient, bestowing any such label is more likely to intensify and prolong incapacity." It has had the effect of demoralizing people, rather than making them more able to cope with life, he argues, and thus overall has tended to prolong, not resolve, people's problems (2001:107). This criticism of the "Syndrome Society" is given added appeal since the fact of the matter is that the expansion of psychiatric diagnosis has manifestly not made people better. At the same time that a culture has emerged in which recognition of illness has come to be considered important, more people have come to think of themselves as ill and more people experience illness as a problem that affects them in the long term.

Objectifying states of mind and their effects on people's ability to act can be considered problematic for another reason. The solution put forward for such illness states almost inevitably emphasizes the importance of professional help. Indeed, there is a very obvious relationship between claims that medicalize problems and the advocacy of a greater degree of recognition of illness, and intervention to treat it, on the part of health professionals in particular.

This relationship between problem construction and the advocacy of expert or professional assistance is evident in many areas. For example, as I argued above, with reference to work by Furedi, there is a clear relationship between constructing parenting as a problem, and claimsmaking that advocates the need for professional support and advice for parents. The idea that parents are best left to their own devices is rarely argued for. It is worth noting that some claims about the problem of PND, and what should be done about this illness, can be situated as part of this development. As I argued in Chapter 6, doing more about the problem of PND now forms part of agendas that aim to address the problems of parenting in both the United States and Britain. A woman's relationship with her partner and her interactions with her child have both become the subject of attention, on the grounds that the former may play a role in making a woman depressed, and the latter will suffer as a result. Depression in mothers, it is argued, has severe consequences for the child, placing his development at risk (and it is boys who are viewed as particularly at risk). It is, in part, on this basis that listening visits carried out by health professionals and greater vigilance on their part in general with regard to the problem of PND are justified. But it is questionable whether interventions of this kind will help people and make their situation better.

It may be an unforeseen consequence of this response to PND, for example, that while purporting to tackle the problem, it may at the same time increase mothers' "paranoia" about whether they are "doing the right thing." As one critic of the current problem of PND, the British nurse Brid Hehir, has noted, it may be the case that current approaches, in Britain at least, may "reinforce the inadequacy many women may already feel by virtue of having been identified as 'depressed' by a health visitor and in need of 'listening visits.'" While supporting the notion that women need a lot of emotional support following childbirth, Hehir contends that "the professional may not be the best person to provide it" and that additionally their intervention may "prolong and intensify [a mother's] problems, and deter women from building their own support network, in the way mothers always have done" (2001b). Rather paradoxically, in this line of reasoning, in the process of aiming to help women get better, their ability to do so is undermined.

Arguably this case could be made about the problem of a range of counseling interventions. The fact that such interventions are now so widely advocated and form a ubiquitous aspect of social life has been taken to mean that we now have a "therapeutic culture" overseen by a "therapeutic state" (J. Nolan 1998; Chriss 1999; Furedi 2003). One U.S. critic of this phenomenon, James Chriss, draws attention to the problems that can be created by this mode of social organization. Drawing on his own experience, of having to engage in marriage counseling before his wedding because this is what his church demanded he and his future wife do, he argues that medical and therapeutic expertise has encroached into "virtually every facet of modern social life." The effect, he contends, is that "persons are systematically disempowered within the contexts of their everyday life, because they systematically lose the ability to discuss and negotiate definitions of the situation informally among themselves, that is within the contexts of family and community" (1999:8).

Bristow has written, similarly, of the range of initiatives in Britain that now aim to "empower people" to cope with the problems of married life: "[D]espite their best intentions, these forms of relationship guidance are counterproductive. . . . the assumption that couples will not cope without advice places them in a dependent, weak position. Ironically . . . relationship guidance inevitably increases the existing level of anxiety and disorientation around intimate relationships" (2002:24). Such observations suggest that while, on the one hand, the "therapeutic society" may have emerged as a response to the weakening of bonds between people and the loss of certainty, in the process of attempting to address this problem, it can make matters worse. At the very least, such observations suggest that there are grounds for caution in advocating that counseling or other professional interventions are in general necessarily either helpful or benign.

To dwell on this point a little further, in particular in relation to problems that people experience in their private life, it is important to note that the widespread encouragement of initiatives that are intended to assist people in this arena (in particular through the provision of therapeutic and other health-oriented interventions) can be considered to be an expression of a shift in thinking about people, their ability to cope, and the consequences of intervention. As Fitzpatrick notes, the development of an array of initiatives and schemes that purport to assist people in this aspect of their lives constitutes "a dramatic reversal of what was traditionally regarded as good medical practice" (in Britain at least) (2001:128). He approvingly refers to the work of the psychotherapist Donald Winnicott, who insisted, "[W]e must never interfere with a home that is a going concern, not even for its own good." Winnicott "carefully distinguished between the legitimate sphere of medical intervention—the treatment of disease—from giving 'advice about life,'" explains

Fitzpatrick. He argued, in clear contrast to the dominant ethos today, that "Doctors and nurses [should] understand that they do not have to settle problems of living for their clients, men and women who are more often more mature persons than the doctor or nurse who is advising" (2001:128–9).

Yet we now live in a culture that tends to strongly subscribe to a view very unlike Winnicott's, one that considers it the case that it is usually beneficial for people to look to others to assist them with their "problems of living." Even if one accepts that perhaps more people than in the past do experience private life as an ordeal, and believe themselves to be in need of professional assistance if they are to sort out their problems, it is necessary to consider whether it is the case that meeting the demand will actually improve the situation.

Asking questions about this aspect of medicalization does not need to spring from hostility to professional help and expertise in the abstract and certainly does not constitute an argument against the need for more well-conducted research about psychiatric illnesses and for the provision of treatment for those who are ill. Indeed, it is apparent that in Britain and even more so in the United States, people who suffer from very serious forms of mental illness are by no means getting the treatment and help that they need (Laurence 2003). But it is legitimate to consider the consequences of the expanding place of expert and professional guidance in contemporary societies. Although the advocacy of support, advice, and treatment in various forms may be motivated by the best possible intentions, it is at least worth asking what its advocacy is predicated upon socially, and whether, in its provision, it will in fact make people "better." Indeed, the notion that such support or assistance may have unforeseen and problematic effects may be given weight by the fact that, in the same way that recognition of illness has coincided with there being more people who are ill, the provision of professional support and intervention has not led to a decrease in the demand for it—to the contrary. In this regard, it is notable that while society has come to place a great deal of import on the idea of evidence-based medicine, the evidence for the efficacy of, for example, counseling, appears to be somewhat lacking.

The overall conclusion this author has drawn from this study is that we need to think about many claims that encourage us to take seriously the mental ill health of others as not simply scientific fact, but as more subjective evaluations about how we should think about people and what they need. In the debate about abortion this point has become clear. The claim that it is right and helpful to view women as victims of Postabortion Syndrome is still considered to be connected with an evaluation of what women need and about how society should be organized. And, in effect, the dispute about it suggests many have decided they do not agree with the views of proponents of this claim about these issues. Many have taken the view that they do not want to live in the kind of society opponents of abortion advocate as best. But what this book has shown is that in most cases, we often appear reluctant to draw connections between processes of medicalization and their underlying dynamics. We have come to accept that many medical labels are objective. Perhaps we might do well to draw some broader lessons from the example of the limits to the medicalization of the abortion problem. It might help us if we strive to make judgments about claims that medicalize problems. We need to be interested in the issue of whether we should always accept that claimsmakers who advocate the use of medical terminology are, in fact, doing something good for others, and consider whether we should critically evaluate these claims and the activities of those who make them.

Notes

CHAPTER 1

1.   These quotations are taken from interviews that the author conducted in 1998 as part of her research for a doctoral thesis.

2.   The "diagnostic criteria" for Postabortion Syndrome developed by Vincent Rue are as follows:

A. Trauma exposure. The abortion event is perceived as the death of one's child, and the individual experiences feelings of fear, helplessness, horror, and impacted grief.

B. Reexperience of abortion trauma in at least one of the following modes:
Recurrent and intrusive recollections
Recurrent dreams of the abortion and/or baby
Reacting as reliving with flashbacks and dissociation
Physiological reactions upon recalling or cue exposure

C. Avoidance or emotional numbing in at least three ways:
Of thoughts and feelings of the abortion
Of information, people, and places related to the abortion
Inability to recall important aspects of abortion trauma
Diminished interest in usual or significant activities
Feelings of detachment or estrangement from others
Restricted range of feelings—loss of loving feelings
Sense of foreshortened future and punishment

D. Associated features—two or more persistent symptoms:
Difficulty with sleep
Irritability or outbursts of anger
Difficulty concentrating
Hypervigilance
Exaggerated startle response
Depression and/or suicidal thinking
Persistent feelings of survivor guilt
Self-devaluation and inability to forgive self
Secondary substance abuse
Symptoms of eating disorder
Loss of sexual interest or sexually acting out

E. Duration. Symptoms in B, C, and D last more than one month.

F. Impairment. Disturbance causes clinically significant distress or impairment in social situations, occupation, or other important areas of functioning.

G. Onset:
Acute (symptoms less than three months)
Chronic (symptoms persist for three months or more)
Delayed (symptoms begin six months or more after stressor)
(Rue and Banhole 1998:25–26).

CHAPTER 3

1. These include a leaflet authored by Wanda Franz, then president of the National Right to Life Committee, titled "What Is Post-Abortion Syndrome?"; a paper by Ann Speckhard; the National Right to Life Committee's report, "The Psychological Aftermath of Abortion"; a paper about PAS by Speckhard and Rue published in 1992; and the 1987 book by Elliot Institute director David Reardon, *Aborted Women—Silent No More* (Rawlinson 1994).

2. These include, for example, a leaflet authored by Wanda Franz; a leaflet titled "The Healing Process, How to Begin" by Terri Fangman, president of Women Exploited by Abortion; "What Is Post-Abortion Syndrome?" by Catherine Souhrada (in which Souhrada refers extensively to the opinions of Vincent Rue and David Reardon); and *The Psychological Safety of Abortion: The Need for Reconsideration,* written by Vincent Rue and published by the Elliot Institute.

CHAPTER 4

1. Koop met privately with twenty-seven groups from both sides of the debate, including representatives of the Association of State and Territorial Health Officials, the Alan Guttmacher Institute, the American Public Health Association, the American College of Obstetricians and Gynecologists, the National Right-to-Life Committee, the Planned Parenthood Federation of America, the Southern Baptist Convention, and the U.S. Conference of Catholic Bishops (House Committee on Government Operations 1989).

2. The following gave verbal or written statements: Nancy Adler, on behalf of the American Psychological Association; Henry David, the American Public Health Association; Jacqueline Darroch Forrest, the Alan Guttmacher Institute; Wanda Franz, National Right to Life Committee; David Grimes, professor of obstetrics and gynecology and preventative medicine, University of North Carolina; Fabian Hulka, professor of obstetrics and gynecology, University of North Carolina; C. Everett Koop, Surgeon General of the United

States; Ralph Reed, U.S. Public Health Service; and Anne Speckhard, psychotherapist.

3. The informed consent provisions in the state of Utah in 1999 are of the most detailed of this kind. They required abortion providers to abide by the following, in order for the state to consider the woman had consented in an informed manner to have an abortion:

> A woman may not obtain an abortion until at least 24 hours after the attending or referring physician, a nurse, nurse-midwife, or physician's assistant orally, in a face-to-face consultation, tells her: (1) the probable gestational age of the "unborn child"; (2) a description of its development; (3) the risks of, and alternatives to, and nature of the proposed abortion procedure, "specifically how the procedure will affect the fetus"; (4) the alternatives to abortion, including private and agency adoption methods; (5) that adoptive parents may legally pay the costs of prenatal care and childbirth; and (6) the medical risks of carrying the pregnancy to term. If the person providing this information at least 24 hours prior to the abortion is not the attending or referring physician, the attending or referring physician must also provide this information in a face-to-face consultation prior to the abortion. In addition, at least 24 hours prior to an abortion, the woman must receive state-mandated information by the attending or referring physician, nurse, nurse-midwife, laboratory technician, psychologist, marriage or family therapist or social worker, orally and in person, that includes: (1) that medical assistance benefits may be available for prenatal care, childbirth, and neonatal care; (2) that the father is liable for child support, even if he offered to pay for an abortion, and that a state agency will assist her in collecting child support; (3) that she has a right to view a free ultrasound of the unborn child and (4) that the department of health produces printed materials and a video that describe gestational stages, abortion methods and public and private agencies and services, including adoption agencies and services, available to assist the woman through pregnancy, upon childbirth and while the child is dependent. In addition, the woman must receive state-prepared printed materials and be asked to view a video immediately or at another designated time and location. A woman who declines to view the video immediately or when designated must be provided a copy. The state-prepared printed materials and video must: (1) describe with pictures, in a manner that conveys the state's preference for childbirth over abortion, the anatomical and physiological characteristics of the "unborn child" at two-week gestational increments, including the possibility of survival; (2) describe abortion methods, the consequences of each procedure to the fetus and

various stages of development, the "possible detrimental psychological effects of abortion," and the medical risks associated with each procedure, including those related to subsequent childbearing; (3) describe
the risks associated with carrying the pregnancy to term; (4) include
information about medical assistance benefits for prenatal care, childbirth and neonatal care and the "father's" liability for child support;
(5) state that a physician who performs an abortion upon a woman
without her "informed consent" may be liable to her for damages in
a civil action and that adoptive parents may legally pay the costs of
prenatal care, childbirth and neonatal care; (6) list public and private
agencies and services available through pregnancy, at childbirth, and
while the child is dependent, including a comprehensive list of names,
addresses and telephone numbers of public and private agencies and
private attorneys whose practices include adoption, and an explanation of possible financial aid available during the adoption process, or
include a 24 hour hotline that may be called to obtain such a list;
(7) present adoption "as a preferred and positive choice and alternative to abortion"; (8) convey the state's preference for childbirth over
abortion; and (9) include a "statement conveying that the state of
Utah prefers childbirth to abortion." In addition to including the information provided in the state-prepared materials, the video must
show an ultrasound of the heartbeat of an "unborn child" in monthly
increments from three weeks' gestational age until 14 weeks' gestational age in a manner designed to convey that state's preference
for childbirth over abortion, and the positive aspects of adoption. A
woman is not required to receive information otherwise required if:
(1) her physician can demonstrate that he or she reasonably believed
imparting the information would have cause a "severely adverse" effect on the woman's physical or mental health; (2) the abortion is necessary to preserve the woman's life; (3) the pregnancy is the result of
rape or incest; (4) the fetus would have been born with grave defects;
or (5) the woman is 14 years or younger. (NARAL 1999)

The state-prepared materials include enlarged color photographs of fetuses and
a twenty-seven-minute-long video called *An Informed Decision*. A version of this
law was challenged in the Utah court in 1994, 1995, and 1996, but most of
the statute was ruled constitutional (NARAL 1999:213).
4.   The Center for Reproductive Law and Policy (1999a) lists the following
states where informed consent laws have been enforced: Idaho, Indiana, Kansas,
Louisiana, Mississippi, Nebraska, North Dakota, Ohio, Pennsylvania, South
Carolina, South Dakota, Utah, Wisconsin. These requirements have been
passed but were blocked subsequently through legal action in Delaware, Ken-
tucky, Massachusetts, Michigan, Montana, and Tennessee.

References

Abma, Joyce C., Linda S. Peterson. 1995. Voluntary childlessness among U.S. women: Recent trends and determinants. Paper presented at the Annual Meetings of the Population Association of America, April 6–8. See www.cpc.unc.edu/pubs/paa_papers/1995/abma.html.

Adams, Cheryll. 2002. Ante and postnatal depression: Where are we now and where should we be going? *Community Practitioner* 75(7):263.

Adler, Nancy E. 1975. Emotional responses of women following therapeutic abortion. *American Journal of Orthopsychiatry* 45(3):446–53.

Adler, Nancy E., Henry P. David, Brenda N. Major, Susan H. Roth, Nancy F. Russo, and Gail E. Wyatt. 1990. Psychological responses after abortion. *Science* 248:41.

Aiken, Cara. 2000. *Surviving Post-Natal Depression.* London and Philadelphia: Jessica Kingsley Publishers.

Aitkenhead, Decca. 1997. A carefree abortion can be embarrassing. *The Guardian,* March 14.

Alan Guttmacher Institute. 2002. Facts in brief: Induced abortion. New York and Washington: Alan Guttmacher Institute.

American College of Obstetricians and Gynecologists. 2001. Assessing the impact of September 11 on pregnancy. Press release. December 12.

———. 2002. Answers to common questions about postpartum depression. Press release. January.

———. N.d. Postpartum depression. Leaflet.

American Psychiatric Association. 1980. *Diagnostic and Statistical Manual of Mental Disorders,* 3rd Ed. Washington, DC: APA Press.

———. 2001. Postpartum depression. Fact sheet. Washington, DC, July.

American Psychological Association. 1987. *Psychological Sequelae of Abortion.* Washington, DC.

Americans United for Life. 1999. "What is a woman's-right-to-know (WRTK) law?" March 15. See www.unitedforlife.com.

Anderson, R. L., D. C. Hanley, D. B. Larson, and R. C. Sider. 1995. Methodological considerations in empirical research on abortion. Pp. 103–115 in *Post-abortion Syndrome—Its Wide Ramifications,* edited by P. Doherty. Dublin: Four Courts Press.

Appleton, Lynn M. 1995. Rethinking Medicalization: Alcoholism and Anomalies. Pp. 59–80 in *Images of Issues,* edited by J. Best. New York: Aldine de Gruyter.

Areias, M. E., R. Kumar, H. Barros, and Figueriedo. 1996. Comparative incidence of depression in women and men, during pregnancy and after childbirth. Validation of the Edinburgh Postnatal Depression Scale in Portuguese mothers. *British Journal of Psychiatry* 169:30–35.

Armstrong, Kathryn. 1997. Women who weep for their 'lost' babies. *Evening Gazette,* January 13.

Ashmore, Russell. 1996. Post-traumatic stress disorder: Symptoms, treatment, prevention. *Mental Health Nursing* 16(2):18–21.

Associated Press. 1989. Panel: UD Suppressed Proof of Abortion Safety. *Chicago Tribune,* December 11.

Association for Post Natal Illness. N.d. History. Fact sheet. See www.apni.org.

Atiyah, P. S. 1997. *The Damages Lottery.* Oxford: Hart Publishing.

Ayers, S., and A. D. Pickering. 2001. Do women get posttraumatic stress disorder as a result of childbirth? A prospective study of incidence. *Birth* June 28, 111–18.

Bailey, Ron. 2001. Causing more grief. September 26. See www.reason.com.

Ballard, C.G., A. K. Stanley, and I. F. Brockington. 1995. Post-traumatic stress disorder (PTSD) after childbirth. *British Journal of Psychiatry* 166: 525–28.

BBC Health Online. N.d. Baby blues or postnatal depression. See www .bbc.co.uk/health.

BBC News Online. 1999a. Depressed mums "need more help." March 12. www.bbc.co.uk.

———. 1999b. Men suffer from baby blues. May 4. See www.bbc.co.uk.

———. 1999c. New fathers get advice. September 10. See www.bbc.co.uk.

———. 1999d. Massage beats baby blues. September 28. See www.bbc.co.uk.

———. 2000. Anti-battering campaign launched. April 30. See www.bbc .co.uk.

———. 2001. Women will be entitled to abortions within three weeks by 2005. September 11.

———. 2002. Scientists investigate post-birth blues. August 6. See www .bbc.co.uk.

Bennett, Catherine. 1996. Abortion debate is still a minefield. *The Guardian,* December 4.

Benvenuti, Paola, Maurizio Ferrara, Carlo Niccolai, Vania Valoriani, and John L. Cox, 1999. The Edinburgh Postnatal Depression Scale: Validation for an Italian sample. *Journal of Affective Disorders* 53(2):137–41.

Berer, Marge. 1988. Whatever Happened to "a woman's right to choose"? *Feminist Review* 29:25–37.

Best, Joel. 1993. But seriously folks: The limitations of the strict constructionist interpretation of social problems. Pp. 129–147 in *Reconsidering So-*

cial Constructionism: Debates in Social Problems Theory, edited by J. A. Holstein and G. Miller. Hawthorne, NY: Aldine de Gruyter.

———. 1995. Typification and social problem construction. Pp. 1–16 in *Images of Issues*, edited by J. Best. Hawthorne, NY: Aldine de Gruyter.

———. 1999. *Random Violence: How We Talk About New Crimes and New Victims*. Berkeley, Los Angeles, and London: University of California Press.

———. 2001. Introduction: The Diffusion of Social Problems. Pp. 1–18 in *How Claims Spread: The Cross-National Diffusion of Social Problems*, edited by Joel Best. Hawthorne, NY: Aldine de Gruyter.

Bewley, C. 2000. Postnatal depression. *Mental Health Practice* 3(7):30–34.

Birth Control Trust. 1989. *Abortion Review* (London) (Winter).

———. 1994a. Medical Briefing: Abortion and Breast Cancer. *Abortion Review* (London) (Autumn).

———. 1994b. *Abortion Review* (London) (Summer).

———. 1997. Kelly and another (defenders). *Abortion Review* (London) (Summer).

———. 1998a. *Abortion Review* (London) (Summer).

———. 1998b. Confidential briefing on anti-choice activities in Britain. London: Birth Control Trust.

Blanchard, Dallas A. 1994. *The Anti-Abortion Movement and the Rise of the Religious Right: From Polite to Fiery Protest*. New York: Twayne Publishers.

Boodman, Sandra G. 1992. Post-abortion trauma existence questioned. *Washington Post*, October 27.

Borrill, Rachel. 1997. UK anti-abortion protesters angry at "lunch-hour termination" offer. *Irish Times*, June 30.

Boseley, Sarah. 2000. Abortion guidelines hailed by campaigners. *The Guardian*, March 13.

Bowman, Phyllis. 1996. *. . . And Still They Weep: Personal Stories of Abortion*. London: SPUC Educational Research Trust.

Boyle, Mary. 1997. *Re-thinking Abortion, Psychology, Gender, Power and the Law*. London: Routledge.

Bracken, Michael B. 1989. Letter. *New York Times*, January 17.

Braxton, Greg. 1992. Protestors target clinic they say misleads women seeking abortions. *Los Angeles Times* (Metro), January 12.

Braynes, Mark. 2001. Even journalists need counselling. *BBC News Online*, September 19.

Brewer, Colin. 1976. Psychoprophylaxis in the shape of abortion. *GP Magazine*, January 23.

———. 1977. Incidence of post-abortion psychosis: A prospective study. *British Medical Journal* 1:476–77.

———. 1978. Post abortion psychosis. Discussion paper written for British Pregnancy Advisory Service. Unpublished.

Brewer, Sarah. 2000. A new baby brings on the blues. *Daily Telegraph*, December 12.

Bridgeman, Jo. 1998. A woman's right to choose? Pp. 76–94 in *Abortion Law and Politics Today*, edited by E. Lee. Basingstoke: Macmillan Press.

Bristow, Jennie. 2002. *Maybe I Do: Marriage and Commitment in a Singleton Society*. London: Institute of Ideas.

British Medical Journal. 1994. Headlines. *British Medical Journal* 309:8.

Brockington, Ian. 1996. *Motherhood and Mental Health*. Oxford: Oxford University Press.

Brockington, I. F., and R. Kumar. 1982. Preface. Pp. vii–viii in *Motherhood and Mental Illness*, edited by I. F. Brockington and R. Kumar. London, Toronto, Sydney, Tokyo, and Montreal: Academic Press.

Brotman, Barbara. 1990. Both sides in abortion issue also remain divided over post-operation stress. *Chicago Tribune*, April 15.

Brown, Gerald. 1997. Women "need advice on quickie abortions." *Manchester Evening News*, June 28.

Brown, G., and T. Harris. 1978. *Social Origins in Depression*. London: Tavistock.

Bruce, Steve. 1988. *The Rise and Fall of the New Christian Right*. Oxford: Clarendon Press.

Brumberg, Joan Jacobs. 1997. From psychiatric syndrome to "communicable" disease: The case of anorexia nervosa, in *Framing Disease: Studies in Cultural History*, edited by C. E. Rosenberg and J. Golden. New Brunswick, NJ: Rutgers University Press.

Burby, Liza N. 2001. Joy derailed. *Newsday*, September 11.

Burgess, Adam. 2003. *Cellular Phones, Public Fears and a Culture of Precaution*. Cambridge: Cambridge University Press.

Butt, Ronald. 1987. Abortion bare of illusion. *The Times* (London), February 26.

Caldwell, Simon. 2000. State snub for pro-life charity. *Catholic Herald*, June 16.

Cannold, Leslie. 2002. Understanding and responding to anti-choice women-centred strategies. *Reproductive Health Matters* 10(19):171–79.

CARAL. 2001. *Crisis Pregnancy Centers in California: The Hidden Threat to Women's Health*. San Francisco, CA: CARAL Pro-Choice Education Fund.

CARE. N.d. Abortion. See www.pregnancy.org.uk.

Carter, Helen. 1999. Women "scared off having abortions." *The Guardian*, November 11.

Center for Reproductive Law and Policy. 1999a. Abortion, Mandatory delays and biased counseling requirements. See www.crlp.org.

———. 1999b. Press release. January 26.

———. 2003. Mandatory delays and biased information requirements; Portrait of injustice: Abortion coverage under the Medicaid program; Restrictions on young women's access to abortion services; Partial-birth abortion ban legislation: By state. Fact sheets. See www.crlp.org.

Chriss, James J. 1999. Introduction. Pp. 1–29 in *Counseling and the Therapeutic State,* edited by J. J. Chriss. Hawthorne, NY: Aldine de Gruyter.

Ciampa, Laura. 2001. Protecting Women's Health. *American Feminist* 8(2) (Summer):10–15.

Clifford, C., A. Day, J. Cox, and J. Werrett. 1999. A cross-cultural analysis of the use of the Edinburgh Post-Natal Depression Scale (EPDS) in health visiting practice. *Journal of Advanced Nursing* (September 30):655–64.

Coates, James. 1986. Abortion battle becomes vigil over "5 old men." *Chicago Tribune,* June 15.

Cohan, Alvin. 1986. Abortion as a marginal issue: The use of peripheral mechanisms in Britain and the United States. Pp. 27–48 in *The New Politics of Abortion,* edited by J. Lovenduski and J. Outshoorn. London: Sage Publications.

Combe, Victoria. 1996. Labour's stance on abortion puts Catholics in dilemma. *Daily Telegraph,* October 21.

Comport, Maggie. 1987. *Towards Happy Motherhood: Understanding Post-Natal Depression.* London: Corgi.

Condor, Bob. 1996. OB-GYNs forced to mind minds. *Chicago Tribune,* September 8.

Connelly, Michael. 1992. Women's center phone book listing to change. *Los Angeles Times,* January 21.

Conrad, Peter. 1979. Types of medical social control. *Sociology of Health and Illness* 1(1):1–11.

———. 1992. Medicalization and Social Control. *Annual Review of Sociology* 18:209–32.

Conrad, Peter, and Deborah Potter. 2000. From hyperactive children to ADHD adults: Observations on the expansion of medical categories. *Social Problems* 47(4):559–582.

Conrad, Peter, and Joseph W. Schneider. 1980. Looking at levels of medicalization: A comment on Strong's critique of the thesis of medical imperialism. *Social Science and Medicine* 14A:75–79.

Cooper, Peter. 2001. The challenges of antenatal prevention of maternal depression. Pp. 9–12 in *Postnatal Depression and Maternal Mental Health: A Public Health Priority,* edited by CPHVA. London: CPHVA.

Cooper, Peter J., and Lynne Murray. 1998. Postnatal depression. *British Medical Journal* 316:1884–86.

Cottle, Michelle. 1999. Selling shyness: How doctors and drug companies created the "social phobia" epidemic. *New Republic,* August 2.

Cotton, Peter. 1996. The precarious self: The rise of post-traumatic stress disorder. *Arena Magazine,* October/November.

Council on Scientific Affairs, American Medical Association. 1992. Induced termination of pregnancy before and after *Roe v Wade:* Trends in the mortality and morbidity of women. *Journal of the American Medical Association* 268(22):3236.

Coward, Rosalind. 1999. *Sacred Cows: Is Feminism Relevant to the New Millennium?* London: HarperCollins.

Cox, John. 1986. *Postnatal Depression: A Guide for Health Professionals.* London: Churchill Livingstone.

CPVHA. 2002. Use of the Edinburgh Postnatal Depression Screening Scale. *Community Practitioner* 75(4) (April):42–43.

Crawley, Janet. 1989. The stakes are high and so are the emotions. *Chicago Tribune,* April 26.

Creedy, D. K., I. M. Shochet, and J. Horsfall. 2000. Childbirth and the development of acute trauma symptoms: Incidence and contributing factors. *Birth* (June 27):104–11.

Crittenden, Ann. 2001. *The Price of Motherhood.* New York: Henry Holt and Company.

Cummins, Fiona, and Jan Jacques. 1999. Exposed: Scandal of the pregnancy 'advisers.'" *The Mirror,* 11 December.

Curham, Siobhan. 2000. *Antenatal and Postnatal Depression.* London: Vermillion.

Cusk, Rachel. 2001. *A Life's Work: On Becoming a Mother.* London: Fourth Estate.

Cuthill, Margaret. 1996. What Is British Victims of Abortion. Pp. xv–xix in *. . . And Still They Weep: Personal Stories of Abortion,* edited by P. Bowman. London: SPUC Educational Research Trust.

Dafoe, Barbara Whitehead, and David Popenoe. 2002. *The State of Our Unions: Why Men Won't Commit.* Paper written for the National Marriage Project, Rutgers State University.

Dagg, P. 1991. The psychological sequelae of therapeutic abortion, denied and completed. *American Journal of Psychiatry* 148(5):578–85.

Dalton, Katharina, and Wendy M. Holton. 2001. *Depression After Childbirth.* Oxford: Oxford University Press.

David, Henry P. 1972. Abortion in psychological perspective. *American Journal of Orthopsychiatry* 42(1):61–68.

———. 1997. Postabortion psychological responses. Pp. 341–47 in *Abortion Matters: Proceedings of the 1996 Amsterdam Abortion Conference,* edited by E. Ketting and J. Smit. London: International Planned Parenthood Federation.

David, Henry P., and Herbert L. Friedman. 1973. Psychosocial research in abortion: A transnational perspective. Pp. 311–37 in *The Abortion Experience: Psychological and Medical Impact,* edited by H. J. Osofsky and J. D. Osofsky. New York: Harper & Row.

David, Miriam. 1986. *The Ideology of the New Right.* Cambridge, UK: Polity Press.

Davidson, J. R. T., and E. B. Foa. 1991. Diagnostic issues in posttraumatic stress disorder: Considerations for DSM IV. *Journal of Abnormal Psychology* 100:346–55.

Davies, Christie. 1992. How people argue about abortion and capital punishment in Europe and America and why. Pp. 101–29 in *Ethics on the Frontiers of Human Existence,* edited by P. Badham. New York: Paragon House.

Daws, Dilys. 1996. Postnatal depression and the family: Conversations that go awry. In *Postnatal Depression: Focus on a Neglected Issue,* edited by B. Knott and J. Carnell. London: The Health Visitors Associations and The National Childbirth Trust.

Dean, Eric T. 1997. *Shook Over Hell: Post-Traumatic Stress, Vietnam and the Civil War.* Cambridge, MA and London: Harvard University Press.

Dench, Sally, Jane Aston, Ceri Evans, Nigel Meager, Matthew Williams, and Rebecca Willison. 2002. *Key Indicators of Women's Position in Britain.* London: Women & Equality Unit.

Department of Health. 1999a. *Procedures for Approval of Private Sector Places for Termination of Pregnancy Under the Abortion Act 1967, as Amended.* London: Department of Health.

———. 1999b. Our healthier nation: Mental health. See www.ohn.gov.uk/ohn/priorities/mental.htm.

———. 1999c. *Saving Lives—Our Healthier Nation.* London: Department of Health.

———. 2001a. *National Strategy for Sexual Health and HIV.* London: Department of Health.

———. 2001b. *Making It Happen: A Guide to Delivering Mental Health Promotion.* London: Department of Health.

———. 2002. Women's mental health: Into the mainstream. See www.doh.gov.uk/mentalhealth.

Devilly, Grant J. 2001. Accountable methods of validation are needed. Letter. *British Medical Journal* 322:1301.

Dillner, Luisa. 1997. Keeping abreast of the facts. *The Guardian* (G2), January 14.

Dineen, Tana. 1999. *Manufacturing Victims: What the Psychology Industry Is Doing to People.* London: Constable and Company.

Doherty, Peter. 1995. *Post-Abortion Syndrome: Its Wide Ramifications.* Dublin: Four Courts Press.

Donnai, D., and R. Harris. 1981. Attitudes of patients after "genetic" termination of pregnancy. *British Medical Journal* 282:621–22.

Double, Duncan. 2002. The limits of psychiatry. *British Medical Journal* 324:900–904.

Downs, Donald. 1996. *More Than Victims: Battered Women, the Syndrome Society and the Law.* Chicago and London: University of Chicago Press.

Dr. Rosemary. 2002. Why new mums need more help. *Daily Express,* September 3.

Drown, Julia. 2000. Better maternity services equal better public health. *The Guardian,* December 4.

Durham, Martin. 1991. *Sex and Politics: The Family and Morality in the Thatcher Years.* Basingstoke: Macmillan.

Dworkin, Ronald W. 2001. The medicalization of unhappiness. *The Public Interest* 144:85–99.

Dyer, Clare. 2002. Veterans sue Ministry of Defence over post-traumatic stress disorder. *British Medical Journal* 324:563.

Education Guardian. 1992. Why deciding is not easy. *The Guardian* (Suppl.), October 27.

Ehrenreich, Barbara, and Deirdre English. 1978. The "sick" women of the upper classes. Pp. 123–43 in *The Cultural Crisis of Modern Medicine,* edited by J. Ehrenreich. New York and London: Monthly Review Press.

Eller, Thomas R. 1996. Informed consent civil actions for post-abortion psychological trauma. *Notre Dame Law Review* 71: 639–70.

Elliot Institute. 1997. A list of major psychological sequelae of abortion. www.afterabortion.org.

———. 2001. *Hope and Healing,* Springfield, IL: Elliot Institute.

Ellis, Simon J. 2001. Logic is flawed. Letter. *British Medical Journal* 322:1301.

Ertelt, Steve. 2001a. British doc changes mind on abortion-breast cancer link. *Pro-Life Infonet,* June 20.

———. 2001b. Abortion doubles breast cancer link. *Pro-Life Infonet,* December 4.

———. 2001c. Coalition on abortion/breast cancer applauds Australian settlement. *Pro-Life Infonet,* December 30.

———. 2002a. Abortion-breast cancer group responds to North Dakota decision. *Pro-Life Infonet,* March 30.

———. 2002b. New campaign says "Women Deserve Better." *Pro-Life Infonet* (e-mail bulletin), July 17.

Evans, Jonathan, Jon Heron, Helen Francomb, Sarah Oke, and Jean Golding. 2001. Cohort study of depressed mood during pregnancy and after childbirth. *British Medical Journal* 323:257–60.

Evening Standard. 1994. Tyranny of freedom of choice. *Evening Standard,* June 28.

Evins, Grace G., and James P. Theofrastous. 1997. Postpartum depression: A review of postpartum screening. *Primary Care Update for Ob/Gyns* 4(6):241–46.

Fanon, Frantz. 1978. Medicine and colonialism. Pp. 229–51 in *The Cultural Crisis of Modern Medicine,* edited by J. Ehrenreich. New York and London: Monthly Review Press.

Farrell, Kirby. 1998. *Post-traumatic Culture, Injury and Interpretation in the Nineties.* Baltimore and London: Johns Hopkins University Press.

Feinmann, Jane. 1997. *Surviving the Baby Blues.* London: Ward Leech.

Feminists for Life. 2000. The feminist case *against* abortion. See www .feministsforlife.org.

Ferris, Paul. 1966. *The Nameless: Abortion in Britain Today.* London: Penguin Books.

Field, L. H. 1999. Post-traumatic stress disorder: A reappraisal. *Journal of the Royal Society of Medicine* 92:35–37.

Figert, Anne E. 1996. *Women and the Ownership of PMS: The Structuring of a Psychiatric Disorder.* Hawthorne, NY: Aldine de Gruyter.

Figes, Kate. 1998. *Life After Birth.* London: Penguin Books.

Finer, Lawrence B., and Stanley K. Henshaw. 2002. Abortion incidence and services in the United States in 2000. *Perspectives on Sexual and Reproductive Health* 35(1):6–15.

Fitzpatrick, Michael. 2001. *The Tyranny of Health: Doctors and the Regulation of Lifestyle.* London and New York: Routledge.

———. 2002. The betrayal of scientific medicine. Pp. 59–76 in *Alternative Medicine: Should We Swallow It?* edited by T. Jenkins. London: Hodder & Stoughton.

Fleck, Stephen. 1973. A psychiatrist's views on abortion. Pp. 179–97 in *Abortion, Society and the Law,* edited by D. F. Walbert and J. D. Butler. Cleveland and London: The Press of Case Western Reserve University.

Fletcher, David. 1996. Skin patch may end post-natal depression. *Electronic Telegraph* 356(April 5).

———. 1997. Counselling cures the baby blues. *Electronic Telegraph* 672 (March 28).

Foa, Edna B., and Barbara Glasov Rothbaum. 1998. *Treating the Trauma of Rape: Cognitive-Behavioural Therapy for PTSD.* New York: Guildford Press.

Fox, Marie. 1998. Abortion decision-making: Taking men's needs seriously. Pp. 198–215 in *Abortion Law and Politics Today,* edited by E. Lee. Basingstoke: Macmillan Press.

Fox, Renee C. 1977. The medicalization and demedicalization of American society. *Daedalus* 106(1):9–22.

Francome, Colin. 1984. *Abortion Freedom: A Worldwide Movement.* London: George Allen and Unwin.

Franklin, Sarah. 1991. Fetal fascinations: New dimensions to the medical-scientific construction of fetal personhood. Pp. 190–205 in *Off-Centre: Feminism and Cultural Studies,* edited by S. Franklin, C. Lury, and J. Stacey. London: HarperCollins.

Franz, Wanda. N.d. What is post-abortion syndrome? Leaflet distributed by British Victims of Abortion.

Freund, Peter and Meredith McGuire. 1991. *Health, Illness and the Social Body.* Upper Saddle River, NJ: Prentice-Hall.

Friedan, Betty. 1963. *The Feminine Mystique.* London: Penguin Books.

Furedi, Frank. 1992. *Mythical Past, Elusive Future, History and Society in an Anxious Age.* London: Pluto Press.

———. 1997. *Culture of Fear, Risk-Taking and the Morality of Law Expectation.* London: Cassell.

———. 2001. *Paranoid Parenting.* London: Penguin Press.

———. 2002a. *Paranoid Parenting,* U.S. Ed. Chicago: Chicago Review Press.

———. 2002b. The institutionalisation of recognition—evading the moral stalemate. Paper given at the conference Demoralisation, Morality, Authority and Power, Cardiff University, April.

———. 2002c. The "second generation" of Holocaust survivors. See www .spiked-online.com.

———. 2003. *Therapy Culture: Cultivating Vulnerability in an Uncertain Age.* London: Routledge.

Gargaro, Carolyn C. N.d. What is a pro-life feminist? See www.gargaro.com.

Gerrard, Janice. 2000. *Postnatal Depression.* London: Nursing Times Books.

Gianelli, Diane M. 1995. Claiming abortion malpractice. *American Medical News,* February 6.

Gilbert, Susan. 1996. Estrogen patch appears to lift severe depression in new mothers. *New York Times,* May 1.

Gilchrist, Anne C., P. Hannaford, P. Frank, and C. Kay. 1995. Termination of pregnancy and psychiatric morbidity. *British Journal of Psychiatry* 167:243–48.

Ginsburg, Faye. 1989. *Contested Lives: The Abortion Debate in an American Community.* Berkeley: University of California Press.

Githens, Marianne, and Dorothy McBride Stetson. 1996. Introduction. Pp. ix–xiii in *Abortion Politics, Public Policy in Cross-Cultural Perspective,* edited by M. Githens and D. McBride Stetson. New York and London: Routledge, 1996.

Glass, Suzanne. 1995. A matter of life and death: British anti-abortion activists have so far shunned the violence of US pro-lifers. But their disturbing presence is ever more insistent. *Independent on Sunday* (Real Life Suppl.), October 15.

Glendon, Mary Ann. 1987. *Abortion and Divorce in Western Law.* Cambridge, MA, and London: Harvard University Press.

Glover, Vivette. 2001. Antenatal and postnatal mood: The effects on the fetus and the child. Pp. 13–15 in *Postnatal Depression and Maternal Mental Health: A Public Health Priority,* edited by CPHVA. London: CPHVA.

Gold-Beck-Wood, Sandra. 1996. Post-traumatic stress disorder may follow childbirth. *British Medical Journal* 313:774.

Goodman, Sherryl H., and Ian H. Gotlib. 2002. Introduction. Pp. 3–9 in

Children of Depressed Parents, edited by S. H. Goodman and I. H. Gotlib. Washington, DC: American Psychological Association.

Goodnow, Cecelia. 2000. When the bough breaks. *Seattle Post-Intelligencer,* August 17.

Goodstein, Laurie. 1993. Breast cancer-abortion link under attack. *Washington Post,* November 1.

Gordon, Alison. 1999. Lunchtime abortion woman to sue clinic. *Mail on Sunday,* June 13.

Green, Jane. 2001. *Babyville.* London: Penguin Books.

Greenwood, V., and J. Young. 1976. *Abortion in Demand.* London: Pluto Press.

Greer, H. S., S. Lal, S. C. Lewis, E. M. Belsey, and R. W. Beard. 1976. Psychosocial consequences of therapeutic abortion: Kings Termination Study III. *British Journal of Psychiatry* 128:74–79.

The Guardian. 1990. Let the new law settle. Editorial. *The Guardian,* April 26.

———. 2000. Food bug trauma "led to job loss." *The Guardian,* May 4.

Guttmacher, Alan F. 1973. The genesis of liberalized abortion in New York: A personal insight. Pp. 63–87 in *Abortion, Society and the Law,* edited by D. F. Walbert and J. D. Butler. Cleveland and London: The Press of Case Western Reserve University.

Hacking, Ian. 1995. *Rewriting the Soul: Multiple Personality and the Sciences of the Memory.* Princeton, NJ: Princeton University Press.

Hadley, Janet. 1994. God's bullies: Attacks on abortion. *Feminist Review* 48:98–111.

———. 1997. The "awfulisation" of abortion. *Choices* 26(1):7–8.

Hall, Celia. 1996. Abortion is linked to higher risk of breast cancer. *Daily Telegraph,* October 12.

———. 1999. Abortion on demand call in conference. *Daily Telegraph,* January 28.

Hall, Toni. 1992. Abortion issue's status elevated. *USA Today,* May 23.

Handy, Jocelyn. 1982. Psychological and social aspects of induced abortion. *British Journal of Clinical Psychology* 21:29–41.

Hansard, 1990. *House of Commons Official Report, Parliamentary Debates,* Tuesday April 24, Vol. 171, No. 92.

Hansen, Bert. 1997. American physicians' "discovery" of homosexuals, 1880–1900: A new diagnosis in a changing society." In *Framing Disease: Studies in Cultural History,* edited by C. E. Rosenberg and J. Golden. New Brunswick, NJ: Rutgers University Press.

Hardyment, Christina. 1995. *Perfect Parents.* Oxford and New York: Oxford University Press.

Hartouni, Valerie. 1997. *Cultural Conceptions: On Reproductive Technologies and the Remaking of Life.* Minneapolis and London: University of Minnesota Press.

Haslam, David. 1996. *Coping with a Termination.* London: Cedar Press.

Hays, Sharon. 1996. *The Cultural Contradictions of Motherhood.* New Haven and London: Yale University Press.

Healy, David. 1997. *The Anti-Depressant Era.* Cambridge, MA, and London: Harvard University Press.

————. 2002. *The Creation of Psychopharmacology.* Cambridge, MA, and London: Harvard University Press.

Hehir, Brid. 2001a. The rise and rise of CAM, March 8. See www.spiked-online.com.

————. 2001b. Is motherhood more depressing than ever? June 21. See www.spiked-online.com.

Helgadottir, Birna. 2000. Why the British are cruel to new mothers. *The Times* (Weekend), May 13.

Henshaw, Stanley K. 1998. Unintended pregnancies in the United States. *Family Planning Perspectives* 30(4):24–49.

Herman, Ellen. 1995. *The Romance of American Psychology: Political Culture in the Age of Experts.* Berkeley, Los Angeles, and London: University of California Press.

Herman, Judith Lewis. 1992. *Trauma and Recovery: From Domestic Abuse to Political Terror.* London: HarperCollins.

Hewlett, Sylvia Ann. 2002. *Baby Hunger.* London: Atlantic Books.

Hill, Amelia. 2001. Extreme fear of birth pain forces women to miscarry. *Observer,* December 16.

Himmelweit, Sue. 1980. Abortion: Individual choice and social control. *Feminist Review* 5:65–68.

Hochschild, Arlie. 1999. The commercial spirit of intimate life and the abduction of feminism: Signs from women's advice books. See http://sociology.berkeley.edu/public_sociology/Hochschild.pdf.

Hofberg, Kristina, and Ian Brockington. 2000. Tokophobia: an unreasoning dread of childbirth. *British Journal of Psychiatry* 176:83–85.

Holden, Constance. 1989. "Koop finds abortion evidence "inconclusive": Right-to-lifers fail to get hoped-for evidence to reverse Roe v. Wade when Supreme Court reconsiders the issue this spring. *Science* 243:730.

Hopkins, Nick, Steve Reicher, and Jannat Saleem. 1996. Constructing women's psychological health in anti-abortion rhetoric. *Sociological Review* 44(3):539–64.

Hordern, Anthony. 1971. *Legal Abortion: The English Experience.* Oxford and New York: Pergamon Press.

Horrie, Chris. 2001. A suitable case for treatment. BBC News Online, January 15.

Horwitz, Allan H. 2002. *Creating Mental Illness.* Chicago and London: University of Chicago Press.

House Committee on Government Operations. 1989. *Hearing on the Medical and Psychological Impact of Abortion. Hearing Before The Human Resources and Intergovernmental Relations Subcommittee of the Committee on Government Operations of the House of Representatives.* 101st Cong., 1st sess. March 16.

Howard, Alex. 1996. *Challenges to Counselling and Psychotherapy.* Basingstoke: Macmillan.

Huget, Jennifer. 2002. What to expect this time. *Washington Post,* May 7.

Hunter, James Davison. 2000. *The Death of Character.* New York: Basic Books.

Huysman, Arlene M. 1998. *A Mother's Tears: Understanding the Mood Swings That Follow Childbirth.* New York: Seven Stories Press.

Illich, Ivan. 1976. *Medical Nemesis.* New York: Pantheon.

Illman, John. 1989. "Vietnam-like guilt" of women haunted by their abortions. *Daily Mail,* October 20.

Ingleby, David. 1982. The social construction of mental illness. Pp. 123–43 in *The Problem of Medical Knowledge: Examining the Social Construction of Medicine,* edited by P. Wright and A. Treacher. Edinburgh: Edinburgh University Press.

Irwin, Aisling. 1999. Post-birth stress "hits one in four mothers." *Daily Telegraph,* July 13.

Jackson, Emily. 2000. Abortion, autonomy and prenatal diagnosis. *Social and Legal Studies* 9(4):467–94.

————. 2001. *Regulating Reproduction.* Oxford and Portland, OR: Hart Publishing.

Jackson, Emily, and Fran Wasoff, with Mavis Maclean and Rebecca Emerson Dobash. 1993. Financial support on divorce: The right mixture of rules and discretion? *International Journal of Law and the Family* 7:230–54.

James, Oliver. 1997. *Britain on the Couch.* London: Arrow.

————. 2002. *They F**** You Up: How to Survive Family Life.* London: Bloomsbury.

Jarmulowicz, Michael. 1992. *The Physical and Psychological Effects of Abortion.* Leamington Spa: Life.

Jenkins, Philip. 1992. *Intimate Enemies: Moral Panics in Contemporary Britain.* Hawthorne, NY: Aldine de Gruyter.

Jenkins, Tiffany. 2002. Introduction. Pp. xi–xix in *Alternative Medicine: Should We Swallow It?* London: Hodder & Stoughton.

Johanson, Richard, Mary Newburn, and Alison Macfarlane. 2002. Has the medicalisation of childbirth gone too far? *British Medical Journal* 324: 892–95.

Johnston, Lucy. 2001. Anti-abortion clinics "duping" pregnant girls. *Sunday Express,* August 26.

Jones, Edgar, and Simon Wessely. 2000. Shell-shock. *Psychiatric Bulletin* 24: 353.

Joseph, S., R. Williams, and W. Yule. 1997. *Understanding Post-traumatic Stress*

———. *A Psychosocial Perspective on PTSD and Treatment.* Chichester, England: John Wiley & Sons.

Kaiser Daily Report. 1993a. National briefing—malpractice: A new weapon in the abortion debate. December 2. See www.kaisernetwork.org.

———. 1993b. National briefing—activists: Pro-life group mails info. on suing providers. September 8. See www.kaisernetwork.org.

———. 1993c. State report—Montana: Waiting period and informed consent proposed. February 5. See www.kaisernetwork.org.

Kaiser Daily Reproductive Health Report. 2000a. Federal judge strikes down Indiana's waiting period abortion law. April 1. See www.kaisernetwork.org.

———. 2000b. "Pro-life" plan: Bankrupt providers through litigation. August 10. See www.kaisernetwork.org.

———. 2000c. Colorado's waiting period amendment fails. November 8. See www.kaisernetwork.org.

———. 2001a. States consider laws requiring warnings on abortion-breast cancer link, despite inconsistent studies. March 2. See www.kaisernetwork.org.

———. 2001b. Virginia senate passes 24-hour waiting period bill; governor to sign. February 7. See www.kaisernetwork.org.

———. 2001c. Arkansas governor signs "Right to Know" Act into law. February 23. See www.kaisernetwork.org.

———. 2001d. Depression during pregnancy more common than after. August 3. See www.kaisernetwork.org.

Kaminer, Wendy. 1993. *I'm Dysfunctional, You're Dysfunctional: The Recovery Movement and Other Self-Help Fashions.* Reading, MA: Addison-Wesley Publishing Company.

Kaplan, Lawrence J., and Rosemarie Tong. 1994. *Controlling Our Reproductive Destiny.* Cambridge, MA: MIT Press.

Kinchin, David. 1998. *Post Traumatic Stress Disorder: The Invisible Injury.* Oxon: Success Unlimited.

Kissling, Frances, and Denise Shannon. 1998. Abortion rights in the United States: Discourse and dissension. Pp. 144–56 in *Abortion Law and Politics Today,* edited by E. Lee. Basingstoke: Macmillan Press.

Kitzinger, Sheila. 1988. Foreword. Pp. 1–2 in *Motherhood: What It Does to Your Mind,* by J. Price. London: Pandora.

———. N.d. Post traumatic stress disorder. See www.babyworld.co.uk.

Kleinman, Arthur. 1988. *The Illness Narratives: Suffering, Healing and the Human Condition.* New York: Basic Books.

Kleinman, Karen, and Valerie Davis Raskin. 1994. *This Isn't What I Expected: Overcoming Postpartum Depression.* New York: Bantam Books.

Knight, India. 2001. Who are they trying to kid? *Sunday Times* (News Review), September 9.

Koerner, Brendan I. 2002. First, you market the disease . . . then you push the pills to treat it. *The Guardian,* July 30.

Kotulak, Ron, and Jon Van. 1989. Study shoots down "abortion syndrome." *Chicago Tribune,* February 19.

Kruckman, Laurence, and Susan Smith. 1998. An introduction to postpartum illness. See www.postpartum.net.

Krum, Sharon. 2000. The women the world forgot. *The Guardian,* January 10.

Kumar, R. 1982. Neurotic disorders in childbearing women. Pp.71–118 in *Motherhood and Mental Illness,* edited by I. Brockington and R. Kumar. London: Academic Press.

Kunkel, Karl. 1995. Down on the farm: Rationale expansion in the construction of factory farming as a social problem. Pp. 239–55 in *Images of Issues: Typifying Contemporary Social Problems,* edited by J. Best. Hawthorne, NY: Aldine de Gruyter.

Kupersanin, Eve. 2002. Americans more willing to seek out treatment. *Psychiatric News* 37(3):1.

Kupferman, Larry. 1994. *A Rachel Rosary: Intercessory Prayer for Victims of Post-Abortion Syndrome.* New York: Resurrection Press.

Kushner Resnick, Susan. 2001. *Sleepless Days: One Woman's Journey Through Postpartum Depression.* New York: St. Martin's Press.

Kutchins, Herb, and Stuart A. Kirk. 1997. *Making Us Crazy, DSM: The Psychiatric Bible and the Creation of Mental Disorders.* New York: Free Press.

Lacey, Hester. 1997. Does abortion really ruin your life? *Independent on Sunday,* August 8.

Lampert, Neil. 1997. The anguish over abortion. *Kent Messenger,* January 23.

Lane Scheppele, Kim. 1996. Constitutionalizing abortion. Pp. 29–54 in *Abortion Politics: Public Policy in Cross-Cultural Perspective,* edited by M. Githens and D. McBride Stetson. London and New York: Routledge.

Lasch, Christopher. 1977. *Haven in a Heartless World: The Family Besieged.* New York: Basic Books.

———. 1980. *The Culture of Narcissism: American Life in an Age of Diminishing Expectations.* New York: Abacus.

———. 1984. *The Minimal Self.* New York and London: W. W. Norton and Company.

Lask, Bryan. 1975. Short-term psychiatric sequelae to therapeutic termination of pregnancy. *British Journal of Psychiatry* 126:173–77.

Latham, Melanie. 2002. *Regulating reproduction: A Century of Conflict in Britain and France.* Manchester: Manchester University Press.

Laurence, Jeremy. 2003. *Pure Madness: How Fear Drives the Mental Health System.* London: Routledge.

Laville, Laura. 2001. Mother of six sues doctors for abortion trauma. *Daily Telegraph,* December 14.

Leary, Warren E. 1989. Koop says abortion report couldn't survive challenge. *New York Times,* March 17.

Lee, Ellie, and Emily Jackson. 2002. Regulating the pregnant body. Pp. 115– 32 in *Real Bodies,* edited by M. Evans and E. Lee. Basingstoke: Palgrave.

Legh-Jonson, Alison. 1989. Abortion: What are the after-effects? *Woman Magazine,* April 29.

Leopold, Kathryn A., and Lauren B. Zoschnick. N.d. Postpartum depression. www.OBGYN.net.

Liebman, Robert C., and Robert Wuthnow (eds.). 1983. *The New Christian Right.* New York: Aldine Publishing Company.

Life. 1992. *Abortion 25 Years on—The Human Cost.* Leamington Spa: Life.

————. N.d. a. A woman's right to choose? Women and the problem pregnancy. Leaflet.

————. N.d. b. Considering abortion? Then please read on. . . . Leaflet.

Linders, Annulla. 1998. Abortion as a social problem: The construction of "opposite" solutions in Sweden and the United States. *Social Problems* 45(4):488– 509.

Litva, Andrea. 2001. Social usefulness of any diagnosis needs consideration. Letter. *British Medical Journal* 322:1301.

Loseke, Donileen R. 1999. *Thinking About Social Problems: An Introduction to Constructionist Prespectives.* Hawthorne, NY: Aldine de Gruyter.

Luker, Kristin. 1984. *Abortion and the Politics of Motherhood.* Berkeley, Los Angeles, and London: University of California Press.

————. 1996. *Dubious Conceptions: The Politics of Teenage Pregnancy.* Cambridge, MA, and London: Harvard University Press.

Lupton, Deborah. 1994. *Medicine as Culture: Illness, Disease and the Body in Western Societies.* London: Sage Publications.

Macdonald, Katy. 1992. The agony of the abortion backlash. *Daily Mail,* September 24.

Macdonald, Victoria. 1994. Commission raises fear on dangers of abortion. *Sunday Telegraph,* June 26.

Macdonald, Victoria, and Roger Todd. 1998. Post-natal depression can make sons delinquent. *Sunday Telegraph,* January 4.

Madigan, Charles M. 1989. Abortion on trial, Supreme Court review sparks adversarial emotions. *Chicago Tribune,* January 15.

Marcé Society, Australasian Branch. 1998. The Marcé Society. Fact sheet. www.wiaru.com/marce/.

Marcus, Laura. 2002. Designer stress. *The Guardian,* July 11.

Marsh, Beezy. 1997. No time to grieve misery of abortion. *Northern Echo,* January 10.

Masden, Lynn. 1994. *Rebounding from Childbirth.* Westport, CT: Bergin and Garvey.

Maternity Care Working Party. 2001. *Modernising Maternity Care.* London: National Childbirth Trust.

Matthewes-Green, Frederica. 2000. Rape and incest are tragic, but abortion doesn't heal the pain. *Citizen Magazine,* October.

Matthey, Stephen, Bryanne Barnett, David J. Kavanagh, and Pauline Howie. 2001. Validation of the Edinburgh Postnatal depression Scale for men, and comparison of item endorsement with their partners. *Journal of Affective Disorders* 64(203):175–84.

Maushart, Susan. 1999. *The Mask of Motherhood.* London: Pandora.

McAdam, Doug, and Dieter Rucht. 1993. The cross-national diffusion of movement ideas. *Annals of the American Academy of Political and Social Science* 528:56–74.

McCarthy, Colman. 1989. The real anguish of abortions. *Washington Post,* February 5.

McNair, Rachel. 1997. Is abortion good for women? Pp. 75–85 in *Swimming Against the Tide, Feminist Dissent on the Issues of Abortion,* edited by A. Kennedy. Dublin: Open Air.

McNeil, Maureen. 1991. Putting the Alton Bill in context. Pp. 149–59 in *Off-Centre: Feminism and Cultural Studies,* edited by S. Franklin, C. Lury, and J. Stacey. London and New York: HarperCollins.

McVeigh, Tracey. 2001. Bullies prey on half of children. *The Guardian,* January 7.

Meek, James. 2002. Judges close cloning loophole. *The Guardian,* January 19.

Menage, Janet. 1993. Post-traumatic stress disorder in women who have undergone obstetric and/or gynaecological procedures. *Journal of Reproductive and Infant Psychology* 11:221–28.

Mezey, Gillian, and Ian Robbins. 2001. Usefulness and validity of post-traumatic stress disorder as a psychiatric category. *British Medical Journal* 323:561–63.

Michels, Nancy. 1988. *Helping Women Recover from Abortion.* Minneapolis, MN: Bethany House Publishers.

Mihill, Chris. 1990. Room for action late in pregnancy. *The Guardian,* April 26.

Miller, Laura J., and Alpa Shah. 1999. Major mental illness during pregnancy. *Primary Care Update for OB/GYNS* 6(5):163–68.

Millns, Sue, and Sally Sheldon. Abortion. Pp. 6–23 in *Conscience and Parliament,* edited by P. Cowley. London: Frank Cass.

Mohr, James. 1978. *Abortion in America.* New York: Oxford University Press.

Moore, Alison. 1998. Healthfront: Post-natal counselling. *Daily Telegraph,* January 17.

Moore, Anna. 2001. A fear is born. *Sunday Times Magazine,* January 26.

Moore, Suzanne. 1992. Looking for trouble: Unwanted pain of an unwanted pregnancy. *The Guardian,* October 8.

Moorhead, Joanna. 1989. Post abortion syndrome a reality, pro lifers insist. *Catholic Herald,* June 23.

Morris, Lois B. 2000. New motherhood: For the partum blues, a question of whether to medicate. *New York Times,* June 25.

Moynihan, Ray, Iona Heath, and David Henry. 2002. Selling sickness: The pharmaceutical industry and disease mongering. *British Medical Journal* 324:886–91.

Murkoff, Heidi E., Arlene Eisenberg, and Sandee Hathaway. 2002. *What to Expect When You're Expecting.* New York: Workman Publishing.

Murray, Lynne. 2001. How postnatal depression can affect children and their families. Pp. 20–23 in *Postnatal Depression and Maternal Mental Health: A Public Health Priority,* edited by CPHVA. London: CPHVA.

Murray, Lynne, and Peter J. Cooper. 1997. *Postpartum Depression and Child Development.* New York and London: Guildford Press.

Napier, Michael, and Kay Wheat. 1995. *Recovering Injuries for Psychiatric Injury.* London: Blackstone Press.

NARAL. 1999. *Who Decides? A State-By-State Review of Abortion and Reproductive Rights.* Washington, DC: NARAL Foundation.

National Abortion Campaign. 1994. Leading anti-abortionists head "private commission." Press release. February 12.

National Institute of Mental Health. 1996. *Attention Deficit Hyperactivity Disorder.* NIH Publication 96-3572. Booklet. Bethesda, MD: National Institutes of Health.

———. 1999. Welcome. See www.nimh.nih.gov/about/index/cfm.

———. 2000. Depression: What every woman should know. Bethesda. MD: National Institutes of Health, August.

———. 2001a. Post-traumatic stress disorder. Fact sheet.

———. 2001b. Prevention and treatment of depression in pregnancy and the postpartum period. See www.nimh.nih.gov/wmhc/matdepsum.cfm.

National Office of Post-Abortion Reconciliation and Healing. N.d. Aftermath. www.marquette.edu/rachels.

National Right to Life Committee. 1987. A report on the psychological aftermath of abortion. Unpublished.

———. 2003. National Sanctity of Human Life Day, 2003. By the President of the United States of America. A Proclamation. Mailing sent by e-mail. January 14.

———. N.d. Is abortion safe? Psychological consequences. Leaflet.

Nelson, Melissa. 2002. Mrs. Bush pushes for early education. *Associated Press,* April 30.

Newman, Karen. 1996. *Fetal Positions: Individualism, Science, Visuality.* Stanford, CA: Stanford University Press.

Newsweek. 2001. Making scare tactics legal. *Newsweek* (Periscope Section), March 12.

Nicolson, Paula. 1998. *Post-Natal Depression, Psychology, Science and the Transition to Motherhood.* London: Routledge.

Niswander, Kenneth. 1973. Abortion practices in the United States: A medical viewpoint. Pp. 199–222 in *Abortion, Society and the Law,* edited by D. F. Walbert and J. D. Butler. Cleveland and London: The Press of Case Western Reserve University.

Nolan, David. 1998. Abortion: Should men have a say? Pp. 216–31 in *Abortion Law and Politics Today,* edited by E. Lee. Basingstoke: Macmillan Press.

Nolan, James. 1998. *The Therapeutic State: Justifying Government at Century's End.* New York: New York University Press.

Nordenberg, Tamar. 2000. Escaping the prison of a past trauma: New treatment for post-traumatic stress disorder. *FDA Consumer Magazine,* May/June.

Northern, Kathy Seward. 1998. Procreative torts: Enhancing the common-law protection for reproductive autonomy. *University of Illinois Law Review* (2): 489–546.

Oakley, Ann. 1992. *Social Support and Motherhood.* Oxford: Blackwell.

O'Brien, Stephen L. 1998. *Traumatic Events and Mental Health.* Cambridge, England: Cambridge University Press.

O'Connor, Karen. 1996. *No Neutral Ground? Abortion Politics in an Age of Absolutes.* Boulder, CO: Westview Press.

Office for National Statistics. 2000. *Statutory Grounds,* Series AB, no. 27. London: Office for National Statistics.

———. 2001. *Social Trends 31.* London: Office for National Statistics.

O'Hara, Michael W. 1997. The nature of postpartum depressive disorders. Pp. 3–34 in *Postpartum Depression and Child Development,* edited by L. Murray and P. J. Cooper. New York and London: Guildford Press.

Okie, Susan. 1989. Abortion report Koop withheld released on Hill. *Washington Post,* March 17.

O'Neil, John. 2001. Childbirth: Prepartum depression also an issue. *New York Times,* August 14.

Paintin, David. 1998. A medical view of abortion in the 1960s. Pp. 12–19 in *Abortion Law and Politics Today,* edited by E. Lee. Basingstoke: Macmillan.

Pantlen, A., and A. Rohde. 2001. Psychologic effects of traumatic live deliveries. *Zettralblatt für Gynäkologie* 123:42–47.

Parkinson, Frank. 1995. *Post-Trauma Stress.* London: Sheldon Press.

Patai, Daphne. 1998. *Heterophobia, Sexual Harassment and the Future of Feminism.* Lanham, MD: Rowman & Littlefield.

Payne, E., A. Kravitz, and M. Notaman. 1976. Outcome following therapeutic abortion. *Archives of General Psychiatry* 33:725–33.

Pearson, Allison. 2002. *I Don't Know How She Does It.* London: Chatto and Windus.

Peele, Stanton. 1995. *Diseasing of America: How We Allowed Recovery Zealots and the Treatment Industry to Convince Us We Are Out of Control.* San Francisco: Jossey-Bass.

Petchesky, Rosalind. 1990. *Abortion and Woman's Choice.* Boston: Northeastern University Press.

Phillips, Joan. 1988. *Policing the Family: Social Control in Thatcher's Britain.* London: Junius Publications.

Pitt, Brice. 1985. The puerperium. Pp. 147–72 in *Psychological Disorders in Obstetrics and Gynaecology,* edited by R. G. Priest. London: Butterworth & Co.

Pollitt, Katha. 1999. The solipsister. *New York Times* (Book Reviews), April 18.

Postpartum Resource Center. N.d. Learning about postpartum depression. Fact sheet. See www.postpartum.net.

Postpartum Support International. 2001. More About Melanie Stokes. June 28. See www.postpartum.net.

————. N.d. About postpartum support international. Fact sheet. See www.postpartum.net.

Potts, Malcolm, Peter Diggory, and John Peel. 1977. *Abortion.* Cambridge, London, and New York: Cambridge University Press.

Price, Jane. 1988. *Motherhood: What It Does to Your Mind.* London: Pandora.

Priest, R. 1978. Introduction. Pp. 1–4 in *Mental Illness in Pregnancy and the Puerperium,* edited by M. Sandler. Oxford: Oxford University Press.

Pro-Choice Alliance. 1994. Private commission of inquiry on abortion. Press release. March 1.

Pupavac, Vanessa. 2001. Therapeutic governance: Psycho-social intervention and trauma risk Management. *Disasters* 25(4):358–72.

Putnam, Robert D. 2000. *Bowling Alone.* New York: Simon & Schuster.

Rachel's Vineyard. N.d. Symptoms of post abortion trauma. See www.rachelsvineyard.org.

Radcliffe-Richards, Janet. 1982. *The Sceptical Feminist: A Philosophical Enquiry.* London and New York: Routledge.

Raitt, Fiona E., and Suzanne Zeedyk. 2000. *The Implicit Relation of Psychology and Law: Women and Syndrome Evidence.* London and Philadelphia: Routledge.

Ralph, K., and J. Alexander. 1994. Post-traumatic stress disorder. Borne under stress. *Nursing Times* 90(12):29–30.

Randall, Peter. 1996. Introduction. Pp. ix–xiv in . . . *And Still They Weep: Personal Stories of Abortion,* edited by P. Bowman. London: SPUC Educational Research Trust.

Rawlinson, Lord. 1994. The physical and psycho-social effects of abortion on women: A report by the Commission of the Inquiry into the Operation and Consequences of the Abortion Act. London: Christian Action Research and Education.

Reardon, David C. 1995. Revisiting the "Koop Report." *Post Abortion Review* 3(3):1–2.

————. 1996a. *Making Abortion Rare: A Healing Strategy for a Divided Nation.* Springfield, IL: Acorn Books.

————. 1996b. *The Jericho Plan: Breaking Down the Walls Which Prevent Post-Abortion Healing.* Springfield, IL: Acorn Books.

Reid, Sue. 2001. "Abortion is legalized killing. This is a fact." *Marie Claire,* August.

Reighard, Fredel T., and Marilyn L. Evans. 1995. Use of the Edinburgh Postnatal Depression Scale in a southern, rural population in the United States. *Progressive Neuro-Psychopharmacology and Biological Psychiatry* 19:1219–24.

Reisser, Teri, with Paul Reisser. 1999. *A Solitary Sorrow: Finding Healing & Wholeness after Abortion.* Colorado Springs, CO: Waterbrook Press.

Rice, D. 2000. Abortion link to breast cancer. *Daily Express,* August 14.

Roan, Sharon L. 1998. *Postpartum Depression: Every Woman's Guide to Diagnosis, Treatment and Prevention.* Holbrook, MA: Adams Media Corporation.

Rogers, Lois. 1994. Living with choice. *Sunday Telegraph* (Style and Travel), July 3.

Rogers, Paul, and Sheena Liness. 2000. Post-traumatic stress disorder. *Nursing Standard* 14(22):47–52.

Rosenberg, Joshua. 2002. No law against human cloning, says judge. *Daily Telegraph,* January 28.

Rothman, Barbara. 1987. *The Tentative Pregnancy.* New York: Penguin.

Rourke, Mary. 1995. Forgive—but not forget. *Los Angeles Times,* July 19.

Rowbotham, Sheila. 1997. *A Century of Women: The History of Women in Britain and the United States.* London: Penguin Books.

Royal College of Obstetricians and Gynaecologists. 2000. *The Care of Women Requesting Induced Abortion.* London: RCOG Press.

Royal College of Psychiatrists. 1994. The Royal College of Psychiatrists' response to the Rawlinson report on "The physical and psychosocial effects of abortion." Press release. July 1.

———. 1997. Post natal depression. Fact sheet. June. See www.rcpsych .ac.uk.

———. 1999. Tokophobia: An unreasoning dread of childbirth. Press release. December 1.

———. 2001. Mental illness after childbirth. Fact sheet. See www.rcpsych .ac.uk.

Rue, Vincent. 1981. *Abortion and Family Relations.* Testimony presented before the Subcommittee on the Constitution, U.S. Senate Judiciary Committee, 97th Cong.

———. 1984. The victims of abortion. Speech given at the National Right to Life Committee Convention, Kansas City, MO.

———. 1986. Post-abortion syndrome. Proceedings of the First National Conference on Post-Abortion Counseling, University of Notre Dame, South Bend, IN.

———. 1995. Post-abortion syndrome: A variant of post-traumatic stress disorder. Pp. 15–28 in *Post-abortion Syndrome—Its Wide Ramifications,* edited by P. Doherty. Dublin: Four Courts Press.

———. 1997. The psychological safety of abortion: The need for reconsideration. *Post Abortion Review* 5(4)(Fall):7–10.

Rue, Vincent, and Naomi Banhole. 1998. Postabortion counselling. *British Journal of Sexual Medicine* (January/February):25–26.

Russo, Nancy Felipe, and Jean E. Denious. 1998. Why is abortion such a controversial issue in the United States? Pp. 25–60 in *The New Civil War: The Psychology, Culture and Politics of Abortion,* edited by Linda J. Beckman and Marie S. Harvey. Washington, DC: American Psychological Association.

Sachdev, Paul. 1981. Introduction (to section on the psychological effects of abortion). Pp. 63–64 in *Abortion Readings and Research,* edited by P. Sachdev. Toronto: Butterworths.

Sacher, David. 2001. *Mental Health: Report of the Surgeon General.* See www.surgeongeneral.gov/library/mentalhealth/home.

Sarler, Carol. 2001. Tales every mother wants to tell. *Observer,* September 9.

Sarvis, Betty, and Hyman Rodman. 1974. *The Abortion Controversy.* New York and London: Columbia University Press.

Scarisbrick, J. 2001a. Letter. *The Guardian,* December 19.

———. 2001b. Letter. *Daily Telegraph,* November 28.

Schlenger, William E., Juesta M. Caddell, Lori Ebert, Kathleen Jordan, Kathryn M. Rourke, David Wilson, Lisa Thalji, Michael Dennis, John A. Fairbank, and Richard A. Kulka. 2002. Psychological reactions to terrorist attacks. *Journal of the American Medical Association* 288(5):581–88.

Schmich, Mary T. 1989. An explosive issue's leading crusaders strategies are being remapped as the action moved back to the states. *Chicago Tribune,* July 24.

Schneider, Carl E., and Maris A. Vinovskis. 1980. *The Law and Politics of Abortion.* Lexington, MA, and Toronto: Lexington Books.

Schwartz, Richard A. 1973. Abortion on request: The psychiatric implications. Pp. 139–178 in *Abortion, Society and the Law,* edited by D. F. Walbert and J. D. Butler. Cleveland and London: The Press of Case Western Reserve University.

Scott, Michael J., and Stephen G. Stradling. 1992. *Counselling for Post-Traumatic Stress Disorder.* London: Sage Publications.

Scott, Wilbur J. 1990. PTSD in DSM III: A case in the politics of diagnosis and disease. *Social Problems* 37:294–310.

Scottish Catholic Observer. 1992. Abortion claims 3.5 million child victims— and 350,000 mothers. *Scottish Catholic Observer,* September 25.

Sebastian, Linda. 1998. *Overcoming Postpartum Depression and Anxiety.* Omaha, NE: Addicus Books.

Seng, Julia S., Deborah J. Oakley, Carolyn M. Sampselle, Cheryl Killion, Sandra Graham-Bermann, and Israel Liberzon. 2001. Posttraumatic stress disorder and pregnancy complications. *Obstetrics and Gynaecology* 97(1):17–22.

Sennett, Richard. 1998. *The Corrosion of Character: The Personal Consequences of Work in the New Capitalism.* London: Norton.

Shakespeare, Judy. 2002. Evaluation of screening for postnatal depression against the NSC Handbook literature. Document prepared for a National Screening Committee workshop. See www.nelh.nhs.uk.

Shalev, Arieh Y. 2001. Disorder takes away human dignity. Letter. *British Medical Journal* 322:1301.

Sharkey, Joe. 1997. It's a mad, mad, mad, mad world; you're not bad, you're sick. It's in the book. *New York Times,* September 28.

Shaw, Russell. 1969. *Abortion on Trial.* London: Robert Hale.

Sheldon, Sally. 1997. *Beyond Control: Medical Power and Abortion Law.* London: Pluto Press.

Shepherd, Ben. 2000. *A War of Nerves: Soldiers and Psychiatrists 1914–1994.* London: Jonathan Cape.

Showalter, Elaine. 1987. *The Female Malady.* London: Virago Press.

———. 1997. *Hystories, Hysterical Epidemics and Modern Culture.* Basingstoke: Picador.

Simms, Madeleine. 1985. Legal abortion in Britain. Pp. 78–95 in *The Sexual Politics of Reproduction,* edited by H. Homans. Aldershot, England, and Brookfield, VT: Gower.

Simms, Madeleine, and Hindel Keith. 1971. *Abortion Law Reformed.* London: Peter Owen.

Simon, Stephanie. 2002. Abortion foes seize on reports of cancer link in new campaign. *Los Angeles Times,* March 24.

Simpson, Helen. 2000. *Hey Yeah Right, Get A Life.* London: Jonathan Cape.

Simpson, John H. 1983. Moral issues and status politics. Pp. 188–207 in *The New Christian Right,* edited by R. C. Liebman and R. Wuthnow. New York: Aldine Publishing Company.

Slater, Lauren. 2001. Beginning and end. *New York Times,* July 8.

Sobie, Amy. 1998. One voice now: The first National Women at Risk Conference. *Post Abortion Review* 6(3):3.

Social Exclusion Unit. 1999. *Teenage Pregnancy.* London: Social Exclusion Unit.

Society for the Protection of Unborn Children. N.d. Aims of the society. See www.spuc.org.uk.

Solinger, Rickie. 2002. *Beggars and Choosers: How the Politics of Choice Shapes Adoption, Abortion and Welfare in the United States.* New York: Hill & Wang.

Somerville, Jennifer. 2000. *Feminism and the Family: Politics and Society in the UK and the USA.* Basingstoke: Palgrave.

Speckhard, Ann, and Vincent Rue. 1992. Postabortion syndrome: An emerging public health concern. *Journal of Social Issues* 48(3):95–119.

Specter, Michael. 1989. Agency censored abortion data, Hill report says. *Washington Post,* December 11.

———. 1990. Psychiatric panel condemns abortion restrictions. APA annual meeting told limits on right to choose do more harm than the procedure itself. *Washington Post,* May 16.

Staggenborg, Suzanne. 1991. *The Pro-Choice Movement: Organization and Activism in the Abortion Conflict.* New York and Oxford: Oxford University Press.

Steadman-Rice, John. 1996. *A Disease of One's Own: Psychotherapy, Addition, and the Emergence of Co-Dependency.* New York: Transaction Publishers.

Stein, G. 1982. The maternity blues. Pp. 119–54 in *Motherhood and Mental Illness,* edited by I. Brockington and R. Kumar. London: Academic Press.

Steinberg, Deborah Lynn. 1991. Adversarial politics: The legal construction of abortion. Pp. 175–89 in *Off-Centre: Feminism and Cultural Studies,* edited by S. Franklin, C. Lury, and J. Stacey. London and New York: Harper-Collins.

Stetson, Dorothy McBride. 1996. Abortion policy triads and women's rights in Russia, the United States, and France. Pp. 79–118 in *Abortion Politics, Public Policy in Cross-Cultural Perspective,* edited by M. Githens and D. McBride Stetson. London and New York: Routledge.

Stotland, Nada L. 1992. The myth of the abortion trauma syndrome. *Journal of the American Medical Association* 268(15):2078–79.

Studlar, Donley T., and Raymond Tatalovich. 1996. Abortion policy in the United States and Canada: Do institutions matter? Pp. 75–96 in *Abortion Politics: Public Policy in Cross-Cultural Perspective,* edited by M. Githens and D. McBride Stetson. London and New York: Routledge.

Summerfield, Derek. 1999. A critique of seven assumptions behind psychological trauma programmes in war-affected areas. *Social Science & Medicine* 48:1449–62.

———. 2001. The invention of post-traumatic stress disorder and the social usefulness of a psychiatric category. *British Medical Journal* 322:95–98.

Summerfield, D., and F. Hume. 1994. May not need treatment in war veterans. Letter. *British Medical Journal* 309:873.

Sumner, L. W. 1981. *Abortion and Moral Theory.* Princeton, NJ: Princeton University Press.

Sutherland, John. 2002. Just can't get enough. *The Guardian,* June 17.

Szasz, Thomas. 1977. *The Manufacture of Madness.* London: HarperCollins.

Tavris, Carol. 1992. *The Mismeasure of Woman.* New York: Simon and Schuster.

Taylor, Mike. 2001. High court bid to stop ex-girlfriend having an abortion. *PA News,* March 16.

Thompson, Dick. 1989. A setback for pro-life forces. New studies find abortions pose little danger to women. *Time,* March 27.

Thompson, Simon B. N. 1997. War experiences and post-traumatic stress disorder. *The Psychologist* 10(8):349–50.

Thorpe, Vanessa. 1996. "Abortion wrecks your life" claims group. *Independent on Sunday,* December 29.

Tierney, Kathleen J. 1982. The battered women movement and the creation of the wife beating problem. *Social Problems* 29(3):207–20.

The Times. 1997. Mental problems "mainly in the minds of their psychiatrists." *The Times,* November 27.

Tinsley, Elisa. 1989. Koop abortion study finds "no conclusion." *USA Today,* January 11.

Toner, Robin. 2001. The abortion debate, stuck in time. *The Nation,* January 21.

Toolis, Kevin. 1999. Shock tactics. *The Guardian,* November 13.

Townsend, Liz. N.d. Help and hope for women and their babies. See www.nrlc .org/news (NRLC website).

Tribe, Laurence. 1990. *Abortion and the Clash of Absolutes.* New York and London: W. W. Norton & Company.

Turner, Bryan. 1995. *Medical Power and Social Knowledge.* London: Sage Publications.

Twiston Davies, Bess. 2001. Psychological perils of abortion. *Catholic Times,* February 18.

Urquhart, D. R., and A. A. Templeton. 1991. Psychiatric morbidity and acceptability following medical and surgical methods of induced abortion. *British Journal of Obstetrics and Gynaecology* 98:396–99.

U.S. Census Bureau. 2000. *Statistical Abstract of the United States: 2000.* Washington, DC: U.S. Census Bureau.

Vogel, Ann. 1999. In the vineyard. *Post-Abortion Review* 7(4):4.

Vogt, Amanda. 1992. Doubt cast on trauma in abortions. *Chicago Tribune,* October 23.

Wainwright, David, and Michael Calnan. 2002. *Work Stress: The Making of a Modern Epidemic.* Buckingham and Philadelphia: Open University Press.

Walbert, David F., and J. Douglas Butler (eds.). 1973. *Abortion, Society and the Law.* Cleveland and London: The Press of Case Western Reserve University.

Wallwork Winik, Lyric. 2000. The demise of child-rearing. *The Public Interest* 141(Fall):41–51.

Warner, Judith. 2001. A quartet of new books diagnoses the plight of women and the less-than-happy American family. *Washington Post,* October 7.

Wastell, David, Tom Baldwin, and Jo Knowsley. 1996. Blair: I'm against abortion. *Sunday Telegraph,* October 27.

Weeks, J. 1989. *Sex, Politics & Society.* London and New York: Longman.

Welburn, Vivienne. 1980. *Postnatal Depression.* London: Fontana Paperbacks.

Welford, Heather. 2002. *Feelings After Birth.* Cambridge: NCT Publishing.

Wessely, Simon. 1995. Liability for psychiatric illness. *Journal of Psychosomatic Research* 39:659–69.

———. 1999. In the culture of counselling, we all risk becoming victims. *The Independent,* May 30.

West, Juliet. 1997. Women haunted for life by their abortions. *Daily Mail,* January 10.

Westervelt, Saundra Davis. 1998. *Shifting the Blame: How Victimization Became a Criminal Defense.* New Brunswick, NJ: Rutgers University Press.

Whitton, A., R. Warner, and L. Appleby. 1996. The pathway to care in postnatal depression: Women's attitudes to post-natal depression and its treatment. *British Journal of General Practice* 46(408):427–28.

Wijma, Klaas, Johan Soderqvist, and Barbro Wijma. 1997. Posttraumatic stress disorder after childbirth: A cross sectional study. *Journal of Anxiety Disorders* 11(6):587–97.

Wilcox, Brian L., Jennifer K. Robbenolt, and Janet E. O'Keefe. 1998. Federal abortion policy and politics: 1973 to 1996. Pp. 3–24 in *The New Civil War: The Psychology, Culture and Politics of Abortion,* edited by L. J. Beckman and S. Marie Harvey. Washington, DC: American Psychological Association.

Williams, Simon J., and Michael Calnan. 1996. The "limits" of medicalization? Modern medicine and the lay populace in "late" modernity. *Social Science and Medicine* 42(12):1609–20.

Wilmoth, Gregory H. 1992. Abortion, public health policy, and informed consent legislation. *Journal of Social Issues* 48(3):1–17.

Winter, Eugenia B. 1988. *Psychological and Medical Aspects of Induced Abortion, A Selective Bibliography 1970–1986.* New York and London: Greenwood Press.

Wintour, Patrick. 1990. MPs pledge to fight vote on abortion. *The Guardian,* April 26.

Wolf, Naomi. 2001. *Misconceptions, Truth, Lies and the Unexpected on the Journey to Motherhood.* London: Chatto and Windus.

Woliver, Laura R. 1996. Rhetoric and symbols in American abortion politics. Pp. 5–28 in *Abortion Politics: Public Policy in Cross-Cultural Perspective,* edited by M. Githens and D. McBride Stetson. London and New York: Routledge.

Womack, Sarah. 2002. Majority of depressed mothers go untreated. *Daily Telegraph,* August 28.

Women's Health Advisor. N.d. Postpartum depression. See www.medinformation.com.

Wright, Peter, and Andrew Treacher. 1982. *The Problem of Medical Knowledge: Examining the Social Construction of Medicine.* Edinburgh: Edinburgh University Press.

Wynn Jones, Ros. 1997. Abortion: As the shouting grows louder, is anyone listening to pregnant women? *Independent on Sunday,* March 16.

Yeoman, Barry. 2001. The quiet war on abortion. *Mother Jones,* September/October.

Yorkshire Post. 1999. "Dismay" as group calls for abortion on request. *Yorkshire Post,* January 28.

Yoshida, K., M. N. Markes, N. Kibe, R. Kumar, H. Nakaono, and N. Tashiro. 1997. Postnatal depression in Japanese women who have given birth in England. *Journal of Affective Disorders* 43:69–77.

Young, Allan. 1995. *The Harmony of Illusions: Inventing Post Traumatic Stress Disorder.* Princeton, NJ: Princeton University Press.

Young, Cathy. 1989. The aborted logic of victimhood. *Washington Post,* November 12.

———. 1999. *Ceasefire! Why Women and Men Must Join Forces to Achieve True Equality.* New York: Free Press.

Zimmerman, Mary. 1981. Psychosocial and emotional consequences of elective abortion: A literature review. Pp. 65–75 in *Abortion Readings and Research,* edited by P. Sachdev. Toronto: Butterworths.

Zola, Irving Kenneth. 1978. Medicine as an institution of social control. Pp. 80–100 in *The Cultural Crisis of Modern Medicine,* edited by J. Ehrenreich. New York and London: Monthly Review Press.

Zolese, G., and C. V. R. Blacker. 1992. The psychological complications of therapeutic abortion. *British Journal of Psychiatry* 160:742–49.

Index

Abortion Act of 1967 (Great
    Britain), 81–82, 84, 88,
    91–92, 142, 145–146,
    163–166, 168, 171
Abortion law (*see also specific cases and
    legislation*)
  civil liability laws and, 129–131
  in Great Britain
    "abortion on request," 40
    courts, 90–92
    features of, 81–84
    medicalization of abortion, 82–
      83
    parliamentary debate (1967–
      1989), 84–87
    reform (1990), 87–90
  informed consent regulations and,
      123–129
  Postabortion Syndrome and, 38–
      39
  in United States
    funding for abortion, 104–106
    Koop inquiry, 94–95
    state legislation, 106–109
    "Women's Right to Know" laws
      and, 39–40, 124–126, 128,
      136
Abortion Malpractice Litigation
    Campaign, 134
Abortion pill (RU 486), 40
ACOG, 176, 203–204, 217, 219
Addiction, use of term of, 44
ADHD, 48, 58, 73
Adler, Nancy, 119, 155
Alan Guttmacher Institute, 4

Alcoholism, 9
Alternative medicine and medical-
    ization, 9–10
Alton Bill (1987), 84, 86
AMA, 120–121, 176
American College of Obstetricians
    and Gynecologists (ACOG),
    176, 203–204, 217, 219
American Law Institute, 175
American Medical Association
    (AMA), 120–121, 176
American Medical Women's Associ-
    ation, 176
American Psychiatric Association
    (APA), 12, 26, 31, 45, 57,
    187, 193
American Psychological Association
    (APA), 120–121, 148, 152,
    157, 176, 208
American Public Health Associa-
    tion, 176
Americans United for Life, 39
American Victims of Abortion, 23
. . . *And Still They Weep* (British pub-
    lication), 143–144
Anorexia nervosa, 8–9
Antiabortion movement (*see also spe-
    cific organizations*)
  change in argument, 1–5, 19–
      20
  feminism and, 36–41
  fetal-centered claims of, 2, 20
  literature (1970s and 1980s), 2
  mental illness and abortion and,
      19–20, 43

Antiabortion movement (*cont.*)
  Postabortion Syndrome and, 17,
    19–20
  Right to Life and, 102–109
APA (*see* American Psychiatric Asso-
    ciation; American Psycho-
    logical Association)
Association for Post-Natal Illness
    (APNI), 199–200
Attention Deficit Hyperactivity
    Disorder (ADHD), 48, 58,
    73

Baby blues, 182, 198, 214 (*see also*
    Postnatal Depression
    [PND])
Battered Child Syndrome, 6, 16
Battered Woman's Syndrome
    (BWS), 15–16, 32, 44, 66–
    68
Blackmun, Harry, 122, 164
Bourne ruling, 166, 173, 175
Bowlby, John, 169–170
Breast cancer and abortion, 112
Brewer, Colin, 154, 156, 160, 170–
    171
Brind, Joel, 112–113
British Medical Association (BMA),
    98, 146, 165
British Pregnancy Advisory Service
    (BPAS), 40
British Victims of Abortion (BVA),
    23, 29, 36, 93–94
Brockington, Ian, 1, 158, 171, 182,
    187, 191–192, 196, 218–
    219
Bush, George W., 110–111, 133

CARE, 21, 39, 137
Casey v. Planned Parenthood (1992),
    108–109, 122, 125–127
Catholic Church, 24, 100, 110

Center for Reproductive Law and
    Policy (CRLP), 124–126
Childbirth
  anticipation of, 240
  expectations about, 240–241
  Posttraumatic Stress Disorder
    and, 5, 216–220
  September 11 (2001) terrorist at-
    tacks and, 219
  "tokophobia" and, 219, 228
Christian Action Research and Edu-
    cation (CARE), 21, 39, 137
*City of Akron v. Akron Center for Re-
    productive Health* (1983), 122
Civil liability laws, 129–131
Civil Rights Act, 129
Cloning, reproductive, 113–114
Combat neurosis, 66 (*see also* Post-
    traumatic Stress Disorder
    [PTSD])
"Commitment phobia," 239–240
Community Practitioners' and
    Health Visitors' Association
    (CPHVA), 205
Complementary alternative medi-
    cine (CAM) and Syndrome
    Society, 60–61
Concept slippage, 29
Conference of Catholic Bishops, 100
Conrad, Peter, 7–9, 12–13, 223–
    224
Contextual constructionist approach
    to social problems, 3
Corrie Bill (1979), 84, 86
Counseling provisions
  in Great Britain, 144–145
  in United States, 131–134
CPCs, 24, 131–133
Crisis Pregnancy Centers (CPCs),
    24, 131–133
Crittenden, Ann, 241
Crutcher, Mark, 134

Culture
  child-centered, 241
  medicalization and, 11–12
  parenting and, 244–245
  posttraumatic, 74–79
  shift in, 212
Cusk, Rachel, 233, 235

Danforth v. Planned Parenthood
  (1976), 107
DART program, 46, 203
David, Henry P., 26, 155, 181
De-moralization
  of abortion, 82, 92
  of society, 101
Decriminalization of abortion, de-
  mand for, 172
Demedicalization of abortion
  limits of medicalization and, 4
  opposition to Postabortion Syn-
  drome and, 17, 151, 222–
  223
Department of Health (DoH) (Great
  Britain), 45, 49, 69, 140–
  141, 202–203
Department of Health and Human
  Services (U.S.), 23
Depression, 226 (*see also* Postnatal
  Depression [PND])
Depression After Delivery, 199, 220
Depression Awareness, Recognition,
  and Treatment (DART) pro-
  gram, 46, 203
*Diagnostic and Statistical Manual of
  Mental Disorders* (DSM), 26–
  27, 45, 49, 57, 59, 76, 185,
  187
Dineen, Tana, 56, 70
Doe v. Bolton (1973), 96–97
Double shift, women's, 212, 234–
  235
Downs, Donald, 44, 66–67

DSM, 26–27, 45, 49, 57, 59, 76,
  185, 187
DSM IV, 186
DSM-III-R, 32, 50, 52

Edinburgh Postnatal Depression
  Scale (EPDS), 195–196,
  204–206
Elliot Institute, 23, 28, 30, 38, 129,
  132

Family Research Council, 23
Farrell, Kirby, 72, 76, 78
Federal Employees Benefits Pro-
  gram, 105
Feinmann, Jane, 197–198, 218–
  219, 231
Feminism
  antiabortion movement and, 36–
  41
  Battered Woman's Syndrome and,
  15, 68–69
  medicalization and, 13
  medicine and scientific knowl-
  edge and, 8
  Postnatal Depression and, 210–
  213
Feminists for Life, 23, 25, 36–37
Fetal-centered claims against abor-
  tion, 2, 20
Figes, Kate, 210, 213–215, 218,
  231, 234–235, 241
Fitzpatrick, Michael, 9, 11, 246,
  248–249
Food and Drug Administration, 56
Friedan, Betty, 237
Funding for abortion, 104–106
Furedi, Frank, 44, 63, 243–244, 247

Germany, childbirth and Posttraumatic Stress Disorder and,
  217–218

Great Britain
  "abortion on request," 40
  medicalization of abortion, 82–
    83
  parliamentary debate (1967–
    1989), 84–87
  counseling provisions in, 144–
    145
  debating Postabortion Syndrome
    in
  . . . And Still They Weep, 143–
    144
  counseling, 144–145
  litigation, 145–149
  Rawlinson Commission, 137–
    143
  litigation after abortion in, 145–
    149
  Moral Majority in, 86
  pregnancy and mental illness in
    changing constructions of men-
      tal health, 166–168
    psychiatric exception, 164–
      166
    unwanted children, 168–170
Guttmacher, Alan, 161, 172, 174,
  177

Harris v. McRae (1980), 104–105
Hatch Amendment, 107
Hays, Sharon, 241
Health of the Nation (Great Britain),
  202
Herman, Ellen, 15, 178–179
Herman, Judith Lewis, 33, 66
"Hidden victims," 73
Hillsborough football stadium disas-
  ter, 71
Hochschild, Arlie, 212, 234
Hodgson v. Minnesota (1990), 108
Homosexuality, 1, 12, 59
Horwitz, Allan H., 43–44, 56

Human Fertilisation and Embryol-
  ogy Act, 21, 81–82, 142
Hyde Amendment, 104, 106
Hysteria, 66

ICD, 45, 185, 187
Infant Life Preservation Act (1929),
  91
Informed consent regulations, 123–
  129
Intensive mothering, 241
International Classification of Disorders
  (ICD), 45, 185, 187

James, Oliver, 45, 61
Jarmulowicz, Michael, 25, 93

Karlin v. Foust (1997), 128
King's Cross train station fire
  (1987), 71
Kirk, Stuart A., 45, 47, 49, 51, 54,
  57, 59, 69–71
Kitzinger, Sheila, 211, 218
Koop, C. Everett, 94, 115, 117–120
Koop inquiry, 94–95, 116–121,
  126, 129, 132, 138–139,
  148, 152
Kraepelinian definition of psychoses,
  187
Kutchins, Herb, 45, 47, 49, 51, 54,
  57, 59, 69–71

Labor, 216 (see also Childbirth)
Lasch, Christopher, 11, 240
Law, medicalization of, 92 (see also
  specific legislation)
Life (British antiabortion organiza-
  tion), 1, 20–21, 37–40
Life Dynamics Inc., 134
Litigation after abortion
  in Great Britain, 145–149
  in United States, 134–137

Loseke, Donileen R., 31
Luker, Kristin, 161–162, 173–175
"Lunch-hour" abortion, 36

Male violence and war, 63–69
Marie Stopes Clinics, 22, 36, 146
Maternal attachment thesis, 169–170
Maternity Care Working Party (Great Britain), 219
Maushart, Susan, 210, 212–213
Medicaid rulings, 106
Medical profession and medicalization, 9
Medicalization
    of abortion
        British abortion law and, 82–83
        lack of support for, 3
    of alcoholism, 9
    alternative medicine and, 9–10
    of anorexia nervosa, 8–9
    culture and, 11–12
    defined, 6
    feminism and, 13
    of homosexuality, 8, 12
    of human experience, 43–46
    of law, 92
    limits to, 4, 12–16, 221
    medical profession and, 9
    of pregnancy, 17
    problem of, 245–250
    processes, 7–12, 17, 250
    selective, 4, 221–225
    of social problems, 13–14
    Syndrome Society and, 14–16, 43–46, 57–62
    thesis, 5–12
    victim culture and, 11
    of women's experiences, 12–13
Men's Health Forum, 209

Mental health
    changing constructions of
        in Great Britain, 166–168
        in United States, 177–179
    childbearing and, 170–171
    unwanted children and, 168–170
Mental Health Act (1946), 178
Mental Health Act (1959), 167
Mental illness
    abortion and
        antiabortion movement and, 19–20, 43
        demedicalization and, 151
        new problems for women and, 230–236
        scientific claims and, effects of, 225–230
        selective medicalization and, 221–225
    motherhood and, 18, 189–190, 225
    pregnancy and
        continued pregnancies, 160–164
        demedicalization and, 159–164
        in Great Britain, 164–171
        postnatal depression and, 181–188
        psychological effects of abortion and, 152–159
        in United States, 172–180
    women's problems and, 69
"Mexico City" policy, 105
"Mind Out for Mental Health" campaign (2000), 45
Ministry of Defense (MOD) (Great Britain), 71
Model Penal Code, 175
Mood disorders, 203 (*see also* Postnatal Depression [PND])

Moral Majority
    competing rights and, politiciz-
        ing, 98–102
    in Great Britain, 86
    in United States, 85–86, 94, 96,
        98–102
Motherhood and mental illness, 18,
    189–90, 225 (*see also* Post-
    natal Depression [PND])

National Cancer Institute, 112
National Childbirth Trust (Great
    Britain), 199, 216
National Health Service (NHS)
    (Great Britain), 35
National Institute for Mental Health
    (Great Britain), 46
National Institute of Mental Health
    (NIMH), 15, 46, 48, 56,
    179, 203, 205
National Neuropsychiatric Institute
    Act, 178
National Office of Post-Abortion
    Reconciliation and Healing,
    Inc., 24–25
National Organization for Women,
    117
National Right to Life Committee
    (NRLC), 22, 25, 100, 131–
    132
National Sanctity of Life Day, 111
National Screening Committee
    (NCS) (Great Britain), 205
National Society for the Protection
    of Children (NSPCC), 209–
    210
Nicolson, Paula, 194, 196
NIMH, 15, 46, 48, 56, 179, 203,
    205
Northern, Kathy Seward, 124, 128,
    135–136
NRLC, 22, 25, 100, 131–132
NSPCC, 209–210

Oakley, Ann, 211
O'Connor, Sandra Day, 108
Offences Against the Person Act
    (1861), 82
Office for National Statistics, 171
Office of Women's Health (U.S.),
    205
O'Hara, Michael, 185–186, 192–
    193, 195, 206
Ohio v. Akron for Reproductive Health
    (1990), 108

Parenting
    advice, 241–43
    childhood experiences and poor,
        61–62
    culture and, 244–245
    intensive mothering, 241
    irresponsible, 244
    Postnatal Depression and, 207–
        210
    public vs. private, 244–245
PAS (*see* Postabortion Syndrome)
Pearson, Allison, 235
Peele, Stanton, 9
Pitt, Brice, 182, 184
Planned Parenthood Federation of
    America, 117, 135
*Planned Parenthood of Southeastern
    Pennsylvania v. Casey* (1992),
    108–109, 122, 125–127
PMS, 13, 44, 47–48, 186, 193–194
PND (*see* Postnatal Depression)
Politics of abortion
    abortion law in United States and
        competing rights and, 96–98
    features of, 95–96
    "moral right" and, 98–102
    Postabortion Syndrome and
        feminization of antiabortion
        movement and, 36–41
    women as victims and, 32–33
Post-Hysterectomy Syndrome, 32

Postabortion distress (PAD), 29
Postabortion Syndrome (PAS)
  abortion law and, 38–39
  antiabortion movement and, 17,
    19–20
  concept slippage and, 29
  contentiousness of, 4
  denial of, 29–31
  diagnostic criteria for, 25–28
  in Great Britain, 20–22
  incidence of, 1–2
  opposition to, 17, 151, 188, 222–
    223, 249–250
  politics of abortion and
    feminization of antiabortion
      movement and, 31–41
    villains and, constructing, 31,
      33–36
    women as victims and, 32–33
  Posttraumatic Stress Disorder
    and, 24–29
  symptoms of, 1, 19, 23–24
  Syndrome Society and, 147, 221–
    222
  term, emergence of, 22
Postnatal Depression (PND)
  advice literature and, 196–199
  baby massage in treating Post-
    natal Depression, 206
  campaigns for recognition of,
    199–201
  causes of, 192–194
  celebrities suffering from, 189–
    190
  diagnosing, 204–206
  feminism and, 210–215
  health policy and practice and,
    201–210
  historical perspective, 181–183
  identifying, 204–206
  media and, 189–190
  missed diagnosis of, 189
  parenting and, 207–210

  population of patients and, defin-
    ing, 194–196
  psychiatry and, 190–196
  specialism and, 183–185
  status of, 185–188
  symptoms of, 191–192
  treating, 206–207
  visibility of, 4–5, 196–197
  Yates's case and, 201, 219, 226
Postnatal Stress Disorder, concept of,
  229
Postpartum blues, 181, 192 (*see also*
  Postnatal Depression
  [PND])
Postpartum depression, 4–5, 192,
  226 (*see also* Postnatal Depression [PND])
Postpartum Resource Center (New
  York), 199–200
Posttraumatic Stress Disorder
  (PTSD)
  childbirth and, 5, 216–220
  claimsmaking and, 159
  culture and, 74–79
  inventing, 62–72
  new victims and, 66–72
  Northern Ireland wars and, 71
  origins of, 49
  Postabortion Syndrome and, 24–
    29
  recognition of, 31, 63–64, 71
  redefining, 51–55, 76
  September 11 (2001) terrorist at-
    tacks, 77
  symptoms of, 50
  Syndrome Society and, 50–57,
    62–72
  Vietnam War veterans and, 15,
    25, 31, 50–51, 64–66, 218
  war and male violence and, 63–
    69
Pregnancy
  childbirth and, 215–220

Pregnancy (*cont.*)
　medicalization of, 17
　mental illness and
　　continued pregnancies, 160–164
　　demedicalization and, 159–164
　　in Great Britain, 164–171
　　postnatal depression and, 181–188
　　psychological effects of abortion and, 152–159
　　in United States, 172–180
　　risk to woman's health and, 171
Pregnancy Centers Online, 132
Premenstrual Syndrome (PMS), 13, 44, 47–48, 186, 193–194
Pro-Life Alliance, 113
Project Rachel, 24, 94, 132–133
Protestant Church, 100
Prozac in treating Postnatal Depression, 206
Psychological effects of abortion (*see also* Postabortion Syndrome [PAS])
　consensus on, new, 154–157
　counterclaims to Postabortion Syndrome and, 152
　debate of, emerging, 152–154
　women at risk for, 157–159
PTSD (*see* Posttraumatic Stress Disorder)
Public Health Service (U.S.), 116
Puerperal psychosis, 226 (*see also* Postnatal Depression [PND])

Rachel's Vineyard (therapeutic support group), 23–24, 135
Rape Trauma Syndrome, 32, 66–68
Rawlinson Commission, 93, 137–143, 160
RCOG, 98, 112–113, 140, 142, 156, 160, 170

Reagan administration, 105, 148, 222
Reardon, David C., 1, 23–24, 32, 35, 95, 119, 125, 129, 132–134
Reform laws, 96–98 (*see also specific legislation*)
Reproductive cloning, 113–114
Required Standard Operating Principles (RSOPs), 141
Right to Life, 102–109
Right to Life League, 132
Roe v. Wade (1973), 37–38, 96–97, 99–102, 105, 107, 109–111, 122, 163, 176–177
Roman Catholic Church, 24, 100, 110
Royal College of General Practitioners, 156
Royal College of Obstetricians and Gynaecologists (RCOG), 98, 112–113, 140, 142, 156, 160, 170
Royal College of Psychiatrists, 45, 138–139, 194–195, 204
Royal Medico-Psychological Association, 169
RU 486 (abortion pill), 40
Rue, Vincent, 24–34, 38, 93, 126–127
Russo, Nancy Felipe, 125, 144
Rust v. Sullivan (1991), 105

Sarvis, Betty, 178
Savage, Wendy, 147
Scandinavian Psychiatric Association, 217
Scarisbrick, Jack, 22, 40, 113, 146
Schneider, Joseph W., 8, 224
Scientific claims, effects of, 225–230
Scott, Wilbur J., 65
Selective medicalization of reproduction, 4, 221–225

September 11 (2001) terrorist attacks, 77, 219
Sex addiction, 44
Sheldon, Sally, 90
Shepherd, Ben, 64–65
Showalter, Elaine, 211, 246
Social Phobia, 58
Social problems, 3, 13–14 (*see also* Problem of abortion)
Society for the Protection of Unborn Children (SPUC), 1, 39, 84, 93
Speckhard, Anne, 24–27, 29, 38, 127–128
Spitzer, Eliot, 133
SPUC, 1, 39, 84, 93
State legislation on abortion, 106–109
Stenberg v. Cahart, 110
Stotland, Nada, 120–21, 127–128
Summerfield, Derek, 65, 70, 72, 77
Supreme Court (U.S.), 96–97, 104–108, 176 (*see also specific legal cases*)
Syndrome Society
 abortion and, 78–79, 81
 complementary and alternative medicine and, 60–61
 criticism of, 247
 cultural sanction and, 72–74
 medicalization and, 14–16, 43–46, 57–62
 motherhood experiences and, 225
 normal vs. abnormal and, 46–49
 pharmaceutical companies and, 59–60
 political forces and, 58–59
 Postabortion Syndrome and, 147, 221–222
 Posttraumatic Stress Disorder and, 50–57, 62–72

"psychology industry" and, 61–62
 term of, 43–44
Syndrome, use of term of, 44 (*see also specific syndromes*)

Tavris, Carol, 47–48
Thornburgh v. American College of Physicians (1989), 122
Title X family planning program (1987), 105
"Tokophobia" (pathological fear of childbirth), 219, 228
Trauma Aftercare Trust, 72
Trauma, clinical concept of, 72 (*see also* Postabortion Syndrome [PAS]; Posttraumatic Stress Disorder [PTSD])
Treasury-Postal Services Bill, 105
Tribe, Laurence, 96, 105

United Kingdom (*see* Great Britain)
United States (*see also* Supreme Court)
 abortion law in
  funding for abortion, 104–106
  Koop inquiry, 94–95
  state legislation, 106–109
 counseling provisions in, 131–134
 debating Postabortion Syndrome in
  civil liability laws, 129–131
  counseling, 131–134
  informed consent regulations, 123–129
  Koop inquiry, 116–121
  litigation, 134–137
  Supreme Court cases, 121–123
 Department of Health and Human Services, 23
 litigation after abortion in, 134–137

United States (*cont.*)
  Moral Majority in, 85–86, 94,
    96, 98–102
  pregnancy and mental illness in
    psychiatric exception, 172–177
  unwanted children as social
    problem, 179–180
Unwanted children
  mental health and, 168–170
  as social problem, 179–180

Victim culture, 11
Victimization, concept of, 70
Victims of abortion, concept of, 1–3
Vietnam War veterans, 15, 25, 31,
    50–51, 64–66, 218

Webster v. Reproductive Health Services
    (1989), 35, 37, 107, 121–
    122
Wessely, Simon, 65–65, 78
Westervelt, Saundra Davis, 67, 76
White Bill (1974), 84, 86
Wilcox, Brian L., 103–104, 110,
    118

Wilke, John, 25, 103, 117
Winnicott, Donald, 248–249
Wolf, Naomi, 210, 212, 214–215,
    233, 235
Women and Children's Resource Act
    (1999), 133
Women Deserve Better, 23, 37
Women Exploited By Abortion
    (WEBA), 23
Women as victims, 32–33
Women's problems
  mental illness and, 69
  new, 230–236
  new narrative of, 212–215
"Women's Right to Know" Act
    (2001) (Arkansas), 125
"Women's Right to Know" laws,
    39–40, 124–126, 128, 136
World Health Organization
    (WHO), 45, 167, 187

Yates, Andrea, 201, 219, 226
Young, Allan, 66, 70, 77–78

Zola, Irving, 6–8, 10–11

About the Author

Ellie Lee is currently researching the issue of teenage pregnancy in Britain. Before becoming an academic, Ellie worked as a consultant carrying out research projects for a range of U.K. organizations with an interest in improving access to reproductive health services. She is the editor of *Abortion Law and Politics Today* (1998), *Real Bodies* (2002), as well as a number of papers, book chapters and articles on pregnancy and abortion.